Financing SMEs and Entrepreneurs 2024

AN OECD SCOREBOARD

OECD
BETTER POLICIES FOR BETTER LIVES

Please cite this publication as:
OECD (2024), *Financing SMEs and Entrepreneurs 2024: An OECD Scoreboard*, OECD Publishing, Paris, https://doi.org/10.1787/fa521246-en.

ISBN 978-92-64-93681-2 (print)
ISBN 978-92-64-81119-5 (pdf)
ISBN 978-92-64-63190-8 (HTML)
ISBN 978-92-64-61579-3 (epub)

Financing SMEs and Entrepreneurs
ISSN 2306-5257 (print)
ISSN 2306-5265 (online)

Photo credits: Cover © Roman Gorielov/Shutterstock.com.

Corrigenda to OECD publications may be found on line at: www.oecd.org/about/publishing/corrigenda.htm.

Preface

Since 2020, the global economy has been hit by a series of shocks, with strong impacts for small and medium-sized enterprises (SMEs) which make up the vast majority of the business population. The COVID-19 crisis was followed by a surge in inflation. This inflation impacted SMEs in particular, as they have limited ability to pass the increase in input costs to customers without losing competitiveness. The steep increase in policy interest rates in most countries around the world and the tighter lending environment have also impacted the cost and access to finance for SMEs, which traditionally rely on debt to finance operations and investments.

As a result, the 2024 edition of *Financing SMEs and Entrepreneurs: An OECD Scoreboard* documents significant volatility in SME finance. This includes an increase in the cost of SME financing in 2022, unprecedented in the history of the exercise, alongside a significant decline in SME lending. If stringent financing conditions persist, the downward trend in SME financing is likely to continue. Developments in the financing environment also contributed to volatility in equity finance, which declined sharply in 2022 after historically high growth in 2021. Women-led and minority-owned businesses, which typically find it more difficult to access venture capital financing, were disproportionately affected. For the first time, the 2024 edition also provides an analysis of disaggregated data at the subnational level on key Scoreboard indicators, which shows more regional variation in the stock of SME loans compared to the provision of government loan guarantees for SMEs.

Against this backdrop, governments around the world have been taking measures to support SMEs and preserve their access to finance. These measures include both immediate interventions, such as shielding them against the increase in input costs, and more long-term structural initiatives, such as diversifying financial sources and instruments, promoting gender equality in access to capital and streamlining payments. These measures aim to help different types of SMEs and entrepreneurs sustain investments and strengthen their resilience to future challenges. In particular, there is a growing emphasis on the crucial role SMEs must play in building net-zero economies, and the need to harness sustainable finance to foster SME participation in the green transition. However, more needs to be done to close the gap, as SMEs continue to face important constraints in access to and uptake of sustainable finance.

In a context of continued economic volatility and the need to accelerate critical transitions, the Scoreboard will continue to monitor the latest developments in SME financing and the policy landscape in this area, in order to support governments in designing policies that address SME financing needs, enhance their resilience and contribute to a sustainable and inclusive economy.

Lamia Kamal-Chaoui

Director, OECD Centre for Entrepreneurship, SMEs, Regions and Cities

Foreword

Financing SMEs and Entrepreneurs 2024: An OECD Scoreboard provides a comprehensive framework for policymakers and other stakeholders to monitor access to finance by SMEs and entrepreneurs. It also constitutes a valuable tool to support the design and evaluation of policy measures and to monitor the implications of financial reforms on access to finance and financing conditions for SMEs more generally.

This 2024 edition provides information on SME and entrepreneurship financing trends and policy developments after a period of a series of macroeconomic disruptions, including significant inflationary pressures, and a strong tightening of monetary policy, which resulted in a swift increase in borrowing costs and restrictive lending conditions. It also sheds light on the recent policy measures implemented to support SMEs in response to the uncertain economic environment. In particular, it seeks to foster SME resilience through increasing the diversification of SME financing sources and instruments to sustain investments in green and digital, and promoting gender equality on access to finance. Based on data collected for the country profiles and information from demand-side surveys, it includes indicators on debt, equity and asset-based finance, as well as on financing framework conditions complemented by summaries of public and private initiatives to support SME access to finance.

Since the Scoreboard exercise started more than a decade ago, this publication has become an international reference for information on SME and entrepreneurship finance trends and policies. It presents data and policy developments for 47 countries, including Australia, Austria, Belgium, Brazil, Canada, Chile, the People's Republic of China, Colombia, the Czech Republic, Denmark, Estonia, Finland, France, Georgia, Germany, Greece, Hungary, Indonesia, Ireland, Israel, Italy, Japan, Kazakhstan, Korea, Latvia, Lithuania, Luxembourg, Malaysia, Mexico, the Netherlands, New Zealand, Norway, Peru, Poland, Portugal, Serbia, the Slovak Republic, Slovenia, South Africa, Spain, Sweden, Switzerland, Thailand, Türkiye, Ukraine, the United Kingdom and the United States.

Chapter 1 focuses on developments in SME finance and financing conditions based on official data up to 2022, complemented by information available for 2023. It also covers ongoing policy measures drawing on data and information received from experts from participating countries, as well as from external sources. Chapter 2 provides an overview of the sustainable finance landscape for SMEs and focuses on the key challenges that these companies face in seeking out and accessing financing for the green transition. It also provides recommendations to strengthen the provision of financial and non-financial support for SME sustainability.

This publication was prepared by the Entrepreneurship, SMEs and Tourism Division of the Centre for Entrepreneurship, SMEs, Regions and Cities (CFE/EST) under the guidance of the OECD Committee on SMEs and Entrepreneurs (CSMEE) and its Informal Steering Group on SME and Entrepreneurship Financing. The preliminary draft was discussed at the meeting of the CSMEE Informal Steering Group on SME Finance on 6 – 7 September 2023, and a revised draft was presented at the fifth meeting of the CSMEE on 9-10 November 2023. Chapter 2 brings insights from the 2023 survey on 'Financing SMEs for Sustainability: Financial Institution Strategies and Approaches' and builds on the 2022 CSMEE report on 'Financing SMEs for Sustainability: Drivers, Constraints and Policies' developed by the CSMEE and informed by the activities of the OECD Platform on Financing SMEs for Sustainability. The final report was approved by written procedure on 24 January 2024 [CFE/SME(2023)15/CHAP1/FINAL, CFE/SME(2023)15/CHAP2/FINAL and CFE/SME(2023)15/CHAP3/ADD/FINAL].

Acknowledgements

This report was produced by the OECD Centre for Entrepreneurship, SMEs, Regions and Cities (CFE), led by Lamia Kamal-Chaoui, Director, as part of the programme of work of the Committee on SMEs and Entrepreneurship. The development of *Financing SMEs and Entrepreneurs 2024: An OECD Scoreboard* is possible thanks to the country experts from participating OECD member and non-member countries who provided information for the country profiles (see below).

The development of the Scoreboard also benefited from the inputs of Delegates of the OECD Committee on SMEs and Entrepreneurship (CSMEE), chaired by Martin Godel (State Secretariat for Economic Affairs, Switzerland), and members of its Informal Steering Group on SME and Entrepreneurship Financing, chaired by Professor Salvatore Zecchini (Italy).

Data and input provided by Helmut Kraemer-Eis and Frank Lang (European Investment Fund), and Felix Haas (European Association of Guarantee Institutions) are gratefully acknowledged.

The publication has been co-ordinated and edited by Miriam Koreen and María Camila Jiménez, under the supervision of Lucia Cusmano, Acting Head of the SME and Entrepreneurship Division of CFE. Chapter 1 was authored by María Camila Jiménez, and Chapter 2 was authored by Marija Kuzmanovic. Research contributions on Chapter 2 and technical support on the Country Profiles were provided by Hans Robinson Koger. Valuable guidance and comments from Nadim Ahmad, Deputy Director of CFE, are gratefully acknowledged. Heather Mortimer-Charoy and Simone Hegge provided technical support. Support from the CFE Communications and Public Affairs unit is gratefully acknowledged: Shayne MacLachlan and Pauline Arbel for advice on promotion; Pilar Philip for the production process; and Finbar Pearson for outreach efforts.

Country expert team

Australia	Evan Holley	Department of the Treasury
	Ashley Barlett	Department of the Treasury
Austria	Agnes Höld	Federal Ministry of Labour and Economy
Belgium	Christophe Herinckx	Federal Ministry of Economy, SMEs, Self-employed and Energy
Brazil	Pedro Henrique Rincon Amaral	Special Secretary for Micro and Small Enterprises (SEMPE)
Canada	Patrice Rivard	Innovation Science and Economic Development Canada
Chile	Carolina Gutiérrez Castillo	Ministry for the Economy and Industry
China	Wu Bao	China Institute for Small and Medium-sized Enterprises
Colombia	Jose David Quintero Nieto	Ministry of Commerce, Industry and Tourism
Czech Republic	Veronika Spirkova	Ministry of Industry and Trade
Denmark	Håkon Jahr	Ministry of Industry, Business and Financial Affairs
Estonia	Andres Võrang	Ministry of Economic Affairs and Communications
Finland	Tiina Ingman	Ministry of Economic Affairs and Employment
	Kari Virtanen	Ministry of Economic Affairs and Employment
	Henri Tuominen	Ministry of Economic Affairs and Employment
France	Guillaume Richet-Bourbousse	Banque de France

	Loriane Py	Banque de France
	Laura García	Ministry of Economy and Finances
	Guillaume Lourette	Ministry of Economy and Finances
Georgia	Simon Burtchuladze	Ministry Economy and Sustainable Development
	Ketevan Chapidze	Ministry Economy and Sustainable Development
Greece	Thanasis Argyriou	Hellenic Ministry for Economy and Development
	Timotheos Rekkas	Hellenic Ministry for Economy and Development
	Aspasia Sverkou	Hellenic Ministry for Economy and Development
Hungary	Annamária Szukics	Ministry for National Economy
	Laura Kanizsai	Ministry for National Economy
	László Hunyadi	Ministry for National Economy
	Anett Nagy	Ministry for National Economy
Ireland	Cynthia O'Regan	Department of Finance, Banking Policy Division
Israel	Nir Ben-Aharon	Small and Medium Business Agency, Ministry of Economy
Italy	Sabrina Pastorelli	Bank of Italy
Japan	Yoda Yasushi	Small and Medium Enterprise Agency, Ministry of Economy, Trade and Industry
Kazakhstan	Bekzat Imashev	Damu Entrepreneurship Fund
Korea	Meeroo Kim	Korea Development Institute
Latvia	Ilze Baltabola	Ministry of Economics
	Signija Zandere	Ministry of Economics
Lithuania	Viktorija Grybauskaitė	Bank of Lithuania
	Justinas Skurkis	Bank of Lithuania
Luxembourg	Cesare Riilio	National Institute for Statistics and Economic Studies
Malaysia	Rafiza Abdul Rajab	SME Corporation Malaysia
Mexico	Jonathan Alexander Barboza	Ministry of Economy
Netherlands	Samuel Struijker Boudier	Ministry of Economic Affairs
	Jelle Kolkman	Ministry of Economic Affairs
New Zealand	Israelanna Natanielu	Ministry of Business, Innovation and Employment
	Sarah Lambert	Ministry of Business, Innovation and Employment
Norway	Hieu Minh Tran	Statistics Norway
	Torkel Larsen Fuglerud	Ministry of Trade, Industry and Fisheries
Peru	Lourdes del Pilar Álvarez	Ministry of Production
Poland	Magdalena Chudy	Ministry of Economic Development and Technology
Portugal	Nuno Gonçalves	Agency for Competitiveness and Innovation
Serbia	Marija Jokic	National Bank of Serbia
	Ana Ivkovic	National Bank of Serbia
Slovak Republic	Andrea Nagyová	National Agency for SME Development
Slovenia	Tine Janžek	Bank of Slovenia
	Krunoslav Karlovčec	Ministry of the Economy, Tourism and Sport
South Africa	Tebogo Maake	National Treasury, Financial Sector Policy Unit
	Nontobeko Lubisi	National Treasury, Financial Sector Policy Unit
Spain	Víctor García-Vaquero	Bank of Spain
	Ana del Río	Bank of Spain
Sweden	Simon Falck	Swedish Agency for Growth Policy Analysis
Switzerland	Samuel Turcati	State Secretariat for Economic Affairs
	Markus Willimann	State Secretariat for Economic Affairs
Thailand	Nutthawadee Thanyakankornkun	Bank of Thailand
Türkiye	Ufuk Acar	Ministry of Industry and Technology – Small and Medium Enterprise Development Organization of Türkiye
Ukraine	Svitlana Gladchenko	Ministry of Economy
	Oleksandr Melnychenko	Ministry of Economy
United Kingdom	Zach Witton	British Business Bank

	Matt Adey	British Business Bank
United States	Morgan Grantner	Department of Commerce
	Tricia Van Orden	Department of Commerce

Table of contents

Tables

Figures

Boxes

Reader's Guide

Indicators

SME and entrepreneurship financing trends are monitored through core indicators, listed in Table 1, selected on the criteria of usefulness, availability, feasibility and timeliness (see the Annex for a detailed description). In detail, the core indicators describe and monitor the following key dimensions:

Table 1. Core indicators in Financing SMEs and entrepreneurs, 2022

Core indicators	Unit	What they show
The allocation and structure of bank credit to SMEs		
Outstanding business loans, SMEs	Volumes in national currency	SME demand for and access to bank credit. A stock indicator measuring the value of an asset at a given point in time, and thus reflecting both new lending, as well as bank loans that have accumulated over time along with loan repayments.
Outstanding business loans, total	Volumes in national currency	
Share of SME outstanding loans	% of total outstanding loans	
New business lending, total	Volumes in national currency	SME demand for and access to bank credit. A flow indicator, measured over one year, which tends to capture more strongly short-term developments and is therefore more volatile than stocks.
New business lending, SMEs	Volumes in national currency	
Share of new SME lending	% of total new lending	
Short-term loans, SMEs	Volumes in national currency	The structure of SME debt, i.e. the share of outstanding credit with an initial maturity of less than one year and more than one year, respectively. This could be considered as a proxy to gauge the purpose of SME bank loans, i.e. for operational and investment needs.
Long-term loans, SMEs	Volumes in national currency	
Extent of public support for SME finance		
Government loan guarantees, SMEs	Volumes in national currency	These indicators illustrate the extent and uptake of government programmes and instruments supporting SMEs' access to finance.
Government guaranteed loans, SMEs	Volumes in national currency	
Direct government loans, SMEs	Volumes in national currency	
Credit costs and conditions		
Interest rate, SMEs	%	The cost of SME loans and how it compares to large firms.
Interest rate, large firms	%	
Interest rate spread	Percentage points	
Collateral, SMEs	% of SMEs needing collateral to obtain bank lending	Proxies the conditions SMEs face when applying for bank credit.
Percentage of SME loan applications	SME loan applications/ total number of SMEs, in %	The (unmet) demand for and utilisation of credit by SMEs, and willingness of banks to lend.

Rejection rate	1-(SME loans authorised/ requested), in %	
Utilisation rate	SME loans used/ authorised, in %	
	Non-bank sources of finance	
Venture and growth capital investments	Volumes in national currency and year-on-year growth rate in %	The take-up and ability to access non-bank finance instruments, including external equity for start-up, early development and expansion stages, as well as asset-based finance, such as leasing, hire purchases, factoring and invoice discounting.
Leasing and hire purchases	Volumes in national currency	
Factoring and invoice discounting	Volumes in national currency	
	Financial health	
Non-performing loans, total	% of total business loans	The incidence of late or non-payments for SME loans, compared to the overall corporate sector. This proxies the (relative) riskiness of lending to SMEs.
Non-performing loans, SMEs	% of total SME loans	
Payment delays, B2B	Number of days	The occurrence of payment delays in the B2B sector, i.e. the difficulty in paying and being paid, to capture the extent of cash flow problems.
Bankruptcies, SMEs	Number and year-on-year growth rate in %	A proxy for the overall business environment in which SMEs operate and the ability of small firms to survive economic downturns and credit crunches.

Data collection

The Scoreboard data are provided by experts designated by participating countries. Most of the indicators are derived from supply-side data provided by financial institutions, statistical offices and other government agencies. This is supplemented by national and regional demand-side surveys in order to provide a more comprehensive view of the evolution of financing trends and needs. Indicators cover access to finance for employer firms, that is, for SMEs which have at least one employee, and are operating a non-financial business. The data in the present edition cover the period 2007 to 2022. Specific attention is placed on developments occurring in 2021, 2022 and the first half of 2023. In addition, information on government policies to ease SMEs' access to finance is also collected on a systematic basis.

The published print version includes a chapter on emerging trends in SME and entrepreneurship finance, drawing on information provided by participating countries, a thematic chapter, focusing for this edition on the sustainable finance landscape for SMEs and the strategies and approaches from financial institutions towards its SME clients. The printed version also includes an annex and a two-page snapshot for every participating country. This snapshot summarises the state of play regarding SME access to finance in each country, while the full country profiles will be available on the OECD website only.

Cross-country comparability

At the individual country level, the Scoreboard provides a coherent picture of SMEs' access to finance over time and monitors changing conditions for SME financing, as well as the impact of policies. There are limits to possible cross-country comparisons, however. Firstly, the statistical definition of an SME differs among participating countries; while the European Union definition is the most commonly used, participating countries outside of the Union usually define an SME differently, which complicates cross-country comparisons (see the Annex for detailed definitions of SMEs across participating countries).

In addition, differences in the definition and coverage for indicators hamper comparability, with a number of countries not able to adhere to the "preferred definition" of the core indicators. A proxy has been adopted in these instances. For this reason, all country profiles include a table, which provides the definition adopted for each indicator and a reference to the data source. Despite these limitations, it is still possible to compare general trends across countries, as the differences in the exact composition of the single indicator are muted when evaluating rates of change. Country profiles in the printed edition of this publication are abbreviated to two pages with key facts and the table with core indicators, while the full profiles remain available online.

Methodological advances and recommendations for data improvements

There have been important methodological and structural improvements in recent editions of this report. More detailed information regarding the sources and definitions of core indicators have been provided for participating countries. Since June 2016, the Scoreboard data are available on the OECD.Stat website. Data on core indicators can be consulted, downloaded and put to further use, thereby addressing a longstanding demand to improve access to the data, and exposure of the publication to a wider audience. In addition, more information is provided on the uptake of financial instruments other than straight debt, and further endeavours will be undertaken in this area for future editions of the publication.

Furthermore, the Scoreboard now seeks to collect disaggregated data on SME and entrepreneurship finance and financing conditions. The 2023 Scoreboard Highlights was the first edition to present the first early findings and this 2024 edition presented more insights on the disaggregated data by TL2 regions. These efforts, in addition to being in line with the 2022 Updated High-Level Principles on SME Financing and the OECD Recommendation on SME Financing, are a crucial improvement for the Scoreboard, considering the significant heterogeneity of the SME population and the impact that these underlying characteristics have on access to finance and financing conditions. Data collection and related analysis has started by geographical location and by gender of the principal owner, and efforts to improve country and time coverage are continuously being pursued. In particular, additional efforts are needed on the collection of gender disaggregated data, as few countries appear to be collecting this information, despite its high policy relevance. In this context, the OECD is also collaborating with other international initiatives which seeks to strengthen information on access to finance by women-owned businesses.

The collection of additional dimensions (e.g. sector of operation and firm size) is foreseen to be incorporated in the near future. Overall, the incorporation of these dimensions will provide a better understanding of SME and entrepreneurship finance trends, would significantly continue to strengthen the usefulness of the Scoreboard, contribute to a better understanding of the heterogeneity of SME segments, enrich the evidence base and support policy efforts focused on SME and entrepreneurship financing.

Finally, efforts are ongoing to increase the coverage of participating countries and to harmonise the data from already participating countries.

A summary of recommendations to further improve data collection and reporting of core indicators are outlined in Box 1 (see the Annex for a more detailed discussion). Actions in these areas can enable countries to progress in the harmonisation of definitions and facilitate inter-temporal and cross-country analysis of trends in SME and entrepreneurship finance.

Box 1. Recommendations for improving the reporting of core indicators

1. Improve reporting of SME loan variables by:

- Systematically separating reporting of financial information for non-employer and employer-firms;
- Providing both stock and flow data for SME loans;
- Detailing the loan composition, indicating the different underlying products (e.g. overdrafts / lines of credit / leases / business mortgages or credit cards / securitised loans), and disclose such elements in the loan definition.

2. Fill gaps in available data and work towards more comprehensive information for other core indicators in the Scoreboard, including:

- Offer more comprehensive information on government programmes that ease SME access to finance:
  - In the context of specific measures on greening and digitalization, provide information on new or expanded government schemes, including information on eligibility criteria and duration, and if possible, amount of total funding allocated to those schemes. Provide the same information for the specific countries experiencing high energy costs and launching financing schemes for SMEs.
  - Specify the figures that can be attributed to schemes in response to the COVID-19 crisis (e.g. new government guarantee schemes, new lines of direct lending) in the reporting of Scoreboard indicators.
- Provide data on non-performing loans for SMEs and for large firms, the latter to be used as a benchmark;
- Provide more comprehensive data on venture capital investments, including trends by stage and sector;
- Compile SME-specific information on the uptake and use of asset-based finance (versus other beneficiaries);
- Collect information on SME loan fees, in addition to interest applied on the loans;
- Detail the definition of collateral and improve reporting, using demand-side surveys to compensate for lack of supply-side data;
- Advance efforts to compile more disaggregated data on the Scoreboard core indicators, notably by sector of operation, firm size, gender of principal owner and geographical location.
  - On the collection of gender-disaggregated data, provide figures distinguishing between firms that are primarily owned (not managed) by women (e.g. 51% owned by women), firms primarily owned by men, and "dual-owned".
  - On the collection of subnational level data, provide figures at the TL2 level.

3. Work to improve data collection on additional non-bank financing instruments, such as online alternative finance, as well as to provide more comprehensive data on alternative sources of equity financing, including business angel investments, with a view to incorporating this information in the set of core indicators in the future.

Acronyms and abbreviations

AGF	African Guarantee Fund
AECM	European Association of Mutual Guarantee Societies
AUD	Australian dollar
B2B	Business-to-Business
BBLS	Bounce Back Loan Scheme
BLS	Bank Lending Survey
BDC	Business Development Bank of Canada
CAD	Canadian dollar
CCCE	European Commission's Covenant of Companies for Climate and Energy
CEO	Chief Executive Officer
COVID-19	Coronavirus disease 2019
CSMEE	Committee on SME and Entrepreneurship
CSRD	Corporate Sustainability Reporting Directive
EC	European Commission
ECB	European Central Bank
EELS	Energy Efficient Loan Scheme
EERSF	Energy Efficiency and Renewable Sources Fund
EFRAG	European Financial Reporting Advisory Group
EIB	European Investment Bank
EIDL	Economic Injury Disaster Loans
EIF	European Investment Fund
EITI	Extractive Industries Transparency Initiative
ESG	Environment, Social, Governance
ESRS	European Sustainability Reporting Standard
ETS	Emissions Trading Scheme
EU	European Union
EUR	Euro
EVCA	European Venture Capital Association
FCFA	West African CFA franc
FCI	Factors Chain International

FIs	Financial Institutions
FIRA	Fideicomisos Instituidos en la Relación con la Agricultura (Trusted Institutes in Relation to Agriculture)
FOGAPE	Fondo de Garantía para Pequeños Empresarios (Guarantee Fund for Small Businesses)
FRF	Financial Reporting Framework
GBP	British pound
GDP	Gross domestic product
GHG	Greenhouse Gas
GFT	Green Finance Taxonomy
GPFI	G20 Global Partnership on Financial Inclusion
GRI	Global Reporting Initiative
IASB	International Accounting Standards Board
IFRS	International Financial Reporting Standards
IFCMA	Inclusive Forum on Carbon Mitigation Approaches
LPD	Late Payment Directive
IMF	International Monetary Fund
IRR	Internal Rate of Return
ISO	International Organization for Standardization
KPIs	Key Performance Indicators
MSME	Micro, Small and Medium enterprises
NPL	Non-performing loans
NVCA	National Venture Capital Association
OECD	Organization for Economic Cooperation and Development
PCAF	Partnership for Carbon Accounting Financials
PCGSs	Public Credit Guarantee Schemes
PE	Private equity
PFIs	Public Financial Institutions
RIA	Regulatory Impact Assessment
R&D	Research and development
SAFE	Survey on the Access to Finance of Enterprises
SBA	Small Business Administration
SBCI	Strategic Banking Cooperation of Ireland
SEK	Swedish krona
SMEs	Small and Medium Enterprises
SEA	South East Asia
TCFD	Climate-related Financial Disclosure
TANKAN	Business Short-Term Economic Sentiment Survey (Japan)
TRY	Turkish Lire
UNCTAD	United Nations Conference on Trade and Development
UNEP	United Nations Environmental Programme

VC Venture capital

WTO World Trade Organization

ISO Country Abbreviations			
AUS	Australia	**JPN**	Japan
AUT	Austria	**KAZ**	Kazakhstan
BEL	Belgium	**KOR**	Korea
BRA	Brazil	**LTU**	Lithuania
CAN	Canada	**LUX**	Luxembourg
CHE	Switzerland	**LVA**	Latvia
CHN	People's Republic of China	**MYS**	Malaysia
CHL	Chile	**MEX**	Mexico
COL	Colombia	**NLD**	Netherlands
CZE	Czech Republic	**NZL**	New Zealand
DNK	Denmark	**NOR**	Norway
ESP	Spain	**PER**	Peru
EST	Estonia	**POL**	Poland
FIN	Finland	**PRT**	Portugal
FRA	France	**SRB**	Serbia
GBR	United Kingdom	**SVK**	Slovak Republic
GEO	Georgia	**SVN**	Slovenia
GRC	Greece	**SWE**	Sweden
HUN	Hungary	**THA**	Thailand
IDN	Indonesia	**TUR**	Türkiye
IRL	Ireland	**UKR**	Ukraine
ISR	Israel	**USA**	United States
ITA	Italy	**ZAF**	South Africa

Executive Summary

Financing SMEs and Entrepreneurs 2024: An OECD Scoreboard provides information on SME financing trends and policies for nearly 50 countries through the end of 2022, including indicators on debt, equity, and financing conditions, as well as enterprise distress data. Data for 2022 are complemented by information available for 2023, along with demand-side information and recent developments in public policy and private initiatives to support SME finance. Taken together, these indicators form a comprehensive framework for policymakers and other stakeholders to evaluate the financing needs of SMEs. The Scoreboard also constitutes a valuable tool to support the design and evaluation of policy measures and to monitor the implications of financial reforms on access to finance and financing conditions for SMEs over time.

Since 2022, SMEs have been greatly impacted by persistent inflationary pressures and the subsequent strong tightening of monetary policy. At the moment of writing, core inflation, which was persistently high in 2023, is projected to ease in most G20 economies. However, geopolitical tensions in the Middle East, their potential repercussions on energy markets, and rising price pressures due to disruptions in the Red Sea may contribute to rising inflation once again. Central Banks continue to have a restrictive monetary policy to ensure inflationary pressures are well-contained, and as a result, lending conditions remain tight and credit growth continues to be weak.

Findings from the Scoreboard show that in 2022, as a result of the steep increase in policy interest rates in most countries around the world, the cost of SME financing registered an increase unprecedented in the history of the exercise. Against this backdrop, both new lending and outstanding loans to SMEs declined, with some heterogeneity across countries. New SME lending fell, explained in part by a reduced supply of credit. The stock of SME loans also declined, driven by a surge in repayment rates, as many SMEs tried to avoid higher borrowing costs, and by an increase in SME bankruptcies. The persistent stringent credit environment is likely to result in a continued downward trend in SME lending.

Equity finance experienced strong volatility, declining sharply in 2022 after historically high growth in 2021. In the first half of 2022, interest rate hikes contributed to many large-scale investors' decision to turn their investments towards fixed-return asset classes, resulting in a decline in start-up valuations, which put further downward pressure on VC fundraising. Women-led businesses and minority-led businesses, which typically find it more difficult to access VC financing, were disproportionately affected.

Asset-based finance continued to recover, although the strength of the rebound is heterogeneous across instruments. While factoring activities experienced marked growth, with tightening lending conditions incentivising many SMEs to opt for this alternative financing instrument, leasing and hire purchases continue to decline although at a slower pace than 2021. In digital financial services, the rise of open banking has led to more innovative offerings, fuelling the growth of digital banks and online alternative finance platforms. These platforms are gaining popularity among underserved SMEs, particularly in certain regions, such as Southeast Asia and Latin America.

Enterprise distress indicators showed mixed performance. Payment delays have not yet been significantly affected by the negative effects of inflation, sheltered by new measures implemented to streamline payment periods in some countries. On the other hand, bankruptcy rates increased across the board, in part due to the resumption of court activities and adjustments following the pandemic. The increase in bankruptcies is also indicative of a growing number of SMEs facing difficulties in maintaining operations amid elevated borrowing and input costs, although bankruptcy rates generally have not yet exceeded pre-COVID levels.

SME finance policies in 2022 and 2023 evolved rapidly to respond to the uncertain economic environment. Support measures ranged from immediate interventions, such as those aimed at buffering against the spike in energy and raw material costs, to more long-term initiatives like promoting gender equality in access to capital. There was also a growing emphasis on diversifying financial sources and instruments to help SMEs sustain their investments, in particular for the green and digital transitions.

Considering the crucial role of policy to increase the flow of financing for SMEs to take part in the green transition, the Thematic Chapter of this publication provides an overview of the sustainable finance landscape for SMEs. It offers information on financial institution strategies and approaches, government policies and policy recommendations in this area.

Access to finance is currently an important constraint for SMEs' net-zero action and will likely represent an even bigger constraint going forward. Financing conditions are becoming increasingly dependent on sustainability considerations, and financial institutions (FIs) are facing non-financial reporting requirements, placing a reporting burden on SMEs.

The offer of sustainable finance is expanding, but SMEs may not be able to tap into this growing pool of finance. The supply of sustainable finance is increasing, driven by regulatory and stakeholder demand and management of net-zero transition risks. In a 2023 OECD survey, both public and private FIs stated that they are increasingly integrating climate considerations in their operations, including by offering tailored financing solutions for SMEs' investments in net zero through several loan types, credit guarantees, and other financing instruments. However, SMEs may not be able to access sustainable finance due to their limited ability to provide sustainability performance data, which is increasingly sought out by FIs to manage risks, develop financing instruments and meet reporting requirements. Moreover, SMEs also risk losing access to finance if they cannot demonstrate credible transition plans in their advancements to net zero, a significant issue for SMEs in high-emitting and hard-to-abate sectors.

SMEs' limited demand for sustainable finance, often due to lack of information, awareness, capacity constraints and market and regulatory uncertainty, poses additional challenges. In the absence of SME demand, FIs have limited incentives to develop tailored financing solutions for financing SMEs' net-zero investment needs. SMEs need a stronger business case and external support to boost their investments in sustainability and seek related financing.

Public actors have an important role to play in establishing a stable and conducive regulatory and policy environment for sustainable finance and investment, offering both financial (loans, equity, grants or credit guarantees) and non-financial support (information, tools, and ways in which SMEs can measure and report on their sustainability performance). Private sector involvement is also essential to bridge the financing gap. Private financial institutions, Fintechs, ESG intermediaries, accountants and other relevant stakeholders all need to contribute toward creating a conducive ecosystem that provides the right information and conditions to drive SME investment in greening and uptake of sustainable finance.

In a context of continued economic volatility and important transitions, the Scoreboard will continue to monitor developments in the SME financing and policy landscape to support governments in developing policies that meet SME financing needs, strengthen their resilience and contribute to a sustainable and inclusive economy.

Recent developments in SME and entrepreneurship finance

1 Recent trends in SME and entrepreneurship finance

The chapter reports on trends and conditions in SME access to finance. It first provides a brief overview of the developments of the macroeconomic conditions and business environment in the context of high inflation and a significant increase in policy interest rates and tightening lending conditions. It then analyses the provision of SME bank financing and credit conditions in 2022, as well as developments on asset-based finance, equity and Fintech. Trends in bankruptcies, payment delays and non-performing loans and recent developments in government policies are also assessed.

Business environment and macroeconomic context

After weak global growth in the second half of 2022, figures for 2023 show signs of improvement, with global GDP rising to an annual growth rate of 3.1%, compared to 2.8% registered in the second half of 2022 (OECD, 2023[1]). This growth is, however, uneven across countries, with economic output picking up in Brazil, China, Japan and the United States. However, output slowed down in the Euro Area and the United Kingdom (Figure 1.1). In 2024, growth is projected to ease to 2.9% before recovering to 3.0% in 2025 (OECD, 2024[2]).

Figure 1.1. GDP growth in selected major economies

Year-on-year growth rate, as a percentage

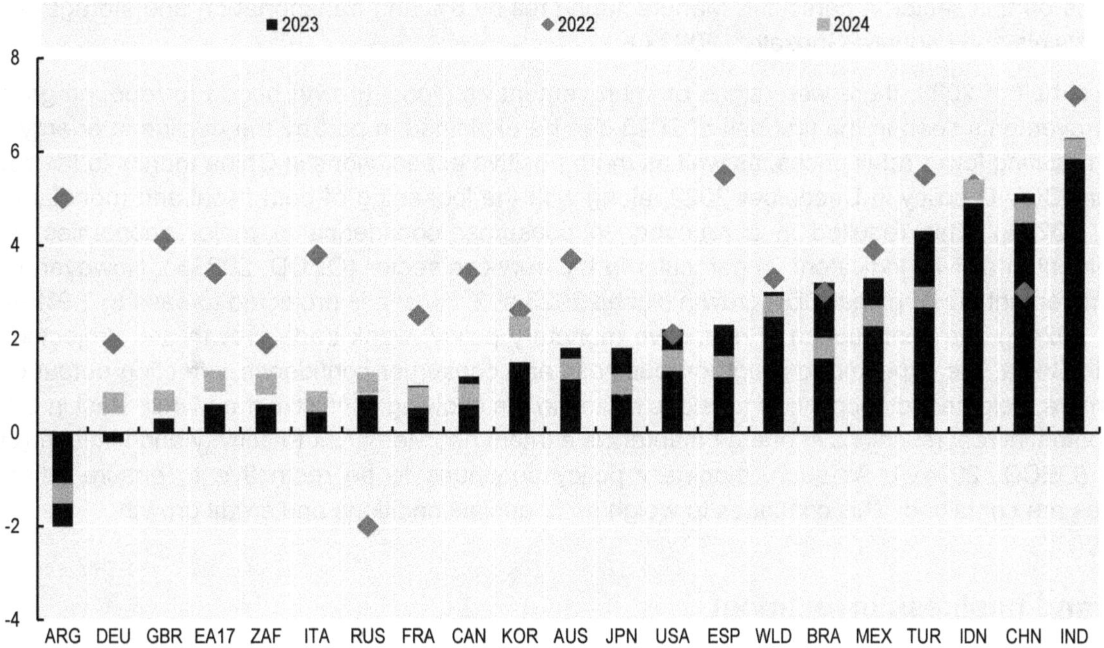

Note: Calculation of World and Euro Area aggregates use nominal GDP weights, using purchasing power parities. Data from India refers to Fiscal Year.
Source: OECD Economic Outlook 113 database, and OECD Interim Economic Outlook 114 database (OECD, 2023[3]) (OECD, 2023[4]) (OECD, 2023[1]).

StatLink https://stat.link/ptl1h6

This uneven growth followed a year of macroeconomic disruptions that had a differential impact across countries. Geopolitical tensions and elevated uncertainty, rooted in Russia's unprovoked aggression against Ukraine, compounded by high inflation, tightening monetary policy, supply chain disruptions and heightened labour shortages, had important impacts on consumer demand and business investment. This, in turn, contributed to a slowdown in most OECD economies, with GDP declining in 15 OECD economies in Q4 2022, predominantly in Europe and Asia Pacific. In 2022, China's GDP experienced a growth rate of only 3%, the lowest in 40 years, except for 2020 during the COVID-19 pandemic (OECD, 2023[3]). While growth in China is expected to pick-up it is expected to be historically subdued, reflecting low domestic demand and stress in the property market, with growth registered at 5.2% in 2023 and projected at 4.7% in 2024 (OECD, 2023[4]) (OECD, 2024[2]).

These macroeconomic developments strongly affected SMEs. In 2022, the sharp increase in inflation, and its consequences on energy and raw material prices, compounded by the phasing out of COVID-19 public financial support, impacted the operations of many SMEs around the world (OECD, 2023[3]). In Europe, for example, inflation-adjusted SME value added declined by 2.3% in 2022 compared to the previous year, with value added in medium-size enterprises experiencing the highest fall at 3% (while small firms declined by 2.6% and micro firms declined by 1.4%). Inflation-adjusted added value in large firms declined by 1% between 2021 and 2022. When compared to 2019, the decline was 2.5%, with medium-sized companies experiencing a stronger hit (-3.9%) compared to small companies (-3.7%). Large firms' inflation-adjusted added value declined by 0.7% in 2022 relative to 2019 (Bella, Katsinis and Laguera-Gonzalez, 2023[5]). When looking at the SME inflation-adjusted value added by sector, construction and manufacturing (where medium-sized enterprises are predominant) were the most affected between 2021 and 2022, declining 5.6% and 3.3%, respectively. When compared between 2022 and 2019, accommodation and food services experienced the largest fall declining 34.4%, as a result of the exceptional impact of the pandemic restrictions on this sector in particular. Manufacturing fell by 5% and transportation and storage by 2.4% (Bella, Katsinis and Laguera-Gonzalez, 2023[5]).

In the first half of 2023, there were signs of improvement as global growth began to rebound gradually. The improvements seen in the first half of 2023 can be explained in part by the decline in energy prices and the resulting lower retail prices, as well as more positive expectations in China thanks to the reversal of its zero-COVID policy in December 2022, along with the loosening of both fiscal and monetary policy (OECD, 2023[3]). This resulted in a recovery in consumer confidence in major economies and an improvement in activity indicators, in particular in the services sector (OECD, 2023[3]). However, despite this improvement in H1, global GDP growth closed 2023 at 3.1% and is projected to ease to 2.9% in 2024 (OECD, 2024[2]) The continuation of restrictive monetary policy, weak trade growth and projected lower growth in China, are expected to weigh on business and consumer confidence, affecting output growth. Furthermore, heightened geopolitical tensions rooted in the evolving conflict in the Middle East in Q4 2023 and its potential repercussions in energy markets is a latent near-term risk to activity and inflation (OECD, 2023[1]) (OECD, 2024[2]). As such, monetary policy continues to be restrictive to ensure inflationary pressures are contained. This continues to weigh on financial conditions and credit growth.

Trade and business investment

Despite the gradual easing of supply bottlenecks in 2022, persistent geopolitical tensions, tighter monetary policy, high commodity prices, slowing industrial production, and high inventory levels resulted in subdued growth in world merchandise trade 2.7% in 2022 (WTO, 2023[6]).

According to the WTO, goods trade was more resilient than expected for the first three quarters of 2022, with merchandise trade volume growing on average by 4.2% quarter-on-quarter (q-o-q) before 2.4% q-o-q decline in Q4, which pulled down the overall performance for the year (WTO, 2023[6]). Several factors contributed to the decline in trade during the last quarter of 2022, but the increase in global commodity prices was the most determinant one, with food and energy prices remaining historically high in Q4 2022, resulting in reduced real income and import demand. On the other hand, the high energy prices had the strongest impact on trade during the winter in the northern hemisphere, in particular in Europe, where gas supplies from Russia stopped (WTO, 2023[6]).

This decline reversed in Q1 2023 when trade volumes recovered partially, rising 1.8% (annualised quarterly rate). The easing of global supply bottlenecks and the reopening of China contributed to this growth. However, there continue to be some vulnerabilities, with transport prices and shipping volumes, as well as demand for manufactured goods and commodities, remaining weak (OECD, 2023[3]). In 2023, global trade growth slowed, in part explained by lagged effects of tight monetary policy, reduced real income and low consumer demand, and the slowdown in economic activity in China (OECD, 2023[4]).

Disruptions in trade flows as a result of the attacks to ships in the Red Sea also weighed on trade growth in 2023. Trade flows have been re-routed, delivery times have lengthened and shipping costs have risen sharply, especially in Asia and Europe. In 2024, despite the projected ease of core inflation, higher shipping charges may increase costs once again, especially for goods. OECD research suggests that the recent 100% increase in shipping costs, if persistent, could raise annual OECD import price inflation by close to 5 percentage points, adding 0.4 percentage points to consumer price inflation after about a year (OECD, 2024[2]).

Business investment, on the other hand, remained high in 2022, in part explained by the delayed and indirect effect of inflation on business investment and, in some countries, the easing of the pandemic's disruptions, which encouraged businesses to invest again to meet the backlog of consumer demand. In 2022, global business investment measured by gross fixed capital formation increased by 5.1% with respect to 2021 (UNCTAD, 2023[7]). This positive trend is expected to reverse, however, with high interest rates and perceptions of a negative economic outlook being associated with lower investment expectations, particularly for SMEs. According to the SME Performance Review by the EC, when interest rates increase by one percentage point, SMEs are 0.83 percentage points less likely to report positive investment expectations compared to 0.65 percentage points for large firms (Bella, Katsinis and Laguera-Gonzalez, 2023[5]). Furthermore, the perception of future economic uncertainty as a major obstacle to investment reduced the probability by 14% among SMEs to report positive investment expectations, versus 10% among large firms (Bella, Katsinis and Laguera-Gonzalez, 2023[5]).

Financial conditions

Credit conditions are increasingly showing the effects of tightening monetary policy. In 2022, policy rates increased, and this had a quick impact on money market rates and bank funding costs (also resulting in banks increasing capital and liquidity buffers, leading to stricter credit conditions for borrowers). In certain countries, interbank interest rates and deposit rates reached levels not seen since the peak of the 2008 global financial crisis. Financing conditions for companies are affected by these developments, as banks passed on the increased policy interest rates to the costs of corporate loans at almost the same pace. The pace of the transmission of these costs from banks to firms differs across countries. Between 2022 and the first quarter of 2023, the largest changes in new bank lending rates[1] were experienced in Australia, Canada, New Zealand, Norway and Sweden, reflecting an earlier tightening of credit conditions (OECD, 2023[3]). In Q3 2023, bank lending slowed sharply in the Euro Area, and some countries are seeing rising loan and credit card delinquency rates and increases in corporate insolvencies (OECD, 2023[4]).

The increase in policy rates in 2022 also impacted corporate debt. Corporate bond yields increased in most advanced economies, but the impact of monetary policy on these yields was less pronounced than in bank lending rates. Corporate bond issuance has decreased significantly, and riskier firms have reduced their bond issuance more than other firms since June 2022, according to Euro Area firm-level data. (OECD, 2023[3]). In Q4 2023 and Q1 2024, as global financial conditions started to ease, financial market participants anticipated the reduction in policy rates could occur earlier and faster than previously expected. Nonetheless, financial conditions remain relatively restrictive in almost all countries and credit growth remains weak (OECD, 2024[2]).

Lending to SMEs

In 2022, lending to SMEs declined in most countries, driven by rising interest rates and reduced credit availability due to increased risk perception among banks. Latin American countries such as Brazil, Colombia and Mexico, however, registered a surge in the flow of credit to SMEs, reflecting a gradual recovery of this indicator after 2020. The stock of SME loans contracted, continuing the downward trajectory documented in 2021, when the stock grew slightly following the phase-out of COVID-19 support. However, there is also some heterogeneity across countries. Some countries maintained their growth, while others experienced a decline due to higher repayment rates and an increase in SME bankruptcies. Moving into 2023, the persistent stringent credit environment can be expected to lead to a continued downtrend in SME lending.

New SME loans

In 2022, the Scoreboard median of new SME loans registered a slight decline, although larger than the one registered in 2021. After declining in 2021 by 0.3%, it registered a 1.8% decline in 2022. The picture is mixed among groups of countries. While both the EU and non-EU high-income countries registered a decline in the median of new SME lending in 2022, with the EU declining by 4%, and non-EU high-income countries declining by 0.1%, upper-middle-income countries registered a increase in new lending, rising by 4% y-o-y. Looking at the developments between 2020 and 2022, the EU registered a large decline in new lending in 2021, with the median declining 12%, and then experienced a smaller drop in 2022 (-4%). In contrast, new lending in upper-middle-income countries declined by 6% in 2020, followed by an increase of 2.5% in 2021 and 4% in 2022.

The small decline in the Scoreboard median growth of new lending can be explained in part by the tighter lending environment, which has affected the supply of credit mainly due to an increased perception of risk among banks (ECB, 2023[8]). Supply-side surveys like the ECB's Bank Lending Survey (BLS) in the EU indicate that banks' risk perceptions have had the largest tightening impact (ECB, 2023[9]). In the United States, the Senior Loan Officer Opinion Survey points to a reduced tolerance for risk as one of the main reasons for tightening lending standards (Federal Reserve, 2023[10]).

Furthermore, the policy rate increases took place at an exceptional pace and magnitude, resulting in a significant increase in the costs of new loans. This implies greater vulnerabilities for firms to borrow in the current context, resulting in a decline in the uptake of loans. In the EU, for example, which registered the largest decline in new loans, the survey on access to finance of enterprises (SAFE) shows fewer firms indicating higher demand for bank loans and credit lines. However, the decline in loan demand has been more pronounced among large firms compared to SMEs (ECB, 2023[11]), reflecting stronger liquidity buffers in large firms compared to SMEs, and the heavy reliance of SMEs on debt finance. In 2022, the annual average of United Kingdom's SMEs that reported that they were currently using external finance was 36%. This was 7 percentage points lower than in 2021 (43%) and the lowest since 2018 (also 36%) (BVA BDRC, 2023[12]).

On the other hand, the increase in the flow of lending in upper-middle-income countries was driven by Latin American countries, namely Mexico (35%), Colombia (16%) and Brazil (8%). The surge can be explained in part by the gradual economic recovery that the region experienced after the COVID-19 pandemic (which also experienced a more moderate impact of the energy crisis compared to other regions), and a rebound of business activity. In Mexico, survey data from SMEs reveal that more businesses acquired credit in 2022. Despite high inflation, they were able to access the credit they requested, although collateral and other requirements were stricter (Banco de México, 2023[13]). Another survey revealed that 62% of SMEs indicated that they were able to navigate inflation and higher input costs and maintain their businesses, and 24% were able to exceed their commercial expectations in 2022 (El Economista, 2022[14]). Colombia experienced a surge in application rates, rising 12 p.p. (see section on SME loan application rates). According to the Central Bank, this was more prevalent for medium-sized companies, but less for microentrepreneurs and small firms who reported reduced access to bank finance and turning instead to cooperatives (Banco de la República, 2022[15]).

Figure 1.2. Growth in new SME lending, 2008-22

Median year-on-year growth rate, as a percentage

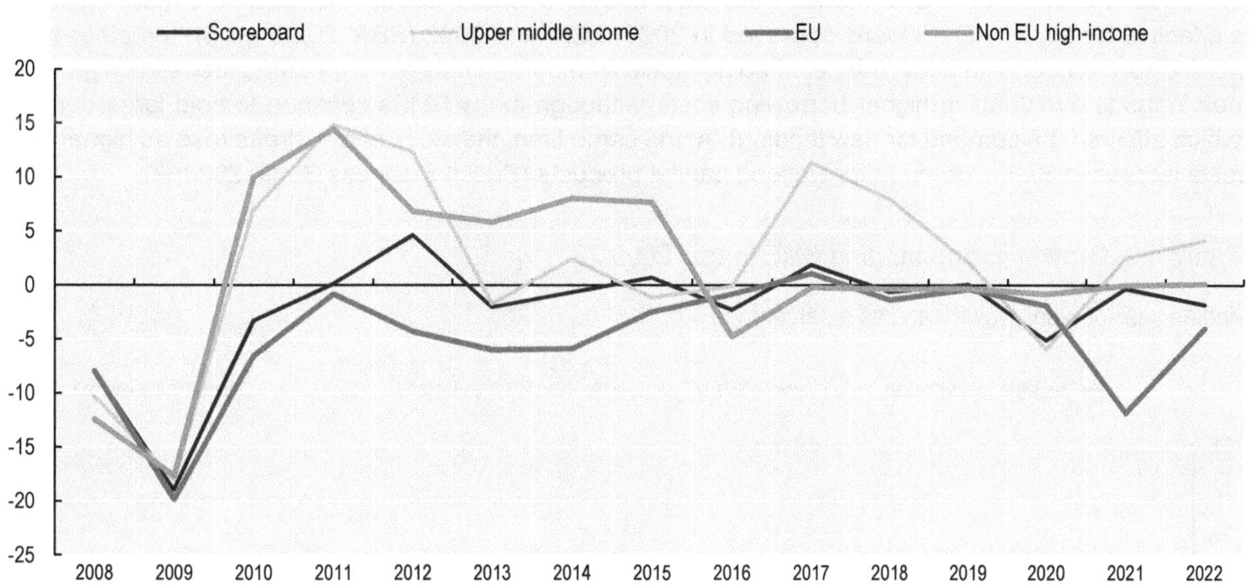

Note: All data are adjusted for inflation using the GDP deflator of each country published in the OECD Economic Outlook database using base year 2007. GDP deflators for non-OECD countries were extracted from the World Development Indicators from the World Bank. Non EU High-income countries include Australia, Canada, Chile, the United Kingdom and the United States. Upper middle-income countries include Brazil, Colombia, Kazakhstan, Mexico and Serbia.
Source: Data compiled from individual country snapshot.

StatLink https://stat.link/hwflav

Outstanding stock of SME loans

In tandem with the decline in new lending in 2022, the growth of the Scoreboard median of the outstanding SME loans dropped by -1.14%. This decline followed negligible growth of 0.25% in 2021, following robust growth of 6.13% in 2020. When looking at the median by group of countries, the EU registered negative growth in the stock of SME loans (-2.58%) continuing the negative trend registered in 2021 when it dropped by -1%. Upper-middle income countries also registered a decline in the stock of loans, dropping by 1.12% in 2022 compared to growth of 3.9% in 2021. Non-EU high-income Scoreboard countries, which include Australia, Canada, Chile, Israel, Japan, Korea, New Zealand, Norway, Switzerland, and the United Kingdom, registered growth of 1.4%, slightly higher than in 2021 (-0.02%).

In the EU, the decline in the stock of loans may also reflect an increase in repayment rates, with many SMEs trying to avoid higher borrowing costs, particularly in light of the repricing of floating-rate debt and the relatively high share of variable rates loans. In fact, in the Euro Area, the average share of variable interest rate loans compared to fixed term loans is 62% (Oesterreichische Nationalbank, 2023[16]) (see Austria country snapshot), prompting many SMEs to repay rather than face higher costs of repayment. According to the ECB, in the last quarter of 2022, the aggregate flow of bank lending became negative, indicating that more loans were maturing or being repaid than loans being issued (ECB, 2023[8]). Another explanation of the decline in this indicator is the increase in SME bankruptcy rates, as banks are required to write off loans, resulting in a decline of the outstanding stock loans.

On the other hand, non-EU high-income countries maintained their growth in the stock of loans despite registering a decline in new loans in 2022. This is consistent with survey data in the United States and

Canada, where the stock of outstanding stock of loans increased (Federal Reserve Bank of Kansas City, 2023[17]) (Government of Canada, 2023[18]), potentially reflecting a slower repayment rate due to the implementation of loan deferrals. In the United States, for example, in March 2022, SBA COVID-19 EIDL loan payments of principal and interest were extended for a total of 30 months. This deferment extension is effective for all COVID-19 loans approved in 2020, 2021 and 2022 (SBA, 2022[19]). On the other hand, in the United Kingdom in 2022, the outstanding stock of loans declined as many SMEs focused on repaying their loans to avoid facing higher borrowing costs, although many SMEs continue to hold large deposits (which affected the demand for new lending). At the same time, the stock of overdrafts rose as higher input costs increased SMEs' demand for working capital products (British Business Bank, 2023[20]).

Figure 1.3. Growth in outstanding SME loans, 2008-22

Median year-on-year growth rate, as a percentage

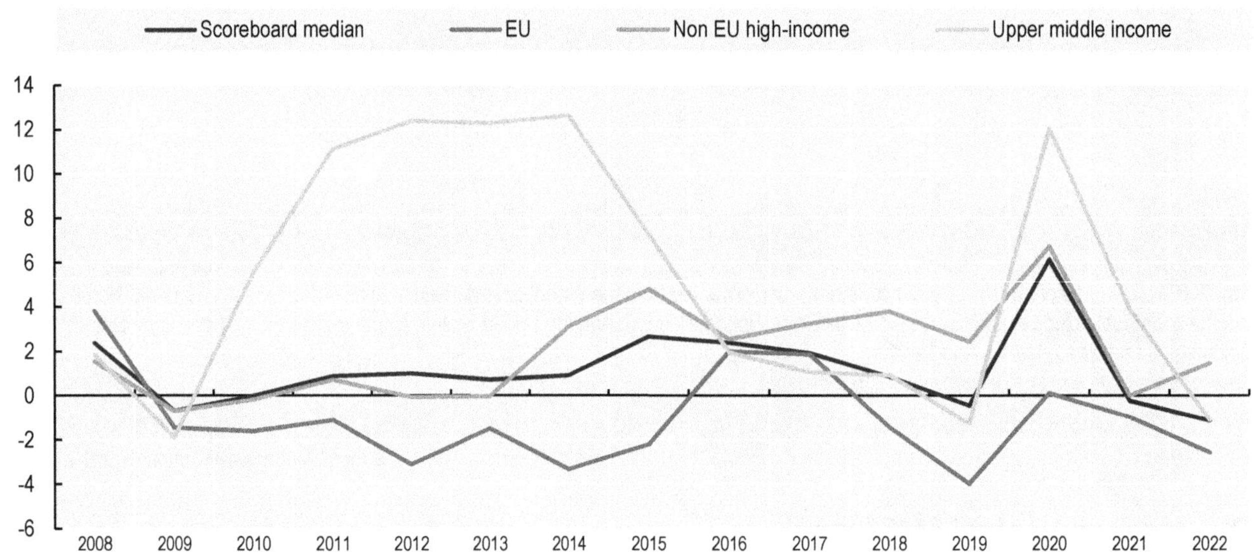

Note: All data are adjusted for inflation using the GDP deflator of each country published in the OECD Economic Outlook database using base year 2007. Data for non-OECD countries were extracted from the World Development Indicators from the World Bank. Non-EU high-income countries include Australia, Canada, Chile, Japan, Korea, New Zealand, the United Kingdom and the United States. Upper middle-income countries include Brazil, Colombia, Kazakhstan, Malaysia, Mexico and Serbia.
Source: Data compiled from information received from individual country Scoreboards.

StatLink https://stat.link/f0yj5v

Developments at the subnational level

Turning to regional differences in outstanding SME loans in 2022, Figure 1.4 presents information on minimum, mean and maximum values in each country[2]. The mean value (i.e. the average of regional values) provides a good indication of the national aggregate value, showing that the volume of SME loans, as a share of GDP, is larger in Türkiye (38%), Portugal (31%) and Belgium (28%), while it is smaller in Indonesia (11%), Peru (9%), and Mexico (1.6%). These figures are affected by the number and size of SME loans, but also by the SME loan definition each country adopts[3], cross-country comparisons should be made with caution. Interestingly, capital regions in the four Western European countries (Belgium, France, Italy and Portugal) feature at the bottom of this ranking, while they are at the top in the two Eastern European countries (Czech Republic and Slovak Republic). While it is difficult to provide a definitive explanation for this without further analysis, the size of regional GDP and the size of the large business sector in regions such as Ile de France (Paris), Lazio (Rome) or Lisbon may help explain the position of these regions at the bottom of the respective national rankings.

Figure 1.4. Outstanding SME loans in relation to regional GDP in selected countries

Percentage of Regional GDP

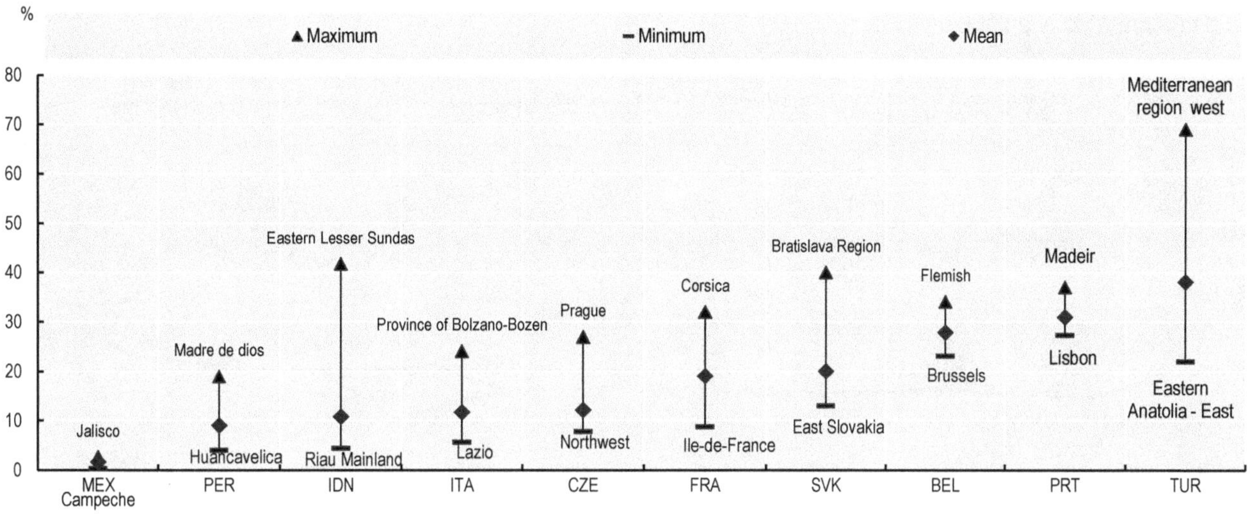

Note: SME loan definitions are not the same across all countries, including within the EU. This especially affects cross-country analysis, but within-country (i.e., regional) analysis is not fully insulated from this problem. Indeed, regional values in relation to GDP will be affected by the national definition of SME loan, as countries in which the SME loan definition is narrower (e.g. in terms of loan size or size of the firm receiving the loan) will tend to show lower national and regional values than those where the SME loan definition is larger. SME loan definitions for the countries covered in this graph are available in Table A A.2 of the 2022 edition of the Scoreboard (OECD, 2022[21]). The data for Belgium is for 2021.

Source: OECD Scoreboard on SME and Entrepreneurship Financing, subnational data collection process.

StatLink https://stat.link/dyo6pr

SME loan shares

In 2022, the Scoreboard median of SME loan shares rose to 47% (up from 43% in 2021) as shown in Figure 1.4. This indicator, which shows the ratio of SME loans to total business loans, offers important information about SME debt financing within the broader business landscape. The four percentage point (p.p.) increase in 2022 shows a more rapid growth compared to the more modest increase experienced in the last five years (on average increasing 0.2 p.p.). The increase likely reflects a faster decline in the total business loans compared to SME loans, with many large businesses opting to repay their loans to avoid higher lending costs. In 2023, however, this is rapidly changing, with many companies facing funding needs in light of PE and bond market volatility (Reuters, 2023[22]).

The data by group of countries, show SME loan shares remaining at levels very similar to 2021. Both the EU and non-EU high-income countries registered a very modest decline in the SME loan share. Going forward, however, the SME loan share could be expected to register a more significant decline. In 2023, the ECB registered a more rapid reduction in the outstanding stock of SME loans relative to the total stock of loans (ECB, 2023[8]). In non-EU high-income countries, some countries registered a decline in the loan share. In the United Kingdom, two factors contributed to the drop in SME loan share: on the one hand, the increase in gross lending to large businesses was higher compared to SMEs, and on the other, gross repayments of bank lending by SMEs reached a record high in 2022, registering 12% increase from 2021 and amounting GBP 73.5 billion according to the Bank of England (see United Kingdom country snapshot). In Israel, the sharp rise in interest rates contributed to a lower flow of lending to SMEs and a lower share of SME loans relative to total loans (see Israel country snapshot). On the other hand, upper-middle-income countries exhibit a slight increase in the proportion of SME loans, rising to 32% (up from 30%).

Figure 1.5. Share of SME outstanding loans, 2008-22

As a percent of total outstanding loans

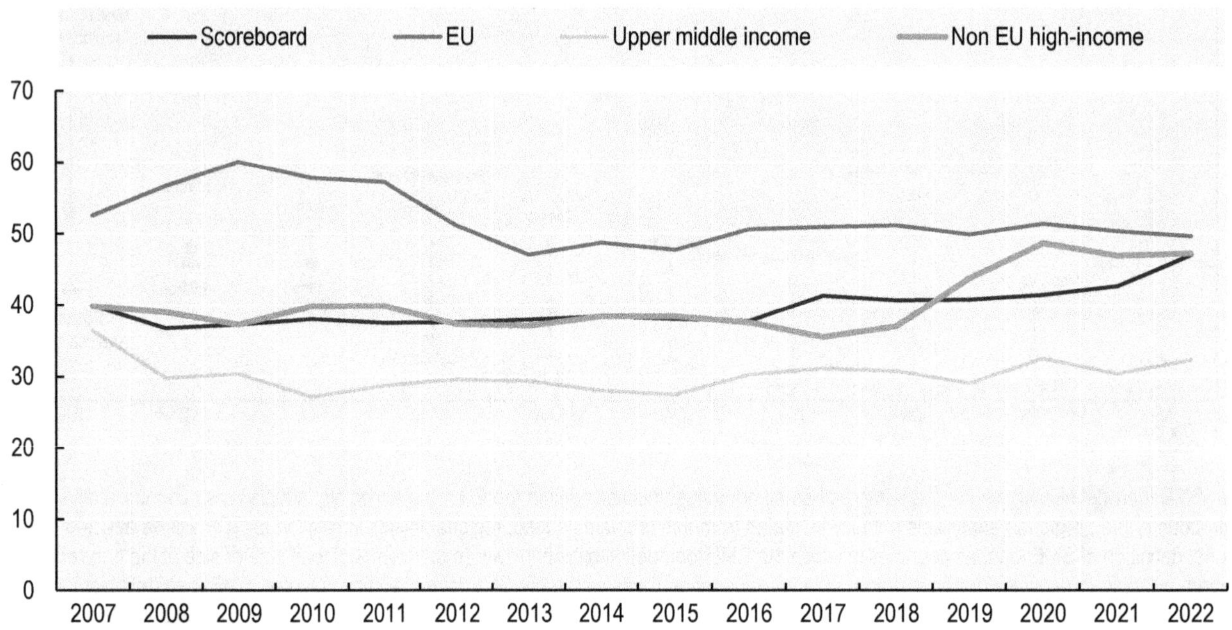

Note: All data are adjusted for inflation using the GDP deflator of each country published in the OECD Economic Outlook database using the base year 2007. Non-EU high-income countries include Australia, Canada, Chile, Israel, Japan, Korea, New Zealand, Norway, Switzerland, United Kingdom,and United States until 2020.
Source: Data compiled from information received from individual country Scoreboards.

StatLink https://stat.link/zu0a6m

Short-term versus long-term lending

Previous editions of the Scoreboard have shown that since 2009 there has been a gradual shift in the SME loan portfolio from short-term loans[4] to loans with longer maturities. Data from 2022 shows a mixed picture, however, with the share of new SME long-term loans declining by 2 p.p. to reach 68%, a first since 2016. On the other hand, the share of the long-term outstanding stock of SME loans increased 2 p.p. to reach 83% in 2022.

The divergence between the two curves can be explained by different factors. First, as explained in the 2023 Scoreboard Highlights, the significant number of loans with long-term durations issued in the years leading up to 2022 has contributed to keeping the proportion of the stock of SME loans high. Second, the implementation of new support measures to help SMEs refinance or extend their existing loans can explain the slight increase in the proportion of long-term outstanding SME loans. The decline in new long-term loans, on the other hand, reflects firms being discouraged from being locked into more expensive long-term loans (in particular in the EU, considering the high share of SMEs that acquire variable-rate loans). As a result, SMEs have used more short-term lending in the hope that longer term rates will begin to fall. Another factor is the increase in SME short-term financing needs[5] in the first half of 2022 due to supply chain disruptions and an increase in input costs (ECB, 2022[23]). This shift is also reflected in the use of credit guarantees, which have moved towards working capital guaranteed loans, which tend to be shorter-term. Indeed, the share of long-term investment capital loan guarantees decreased from more than 80% pre-pandemic to around 50% in the years 2020, 2021 and 2022 (AECM, 2023[24]).

Figure 1.6. Share of long-term SME loans, 2007-22

Percentage of total SME loans, median value

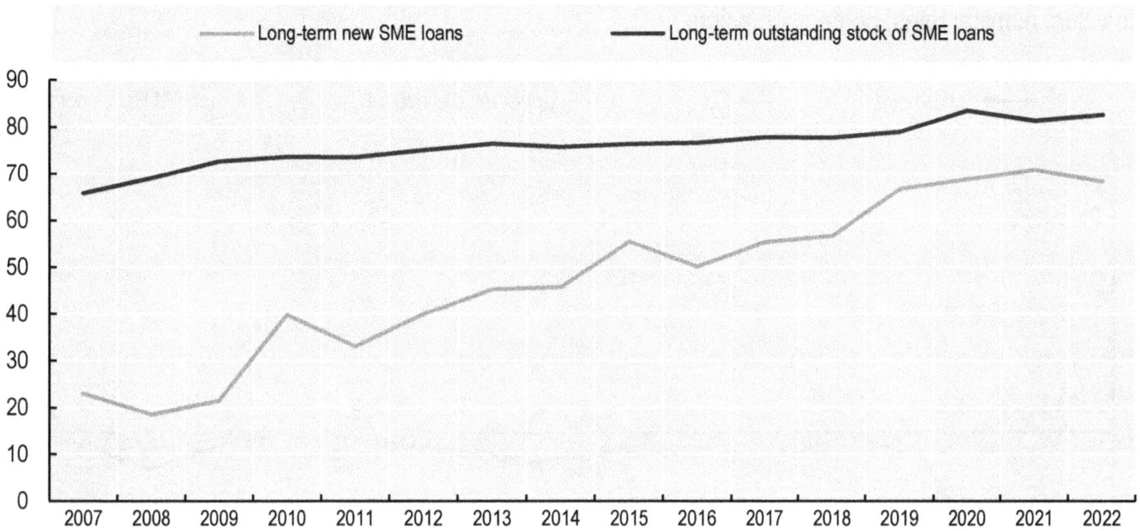

Note: All data are adjusted for inflation using the GDP deflator of each country published in the OECD Economic Outlook database using base year 2007.
Source: Data compiled from information received from individual country Scoreboards.

StatLink https://stat.link/w1d4zf

Credit conditions

This section examines credit conditions for SMEs and entrepreneurs based on data on bank finance costs, collateral requirements and rejection rates. In 2022, many Central Banks moved to increase their policy interest rates, resulting in an increase in the cost of SME finance unprecedented in Scoreboard history (i.e. since 2007). Survey data for 2022 and the first half of 2023 show a significant proportion of SMEs indicating a marked decline in the affordability and accessibility of financing. This has impacted loan demand, even as a growing number of SMEs indicated an increased need for finance. Survey data from banks also indicate tightening terms and conditions due to the increased perception of a more uncertain economic outlook and reduced tolerance for risk.

SME interest rates

In 2022, the cost of finance increased sharply, as governments around the world tightened monetary policy. Years of low interest rates were challenged by rising inflationary pressures which incited a strong response by Central Banks. The rise in policy interest rates was transmitted almost one to one to the real economy and corporate interest rates, including for SME loans, rose accordingly (OECD, 2023[3]). The Scoreboard median increased by 1.1 percentage points, a pace never registered in the Scoreboard history. It is notable that even in 2008, during the great financial crisis, SME interest rates increased by only 0.38 percentage points. In other words, interest rates rose 1.7% in 2008 relative to 2007, while they rose 29% in 2022 relative to 2021. Thus 2022 can be considered to mark the end of a long period of highly accommodative lending, with negative implications for the borrowing costs for SMEs. The rise in interest rates is expected to weigh on the recovery of SME liquidity after the repeated disruptions in the last two years. Empirical analysis from the EC suggests that for every percentage point rise in interest rates in 2021, the profit margins of SMEs is expected to decrease by 0.35 percentage points[6] (European Commission, 2023[25])

Figure 1.7. Changes in SME interest rates

Median value, nominal rates, percentage points

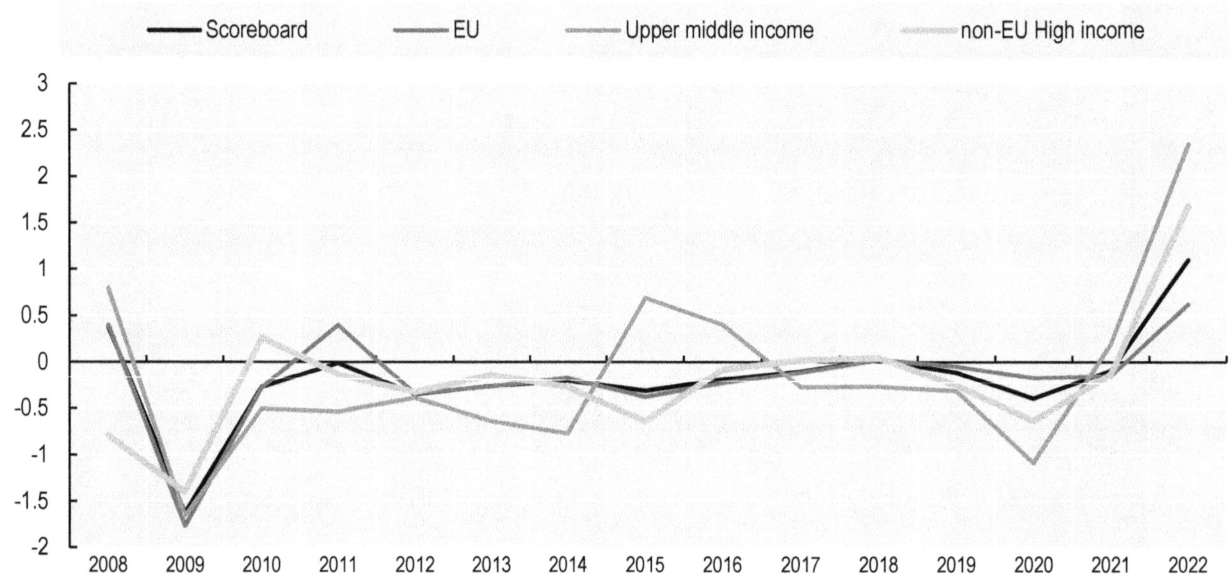

Source: Data compiled from individual country Scoreboards.

StatLink https://stat.link/pb8fxg

All country groups followed the trend of the Scoreboard median, registering hikes in 2022. The highest increase was registered in upper-middle income countries, by 2.3 percentage points, and non-EU high-income countries, by 1.7 percentage points. EU countries also registered an increase in interest rates, although of a lesser magnitude, by 0.6 percentage points. Neither group of countries had registered such an increase in the Scoreboard history. In February 2023, Euro Area firms were paying on average 250 basis points more in interest on new loans than they were at the end of 2021 (ECB, 2023[8]). As of December 2023, forward-looking real interest rates were positive in most major economies, and longer-term interest rates and government bond spreads have also risen in most emerging market economies. Going forward, it is likely that monetary policy will remain restrictive until there are clear signs that inflationary pressures are abating (OECD, 2023[1]).

Figure 1.7 shows the SME interest rates by country. In contrast with 2021, all countries registered an increase in SME interest rates. The highest increases were registered in Colombia (9 p.p.), Hungary (7.5 p.p.), Brazil (5.8 p.p.), Chile (4.8 p.p.) and Kazakhstan (4.3 p.p.). Going forward, the increase in interest rates is expected to reduce the probability of SMEs' reporting positive investment expectations (European Commission, 2023[25]).

Figure 1.8. SME interest rates

Nominal rates, as a percent

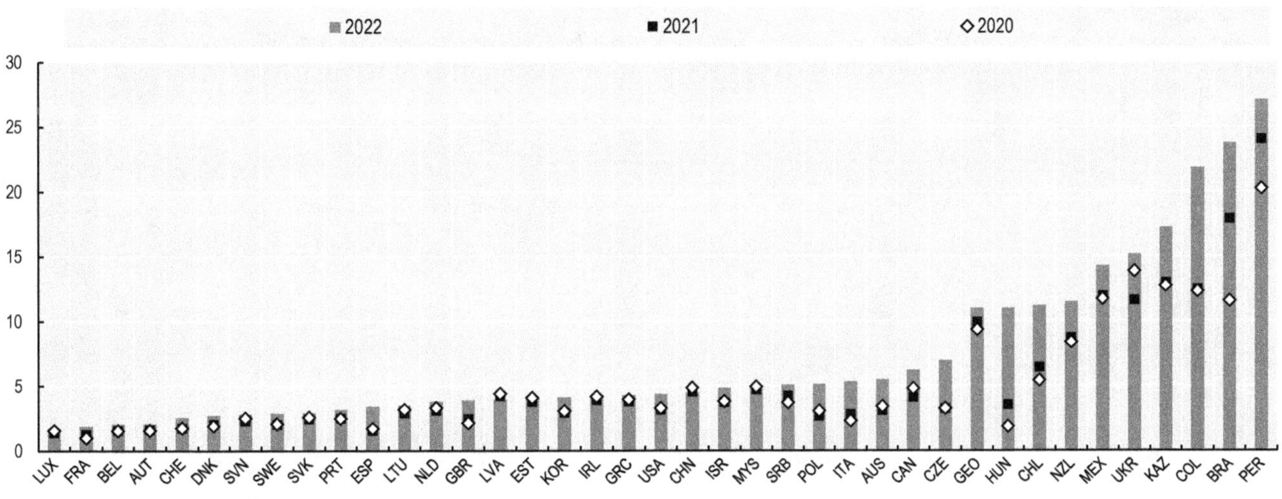

Note: All data are adjusted for inflation using the GDP deflator of each country published in the OECD Economic Outlook database using the base year 2007.
Source: Data compiled from individual country Scoreboards.

StatLink https://stat.link/o6gm5k

Interest rate spreads

The significant increase in interest rates across the board did not translate into a sharp increase in interest rate spreads[7], indicating that borrowing conditions for SMEs in 2022 did not deteriorate more than for large firms. In fact, the Scoreboard median declined, passing from 0.93 percentage points in 2021 to 0.90 percentage points in 2022. Looking at the developments by country, in 2022, 19 out of 36 countries that provided data for this indicator registered narrower interest rate spreads. The largest declines were registered in Ukraine (-2.8 p.p.), the Czech Republic (-1.87 p.p.), Mexico (-1.6 p.p.), Ireland (-0.98 p.p.) and Hungary (-0.95 p.p.), reversing the increase in spreads registered in 2021.

The highest spreads were registered in Peru, Colombia, Brazil, and Chile and the largest increase spreads between 2021 and 2022 was observed in Poland (+1.2 p.p.), Italy (+0.83 p.p.) and Finland (+0.69).

One explanation for the slight decline in interest rate spreads, against the backdrop of increases in interest rates across the board, is the increased perception on the risk to lend to large firms as a result of the negative implications of the interest rate hikes in bond and equity markets, which is causing funding shortages for these firms (S&P Market Intelligence, 2022[26]). In fact, the financial vulnerability indicator, developed within the framework of the SAFE survey to measure firms' financial situation, shows that in 2022, the increase in the share of large firms facing difficulties in running their businesses and servicing their debt was higher compared to the share of SMEs in the same situation (ECB, 2022[27]). However, it is likely that interest rate spreads will increase going forward, with many banks increasingly reporting tighter conditions to SMEs in 2023 to further reduce risk in their operations (ECB, 2023[9]).

Figure 1.9. Interest rate spreads between loans to SMEs and to large firms

Nominal rates, percentage points

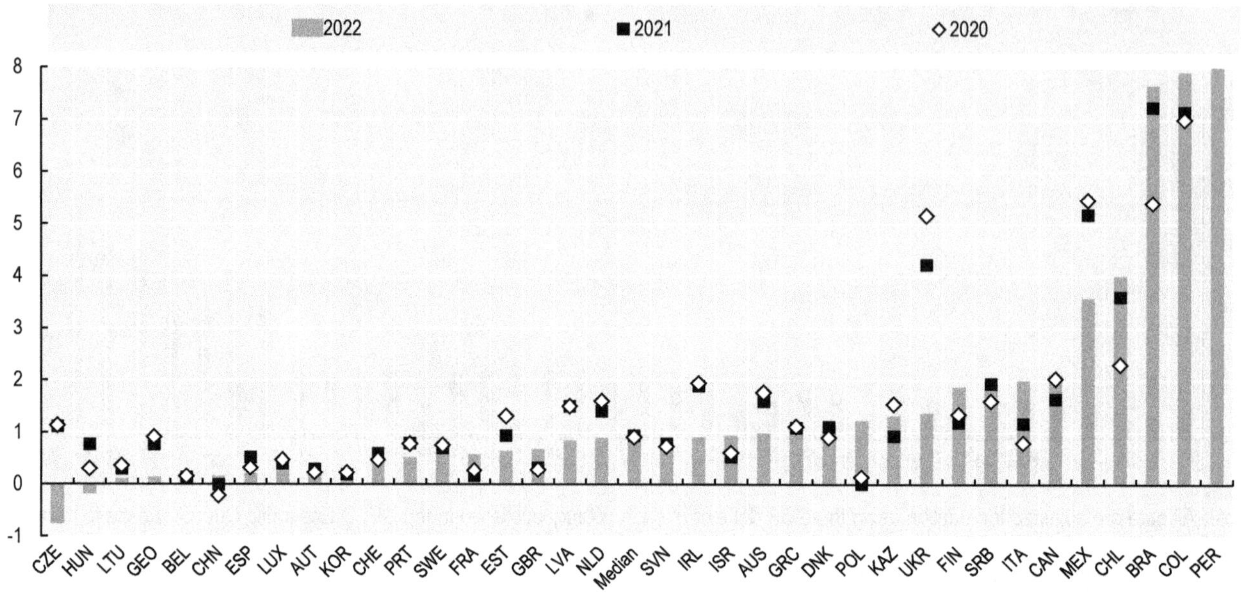

Note: Data from Peru do not enter the graph due to the scale used. In 2020, the interest rate spread was 15.84 p.p. and, in 2021 20.2 p.p. and in 2022 19.85 p.p.
Source: Data compiled from individual country Scoreboards.

StatLink https://stat.link/wuojza

Collateral requirements

Data on collateral requirements comes from demand and supply-side surveys, which may differ in methodology, sampling, and questions asked across different countries. Therefore, cross-country comparisons should be made with caution.

In 2022, the share of SMEs requiring collateral increased by 1.17 p.p., driven by the rise in interest rates and overall tightening of lending conditions. Nonetheless, the increase did not reach the pace experienced in 2008, when the share of SMEs requiring collateral increased by 7.2 p.p. The countries that experienced the largest increase in the share of SMEs requiring collateral include Lithuania (+28.4 p.p.), Greece (+15 p.p.), Ireland (+11 p.p.), the Netherlands (+9 p.p.) and the United Kingdom (+8 p.p.).

Figure 1.10. Collateral requirements

Percentage of SMEs requiring collateral by country (left), median growth rate (right)

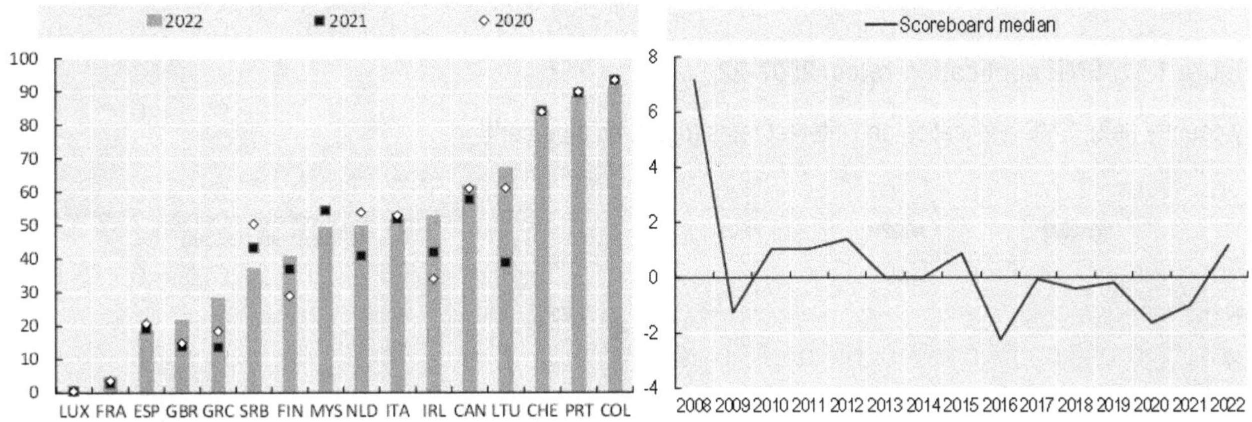

Source: Data compiled from individual country Scoreboards

StatLink https://stat.link/l5imas

The increase in the share of SMEs requiring collateral reflects the rise in the cost of finance and the increased perception of risk from banks. On one hand, higher interest rates are typically associated with a decline in asset prices, which results in a decline in the value of collateral (ECB, 2023[8]). This can lead to immediate adjustments, with lenders requiring more collateral to account for potential price drops to ensure that the value of the collateral does not fall below the loan amount. On the other hand, a higher cost of finance implies higher probabilities of default, as many borrowers may struggle to meet their repayment obligations, leading to higher collateral required for new loans. For example, in the Euro Area, since the end of 2021, firm-level probabilities of default, as reported by banks have increased more strongly for SMEs (ECB, 2023[8]).

SME loan application rates

Since the COVID-19 crisis, lending conditions have experienced notable shifts compared to the more stable evolution after the great financial crisis. In 2021 and 2022, the high inflation environment and subsequent tightening of lending conditions resulted in an increase in SME interest rates of 1.1 p.p., while the application rates of SME loans declined by 2 p.p. in the same period. Half of the countries that provided data for this indicator (7 out of 14) show that SME demand for credit, expressed as the share of SMEs that applied for loans over the total number of SMEs, declined in 2022. The largest declines in SME loan applications were experienced in Luxembourg (-11 p.p.), the United Kingdom (-4 p.p.), and Austria (-3.5 p.p.). On the other hand, the largest increase in application rates was experienced in Colombia (12 p.p.), followed by Slovakia (2 p.p.). In Colombia, access to bank finance was predominant among medium-sized enterprises compared to other size classes (Banco de la República, 2022[15]).

Demand-side surveys of 2022, indicate that the escalating costs of credit have acted as a deterrent for SMEs, discouraging them from seeking debt finance. This is in strong contrast to trends observed in previous years. The left panel of Figure 1.11 shows the evolution of SME interest rates against SME application rates since 2007. The graph shows that after the 2008 crisis, both SME interest rates and loan applications showed a marked decline. From 2009 to 2019, loan applications remained relatively stable, varying from 23% to 28%. During this period, SME interest rates exhibited a gradual decline in response to an accommodative monetary policy, declining from 4.8% in 2009 to 3.9% in 2019 (a decline of 23% relative to the rates in 2009). In 2020, after the shock of the COVID-19 pandemic, the swift policy response to inject liquidity into the economy, and in particular to safeguard SMEs, resulted in a further decline in SME interest rates (-14% relative to rates in 2019), and in an increase in SME loan applications (+13% relative to rates in 2019). In 2022, on the other hand, interest rates rose by 29% while application rates declined by 8%, relative to 2021.

Figure 1.11. SME application rates, 2007-22

By country (left), SME application and interest rates (right), as a percent

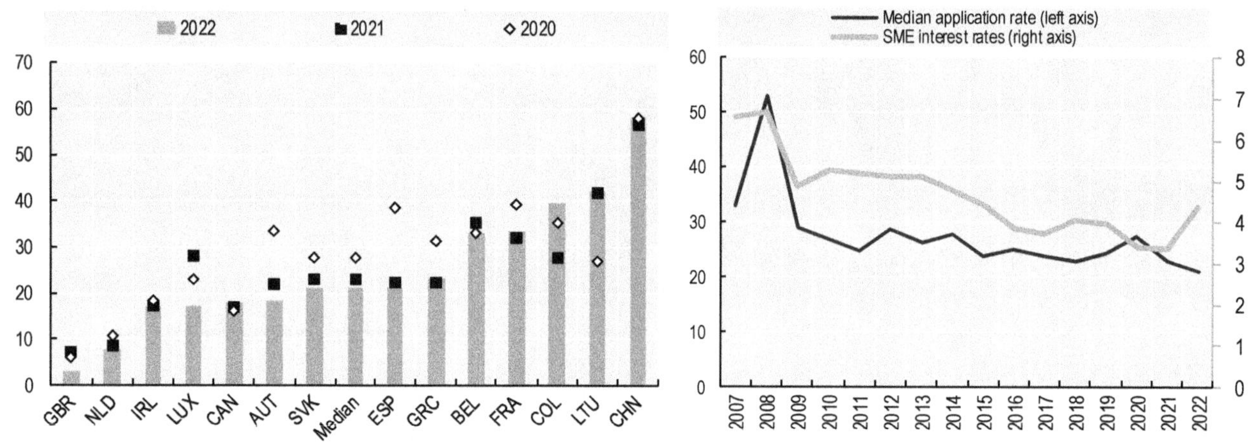

Source: Data compiled from individual country Scoreboards. All data come from demand-side surveys except for China.

StatLink https://stat.link/2lwjte

Rejection rates

Rejection rates provide insights into SME credit supply and overall financing conditions. Higher rates of rejection indicate constraints in the supply of credit and suggest that demand for loans is not being met because the terms and conditions of the loan offers are deemed unacceptable, the average creditworthiness of loan applications has deteriorated, or banks are rationing credit. Nevertheless, rejection rates should be analysed in the context of new lending trends, in order to have a more comprehensive perspective on SME access to finance. Data on rejection rates are usually gathered from demand-side surveys, with limited comparability across countries, however.

The median growth of rejection rates for SMEs in 2022 increased slightly in 2022 by 0.6 p.p., and 11 out of 18 countries that provided data for this indicator registered an increase. The largest increase was experienced in the United Kingdom with a 30 p.p. increase, followed by France (+4.7 p.p.) and Lithuania (+3.5 p.p.). The increase in United Kingdom is likely driven by a number of factors including the end of the Bounce Back Loan Scheme (BBLS) in 2021, which required borrowers to self-declare they met the schemes' eligibility criteria and lenders were not required to assess the affordability or viability of the business. The steep rise in rejection rates was also driven by concerns about businesses' ability to repay debts given deteriorating economic conditions, in particular as a result of a sharp increase in energy costs, with banks looking at the energy rates a business was paying, and profit after energy bills. Rejection rates were also driven by an increase in collateral requirements (Figure 1.10) following the closing of applications for BBLS, which required no collateral, in 2021. Similarly, in France and Lithuania, the increase in rejection rates reflects the tightening of credit standards (ECB, 2022[27]).

Figure 1.12. Rejection rates

As a percentage of loans requested by SMEs

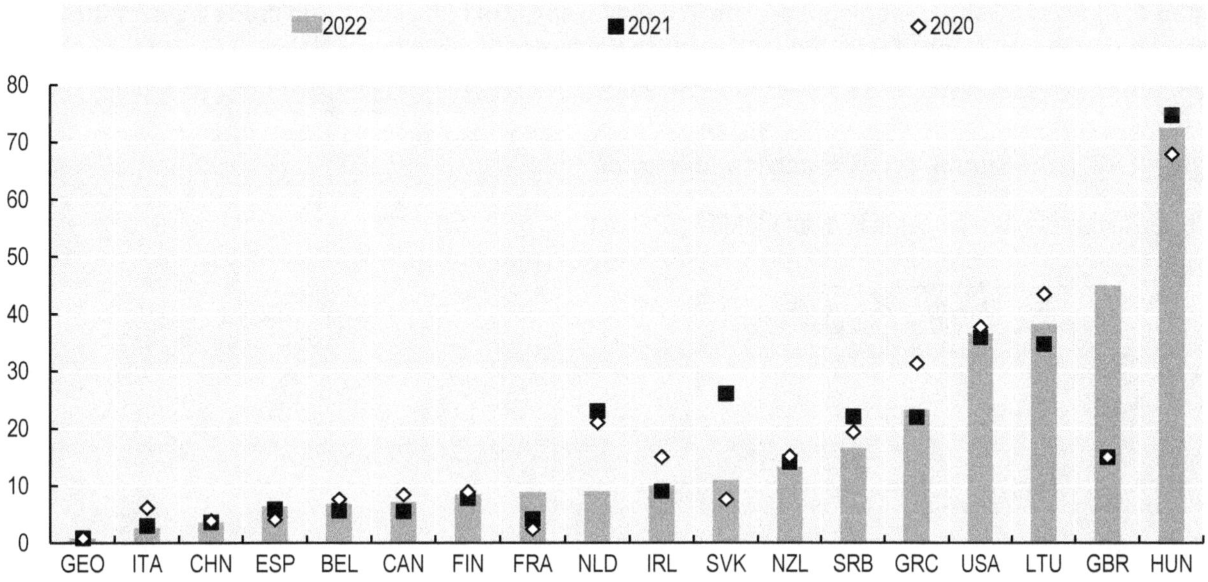

Source: Data compiled from individual country Scoreboards. All data come from demand-side surveys except for China and Giorgia.

StatLink https://stat.link/37qju9

Additional evidence on credit conditions from survey data

Euro Area

The SAFE survey gathers information about the financial situation of European firms, along with the need for and availability of external financing. It is conducted twice a year in spring and fall. The survey conducted in Spring 2023, covering the period from October to March 2023, shows that business activity continues to recover, with firms indicating improvements in turnover but the rebound being stronger for large firms compared to SMEs. Profitability, however, continues to weaken for SMEs, with these companies indicating a more significant decline in their profits (-16%) compared to large firms, which indicated no change in profits. This decline is in part due to an increase in labour, energy and other input costs (ECB, 2022[27]) (ECB, 2023[11]).

With respect to access to finance and financing conditions, firms' responses reflect the monetary policy tightening implemented in the last year. The left panel of Figure 1.13 shows the perceptions of SMEs about the developments in credit conditions (interest and collateral requirements) in the Euro Area. A significant share of firms (the highest levels observed since the survey began in 2009) reported increases in bank interest rates and a significant deterioration in the cost of financing: 87% of firms reported rises in interest rates, from 71% in the previous survey round (Figure 1.13 panel B). This reflects the rapid transmission of monetary policy tightening to costs of corporate lending (see section on Financial conditions).

The tightening of lending conditions has resulted in a decline in demand for finance. In net terms, fewer firms in the Euro Area reported higher demand for external financing across instruments. This decline in demand was predominant for bank loans and credit lines, which is consistent with the overall slowdown in the provision of bank lending to companies registered in Q4 2022 and Q1 2023 of the EC Bank Lending Survey. The decline in demand was also seen for alternative finance instruments such as trade credit, leasing and hire purchases and equity. The deceleration in demand was, however, more predominant in large firms compared to SMEs (ECB, 2023[11]).

The tighter lending environment is also affecting the availability of debt financing. The right panel of Figure 1.13 shows SMEs reporting a decline in the availability of bank loans and credit lines for the second survey round in a row, after several rounds in which firms reported a wide availability (Figure 1.13 panel A). Across size classes, more SMEs reported lower availability compared to large firms.

Figure 1.13. ECB Survey on SME access to finance

Selected indicators as a percentage of total SMEs surveyed

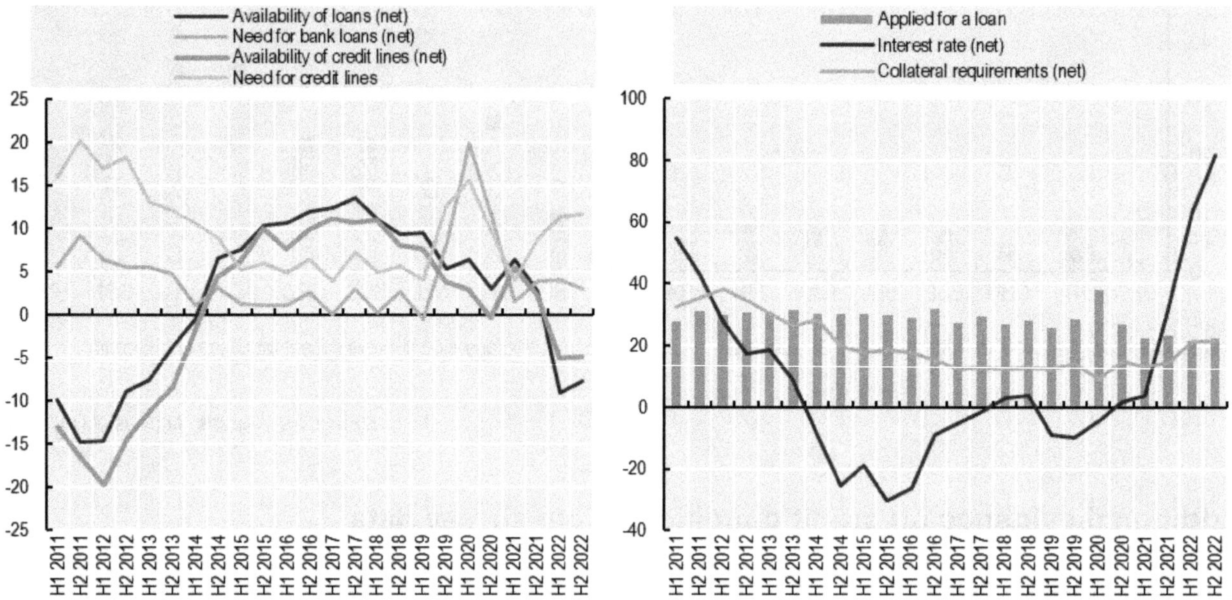

Note: The net percentage is the difference between the percentage of firms reporting that the given factor has improved and the percentage reporting that it has deteriorated, or the difference between the percentage reporting that it has increased and the percentage reporting that it has decreased. H1 2022 refers to round 27 (April to September 2022), published in November 2022. H2 2022 refers to round 28 (October 2022 to March 2023), published in May 2023.
Source: European Central Bank, 2022

StatLink https://stat.link/lvr7t6

United States

The Senior Loan Officer Opinion Survey provides information on the opinion of senior bank officials on lending practices in the United States. In Q1 2023, respondents indicated tightening of lending standards and a decline in the demand for commercial and industrial (C&I) loans across all firm sizes. The most reported areas of tightening were premiums charged on riskier loans, spreads of loan rates over the cost of funds, and costs of credit lines. Additionally, a significant proportion of banks reported having tightened the maximum size of credit lines and collateralisation requirements to firms of all sizes (Federal Reserve, 2023[10]).

A significant share of banks that reported having tightened standards cited a less favourable or more uncertain economic outlook, reduced tolerance for risk, worsening of industry-specific problems, and deterioration in their current or expected liquidity position as important reasons for doing so. Although banks of all sizes cited the same reasons for tightening, mid-sized and other banks more frequently cited the bank's liquidity position, industry-specific problems, and reduced risk tolerance (Federal Reserve, 2023[10]).

The Small Business Lending Survey is conducted every quarter to gather commercial banks' perceptions of their small business lending activities in the United States. In the first quarter of 2023, small business commercial and industrial (C&I) lending declined sharply, falling by 15.9% compared to the same period in 2022, and by 6.8% relative to the previous quarter. This survey round was the fourth consecutive quarter of low loan demand, with the largest proportion of respondents reporting this since the inception of the survey. The weakening of loan demand aligns with the Federal Reserve's stance of monetary policy tightening since mid-2022 (Federal Reserve Bank of Kansas City, 2023[17]).

Japan

The Bank of Japan's Tankan survey reports business confidence and lending attitudes on a quarterly basis. In 2022, lending attitudes tightened for all firm sizes, but in particular for SMEs. This may reflect adjustments after a period of interest-free loans and an increase in the leverage of SMEs (Bank of Japan, 2023[28]).

Figure 1.14. Lending attitudes in Japan

Diffusion Index, in percentage points

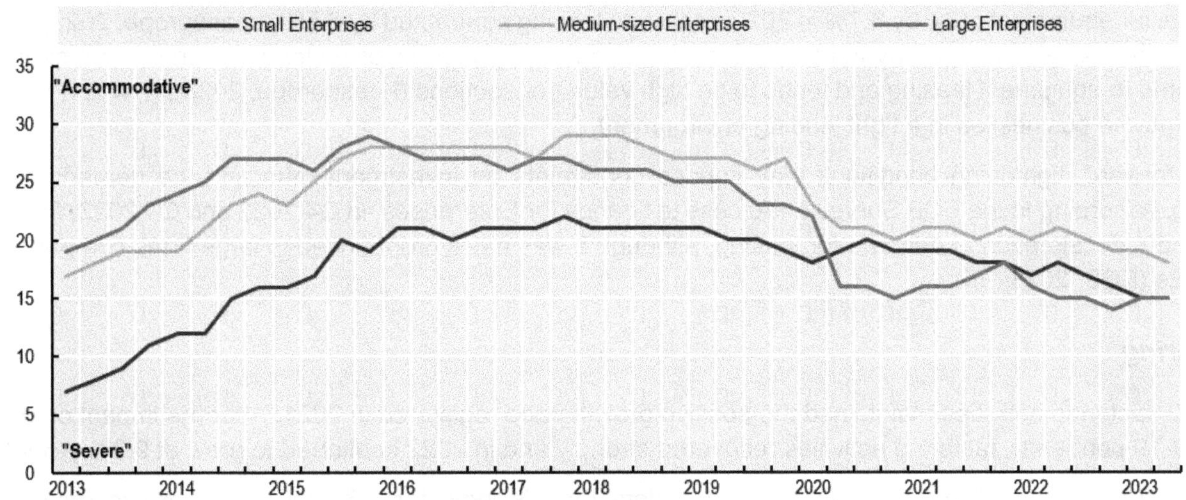

Note: Diffusion index of "Accommodative" minus "Severe", percentage points.
Source: (Bank of Japan, 2023[28])

StatLink https://stat.link/hx3so1

This tightening has occurred in a period where monetary policy has remained accommodative despite inflation exceeding the 2% target in April 2022, and the Bank of Japan announcing that there would be no change in its monetary policy stance (OECD, 2023[3]). This has resulted in exceptionally high uncertainty around baseline inflation projections (IMF, 2023[29]).

In the first quarter of 2023 however, speculation about a potential tightening of monetary policy resulted in companies shifting towards bank loans for longer-term funding. Anecdotal evidence suggests that Japanese loan rates had become more favourable than the cost of selling long-term bonds for businesses capital investment and refinancing needs, which typically decrease in value if interest rates rise. This shift in preference towards loans over bonds for longer-term funding needs indicates a significant change in the business lending landscape in Japan, influenced by the anticipation of potential changes in the country's monetary policy (The Japan Times, 2023[30]).

Asset-based finance

Leasing and hire purchases

Data from the country Scoreboards reveal that in 2022, leasing activities declined by 2.15%. This decline is, however, smaller than the one experienced in 2021, when leasing activities declined by 4%, indicating a gradual recovery of this type of finance (

Figure 1.15). From the 21 countries that provided data for this indicator, 15 experienced a decline in leasing volumes, with Ukraine (-77%), Peru (-34%) and Türkiye (-28%) registering the largest declines.

Information from Leaseurope, the trade association representing the European leasing industry, on the other hand, show positive developments in 2022, with new business volumes growing by 7.3% and the outstanding portfolio expanding by 5.2% compared to 2021 (Leaseurope, 2023[31]). Although the data from Leaseurope are not adjusted for inflation and need to be interpreted with caution considering the large surge in price levels in Europe in 2022, they indicate that leasing activities are recovering from the decline experienced in 2020 and 2021 when many businesses had to pause their activities and opted to use debt finance through COVID-19 government support channelled through banks. Despite the prospects of a gradual recovery in leasing, the rebound is not homogenous across asset classes: while new business volumes for equipment grew by 8.7% in 2022, real state leasing contracted by 6.5% (Leaseurope, 2023[31]). This can be explained in part by the fact that real estate leasing often involves longer-term commitments compared to equipment leasing and tends to be high value transactions (Leaseurope, 2023[32]), which may disincentivise businesses in a tight lending environment.

Going forward, tightening conditions may impose constraints on investment, affecting the demand for leasing. According to the ECB Survey on Access to finance for Enterprises, in Q4 2022 and Q1 2023, firms reported a deceleration in demand for leasing, although it was more pronounced in large firms compared to SMEs (ECB, 2023[11]).

Factoring

In 2022, factoring activities maintained the positive growth pace registered in 2021. After the impact of the COVID-19 pandemic, factoring activities recovered strongly and in 2022 continued to grow at 9.3% y-o-y (

Figure 1.15). Of the 17 countries that provided data for this indicator, 13 registered positive growth. Countries with the strongest growth were Hungary (32%), the United Kingdom (24%) and Belgium (18%). Data from Factors Chain International (FCI), the global association of the factoring, receivables and supply chain finance industry, also show an important growth of factoring activities in 2022. According to FCI, EUR 3 659 billion was transacted globally in 2022, compared to EUR 3 069 billion in 2021, which represents the single biggest increase ever reported in a given year (Factor Chain International, 2023[33]).

Going forward, factoring activities are expected to continue to grow as tightening lending conditions and high borrowing costs can incentivise many SMEs to opt for this alternative finance instrument. On one hand, the increase in the cost of raw materials and operational expenses amid tightening lending criteria may increase the demand for factoring, which can provide working capital more easily than bank finance. On the other hand, as banks are more risk averse, overindebted businesses might be unable to access debt finance to maintain operations, and selling their account receivables at a discount can be a viable option to continue their business activities. In addition, high inflation increases the likelihood that firms will delay payments to their suppliers. Factoring can help firms fill the gap of capital and mitigate the negative effect of late payments on SME liquidity.

Figure 1.15. Leasing and hire purchases and factoring activities

Median growth rate

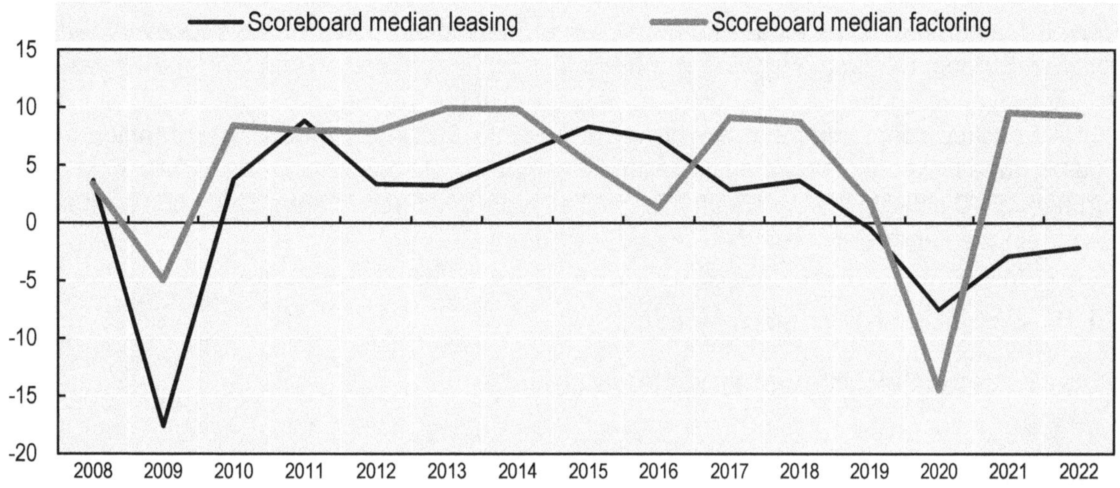

Source: Data compiled from individual country Scoreboards.

StatLink https://stat.link/ix8nuh

Equity finance for SMEs

Venture capital

Venture capital (VC) investments continued to experience strong volatility (Figure 1.16 right panel). They declined sharply in 2022, by 16.2%, after the historic growth experienced in 2021, when VC investment activities increased by 60%. This sharp decline was driven by several events. First, as reported in the 2023 Scoreboard Highlights (OECD, 2023[34]), interest rate hikes, or in some cases the anticipation of interest rate increases, contributed to the decision by large-scale investors including pension funds to turn their investments towards less volatile fixed-return asset classes. This is confirmed by recent survey data from European VC fund managers from Q3 2023, which shows that for 79% of respondents, a prolonged increase in interest rates is impacting investor appetite to invest in VC funds (EIF, 2023[35]).

This shift resulted in a decline in start-up valuations which put further downward pressure on VC fundraising. Data from Preqin show that in 2022 VC down rounds[8] made up 8.6% of all deals worldwide, compared to 6.8% between 2017 and 2021. Down rounds varied across stages, with more down rounds seen in later-stage series C and D (Preqin, 2023[36]).

With many valuations down and VC investors pulling out, VC fund returns suffered. According to Pitchbook data, the rolling one-year IRR for VC dropped to 2.8% in Q2 2022 (its lowest level since Q4 2016), and Q4 2022 registered a sixth consecutive quarter of decline in the IRR (Pitchbook, 2022[37]) (Pitchbook, 2023[38]).

Figure 1.16 show VC investment activities by country, expressed as a share of GDP. 18 out of 28 countries showed a decline in VC investments. In the US, VC volumes as a percent of GDP fell to 0.7% in 2022, down from 1.1% registered in 2021; in Canada they fell to 0.3%, down from 0.5%, and in Finland they fell to 0.1% in 2022, down from 0.3% in 2021. In the US, although the first quarter of 2023 saw a rebound with an increase in VC fundraising of 37% q-o-q growth, fund formation remained subdued (EY, 2023[39]). In Canada, data on investments by the Business Development Bank of Canada showed a marked decline in up rounds between Q2 2022 and Q2 2023, indicating that investors were seeking protection through a lower valuation entry point, resulting in projections indicating a slowing down in capital deployment for 2023 (BDC, 2023[40]). As VC investments decline, women and minority groups are particularly vulnerable. Box 1.1 shows data of VC fundraising performance of female and other demographic groups of entrepreneurs.

Going forward, a number of challenges need to be overcome to support a durable recovery and growth in VC activity. In Europe, for example, there is a need to incentivize more private long-term investors to stay in the market, even in economic downturns, to improve exit markets and to strengthen the availability of funds for VC-backed companies that aim to scale up (EIF, 2023[35]). In other geographies like the US, challenges include limited exit opportunities with rising inability of companies to go public, high geographic concentration of VC activities in the country, as well as a gradual drop in angel and seed rounds provoked by an uncertain market environment (NVCA and Pitchbook, 2023[41]).

Figure 1.16. Venture capital volumes by country

Volumes as a percent of GDP (left), median growth rate (right)

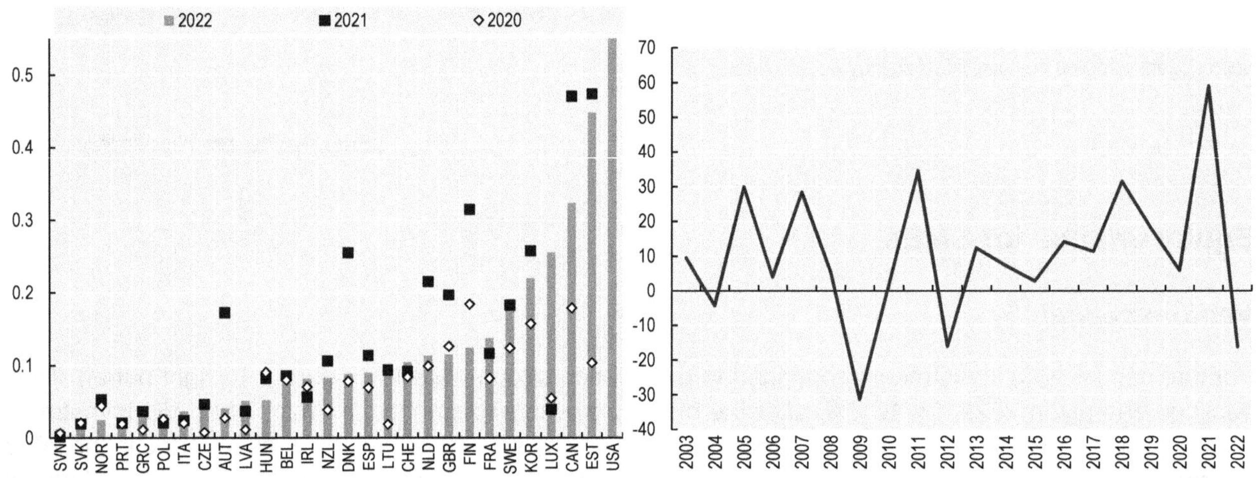

Note: As the volumes are expressed as a share of GDP, precaution on the interpretation of the graph is needed considering the impact of the COVID-19 crisis on GDP. Data from the United States do not appear in the graph due to the scale used. In 2020, the VC volume as a percentage of GDP was 0.6%., in 2021 1.1% and in 2022 0.7%.
Source: OECD Entrepreneurship Finance Database.

StatLink https://stat.link/86zge0

Box 1.1. Gender and minority imbalances in access to venture capital

A persistent issue in VC activities is the unequal access to equity funding for female entrepreneurs compared to their male counterparts. In the United Kingdom just 2% of the total of equity investment in 2022 went to SMEs with all female teams (British Business Bank, 2023[42]) . In Finland, in 2021, women accounted for 11% of the board seats in PE-backed companies and 6% of VC-backed companies (see Finland country snapshot). Worldwide in 2020, businesses owned or led by women received only about 2% of total venture capital investments and the women entrepreneurs who were able to acquire funding received on average only about 70% of the funding that men received (Crunchbase, 2020[43]; OECD, 2023[44]). The problem stems in part from underrepresentation of women in the VC and PE investor base. In Europe, women occupy about 23% of European VC roles, and only one in seven of senior VC investors is a woman. Of those, nine in ten works in male majority teams (EIF, Invest Europe, 2023[45]).

Furthermore, when VC investments decline, women-owned businesses tend to be the most affected, with their VC investments dropping more prominently compared to businesses that have male and female co-founders (Figure 1.17) (Crunchbase, 2020[43]). This also holds true for other demographic groups. In the United States, while total VC investments dropped by 36% in 2022, VC investments to black entrepreneurs dropped by 45% in the same period (Crunchbase, 2023[46]). In the United Kingdom, less than 2% of VC investment value in 2022 went to all ethnic minorities, while 43% of seed stage funding went to graduates from "elite" universities (British Business Bank, 2023[42]). In response to this persistent issue, governments are increasingly taking action to address these gaps in access to finance, in particular with respect to gender gaps (see section Evolution of government policy responses).

Figure 1.17. Global Venture Deal volume to female-only and female/male co-founded companies

Investment volumes Billion USD (left axis), and number of deals (right axis)

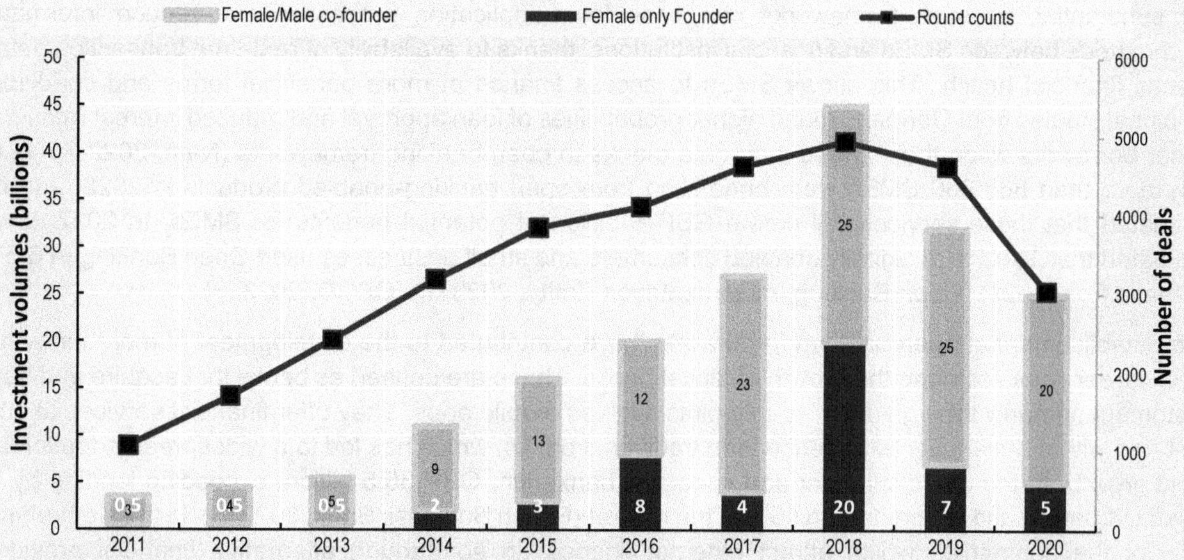

Note: Start-ups without founders listed in Crunchbase and private equity are excluded.
Source: Global VC funding to female founders dropped dramatically this year, (Crunchbase, 2020[43])

StatLink https://stat.link/4hoviz

Fintech developments

In recent years, the Fintech industry has experienced remarkable development, contributing to reshaping the SME financing landscape. Online finance solutions have become more mainstream, with many traditional lenders partnering with online platforms, and with governments expanding the range of institutions they use to channel SME financing support. Furthermore, the growing use of open banking frameworks has contributed to the offer of more innovative products and services, fuelling the growth of digital banks and online alternative finance platforms, which have demonstrated their usefulness in reaching underserved segments of the SME population.

As documented by previous editions of this Scoreboard, online alternative platforms[9] have seen continued and accelerated growth in recent years, and including during the pandemic when volumes of funding transacted through online alternative finance grew 57% y-o-y (OECD, 2023[34]). Such platforms have demonstrated their ability to reach underserved segments of the SMEs. The trend is becoming more prevalent in countries where banks tend to be more risk-averse, and where borrowing costs are high. For example, survey data from Southeast Asian countries[10] show that most users of these platforms are sole traders (78%) and young companies, 1 to 5 years old (56%). Of the MSMEs that raised funding through platforms 65% had previously approached banks for funding. (Cambridge Centre for Alternative Finance, 2022[47]). Similar findings were seen in Latin America[11], where 76% of respondents who secured finance from alternative platforms were sole traders. From the total of respondents, about 80% tried a bank provider but 70% were unable to finance their business through this source (Cambridge Centre for Alternative Finance, 2022[48]).

Furthermore, open banking, which refers to the practice of sharing banking data via standardised and secure interfaces at the request of clients (OECD, 2023[49]), has been gaining traction, as a way to enhance SME access to finance and streamline application procedures. This allows for the secure sharing of SME financial information with financial institutions or with service providers, with the entrepreneurs' consent. According to a new study on open banking frameworks, 25 out of 31 OECD countries taking part in the survey have established such frameworks (OECD, 2023[49]). The implications for SME access to finance are substantial, as such frameworks can ease loan application processes and reduce information asymmetries between SMEs and financial institutions, thanks to availability of real-time transaction data to assess financial health. This allows SMEs to access finance at more beneficial terms and conditions. Empirical studies from Germany found higher probabilities of loan approval and reduced interest rates from riskier borrowers when they shared their data thanks to open banking frameworks (Nam, 2022[50]). In the UK, more than 660 000 SMEs were benefitting from open banking-enabled products in 2022, and it is estimated that these services will create GBP 6 billion of potential benefits for SMEs. In 2022, it was estimated that 10-11% of digitally enabled consumers and small businesses used Open Banking (a 6.57% increase from 2021) (Open Banking Implementation Entity, 2023[51]) (OECD, 2023[49]).

The establishment of open banking frameworks have contributed to the development of more innovative financial services, fostering the growth of digital banks. These are defined as banks that acquire and serve customers primarily through digital touchpoints such as mobile apps. They offer financial services at a low cost and with a better user experience than traditional banks, which has led to a widespread adoption and rapid growth. In the UK, challenger and specialist banks lent GBP 35.5 billion, exceeding lending by the major UK banks, and concentrating 55% of the market (British Business Bank, 2023[52]). In the Netherlands, 40% of the companies which attract external finance do so through alternative financial providers, especially for loans of less than EUR 250 000. In some countries, digital banks have reached market capitalisation nearly as large as some of the largest traditional banks (IMF, 2022[53]).

Payment delays, bankruptcies, and non-performing loans

Enterprise distress indicators reacted to the heightened cost of credit and the uncertain economic environment in 2022, but they also reflect governmental measures aimed at counteracting the negative effects of inflation and credit tightening. Payment delays remained relatively stable due to initiatives streamlining payment periods in some countries, and non-performing loans (NPLs) have continued their long-term downward trend, thanks to constant NPL deleveraging, as well as the implementation of debt restructuring measures. On the other hand, bankruptcy rates increased in almost all group of countries, in part due to the resumption of court activities and adjustments.

Payment delays

In 2022, the Scoreboard median of payment delays stood at 12 days, the same median registered in 2021. Looking at specific country developments, payment delays remained stable in 2022, despite the detrimental effects that rising costs generally have on payment periods. Policy measures to reduce payment periods might have in part contributed to these developments (see section on the Evolution of government policy responses). In 2022, 11 out of 16 countries reduced the payment delays for business-to-business (B2B) transactions (compared to 9 in 2021), 4 countries increased the number of days and one country did not register any change. The countries that increased the number of days are, however, among the group of countries that registered shorter payment periods (ranging from 9 to 14 days), namely Austria, Denmark, Korea, Portugal. From the countries that registered the longest payment periods, including Colombia (97 days), Chile (47 days) and Czech Republic (43 days), Colombia and the Czech Republic appeared to have made progress, reducing the number of payment periods by 16 and 5 days accordingly between 2021 and 2022.

In 2023, if costs continue to increase, the likelihood that firms would experience late receipt of payments and subsequently pay their own suppliers late may materialise. A study from the European Commission, exploring the effects of inflation and decline of GDP on late payments in 2022, estimates that across the EU, the number of days that SMEs will take to collect payments increased by 1.5 due to inflation and 1.6 days due to the reduction in the 2022 GDP growth rate (Bella, Katsinis and Laguera-Gonzalez, 2023[5]). These developments have important implications for firm growth. Already by the end of 2022, 40% of European companies reported that late payment diminished their growth, and 26% indicated it was threatening their survival (Intrum Justicia, 2022[54]). Furthermore, according to the European Commission, late payments are a factor in a quarter of SME bankruptcies (European Commission, 2023[55]). In response to these developments governments are taking action to reduce payment periods (see section on Evolution of government policy responses).

Figure 1.18. Payment delays

By country, number of days

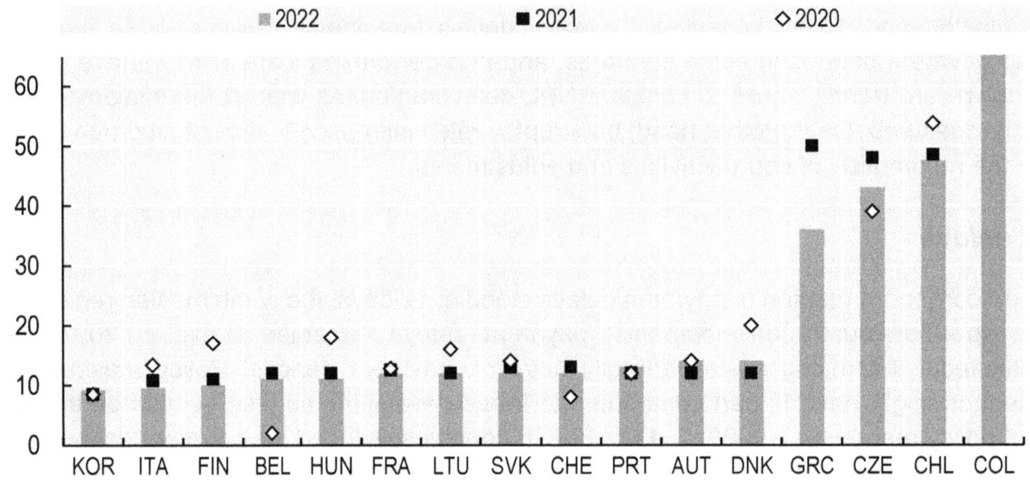

Note: Data from Colombia do not appear in the graph due to the scale used. In 2020, the payment period was 103 days, in 2021 113 days and in 2022 97 days.
Source: Data compiled from individual country Scoreboards.

StatLink https://stat.link/chogsk

Bankruptcies

In 2022, almost all country groups registered an increase in bankruptcies, with the Scoreboard median rising by 21%. EU country bankruptcies increased by 27%, upper-middle economies grew by 16% while non-EU high-income countries declined by 8%.

The overall surge can be attributed to the adjustment after two years of declining bankruptcy rates during the pandemic, as a result of changes in bankruptcy procedures, cessation of court activity and unprecedented financial support provided to SMEs. In 2022, almost all countries had phased out support and resumed court activities. For example, in France, the resumption of legal proceedings in early 2022 led to a 50% jump in cases compared to the same period in 2021 (Le Monde, 2023[56]). Similarly, in the United States, a decrease in the debt threshold for SMEs to declare bankruptcy under the specialized provision known as subchapter V saw a corresponding rise in this indicator (Reuters, 2022[57]). Despite these adjustments, bankruptcies in France and the United States remained below pre-pandemic levels in 2022. In Australia, permanent reforms, including a new formal debt restructuring process and a simplified liquidation pathway, came into effect on 1 January 2021, which are available to incorporated businesses with liabilities of less than AUD 1 million (see Australia country snapshot).

Despite SMEs entering in 2023 with relatively strong liquidity positions, the increase in bankruptcies can also be indicative of a growing number of SMEs that find it difficult to maintain operations amid elevated borrowing and input costs, and increased difficulties in accessing finance. Nevertheless, bankruptcies generally did not exceed pre-COVID levels.

Figure 1.19. SME bankruptcies by group of countries

Median year-on-year growth rate, as a percentage

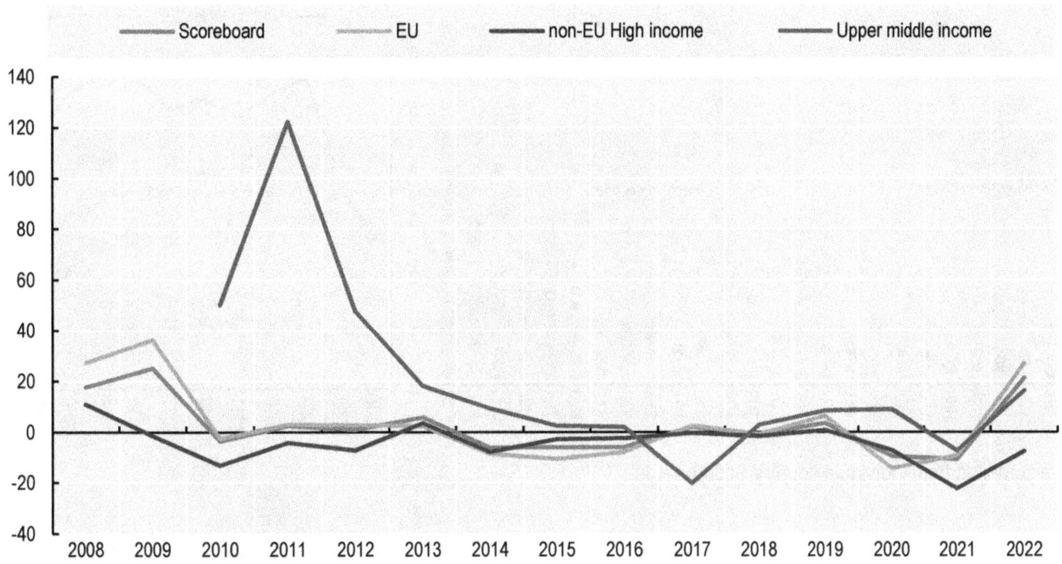

Source: Data compiled from individual country Scoreboards.

StatLink https://stat.link/stxf3u

Non-performing loans

NPLs are overall more prevalent among SMEs than in the general business population. However, the long-term trend shows that, since the 2008 crisis, NPLs have experienced a decline in SMEs and in all firms. Specifically, between 2021 and 2022, despite the tightening of lending conditions for corporate loans, the median of SME NPLs declined to 2.4% (down from 3.3% in 2021) and for all firms dropped to 1.8% (down from 1.9% in 2021)Figure 1.20 (right panel). The negative trend is also evident when looking at the share of SME NPLs by country between 2021 and 2022. From the 25 countries that provided data for this indicator, 18 registered a decline. The most significant drops were experienced in Greece (-7.22%), Türkiye (-2.4%), Chile (-1.9%), Ireland (1.7%), Poland (1.2%) and the Netherlands (1.2%) Figure 1.20 (left panel).

In Greece, NPLs have been declining for eight consecutive years due to the Hercules Programme, which assists commercial banks in securitising and removing them from their balance sheets (see Greece country snapshot). In Türkiye, temporary regulation changes in the definition of NPLs and the increase in the total amount of SME loans resulted in a decline of the SME NPL ratio (see Türkiye country snapshot). In Chile, while the NPL ratio for total businesses increased, the SME NPL ratio declined in part explained by the implementation of debt restructuring measures, as well as interest and fines forgiveness, and payment extensions (see Chile country snapshot) (Ministerio de Economía, Fomento y Turismo, 2022[58]). In Europe, according to the European Banking Authority, the downward trend of SME NPL ratios is due to a constant NPL deleveraging as a result of regulatory changes on the management of non-performing and forborne exposures (European Banking Authority, 2018[59]). This has resulted in banks entering well-prepared to face weaker asset quality due to higher borrowing costs (KPMG, 2022[60]). In addition, European banks have gradually built up provisions for non-performing loan books. In Q3 2022, the NLP coverage ratio of EU banks[12], which indicates the ability of banks to absorb future losses, amounted to 45.5% (European Commission, 2023[61]).

Figure 1.20. Non-performing loans

Volumes as a percent of total SME loans (left), median growth rate (right)

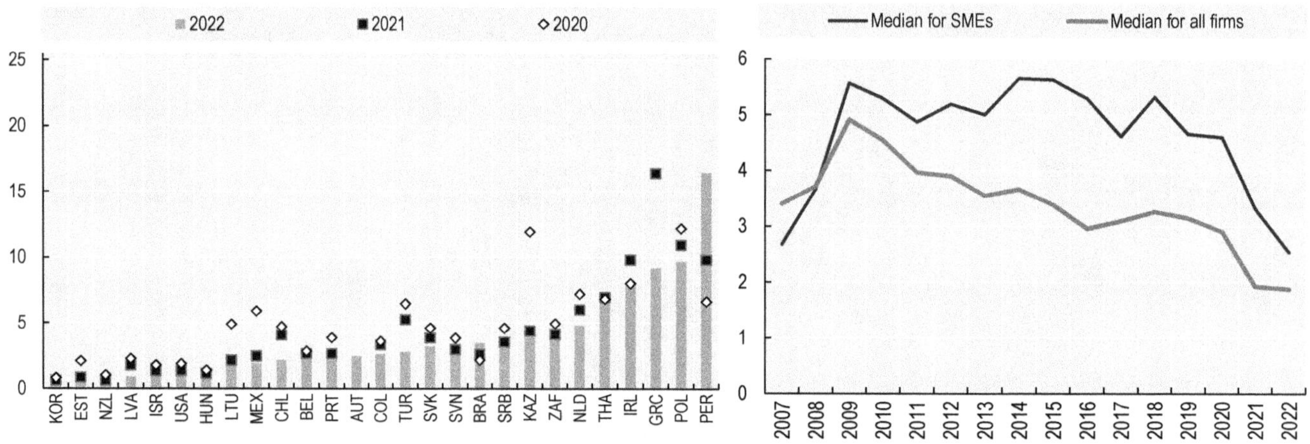

Source: Data compiled from individual country Scoreboards.

StatLink https://stat.link/nasyfo

Evolution of government policy responses

Governments around the world have responded to the high inflation environment by implementing a diverse range of strategies, with the aim of ensuring SMEs have access to the finance they need. Some immediate measures included supporting SMEs to absorb the rise in prices of energy and raw materials and strengthening SME lending amid tight lending conditions. Efforts to alleviate the adverse effects of inflation on SMEs are also being concentrated on minimising late payments in both government-to-business and business-to-business deals and facilitating access to a diverse set of instruments and sources of finance to sustain SME investments, in particular in the green and digital transitions. Measures to promote gender equality in access to capital have also increasingly been implemented.

Table 1.1 summarises the government policies in place in 2021 and 2022 for participating countries. This is not a comprehensive overview of policy initiatives, but rather an overview of broad categories. More information about the policy landscape can be found in the individual country snapshots.

Table 1.1. Government policy instruments to foster SME access to finance, 2021-22

				Support for start-up finance				
Country	Government loan guarantees	Direct lending to SMEs	Subsidised interest rates	Special guarantees and loans for start-ups	Venture Capital funds (direct)	Funds of funds	Business Angel co-investments	Non-financial support for SMEs
Australia	X							X
Austria	X	X		X	X			X
Belgium	X	X						
Brazil								
Canada	X	X	X		X			X

Chile	X	X			X			
China		X	X	X				
Colombia				X		X	X	
Czech Republic	X	X	X		X	X		
Denmark					X	X	X	X
Estonia	X	X						
Finland	X				X	X	X	
France	X	X						
Georgia								X
Germany	X	X		X	X	X	X	X
Greece	X	X	X		X	X	X	X
Hungary	X	X						X
Indonesia								
Ireland	X	X		X	X		X	X
Israel	X	X			X			X
Italy	X							X
Japan	X	X						
Kazakhstan	X	X	X					X
Korea	X	X	X					
Latvia	X	X		X	X			X
Lithuania	X	X	X	X	X		X	X
Luxembourg	X					X		X
Malaysia								X
Mexico		X			X			X
Netherlands	X	X			X	X		X
New Zealand		X			X	X		X
Peru	X	X						
Poland	X	X						X
Portugal	X							X
Serbia	X							
Slovak Republic	X	X	X	X	X			
Slovenia	X	X			X	X		X
South Africa								
Spain	X					X		
Sweden		X						X
Switzerland	X							
Thailand	X							
Turkey	X	X		X	X	X	X	X
Ukraine	X	X						
United Kingdom	X	X		X	X	X	X	X
United States	X	X				X		X

Note: Country snapshots may not contain references to all initiatives.
Source: Individual Scoreboard country snapshots.

Based on information from participating countries, a number of broad emerging trends can be discerned and are presented below along with recent policy examples. Full country snapshots provide more detailed information on policy initiatives.

Financial support targeted SMEs affected by inflation and high energy costs

SMEs have been facing a number of shocks in recent years that have threatened their development, growth and even survival. On the heels of the COVID-19 crisis, SMEs were hit by a significant increase in input costs, resulting in soaring inflation rates. This challenge was exacerbated in regions that have, at the same time, been hit hard by the energy crisis caused by Russia's aggression against Ukraine. Governments have moved to provide support to SMEs, especially those in regions or sectors heavily dependent on Russian energy imports, or those that are finding difficult to navigate the steep increase in input and energy costs (OECD, 2023[62]).

Australia is progressing in several initiatives to improve the operating environment for SMEs, for example, reducing energy price pressures. These initiatives include the provision of electricity bill relief to eligible small businesses and households through the Energy Bill Relief Fund, in partnership with state and territory governments, with approximately one million small businesses projected to receive support through this fund. In addition, Australia introduced the Small Business Energy Incentive, a bonus 20% tax deduction for eligible assets to help small and medium businesses with an annual turnover of less than AUS 50 million electrify and save on their energy bills. Subject to the passage of legislation, the incentive would apply from 1 July 2023 until 30 June 2024. This builds on the Energy Efficiency Grants Program committed in 2021-22 (see Australian country snapshot).

In Austria, a series of relief packages have been implemented to support SMEs facing high energy costs. In May 2023, the fourth package was approved, which includes EUR 400 million to extend the suspension of electricity and natural gas taxes until the end of 2023 for SMEs. In parallel, the Federal Government implemented an energy cost subsidy covering 30% of the price difference compared to the previous year for electricity, gas and fuel. Furthermore, an additional relief package, which subsidises high energy costs (the so-called "EKZ 2") was introduced in 2023. For SMEs a flat rate subsidy is offered in addition to the energy cost subsidy (see Austria country snapshot). In the Belgian region of Flanders, SMEs facing liquidity needs as a result of the Ukraine crisis and the energy crisis can benefit from a bridge loan raging from EUR 10 000 to EUR 2 million. The maximum loan amount is limited to 15% of the average annual turnover of 3 calendar years prior to the application. The programme started in Q1 2022 until the end of 2023 (see Belgium country snapshot). Going forward, and as global energy prices start to decline, it is expected that these measures will be phased out in 2024.

Targeted government guarantees are being put in place to strengthen SME lending in light of tighter conditions

With many SMEs finding difficult to access the necessary capital to maintain operations in the current context, a number of governments are launching new financial support measures, including credit guarantees targeted to specific objectives, purposes and profiles of firms.

Despite the overall decline in the use of government credit guarantees after the pandemic, with the Scoreboard median of credit guaranteed loans declining by 21% in 2022, the contribution of government guaranteed loans to the SME loan stock has increased to reach 8% (up from 6.9% in 2021) Figure 1.21. This indicates that, despite the decline in the total stock of SME loans, a larger volume of this was backed by government guarantees in 2022. Looking by group of countries, the increase is more marked in the EU, where it rose to reach 9% (up from 6.6% in 2021). Similarly, in upper-middle-income economies, the median increased to 8% (up from 7.4% in 2021). In non-EU high-income countries, however, the median continued its downward trend since 2020.

Figure 1.21. The median contribution of government guaranteed loans to SME loan stock

Median year-on-year growth rate, as a percentage

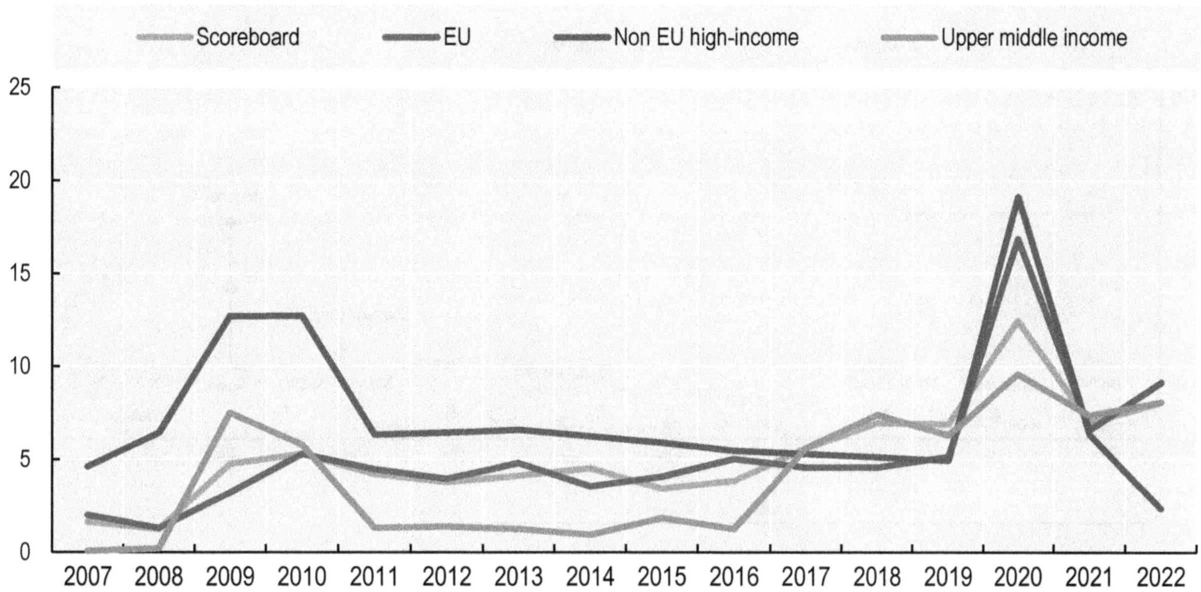

Source: Data compiled from individual country Scoreboards.

StatLink https://stat.link/6gkoae

In Belgium, the European Investment Fund (EIF) has signed four new guarantee agreements backed by the Invest EU programme. The new schemes will unlock EUR 608.5 million in new financing for Belgian SMEs ranging from microfinancing to small mid-caps. In particular for SMEs in Brussels, finance&invest.brussels will receive EUR 78 million in new lending. The InvestEU backing for this transaction focuses on SME competitiveness and sustainability. The focus is also on supporting seed financing and backing start-ups with subordinated lending. In Flanders, a direct EIF guarantee with PMV Group will cover a loan portfolio of EUR 132.5 million (EIF, 2023[63]). In Chile, the guarantee fund for SMEs (FOGAPE) has included flexible payment agreements for tax owed by SMEs affected by high interest rates and higher input prices, as well as SMEs that have not yet received support from other FOGAPE programmes. The objective will be the financing of working capital, refinancing and investment with guarantees of up to 95% for microenterprises, 90% small and 85% for medium, with a maximum rate of TPM + 5% (see Chile country snapshot).

At the subnational level, Figure 1.20 shows that among countries for which information is available, government loan guarantees were more common in Hungary, Italy and Poland, where there is indeed a strong tradition in the use of this policy instrument. Regional variance, measured through the standard deviation of regional values (i.e. regional government loan guarantees in relation to regional GDP), is stronger in Poland (0.9 percentage points) and Italy (0.6 percentage points). Government loan guarantees as a share of GDP are larger in less well-off regions in the case of Poland (Mazoweicki region) and Hungary (Southern Great Plain). However, this is not the case in Italy, where the top six regions are all from the better-off north and centre of the country[13] , which might signal risk aversion among Italian banks as well as especially difficult financing conditions in Italy's South.

Figure 1.22. Government Loan Guarantees for SMEs at the regional level, 2022

Percentage of Regional GDP

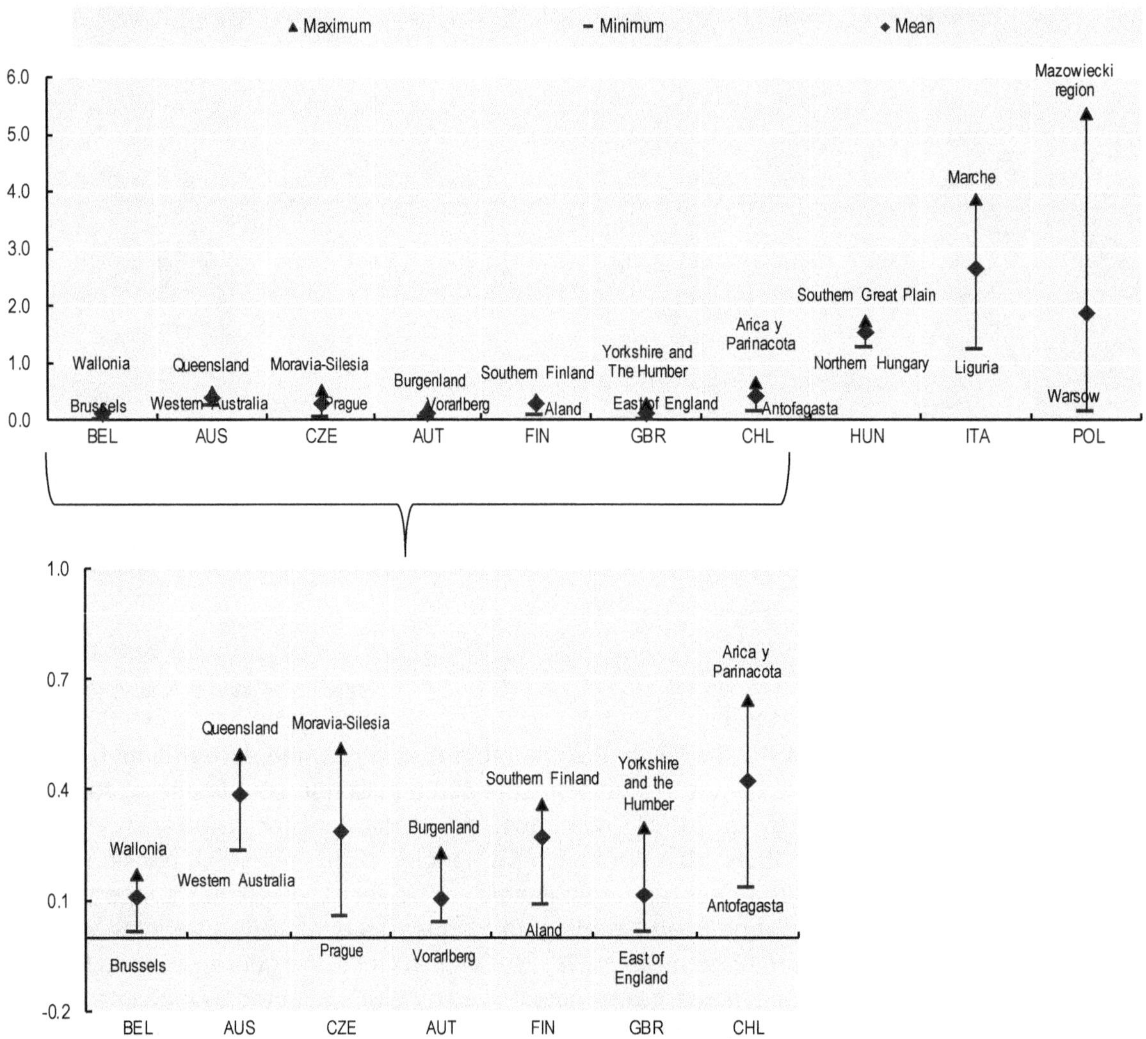

Source: Data compiled from individual country Scoreboards.

StatLink https://stat.link/cni8ye

Additional efforts to reduce late payments are part of the policy mix to strengthen SME liquidity

Late payments from public and private customers are a longstanding issue for SMEs, for whom payments serve to provide access to liquidity without taking on debt. In the current challenging context, many governments have put in place new laws and directives to enhance prompt payments and strengthen SME liquidity, with the aim of increasing the financial resilience of SMEs. The European Commission (EC) has included the revision of the Late Payment Directive (LPD) in its work programme for 2023. The goal of this revision is to create a more robust legal system with clearly defined maximum payment terms for B2B transactions and improve enforcement and monitoring. Additionally, it seeks to provide SMEs with easy access to effective mediation tools and clarify provisions to prevent unfair practices and abuses (DG GROW, 2023[64]). More recently, as part of the SME Relief Package, the EC has proposed a revision of the late payment rules to replace the existing LPD with a binding regulation with maximum payment terms of 30 days for all commercial transactions. It will make the payment of compensatory fees and interest automatic in case of late payment and bind these new measures with a robust enforcement framework. The proposal also makes it easier for companies to claim their rights by reducing the burden of, and facilitating access to, effective redress via mediation (European Commission, 2023[65]).

Other governments have announced reviews to assess the efficacy of their current late payment laws. In Australia, three measures aim to improve payment times for small businesses. The first one is the Payment Times Reporting Scheme, where transparency around payment performance encourages large businesses and government enterprises to improve their payment practices. On 6 December 2022, the Australian Government announced an independent review of the Payment Times Reporting Act 2020 as required under the legislation. The second measure is the Payment Times Procurement Connected Policy, which leverages Australian Government procurement to improve payment times to small businesses in the supply chains of government contracts. Finally, the third is the Supplier Pay On-Time or Pay Interest Policy, which requires Australian Government agencies pay invoices in 20 calendar days (and invoices in 5 calendar days) or pay interest on late payments (see Australia country snapshot).

At the end of 2022, the UK government also launched a review to tackle late business payments. The review, known as the *Prompt Payment and Cash Flow Review,* aims to examine existing payment practices and measures. In the past years, the government has introduced regulations that have improved payment practices, such as the Prompt Payment Code and the establishment of the Small Business Commissioner to hold non-compliant businesses to account (Department for Business, Energy and Industrial Strategy, 2023[66]). In the current framework, the payment date for business-to-business (B2B) transactions usually has to be within 60 days of the customer receiving an invoice or within 60 days of receiving the goods or services. For public authorities, the rules are stricter. Public sector contracts must be paid no more than 30 days after invoicing or delivery. Businesses that fail to pay their suppliers within the legal timeframe are liable to pay interest or debt recovery fees to the payee (UK Government, 2023[67]).

Governments are increasingly implementing measures to address the gender gap in access to finance

In recent years, the gender disparity in access to finance for female entrepreneurs has been increasingly acknowledged in many countries. This has led to a series of policy initiatives aimed at addressing the gender gap, as many governments recognise the multiplier effect that investing in women-led businesses can have on creating inclusive economic growth and resilience (OECD, 2023[44]). It is estimated that gender parity in entrepreneurship could add USD 5 to 6 trillion in net value to the global economy (Women Entrepreneurs Finance Initiative, 2022[68]), which represents a USD 1.7 trillion in growth opportunity for financial institutions (World Bank, 2020[69]).

A notable trend is the establishment of government-backed funds specifically designed to strengthen women-led enterprises. These funds typically target early-stage businesses, supplying women entrepreneurs with the capital required for growth. One such example is the Women in Technology Venture Fund, introduced by the Canadian government in 2018. The Fund, managed by the Business Development Bank of Canada, has a portfolio of CAD 200 million and targets women-led technology companies in the seed to series B investment stages (BDC, 2022[70]). Other initiatives include Enterprise Ireland's Competitive Start-Fund for Female Entrepreneurs which have expanded considerably under the 6-year plan for Women in Business launched in 2020. It offers EUR 50 000 in equity funding to early-stage startups led by women that show the potential to employ over ten people and achieve EUR 1 million in export sales within three years. The fund's size has doubled since 2016, reaching EUR 1 million in 2020 (Enterprise Ireland, 2021[71]). In France, a debt guarantee dedicated to support women entrepreneurs “Garantie EGALITE Femmes” was implemented by Bpifrance and France Active. It aims to facilitate women’s access to bank credit to finance the creation, takeover or development of their business (bpifrance, 2023[72]). In Switzerland, there is also a dedicated guarantee scheme SAFFA, to support women that wish to become self-employed or that wanted to take over or expand an existing business (SAFFA, 2023[73]).

Alongside this financial support, there are initiatives designed to provide female entrepreneurs with skills and networks to successfully secure funding. These initiatives include mentorship schemes, networking events, and capacity-building workshops. The SBA in the United States runs Women's Business Centers (WBCs) across the country. These centres offer business training, mentoring, and networking opportunities to women entrepreneurs. They also provide assistance in accessing capital, including guidance on preparing a strong loan application.

Additionally, there has been a push for greater transparency in access to finance by gender. This includes efforts to collect and publish data on the gender breakdown of entrepreneurs receiving different types of finance. The goal is to highlight the extent of the gender gap and encourage more equitable funding practices. In 2013, the G20 recognised the importance of data collection and analysis as a priority action in addressing the SME finance gender gap and developed a basic set of gender-disaggregated financial indicators, as part of the G20 Global Partnership on Financial Inclusion (GPFI) and its SME Finance Subgroup indicators (World Bank, 2020[69]). The 2022 Updated G20/OECD High-Level Principles on SME Financing, which were embodied in a new Recommendation on SME Financing approved by the OECD Council at Ministerial level in June 2023, also call for gender-disaggregated data collection (OECD, 2023[74]). Additionally, the present Scoreboard is working to mainstream the collection of gender-disaggregated data and information, following a pilot exercise which revealed the limited availability of gender-disaggregated data in Scoreboard countries. Another case in point is the Women Entrepreneurs Finance (We-Fi) Code[14], a global multi-stakeholder effort seeking to expand the quality and quantity of data on women-led firms' financing across a larger group of countries.

Specific country initiatives to enhance the transparency on the gender dimension on SME access to finance are also worth noting. In the UK, the Investing in Women Code is a case in point. In 2019, the government introduced a voluntary public-private partnership with the objective to strengthen the quantity and quality of information on gender gaps in access to finance and mobilise financial institutions to help bridge this gap (UK Department for Business and Trade, 2022[75]). As of June 2023, 204 organisations had signed up to the code, and the impact has been visible. As of H2 2023, VC signatories represented a record large share of the market, and the number of deals made by these VCs with all female teams rose 3 p.p. between 2021 and 2022 (UK Department for Business and Trade, 2023[76]). In Mexico, in 2014, the Government approved the Financial Reform law, with the mandate to promote gender equality in access to financial services and in programmes led by national development banks (Data2x, 2019[77]). This contributed positively to fostering financial inclusion in the country. In 2015, soon after the reform took place, the gender gap in the holding of an account declined by 4.3 p.p. with stronger improvements in rural areas compared to urban areas according to a report from the National Council for Financial Inclusion (National Council for Financial Inclusion, 2016[78]).

Measures to promote alternative financing instruments to sustain SME investments in the twin transition are being introduced

In addition to the "build back better" measures launched in the wake of the COVID-19 pandemic, which included measures to help SMEs adapt to the green and digital transitions (OECD, 2022[21]), governments are continuing to work to build SME resilience in light of new macroeconomic shocks. The current tightening of lending conditions has led many SMEs to reduce their investments, with implications for their ability to adapt to the twin transition. This is in part due to the fact that higher interest rates often disincentivise business investment, with firms finding more attractive to place retained earnings on deposits or in interest-bearing financial instruments rather than using them to fund investment and working capital (ECB, 2023[8]).

What is more, the expected decline in business investment also impacts on firms' resource efficiency actions and digital transformations. Studies looking at investment dynamics in Europe found that in periods with high inflation, the share of companies not undertaking resource-efficient investments increase by 13 p.p., and interviews with SMEs also indicate to the postponement of substantial and long-term investments related to the green transition (Kalemli-Özcan, Laeven and Moreno, 2019[79]). However, this phenomenon in the current context may have been mitigated by the high energy prices, with the probability of SMEs investing to be more energy-efficient increasing by 6 p.p. (Bella, Katsinis and Laguera-Gonzalez, 2023[5]).

Recognising the importance of maintaining SME investments to adapt to the green and digital transitions, many governments have implemented measures. The Flemish Region in Belgium introduced a new quasi-equity instrument to incentivize these investments. The "Breakthrough loan" programme started in Q1 2022 with the objective of accelerating ambitious projects around digital transformation, sustainability transition, and internationalisation. The Breakthrough loan offers a unique form of financing that blends risk capital and subsidies. To be eligible, SMEs need to pass a validation to demonstrate financial sustainability. The financing terms of the Breakthrough loan include a ticket size ranging from 50 000 to 250 000 EUR and a term duration of 2 to 8 years. For the initial three years, capital repayments are not permitted. The loan carries a fixed interest rate of 4%. Companies that achieve a "breakthrough" can expect active guidance from the project partners (see Belgium country snapshot). In Türkiye, KOSGEB introduced two programmes to support SME innovation: the Advanced Entrepreneurship Support Programme with a budget up to TRY 1 million in Q4 2022, and the R&D, Innovation and Product Development Support Programme in Q1 2021. In the latter, public support include on R&D, innovation and product development projects up to TRY 1.1 million or up to TRY 6 million via calls for specified sectors. SMEs that have successfully completed R&D and P&D processes within the scope of digital transition can benefit from the SME Techno-Investment Support Programme which provides up to TRY 10 million support for the commercialization of their products (see Türkiye country snapshot).

Looking ahead

In 2022, against the backdrop of tight monetary policy, high borrowing costs and low availability of finance, both the stocks and flows of SME loans declined. With the steep increase in policy interest rates in most countries around the world, the cost of SME financing registered an increase unprecedented in the history of the Scoreboard which has resulted in a lower uptake of SME loans. Equity finance also exhibited a decline, in part explained by the cyclical nature of this type of finance, with investors seeking out other types of fixed return investments in response to interest rate hikes.

In 2022 and 2023, SME finance policy responded to these developments and the uncertain economic environment, characterised by elevated inflation and input costs, and a subsequent strong tightening of lending conditions. Governments have deployed a number of measures to support SMEs, ranging from immediate interventions, such as buffering against the spike in energy and raw material costs, to more long-term initiatives like streamlining payments and diversifying financial sources and instruments to help SMEs sustain their investments. Furthermore, the government focus on maintaining SME investments on green and digital transitions showcase the future pathways for SMEs to achieve sustainable businesses and contribute to a resilient economy. In addition, the growing emphasis on achieving gender equality in accessing finance recognises that sustainable and inclusive economic growth depends not only on economic robustness, but also on creating a fair and inclusive environment for all entrepreneurs.

The new OECD Recommendation on SME Financing provides important guidance to governments in their efforts to foster access to a diverse range of financing instruments for SMEs and to build evidence-based policies in this area (OECD, 2023[74]). The strong political consensus around SME finance issues was further underlined during the June 2023 meeting of the OECD Committee on SMEs and Entrepreneurship at Ministerial level[15].

While there are indications that many SMEs have been able to adapt to the less favourable financing environment thanks to better liquidity positions compared to the onset of the pandemic crisis, there is no room for complacency. The Scoreboard will continue to evolve in order to help monitor countries' progress against their commitments, along with developments in the SME financing and policy landscape, to support governments in developing policies that meet SME financing needs, foster greater resilience and contribute to a sustainable and inclusive economy.

References

AECM (2023), *AECM members' support to SMEs affected by the war in Ukraine*, https://aecm.eu/wp-content/uploads/2023/02/20230224_AECM-brochure-on-Ukraine-measures-1.pdf. [98]

AECM (2023), *AECM Statistical Yearbook 2022*, https://www.flipsnack.com/aecmeurope/202305_aecm-statistical-yearbook-2022.html. [24]

Amundi (2023), *Bonds are back: credit markets in focus during 2023*, https://research-center.amundi.com/article/bonds-are-back-credit-markets-focus-during-2023. [85]

APEC (2022), *Public Policy, Fintech and SMEs: Recommendations for Promoting a New Financing Ecosystem*, https://www.apec.org/docs/default-source/publications/2022/8/public-policy-fintech-and-smes-recommendations-for-promoting-a-new-financing-ecosystem/222_smewg_public-policy-fintech-and-smes.pdf?sfvrsn=ff6f0c35_2. [90]

Australian Government (2023), *Energy Bill Relief Fund*, https://www.energy.gov.au/energy-bill-relief-fund. [94]

Australian Government - The Treasury (2023), *Small Business Energy Incentive*, https://www.ato.gov.au/about-ato/new-legislation/in-detail/businesses/small-business-energy-incentive. [95]

Banco de la República (2022), *Reporte de la situación del crédito en Colombia*, https://repositorio.banrep.gov.co/bitstream/handle/20.500.12134/10595/RSCC.pdf. [15]

Banco de México (2023), *Evolución del Financiamiento a las Empresas durante el Trimestre Octubre - Diciembre de 2022*, https://www.banxico.org.mx/publicaciones-y-prensa/evolucion-trimestral-del-financiamiento-a-las-empr/%7BD5CA1289-F2D7-09C2-7B2D-423C8E37F21D%7D.pdf. [13]

Bank of Japan (2023), *Tankan Outline (June 2023) : 日本銀行 Bank of Japan*, https://www.boj.or.jp/en/statistics/tk/yoshi/tk2306.htm (accessed on 27 July 2023). [28]

Banque de France (2022), *Loans by size of firms – September 2022*, https://www.banque-france.fr/sites/default/files/webstat_pdf/cre_tai_ent_2258_en-gb_si_credits_taille_entreprises_202209_en.pdf. [96]

BDC (2023), *Canada's Venture Capital Landscape*, https://www.bdc.ca/globalassets/digizuite/41066-report-canada-venture-capital-landscape-2023.pdf. [40]

BDC (2022), *Women in Technology Venture Fund*, https://www.bdc.ca/en/bdc-capital/venture-capital/funds/women-tech-fund. [70]

Bella, D., L. Katsinis and A. Laguera-Gonzalez (2023), "Annual Report on European SMEs 2022/2023", *GROW and JRC SME Performance Review - European Commission*, https://single-market-economy.ec.europa.eu/system/files/2023-06/Annual%20Report%20on%20European%20SMEs%202023.pdf (accessed on 24 July 2023). [5]

Board of Governors of the Federal Reserve System (2023), *Federal Reserve Supervision and Regulation Report*, https://www.federalreserve.gov/publications/2023-may-supervision-and-regulation-report-banking-system-conditions.htm. [97]

bpifrance (2023), *Garantie EGALITE Femmes*, https://bpifrance-creation.fr/encyclopedie/financements/dispositifs-garantie/garantie-egalite-femmes. [72]

British Business Bank (2023), *Challenger and specialist bank lending reached record high of £35.5bn in 2022, finds latest British Business Bank research*, https://www.british-business-bank.co.uk/press-release/challenger-and-specialist-bank-lending-reached-record-high-of-35-5bn-in-2022-finds-latest-british-business-bank-research/. [52]

British Business Bank (2023), *Finding what works: Pathways to Improve Diversity in Venture Capital Investment*, https://www.british-business-bank.co.uk/wp-content/uploads/2023/07/BBB_What_Works_in_VC_Report.pdf. [42]

British Business Bank (2023), *Small Business Finance Market 2022/23*, https://www.british-business-bank.co.uk/wp-content/uploads/2023/02/J0189_BBB_SBFM_Report_2023_AW.pdf. [20]

British Business Bank (2022), "Small Business Equity Tracker", https://www.british-business-bank.co.uk/small-business-equity-tracker-2022/ (accessed on 11 April 2023). [99]

British Business Bank (2022), *SME Finance Survey*, https://www.british-business-bank.co.uk/wp-content/uploads/2022/02/SME-Finance-Survey-2021-Report.pdf. [88]

BVA BDRC (2023), *SME Finance monitor*, https://www.bva-bdrc.com/sme-finance-monitor/. [12]

Cambridge Centre for Alternative Finance (2022), *The ASEAN Access to Digital Finance Study*, https://www.jbs.cam.ac.uk/wp-content/uploads/2022/12/2022-ccaf-asean-access-to-digital-finance-study.pdf. [47]

Cambridge Centre for Alternative Finance (2022), *The SME Access to Digital Finance Study*, https://www.jbs.cam.ac.uk/wp-content/uploads/2022/08/2022-08-30-ccaf-report-sme-access-to-digital-finance-latam.pdf. [48]

Crunchbase (2023), *Special Series: VC Dollars To Black Startup Founders Fell More Than 50% In 2022*, https://news.crunchbase.com/diversity/venture-funding-black-startups-2022/. [46]

Crunchbase (2020), *Global VC Funding To Female Founders Dropped Dramatically This Year*, https://news.crunchbase.com/venture/global-vc-funding-to-female-founders/. [43]

Data2x (2019), *Enabling Women's Financial Inclusion through Data: The Case of Mexico*, https://data2x.org/wp-content/uploads/2019/08/WFID-Mexico-Case-Study_FINAL.pdf. [77]

Department for Business, Energy and Industrial Strategy (2023), *Payment and Cashflow Review: The Reporting on Payment Practices and Performance Regulations 2017 - Government Consultation*, https://assets.publishing.service.gov.uk/government/uploads/system/uploads/attachment_data/file/1132949/amendments_payment_practices_and_performance_regulations_2017.pdf (accessed on 28 July 2023). [66]

DG GROW (2023), *Management Plan 2023 - Directorate-General Internal Market, Industry, Entrepreneurship and SMEs*, https://commission.europa.eu/system/files/2023-05/grow_mp_2023_en.pdf (accessed on 28 July 2023). [64]

ECB (2023), *Monetary policy tightening and the financing of firms*, https://www.ecb.europa.eu/press/key/date/2023/html/ecb.sp230419~09fe9b3295.en.html (accessed on 3 August 2023). [8]

ECB (2023), *Survey on the Access to Finance of Enterprises in the Euro Area - October 2022 to March 2023*, https://www.ecb.europa.eu/stats/ecb_surveys/safe/html/ecb.safe202306~58c0da48d6.en.html#toc2 (accessed on 26 July 2023). [11]

ECB (2023), *The Euro Area Bank Lending Survey (ECB)*, https://www.ecb.europa.eu/stats/ecb_surveys/bank_lending_survey/html/ecb.blssurvey2023q2~6d340c8db6.en.html (accessed on 3 August 2023). [9]

ECB (2022), *Survey on the Access to Finance of Enterprises in the Euro Area - April to September 2022*, https://www.ecb.europa.eu/stats/ecb_surveys/safe/html/ecb.safe202212~6bc3312ea1.en.html (accessed on 26 July 2023). [27]

ECB (2022), *The Euro Area Bank Lending Survey (ECB)*, https://www.ecb.europa.eu/stats/ecb_surveys/bank_lending_survey/pdf/ecb.blssurvey2022q1~fd61911ffd.en.pdf. [23]

EIF (2023), *2023 wave of the EIF VC and PE Mid-Market Survey*. [35]

EIF (2023), *Belgian regional investment companies to extend over €600 million in new lending for SMEs thanks to EIF and InvestEU*, https://ec.europa.eu/commission/presscorner/detail/en/ip_23_3703. [63]

EIF (2022), *The European Small Business Finance Outlook*, https://www.eif.org/news_centre/publications/eif_working_paper_2022_84.pdf. [86]

EIF, Invest Europe (2023), *The VC factor: Data-driven insights about European VC and its gender diversity trends*, https://www.eif.org/news_centre/publications/TheVCfactorGenderLensEdition.htm. [45]

El Economista (2022), *Comercio fue favorable para pymes en 2022: ¿Qué esperar para 2023?*, https://www.eleconomista.com.mx/el-empresario/Comercio-fue-favorable-para-pymes-en-2022-Que-esperar-para-2023-20221221-0069.html. [14]

Enterprise Ireland (2021), *Enterprise Ireland Action Plan for Women in Business*, https://www.enterprise-ireland.com/en/start-a-business-in-ireland/startups%20led%20by%20ambitious%20women/. [71]

European Banking Authority (2018), *Guidelines on management of non-performing and forborne exposures*, https://www.eba.europa.eu/regulation-and-policy/credit-risk/guidelines-on-management-of-non-performing-and-forborne-exposures. [59]

European Commission (2023), *Communication from the Commission to the European Parliament, the Council, the European Economic and Social Committee*, https://single-market-economy.ec.europa.eu/system/files/2023-09/COM_2023_535_1_EN_ACT_part1_v12.pdf. [65]

European Commission (2023), *European Financial Stability and Integration Review 2023*, https://finance.ec.europa.eu/system/files/2023-06/european-financial-stability-and-integration-review-2023_en_0.pdf. [61]

European Commission (2023), *Late payments - update of EU rules*, https://ec.europa.eu/info/law/better-regulation/have-your-say/initiatives/13665-Late-payments-update-of-EU-rules_en. [55]

European Commission (2023), *SMEs and High inflation - Final Report*, https://single-market-economy.ec.europa.eu/system/files/2023-12/SMEs%20Inflation%20Final%20Report%20v3.1.pdf. [25]

EY (2023), *Q1 VC investment rises, with headwinds increasing for 2023*, https://www.ey.com/en_us/growth/venture-capital/q1-2023-venture-capital-investment-trends. [39]

Factor Chain International (2023), *FCI Annual Review 2023*, https://fci.nl/en/annual-review?language_content_entity=en. [33]

Federal Reserve (2023), *Senior Loan Officer Opinion Survey on Bank Lending Practices*, https://www.federalreserve.gov/data/sloos/sloos-202304.htm (accessed on 26 July 2023). [10]

Federal Reserve Bank of Kansas City (2023), *Small Business Lending Survey*, https://www.kansascityfed.org/surveys/small-business-lending-survey/ (accessed on 26 July 2023). [17]

Federal Reserve Bank of Saint Louis (2022), *A Look at Fed Tightening Episodes since the 1980s: Part I*, https://www.stlouisfed.org/on-the-economy/2022/apr/fed-tightening-episodes-since-1980s-part-one. [82]

Finnovista (2021), *With 67 new companies, the Fintech ecosystem in Chile grows at a rate of 38% per year, reaching 179 startups in 2021*, https://www.finnovista.com/radar/con-67-empresas-nuevas-el-ecosistema-fintech-en-chile-crece-a-un-ritmo-de-38-anual-llegando-a-las-179-startups-en-2021/. [89]

Goldman Sachs (2022), *Preparing for the rising tide of rates*, https://www.gsam.com/content/gsam/us/en/institutions/market-insights/gsam-insights/2022/preparing-for-the-rising-tide-of-rates.html. [87]

Government of Canada (2023), *Biannual Survey of Suppliers of Business Financing*, https://ised-isde.canada.ca/site/sme-research-statistics/en/survey-data-and-analysis/biannual-survey-suppliers-business-financing (accessed on 3 August 2023). [18]

HASCAP Canada (2021), “Will the HASCAP Loan Program be Extended into 2022?”, https://hascap.ca/will-the-hascap-loan-program-be-extended-into-2022/ (accessed on 3 August 2023). [80]

IMF (2023), "Japan: 2023 Article IV consultation-press release; Staff Report; and Statement by the Executive Director for Japan", https://www.google.com/url?sa=i&rct=j&q=&esrc=s&source=web&cd=&ved=0CAIQw7AJahcKEwilvY602q6AAxUAAAAAHQAAAAAQAw&url=https%3A%2F%2Fwww.elibrary.imf.org%2Fdownloadpdf%2Fjournals%2F002%2F2023%2F127%2F002.2023.issue-127-en.xml&psig=AOvVaw24wveDGgpj2qOx5iTT_gG3&ust=1690540899247362&opi=89978449 (accessed on 27 July 2023). [29]

IMF (2022), *The rapid growth of Fintech*, https://www.elibrary.imf.org/display/book/9798400205293/CH003.xml. [53]

IMF (2018), *Challenges for Monetary Policy in emerging markets as global financial conditions normalize*. [81]

Intrum Justicia (2022), *European Payment Report 2022*, https://www.intrum.com/press/news-stories/the-damaging-effect-of-late-payment/. [54]

Kalemli-Özcan, S., L. Laeven and D. Moreno (2019), *Debt overhang, rollover risk, and corporate investment: evidence from the European crisis*, https://www.ecb.europa.eu/pub/pdf/scpwps/ecb.wp2241~cbea165b30.en.pdf. [79]

KPMG (2022), *Non-performing loans: Early signs points towards an increase next year*, https://kpmg.com/xx/en/home/insights/2022/11/non-performing-loans-early-signs-point-towards-an-increase-in-2023.html. [60]

Le Monde (2023), *In France, business bankrupcies in 2022 were up by nearly 50%*, https://www.lemonde.fr/en/economy/article/2023/01/18/in-france-business-bankrupcies-in-2022-were-up-by-nearly-50_6011994_19.html. [56]

Leaseurope (2023), *Leaseurope Response to the Leases Discussion Paper*, https://www.efrag.org/Assets/Download?assetUrl=%2Fsites%2Fwebpublishing%2FProject%20Documents%2F108%2FCL%2008b%20-%20Leases%20-%20Leaseurope.pdf. [32]

Leaseurope (2023), *Preliminary 2022 survey results for the leasing sector*, https://www.leaseurope.org/preliminary-2022-survey-results-leasing-sector. [31]

Ministerio de Economía, Fomento y Turismo (2022), *Nuevo Fogape y medidas de alivio tributario son aprobadas con unanimidad y despachadas para su promulgación*, https://www.economia.gob.cl/2022/10/19/nuevo-fogape-y-medidas-de-alivio-tributario-son-aprobadas-con-unanimidad-y-despachadas-para-su-promulgacion.htm. [58]

Nam, R. (2022), *Open Banking and Customer Data Sharing: Implications for Fintech Borrowers*, https://www.ecb.europa.eu/pub/conferences/ecbforum/shared/pdf/2023/EFCB_2023_Rachel_Nam_Paper.pdf. [50]

National Council for Financial Inclusion (2016), *National Policy for Financial Inclusion*, https://www.gob.mx/cms/uploads/attachment/file/199615/Mexico_s_National_Policy_Financial_Inclusion.pdf. [78]

NVCA and Pitchbook (2023), *2023 Yearbook*, https://nvca.org/wp-content/uploads/2023/03/NVCA-2023-Yearbook_FINALFINAL.pdf. [41]

OECD (2024), *OECD Economic Outlook, Interim Report February 2024*, https://www.oecd-ilibrary.org/docserver/0fd73462-en.pdf?expires=1707209799&id=id&accname=ocid84004878&checksum=2D0F89407E88D9C04B6F61660106475D. [2]

OECD (2023), *Joining Forces for Gender Equality: What is Holding us Back?*, https://www.oecd-ilibrary.org/sites/67d48024-en/1/3/29/index.html?itemId=/content/publication/67d48024-en&_csp_=cf1b2c60a6e37adbf8a9ecf7b480f228&itemIGO=oecd&itemContentType=book. [44]

OECD (2023), *OECD Economic Outlook, Interim Report September 2023*, https://www.oecd.org/economic-outlook/september-2023/. [4]

OECD (2023), *OECD Economic Outlook, Volume 2023 Issue 1*, OECD Publishing, Paris, https://doi.org/10.1787/ce188438-en. [3]

OECD (2023), *OECD Economic Outlook, Volume 2023 Issue 2*, https://www.oecd-ilibrary.org/sites/7a5f73ce-en/1/3/1/index.html?itemId=/content/publication/7a5f73ce-en&_csp_=ff1338015957b6cc89df6710d74ff9f1&itemIGO=oecd&itemContentType=book. [1]

OECD (2023), *OECD Financing SMEs and Entrepreneurs Scoreboard: 2023 Highlights*, https://www.oecd-ilibrary.org/docserver/a8d13e55-en.pdf?expires=1690213603&id=id&accname=ocid84004878&checksum=2C70B36E4629C879258E22C68282ABE4 (accessed on 24 July 2023). [34]

OECD (2023), *Recommendation of the Council in SME Financing*, https://legalinstruments.oecd.org/en/instruments/OECD-LEGAL-0493. [74]

OECD (2023), *Shift from open banking to open finance*, https://www.oecd-ilibrary.org/docserver/9f881c0c-en.pdf?expires=1696582516&id=id&accname=ocid84004878&checksum=E461EF4EE5179C27CAC18E3CEC873E0F. [49]

OECD (2023), *SME policy responses to the 2022/2023 energy crisis*, OECD Publishing, https://doi.org/10.1787/80012fbd-en. [62]

OECD (2022), *Financing SMEs and Entrepreneurs 2022: An OECD Scoreboard*, OECD Publishing, Paris, https://doi.org/10.1787/e9073a0f-en. [21]

OECD (2012), *Financing SMEs and Entrepreneurs: An OECD Scoreboard*, https://www.oecd-ilibrary.org/docserver/9789264166769-en.pdf?. [93]

Oesterreichische Nationalbank (2023), *Data and Analytics Austrian Financial Institutions*, https://www.oenb.at/Publikationen/Statistik/Statistiken---Daten-und-Analysen.html. [16]

Open Banking Implementation Entity (2023), *Open Banking Impact report*, https://openbanking.foleon.com/live-publications/the-open-banking-impact-report-march-2023/intermediate-outcomes-adoption. [51]

Pitchbook (2023), *Global Fund Performance Report*, https://files.pitchbook.com/website/files/pdf/2023_Global_Fund_Performance_Report_as_of_Q4_2022_with_preliminary_Q1_2023_data.pdf. [38]

Pitchbook (2022), *Global Fund Performance Report*, https://files.pitchbook.com/website/files/pdf/2022_Global_Fund_Performance_Report_as_of_Q2_2022_with_Preliminary_Q3_2022_Data.pdf. [37]

Preqin (2023), *Venture Capital Q1 2023: Preqin Quarterly Update | Preqin*, https://www.preqin.com/insights/research/quarterly-updates/q1-2023-venture-capital (accessed on 4 August 2023). [36]

Reuters (2023), *Bank of Israel says too soon to lower rates due to war uncertainty*, https://www.reuters.com/world/middle-east/bank-israel-again-holds-key-interest-rate-475-during-war-2023-11-27/. [92]

Reuters (2023), *Recession risk, rate rises drive down private equity deal volumes to 4-year low*, https://www.reuters.com/markets/global-markets-private-equity-graphic-2023-06-26/. [22]

Reuters (2022), *Bankruptcy filings are creeping back up in early 2022*, https://www.reuters.com/legal/transactional/bankruptcy-filings-are-creeping-back-up-early-2022-2022-04-05/. [57]

S&P Market Intelligence (2022), *Outlook for private equity dealmaking sours as inflation, interest rates rise*, https://www.spglobal.com/marketintelligence/en/news-insights/latest-news-headlines/outlook-for-private-equity-dealmaking-sours-as-inflation-interest-rates-rise-70689997. [26]

SAFFA (2023), *SAFFA*, https://www.saffa.ch/de/saffa. [73]

SBA (2022), *SBA Administrator Guzman Announces Key Policy Change: Existing COVID Economic Injury Disaster Loan Program Borrowers to Receive an Additional Deferment | U.S. Small Business Administration*, https://www.sba.gov/article/2022/mar/15/sba-administrator-guzman-announces-key-policy-change-existing-covid-economic-injury-disaster-loan (accessed on 3 August 2023). [19]

Suryanto, Rusdin and R. Dai (2020), *Fintech as a Catalyst for Growth of Micro, Small and Medium Enterprises in Indonesia*, https://www.abacademies.org/articles/Fintech-as-a-catalyst-for-growth-of-micro-small-and-medium-enterprises-in-Indonesia-1939-6104-19-5-599.pdf. [91]

The Guardian (2023), *MPs challenge VC firms over record on female and minority-led firms*, https://www.theguardian.com/business/2023/jul/24/mps-challenge-vc-firms-over-record-on-female-and-minority-led-firms?CMP=Share_AndroidApp_Other. [83]

The Japan Times (2023), *Japanese firms turn to loans for longer-term funding amid BOJ risks - The Japan Times*, https://www.japantimes.co.jp/news/2023/03/16/business/economy-business/companies-bank-loans/ (accessed on 27 July 2023). [30]

U.S. Bank (2023), *How rising interest rates impact the bond market*, https://www.usbank.com/investing/financial-perspectives/market-news/interest-rates-affect-bonds.html. [84]

UK Department for Business and Trade (2023), *Investing in Women Code closing the finance gap*, https://www.gov.uk/government/news/investing-in-women-code-closing-the-finance-gap#:~:text=The%20Investing%20in%20Women%20Code%20is%20a%20commitment%20to%20support,need%20to%20achieve%20their%20goals. [76]

UK Department for Business and Trade (2022), *Overview of the UK Investing in Women Code*, https://we-fi.org/wp-content/uploads/2022/07/Overview-of-the-UK-Investing-in-Women-Code.pdf. [75]

UK Government (2023), *Late commercial payments: charging interest and debt recovery*, https://www.gov.uk/late-commercial-payments-interest-debt-recovery (accessed on 28 July 2023). [67]

UNCTAD (2023), "World Investment Report 2023", https://unctad.org/system/files/official-document/wir2023_en.pdf (accessed on 24 July 2023). [7]

Women Entrepreneurs Finance Initiative (2022), *The case for investing in women entrepreneurs*, https://we-fi.org/wp-content/uploads/2022/06/We-Fi-Case-for-Investment.pdf. [68]

World Bank (2020), *G-20: Data enhancement and coordination in SME Finance Stocktaking Report*, https://www.gpfi.org/sites/gpfi/files/g20_SME_stock_2020.pdf. [69]

WTO (2023), "Global Trade Outlook and Statistics", https://www.wto.org/english/res_e/booksp_e/trade_outlook23_e.pdf (accessed on 24 July 2023). [6]

Notes

[1] Computed between the date of the first rate increase and March 2023.

[2] Subnational data is presented in relation to regional GDP to account for the different size of regions. Information is presented for ten countries: eight OECD members (Belgium, Czech Republic, Italy, France, Mexico, Portugal, Slovak Republic, and Türkiye) and two non-OECD members (Indonesia and Peru). Data on regional SME loans from Georgia and Kazakhstan could not be matched to regional GDP data, which is the reason why these two countries are not covered in the analysis, although subnational data is available for these two countries on this indicator.

[3] SME loan definitions are not the same across all countries. This means that countries in which the SME loan definition is narrower (e.g. in terms of loan size or size of the firm receiving the loan) will tend to show lower national and regional values than those where the SME loan definition is broader. SME loan definitions in the OECD Scoreboard countries are available in Table A A.2 of the 2022 edition of the Scoreboard (OECD, 2022[21]).

[4] Short-term loans are defined as loans with maturities of less than a year and are often used to provide working capital. Long-term loans, on the other hand, are often used to finance investments, but can also indicate a strategy used by SMEs to lock in lower interest rates. Small loans with short-term maturities typically carry high-interest rates largely explained by the presence of fixed screening costs given higher risk of default compared to long-term loans (EIF, 2022[86]).

[5] In Austria, for example, financing needs for storage and working capital were the dominant reason behind the increase in demand for short-term credit (see Austrian country snapshot).

[6] Empirical analysis is based on Orbis as of 2021. Due to the temporal limitation of Orbis, which only covers a period during which the ECB had not yet raised interest rates to excessive levels, it could also be that the effect of interest rates is driven by non-Eurozone Member States (European Commission, 2023[25]).

[7] The interest rate spread between loans to SMEs and large companies offers additional insights regarding SME credit conditions. Given the inherently riskier profiles that SMEs have as borrowers, they are usually charged higher interest rates compared to large enterprises. As such, a narrowing interest rate spread generally indicates more favourable lending conditions for SMEs, while a widening spread indicates tighter lending conditions (OECD, 2012[93]).

[8] A down round is a financing round where the start-up has a lower valuation compared to the previous round. Down rounds often reflect a shift in investor sentiment.

[9] Online alternative finance involves raising funds through an intermediary platform. It's divided into debt, equity, and non-investment models. Debt-based models include P2P/marketplace lending, while equity-based models involve issuing unlisted shares or securities through equity-crowdfunding. Non-investment-based models include reward-based and donation-based crowdfunding.

[10] Countries included in the study were Indonesia, Malaysia, the Philippines, Singapore and Thailand. The survey was conducted in Spring 2022.

[11] Countries included in the study were Argentina, Brazil, Chile, Colombia, Peru and Mexico. The survey was conducted in Spring 2021.

[12] The NPL coverage ratio is the total allowance for loan losses divided by the total amount of NPLs.

[13] In order, they are Marche, Umbria, Veneto, the Province of Bolzano, Tuscany and Emilia-Romagna.

[14] Women Entrepreneurs Finance Initiative | Women Entrepreneurs Finance Initiative (we-fi.org)

[15] OECD Recommendation on SME Financing - OECD

2 Sustainable finance for SMEs: Challenges and opportunities

This chapter provides an overview of the sustainable finance landscape for SMEs and focuses on the key challenges that these companies face in seeking out and accessing financing for the green transition. It also provides recommendations to strengthen the provision of financial and non-financial support for SME sustainability.

Glossary of Terms

- **Bridge loans** refers to a financing instrument that allows SMEs to have capital until permanent or next stage financing can be obtained.
- **Carbon pricing** is a pricing scheme where a tax is directly applied to the production of carbon emissions or fuels that release GHG gasses.
- **Environmentally sustainable finance** is all finance that considers environmental performance as a criterion for the financing decision or for determining the financing conditions, regardless of the purpose of use of the funds.
- **ESG integration** is an investment/financing strategy that considers environmental as well as social and governance impacts as factors of risk and opportunity in the financing and investment strategies of financial institutions and institutional investments, alongside maximizing financial returns.
- **Exclusionary screening** is an investment/financing strategy that prohibits financing/investments in specific industries or activities (e.g. extraction of fossil fuels, agricultural activities associated with deforestation).
- **Green asset ratio** is a metric used to assess the sustainability of a company or portfolio, calculated by dividing the total value of an entity's environmentally friendly assets by the total value of all of its assets.
- **Green equity** refers to either Venture Capital or Private Equity aimed specifically at funding innovative solutions to address environmental challenges.
- **Green loans** are a debt instrument committed exclusively to finance green projects.
- **Green revolving credit** is a form of credit where the requested amount is available and once used and repaid, the credit replenishes. Only available for green projects (e.g. energy efficiency, renewable energy, etc.).
- **Green supply chain financing/green factoring** involves a buyer approving its supplier invoices for financing by a bank when a product or service is provided. This type of financing helps the supplier get short-term credit and optimize working capital, while the buyer gets more time to pay off balances. Preferential rates are given depending on the sustainability performance of the supplier.
- **Green transition** is a shift towards an economical model that allows for sustainable growth without negatively impacts on the environment.
- **Green washing** a practice whereby sustainability related statements, declarations, actions or communications, do not clearly and fairly reflect the underlying sustainability profile of an entity, a financial product, or financial service. This practice may be misleading to consumers, investors or other market participants.
- **Hard-to-abate** refers to firms that have emissions that are extremely costly or difficult to reduce with the currently available technologies.
- **Hybrid financing/hybrid instruments** are instruments/investments that combine debt and equity.
- **Impact investing** is an investment strategy that pursues or seeks to maximize environmental and social returns, even if they come at the expense of financial returns.
- **Nature positive** refers to sustainable development outcomes that have a net positive impact on the natural world. This concept goes beyond net zero, focusing on actions that preserve biodiversity, improve natural capacity to absorb pollution, and decrease the vulnerability of natural ecosystems.
- **Net zero** refers to the target of reducing greenhouse gas emissions to zero by balancing the amount released into the atmosphere with the amount removed and stored by carbon sinks. An

entity can achieve net zero by reducing carbon emissions and offsetting any emissions that cannot be eliminated.

- **Non-financial disclosure/reporting** is a form of transparency reporting whereby companies formally disclose information not related to their finances, including information on environmental impacts and human rights. For example, non-financial disclosures related to climate include information on carbon emissions. On the one hand, climate related non-disclosure requirements enable companies to demonstrate foresight in their consideration of climate issues. On the other hand, it helps inform investors to efficiently allocate capital towards a lower emissions economy.
- **Public Financial Institutions** refer to government-owned entities that offer a host of financial services/products, such as direct financing and guarantees, to support SMEs' access to finance.
- **Partnership for Carbon Accounting Financials (PCAF) Methodology** is a methodology that enables financial institutions to measure and disclose GHG emissions for loans and investments.
- **Scope of emissions** describe the three different levels by which the coverage of climate-related disclosure requirements differs. While Scope 1 and 2 emissions include GHG emissions that the company is directly responsible for (1) or indirectly produces through energy consumption (2), Scope 3 emissions encompasses all other emissions that are outside of the company's control. The hard-to-measure scope 3 emissions stem from upstream activities such as commuting of employees or purchases goods as well as from downstream activities such as treatment of waste or operations of franchises.
- **Sustainable finance** is finance that takes into consideration environmental, social and governance factors (ESG) in financing decisions.
- **Taxonomy** is a framework to establish a common definition what activities are considered environmentally sustainable.

Overview

Financing SMEs' transition to sustainability is an important priority to meet climate objectives. SMEs on aggregate account for about 40% of the greenhouse gas (GHG) emissions of the business sector; yet most are only at the beginning of the journey to net zero (OECD, 2023[1]). Likewise, few SMEs have developed transition plans or made commitments to reach net zero (OECD, 2022[2]). In the current context of high interest rates and more difficult access to finance for SMEs (see Chapter 1), these firms must nevertheless push ahead to drive the green transition and green their business practices.

Access to finance is an important constraint for SMEs' net-zero action. In a recent survey of nearly 350 SMEs globally, 55% of respondents identified the lack of funds as a key reason for limited action on climate change and nearly 70% stated that they need additional funds to take action or accelerate their progress on emission reductions (SME Climate Hub, 2023[3]). Access to finance will likely represent an even bigger constraint for climate action, as financing conditions become increasingly dependent on sustainability considerations and as financial institutions (FIs) face non-financial reporting requirements, both of which place a reporting burden on SMEs. Ensuring that SMEs have access to tailored sustainable financing solutions to meet their net-zero investment needs is critical for the net-zero transition.

The supply of sustainable finance is growing rapidly in response to regulatory and stakeholder demand and management of risks in the net-zero transition. In a 2023 survey by the OECD Platform on Financing SMEs for Sustainability[1], both public and private financial institutions (FIs) stated that they are increasingly integrating climate considerations in their operations, including in developing institutional objectives and plans and assessing some or all financing/investment opportunities. Some FIs are also providing dedicated financing programmes or more advantageous conditions for investments focused on green objectives. Most FIs are providing tailored financing solutions for SMEs' investments in net zero and greening, including through medium- and long-term loans, short-term loans and factoring, credit guarantees, and other financing instruments.

However, SMEs may not be able to tap into this growing pool of sustainable finance. Financial institutions increasingly need and seek out granular data on their clients' sustainability performance to manage risks, develop financing instruments and meet reporting requirements. Yet SMEs are not as well equipped to provide these data as large entities due to their relatively limited capacities to identify, measure and report on their environmental performance. This poses potential risks to SMEs' ability to access financing in the future. SMEs also risk losing access to finance if they cannot advance (sufficiently rapidly) on the journey to net zero and/or cannot demonstrate credible transition plans. This is a particularly strong risk for SMEs in high-emitting and hard-to-abate sectors.

SMEs' limited demand for sustainable finance is also an important challenge, which often stems from lack of information and awareness, as well as capacity and resource constraints. SMEs also face high technical, market and regulatory uncertainty. This has several important implications for policy and finance. SMEs need a stronger business case and external support to boost their investments in sustainability and to seek the related financing. In the absence of SME demand, public and private FIs have limited incentives to develop tailored financing solutions for financing SMEs' net-zero and other investment needs. Furthermore, if they do not invest in improving their sustainability performance or cannot provide credible transition plans, SMEs risk losing access to finance even for other investment needs, as noted above.

Public actors have an important role to play in establishing a stable and conducive regulatory and policy environment for sustainable finance and investment and providing relevant financial and non-financial support to enhance SME access to and uptake of sustainable finance. Financial support can entail the provision of direct financing through loans, equity, grants and other instruments; or it may entail the mobilisation of private financing through credit guarantees and other de-risking instruments. Public financial institutions can also help SMEs by facilitating their participation in capital markets and supporting financial innovation to foster the development of relevant digital financial solutions. Non-financial support may include information and tools to help SMEs in strengthening their awareness about the sustainability journey, the available technologies and resources they can tap into, and the ways in which they can measure and report on their sustainability performance.

Private actors, too, need to drive the transition. The large financing gap cannot be filled by the public sector alone. Private financial institutions, Fintechs, ESG intermediaries, such as rating agencies, accountants and other relevant stakeholders, all need to contribute toward creating a conducive ecosystem that provides the right information, incentives and conditions to drive SME investment in greening and their uptake of relevant financing instruments to meet these needs.

In order to help foster the provision and uptake of sustainable finance for SMEs, and to maximise the potential for private actors to the contribute to the transition, public institutions need to take into account the following considerations:

- Understand SMEs' diverse needs and pathways to net zero and nature positive;
- Devise sustainability-related policies and regulations that take into consideration the impact on SMEs;
- Strengthen the transparency and interoperability of sustainability-related data, definitions and standards;
- Ensure that a stable, transparent and comprehensive policy and regulatory framework is in place to support investment and financing of the green transition;
- Provide financial support to address challenges impeding SME access to sustainable finance;
- Provide non-financial support for SMEs to foster their access to, but also uptake of sustainable finance;
- Foster the sustainable finance ecosystem for SMEs by promoting dialogue and knowledge-sharing among the diverse actors.

This thematic chapter of the Scoreboard aims to shed light on timely issues and provide additional context and information to enrich the trends documented in this report. Following the 2022 edition, which analysed how COVID-19 and build-back-better support measures contributed to SME access to finance, this chapter provides information on the latest state of play in sustainable finance for SMEs, offering information on financial institution strategies and approaches, relevant financing support and technical assistance provided to small businesses and policy recommendations. It takes into account guidance provided in the OECD Recommendation on SME Financing and insights shared at the 2023 CSMEE meeting at Ministerial Level (OECD, 2023[4]), (OECD, 2022[5]). It brings insights from the 2023 survey "Financing SMEs for Sustainability – Financial Institution Strategies and Approaches" and builds on the 2022 report on "Financing SMEs for Sustainability: Drivers, Constraints and Policies", developed by the OECD Committee on SMEs and Entrepreneurship and informed by the activities of the OECD Platform on Financing SMEs for Sustainability (OECD, 2023[6]) (OECD, 2022[2]) (OECD, 2023[7]).

Introduction

Financing the net-zero transition of millions of SMEs is an important priority for the coming decades. SMEs account for a significant share of the global greenhouse emissions: about 40% of business sector GHG emissions in EU countries, according to recent OECD estimates, and about 50% globally according to the International Trade Centre (ITC) (OECD, 2023[1]; ITC, 2021[8]). Despite this, SMEs have not been a strong focus for national and international climate policies, which have most often targeted larger firms. According to the International Energy Agency (IEA), as of mid-2021, less than 100 of more than 6 000 environmental and energy policy measures, concerned specifically SMEs and 150 start-ups and entrepreneurship (OECD, 2021[9]). Similarly, an OECD analysis of post-COVID national recovery and resilience plans from

91 countries suggests that SME-specific policies represent only about 5% of the total number of climate-related policies and about 2.4% of total allocated funding for the implementation of these policies (OECD, 2022[10]).

Furthermore, and in part as a result, SMEs themselves have also taken only limited actions toward the net-zero transition. For example, a 2023 survey of nearly 350 SMEs showed that while most SMEs (82%) recognise that the green transition is a high priority, the large majority have taken only elementary steps toward greening their business models, such as the introduction of energy efficiency measures and waste reduction (76%), reducing energy consumption (71%) and employee education (66%) (SME Climate Hub, 2023[3]). SMEs also have an important role to play in developing the innovative technologies, products and processes that advance the global net-zero agenda. For example, SMEs account for an estimated 70% and 90% of clean tech companies in the UK and Finland respectively (ETLA, 2015[11]) (Carbon Trust, 2013[12]).

Most entrepreneurs and SMEs cite access to finance as an important obstacle to their green and net-zero transition. In the above-mentioned survey, 55% of SMEs identified the lack of funds as a key reason for limited action on climate change and nearly 70% stated that they need additional funds to take action or accelerate their progress on emission reductions (SME Climate Hub, 2023[3]). Access to finance is likely to become an even bigger constraint as sustainability considerations are increasingly linked to financing decisions and as financial institutions (FIs) face non-financial reporting requirements that place a reporting burden on SMEs. Ensuring that SMEs have access to tailored sustainable financing solutions that can meet their net-zero investment needs is a critical factor for the net-zero transition.

However, ensuring that there is sufficient demand and uptake of sustainable finance among SMEs is also an important challenge. SMEs often lack awareness about the net-zero transition and the actions they need to take to reach net zero. A 2021 survey conducted by the UK Chamber of Commerce shows that only one in ten SMEs currently measure their GHG emissions (one in 20 for microenterprises). Moreover, 22% of SMEs do not fully understand the term 'net zero,' and almost a third have yet to seek advice or information to help them develop a net-zero roadmap or improve their environmental performance (British Chambers of Commerce, 2021[13]). Yet, even when they are aware of the importance of the green transition, SMEs may not see the business case for net-zero investments given that these investments often entail high upfront costs with uncertain long-term returns due to changes in the regulatory environment, varying consumer demand, technological progress and other factors. Lack of relevant knowledge and skills, time and other resources can also deter SMEs from taking action on climate change. Nearly 60% of SMEs globally have cited lack of skills and 44% lack of time as constraints to climate action (SME Climate Hub, 2023[3]). Similarly, survey data from Korea show that 31% of SMEs find the lack of information on the methods to reduce their carbon footprint to be a main constraint to achieving net zero (Korea Chamber of Commerce and Industry, 2021[14]). This means that even if tailored financing instruments and support are put in place, uptake can pose a challenge for SME clients. Non-financial support, therefore, has an important role to play in bolstering SME demand for net-zero financing and investment and supporting the effective financing of SMEs' transition.

This chapter builds on the 2023 survey "Financing SMEs for Sustainability – Financial Institution Strategies and Approaches" and the 2022 report "Financing SMEs for Sustainability: Drivers, Constraints and Policies" of the OECD Committee on SMEs and Entrepreneurship and informed by the work of the OECD Platform on Financing SMEs for Sustainability (OECD, 2022[2]; OECD, 2023[15]) (OECD, 2023[6]). This chapter focuses specifically on the environmental angle of sustainable finance. It outlines the key challenges and opportunities in the provision and uptake of sustainable finance by SMEs and explores the role that regulations, policies as well as public financial and non-financial support can play in supporting SMEs as they tap into the growing pool of sustainable finance and mobilise investments towards net zero.

The chapter is divided into four sections. The first section explains what sustainable finance is and why it matters for SMEs. The second section explores how sustainable finance is changing the financing landscape for SMEs and what this implies for SMEs in terms of their ability to access finance and their incentives for greening their business models. The third section focuses on the challenge posed by SMEs' limited demand for and uptake of sustainable finance. Finally, the last section elaborates on the importance of creating a conducive ecosystem for the provision and uptake of sustainable finance for SMEs. It focuses in particular on the role public actors, including regulators, policy makers and public financial institutions, can play in providing financial and non-financial support to drive and accelerate SMEs' transition to sustainability.

Box 2.1. Green/sustainable taxonomies are being developed to define green and sustainable activities

Purpose and function of green/sustainable taxonomies

Green/sustainable taxonomies seek to provide greater clarity on the environmental sustainability of specific financing and investment activities by establishing clear criteria for what assets can be defined as green or sustainable.

The adoption of green/sustainable taxonomies helps mobilise resources to sustainable investments by providing a shared definition, reducing the incidence of greenwashing, and by incentivising firms to offer additional non-financial disclosures.

Examples of green taxonomies across the world

The EU green taxonomy defines six categories of environmental objectives: 1) climate change mitigation; 2) climate adaptation; 3) sustainable use of water and marine resources; 4) transition to a circular economy; 5) pollution prevention; 6) protection and restoration of biodiversity and ecosystems.

For an economic activity to be qualified as sustainable, it must contribute substantially to one or more of the above environmental objectives while doing no significant harm to any of the other listed objectives. Sustainable investments must also comply with minimum social safeguards, aligning with several international standards (ex: OECD Guidelines for Multinational Enterprises, UN Guiding Principles on Business and Human Rights, International Labour Organisation's declaration on Fundamental Rights and Principles at Work, etc.). To facilitate the adoption of the above requirements, the EU has incorporated a set of guiding metrics, principles and online platforms to which firms can refer.

There are certain mandatory requirements, including requirements for providers of financial products to disclose which of their investments comply with the sustainability criteria of the taxonomy. Large enterprises and all listed companies must also disclose what share of their turnover and capital expenditure are sustainable in line with the taxonomy criteria.

The green taxonomy also has provisions that consider investments enabling green activities and transitional activities that are not sustainable but have lower carbon emissions (e.g. nuclear power and natural gas).

Colombia in 2022 launched its own green taxonomy plan, the first country in the Latin American region to do so. The national government used the EU Green Taxonomy as a baseline with many of the same environmental goals and guidelines. Additional technical criteria were introduced to adapt the policy to fit the socio-economic context of the country and align it with local environmental strategies.

In Korea, the government has developed a Korean Green Classification System (K-taxonomy). The taxonomy defines a subset of economic activities that can be considered green, including activities in the energy, industrial, and transportation sector. The taxonomy also makes additional classifications for transitional activities.

In **Mexico**, the sustainable taxonomy was launched in March 2023. The taxonomy covers both environmental and social activities, including climate change mitigation, climate change adaptation and gender equality.

In Singapore, the Green Finance Industry Taskforce has begun the development of a taxonomy that would be used by Singapore-based financial institutions which are also active in the ASEAN region.

In **South Africa**, the National Treasury launched in April 2022 its Green Finance Taxonomy (GFT) which builds on the technical content of the EU Sustainable Finance Taxonomy.

China has an informal taxonomy that is a combined set of regulations defining green credit and green bonds. These regulations offer lending guidelines with accompanying KPIs and require banks to report bi-annually on what percentage of their portfolio is green and their combined impact on emission reduction and water savings.

The UK Green Technical Advisory Group is advising the Government on the development of a UK taxonomy.

In **Canada**, the development of the so-called Transition Taxonomy has been led by the private sector (six major banks, pension funds and insurance companies). The government in 2021 began preparing recommendations for the establishment of a green and transition finance taxonomy, establishing a technical group from the Sustainable Finance Action Council to provide guidance.

Other countries that have taken steps to develop and implement green taxonomies include Chile, Georgia, Malaysia and Mexico.

Transition taxonomies

Transition taxonomies differ from traditional green taxonomies, focusing instead on providing finance to high-carbon emitting firms that intend to decarbonize their operations. Transition taxonomies help promote long-term strategic GHG emission reduction by establishing clear guidelines and reporting frameworks for decarbonization.

Several countries have begun to establish transition taxonomies to address these needs. In 2021, **Japan** published Basic Guidelines on Climate Transition Finance that require recipients of transition finance to develop and report on their transition progress to financial institutions and provides guidance on aligning reporting with international standards. Korea, as noted above also has additional clarifications within its green taxonomy defining transitional activities. Likewise, Canada's taxonomy roadmap report establishes transition finance mechanisms for activities with viable decarbonization pathways.

Source: (OECD, 2020[16]), (European Commission, 2023[17]), (Reuters, 2022[18]), (bnamericas, 2022[19]), (IBK, 2023[20]), (Modern Mining, 2022[21]), (Green Finance Institute, 2023[22]), (Natixis, 2021[23]), (Lexology, 2022[24]), (OECD, Forthcoming[25]), (Canada, 2023[26]) (Gobierno de México, 2023[27])

What is sustainable finance and why does it matter for SMEs?

Sustainable finance takes into consideration environmental, social and governance factors (ESG) in financing decisions (OECD, 2020[28]), with the "E" pillar including all financing that considers environmental performance as a criterion for the financing decision or for determining the financing conditions, regardless of the purpose of use of the funds. Sustainable finance therefore goes beyond the financing of greening or environmentally sustainable investments/projects as defined by relevant green and sustainable taxonomies (Box 2.1). This chapter focuses on environmentally sustainable finance, and in particular on the climate/net-zero dimension.

The consideration of environmental factors in financing can take many forms. Exclusionary screening or divestment prohibits financing/investments in specific industries or activities (e.g. extraction of fossil fuels, agricultural activities associated with deforestation). ESG (environmental, social, governance) integration considers environmental (as well as social and governance impacts) as factors of risk and opportunity in the financing and investment strategies of financial institutions and institutional investors, alongside maximising financial returns. The active engagement approach targets companies with high emissions but a strong propensity for improvement in their ESG performance. On the other end of the spectrum, impact investing pursues or seeks to maximise environmental and social returns, even if they come at the expense of financial returns (OECD, 2020[29]) (Eurosif, 2016[30]) (Busch, Bauer and Orlitzky, 2016[31]; Busch, Bauer and Orlitzky, 2016[32]). Depending on the nature of their enterprise, FIs and (institutional) investors may employ one or more of these approaches or instruments when incorporating environmental factors in their operations.

Whatever the approach taken, the inclusion of environmental factors in financial institutions' investment decisions and broader operations has important implications. One of the main implications is that financial institutions (FIs) increasingly need to obtain sustainability-related data on their clients for the purposes of making financing decisions, devising relevant tailored financing instruments, managing the risks of their financed portfolios and meeting emerging reporting requirements. Likewise, companies in high emitting sectors or sectors with a high and hard-to-abate environmental footprint face greater risks of being excluded from access to external financing, especially if they cannot provide credible transition plans to net zero or towards improved environmental performance (OECD, 2022[33]). The challenges are further exacerbated for the inclusion of considerations such as transition to nature positive and enterprises' impacts on biodiversity and ecosystem services, which are even more difficult to identify and measure (OECD, 2023[34]).

The emergence of sustainable finance has even stronger implications for SMEs. Some of these implications, which will be further elaborated in the following sections, include:

- SMEs that adopt green business models or improve their environmental performance could tap into a growing pool of finance to meet their investment needs. They could also benefit from financing at better conditions (e.g. lower interest rates, etc), if they are able to produce relevant data to demonstrate their sustainability performance. Conversely, SMEs could risk losing access to external financing if they cannot produce data on their sustainability performance, due to their relatively limited capacities to identify, measure and report on their environmental performance.
- Similarly, while SMEs may increasingly face stronger incentives to green their business models, they may risk losing access to finance if they cannot advance (sufficiently rapidly) on the journey to net zero and/or cannot demonstrate credible transition plans. This is a particularly strong risk for SMEs in high-emitting and hard-to-abate sectors.
- The evolution of the financing landscape requires SMEs to interact with an even wider range of ecosystem actors, including various ESG intermediaries and sustainability-related service providers that can support SMEs in measuring, reporting on and improving their environmental performance. This has implication for resources and their allocation within the SME (OECD, 2022[35]).

The supply of sustainable finance is growing…

Sustainable finance is growing rapidly in response to stakeholder demand

Sustainable finance has seen tremendous growth over the past decade. ESG integration now accounts for about USD 40 trillion in assets under management, and financial institutions around the globe are increasingly pledging to integrate ESG factors into their operations as well as to align their portfolios with net zero, the Sustainable Development Goals or other sustainability metrics (Global Sustainable Investment Alliance, 2020[36]) (BNP Paribas, 2021[37]).

Emerging non-financial disclosure and other regulatory requirements for financial institutions and large enterprises are one of the key drivers for the growth of sustainable finance. In a 2023 OECD survey of public development banks and private financial institutions (Box 2.2), regulatory demand was identified as the most important driver of climate action (Figure 2.1). FIs in a growing number of countries need to disclose the sustainability of their own operations as well as the operations of their clients. These requirements can entail reporting on financed emissions, the share of the portfolio that is aligned with the nationally applicable taxonomy, a green asset ratio and other similar indicators, which creates incentives for FIs to allocate more financing toward green and sustainable activities.

The increase in the supply of sustainable finance has also been driven by investors,' consumers' and employees' growing awareness of the importance and urgency of tackling the climate crisis and other environmental and social challenges. According to a 2022 poll, 88% of institutional investors place sustainability on par with operational and financial considerations when making investment decisions. Furthermore, 60% of respondents base their decision on where to work on their beliefs and values and 58% buy or advocate for brands that match their values (Edelman, 2022[38]). Shareholder and client demand were identified as important drivers for climate action in the OECD survey of financial institutions (Figure 2.1). In combination with increased sustainability reporting mandates for FIs and the associated reputational considerations, the changing investor and consumer preferences create increasingly powerful incentives for FIs to integrate sustainability considerations in financing decisions.

Besides growing awareness and value-based investment decision-making, purely financial considerations also drive investors' and FIs' growing allocation of financing toward sustainable or sustainability aligned activities. In the OECD survey, implications for the long-term financial and operational performance of the FI were the second most important driver of climate action (Figure 2.1). Other survey data show that 83% of early-stage investors in Europe prefer to invest in more environmentally sustainable start-ups, as they are likely to perform better when they have sustainability goals in their business models. Likewise, 59% of investors said that they have declined an investment opportunity in the last year due to sustainability concerns (SME guidance for business growth, 2022[39]).

Figure 2.1. Factors driving action on climate change in FIs

Please rate the importance of the following factors in driving action on climate/net zero in your institution (% of all respondents)

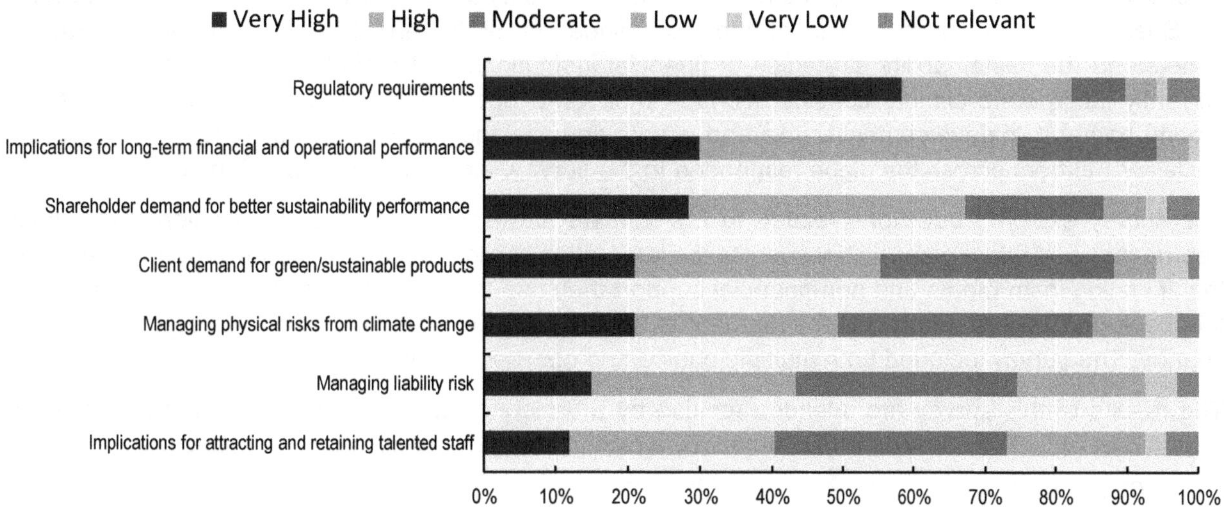

Source: (OECD, 2023[6]).

StatLink https://stat.link/32jvru

The OECD survey shows that financial institutions are taking steps toward integrating climate considerations in their SME and overall operations. Over 60% of FIs consider climate implications when developing strategies and business plans, and nearly half set climate-related criteria for their suppliers. Over 75% of public and 60% of private FIs also assess the climate related impacts of some or all of their financing/investment decisions (OECD, 2023[6]) (Figure 2.2).

Box 2.2. OECD Survey – Financial Institution Strategies and Approaches

The OECD **Survey *Financing SMEs for Sustainability-Financial Institution Strategies and Approaches***, conducted in the spring and summer of 2023 by the OECD Platform on Financing SMEs for Sustainability under the aegis of the Committee on SMEs and Entrepreneurship, sought to understand the sustainability strategies of financial institutions and provide a snapshot of how they currently incorporate climate considerations in their SME operations. The survey was administered among both public development banks and private financial institutions serving SMEs on a voluntary basis. 67 FIs from across the globe responded to the survey, including 45 private banks.

The survey explored questions related to FIs' climate strategies, targets and transition plans, their approaches and future plans with respect to the integration of climate considerations in SME operations, the financing instruments and non-financial support they use to enable SMEs' net-zero transition, and feedback on how the regulatory environment is affecting SMEs' access to and uptake of sustainable finance. The survey included both multiple choice and open-ended questions.

The results of this survey are intended for use by a variety of stakeholders (governments, financial institutions, etc). They provide a benchmark by which to measure future progress in this area.

Source: (OECD, 2023[6])

Figure 2.2. Most public and private FIs take climate considerations into account in their (SME) operations

How (if at all) does your institution integrate climate considerations in its financing/investment decisions? (% of respondents)

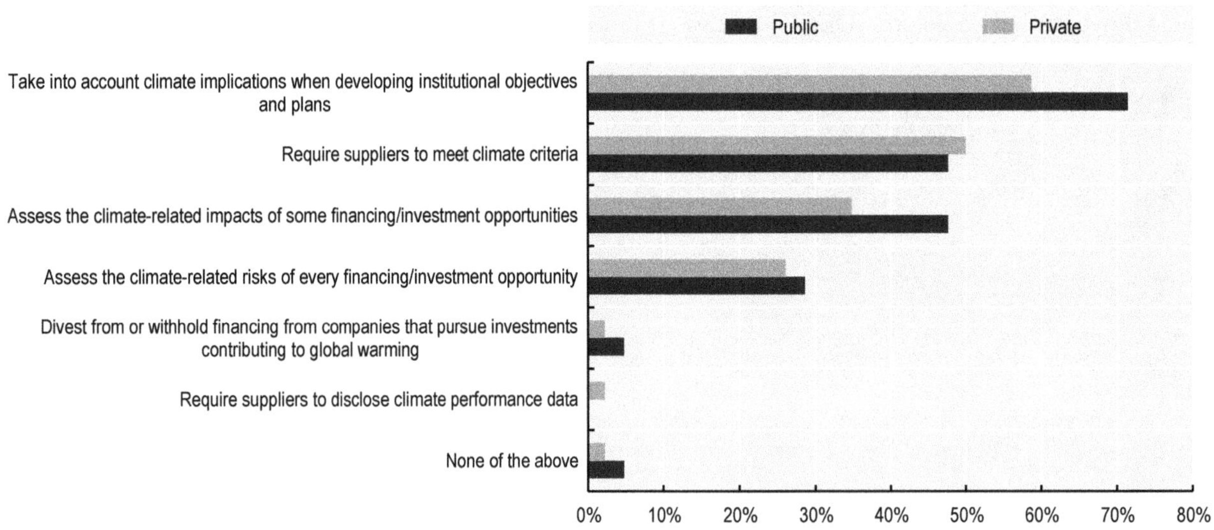

Source: (OECD, 2023[6]).

StatLink https://stat.link/4rgofm

FIs are expanding their offer of green and sustainable financing products through a range of instruments

Environmental considerations can be integrated into financing products in different ways. As the typology in Table 2.1 illustrates, products can range from green debt or equity that are financing specific greening investment or sustainability-linked financing. The latter links financing – regardless of purpose – with the sustainability performance of the investment or investee (Table 2.1).

Table 2.1. Types of sustainable finance products

Instrument	Type	Actors involved	Characteristics	Environmental aspects of the instrument
Green loans	Debt	PFIs, Banks	Lending to finance SME greening can be enhanced through targeted SME lending portfolios or green credit lines.	Green loans are committed exclusively to finance green projects such as those addressing climate change, natural resource depletion, biodiversity loss, and air, water and soil pollution. These instruments involve periodic reporting by the borrower to the lender of the actual use of proceeds, through qualitative or quantitative performance measures (e.g. electricity generation, or reduction of GHG emissions).
Green concessional loans	Debt	PFIs, Non-Commercial banks	As PFIs support governments to achieve policy goals, they are in a position to provide loans with favourable terms for SMEs, i.e. grace periods and low interest rates	Green concessional loans are used specifically for environmental investments and granted with (substantially) more favourable terms compared to market loans (below-the market interest rates, longer grant periods or a combination of both). Such loans may be conditional on measures beyond regulatory requirements (e.g., use of best available techniques or best management practices).
Bridge loans	Debt	PFIs, Investors	Bridge loans can be crucial for the survival of green projects. Given the large risk of sustainable projects, this instrument allows the SME to have capital until permanent or next stage financing can be obtained.	Bridge loans are particularly useful for green pioneer companies facing high upfront costs and risks in early-stage development phases and between funding rounds, (e.g. developing cutting-edge technologies in areas such as clean energy or mobility).
Green revolving credit	Debt	PFIs, Banks	Revolving credit gives flexibility to green SMEs as they can use funds when they need it. The requested amount is available, once used and repaid, the credit replenishes.	Green revolving credits are often dedicated to fund energy efficiency, renewable energy, and/or sustainability projects that generate cost savings. A portion of the savings are used to replenish Green Revolving Funds allowing reinvestment in future similar projects.
Green guarantees to banks	Debt	PFIs, Banks, Mutual Guarantee Societies	PFIs and guarantee societies can incentivize bank lending by providing guarantees to green credit lines. Eco-credits are examples of loan guarantees to promote energy efficiency projects	Green credit guarantees have specific eligibility criteria aligned with environmental objectives that can be based on the use of proceeds and/or on the characteristics of borrowers. Green guarantees may have monitor and evaluation frameworks to measure and report climate performance and disclose the carbon footprint of the guaranteed portfolio.
Green supply chain financing/ green factoring	Debt	PFIs, Banks, Enterprises	Financial institutions as well as enterprises can use this instrument to support SME greening in supply chains.	Supply chain finance involves a buyer approving its supplier invoices for financing by a bank when a product or service is provided. This type of financing helps the supplier get short-term credit and optimize working capital, while the buyer gets more time to pay off balances. Green supply chain finance entails the provision of financing at preferential rates upon demonstrated sustainability performance. Such

				preferential rates can potentially improve along with sustainability scores.
Grants for green projects	Grants	PFIs	PFIs can channel governmental grants for green SME projects. Grants can include cash transfers as well as technical support.	While green subsidies are specifically used to help firms offset high upfront costs related to the implementation of green technologies and/or processes, green grants can be used for a broader set of purposes (e.g. incentivize production of green products and services).
Green equity	Equity	Impact Investors, PFIs, Venture capital funds	Equity is one of the main instruments used by impact investors but it can also be used by PFIs and private financial institutions	Green Equity includes both Venture Capital and Private Equity aimed specifically at funding innovative solutions to address environmental challenges (e.g. Green-tech, sustainability start-ups). Green VC typically fund the development of pilot-scale green projects where investments can have long funding periods. It has continuous monitoring and reporting, and investors are directly involved in corporate governance to ensure products and processes are aligned to climate objectives. PE fund green start-ups in advanced stages, and also incorporate green indicators to evaluate performance.
Hybrid Financing	Equity and Debt	Impact Investors, PFIs	Hybrid instruments combine debt and equity. It is useful for SMEs as they can convert outstanding debt into equity.	Using hybrid financing instruments, PFIs are able to offer additional incentives for SMEs' green transition. SMEs are likely to benefit more from green investments as compared to alternative investments because of favourable financing conditions (e.g. when a green loan is connected to a grant). For example, PFIs can provide a certain percentage of the green loan in the form of a grant if the company uses the grant for targeted green measures such as investment in renewable energies or energy efficiency.
Mini-green bonds	Capital Markets	Banks, PFIs, Impact Investors	They are smaller green bonds to allow the access of unlisted SMEs to capital markets. Mini bonds can complement large green bonds. The downside is that they are often perceived as risky investments, thus they are guaranteed by public institutions.	Mini-green bonds are committed exclusively to financing environmental or climate projects. These bonds are issued by green start-ups or SMEs. They often cannot be traded and must be held until maturity, as they do not usually have a secondary market for investors to exit early. Green mini bonds are also less regulated and given their high perceived risk they offer higher returns compared to traditional bonds.
Sustainability-linked instruments	Debt, capital markets	Banks, PFIs, Impact investors	Loans or bonds whose financing conditions are tied to the sustainability/ESG performance of the issuer.	Sustainability-linked loans have a dynamic interest rate linked solely to selected sustainability performance indicators, such as carbon emissions or a specific ESG target. Beneficial conditions are not tied to the use of proceeds (like in green concessional loans). ESG-linked bonds have coupons linked to sustainability performance targets (e.g. EU Taxonomy, UN Sustainable Development Goals related to climate change or environmental degradation).

Source: (OECD, 2022[2]) based on (ASEAN, 2019[40]), (European Commission, 2017[41]), (European Parliamentary Research Service, 2021[42]), (FCA, 2022[43]), (KFW, 2022[44]), (McDaniels and Robins, 2017[45]), (OECD, 2015[46]), (Sustainalytics, 2022[47]), (The Montreal Group, 2016[48]), (Kim et al., 2022[49]), (US Department of Energy, 2021[50]), (World Bank, 2021[51]) and (Lin, 2022[52]).

FIs can use green or sustainable instruments to align their portfolios with national, supranational or individually defined taxonomies. This, in turn, can help FIs manage sustainability-related risks in their portfolios and improve portfolio alignment for the purposes of disclosure and managing reputational risks. It can also allow for the provision of more favourable financing conditions for such investments recognising their better long-term financial performance.

In the OECD survey of financial institutions, most FIs indicated that they offer tailored financing solutions to SMEs. Most banks have products labelled as green and sustainable, but fewer offer ESG-linked instruments or transition finance (Figure 2.3 Panel A).

Most FIs offer debt instruments – medium- and long-term debt and short-term loans and factoring – but equity and quasi-equity financing remain relatively limited. Loan guarantees are important instruments that public financial institutions use to mobilise financing for SMEs' green and sustainable investments (Figure 2.3 Panel B).

The introduction and implementation of sustainable financing instruments requires regular monitoring of sustainability performance or pre-defined KPIs related to that financing (Table 2.1). Yet SMEs have limited capacities to provide such data, making it more difficult for them to benefit from these financing products. This in turn also makes financial institutions more reluctant to extend such tailored products for SMEs as they risk being labelled as greenwashing if they cannot produce relevant firm-level data. Demand-side constraints also limit SMEs' ability to profit from this growing pool of tailored financing solutions.

Figure 2.3. Banks provide a variety of sustainability related financing products.

A. Does your institution provide any financing/investment products classified as:

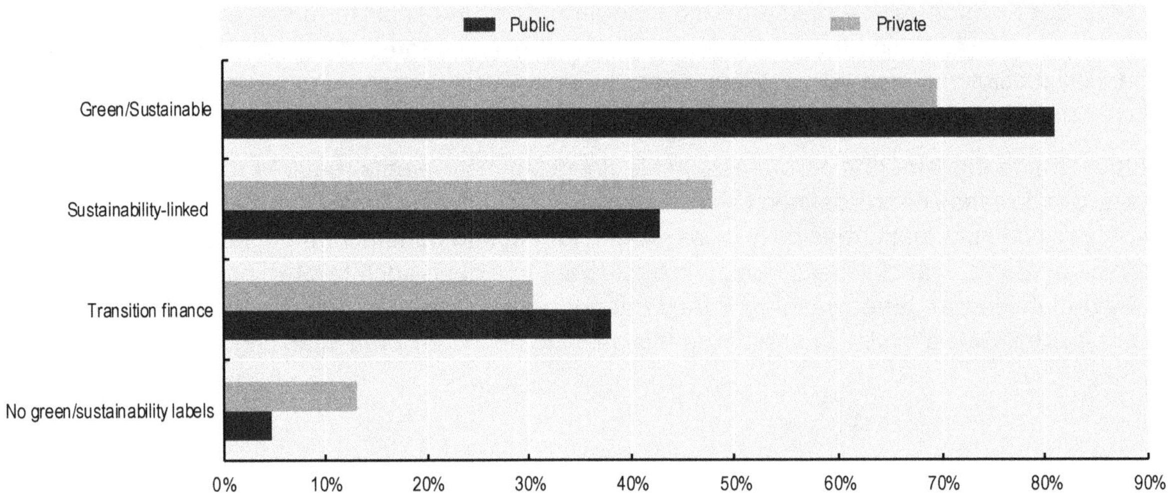

B. Which of the following types of tailored instruments does your institution use to finance SMEs' sustainable or green investments?

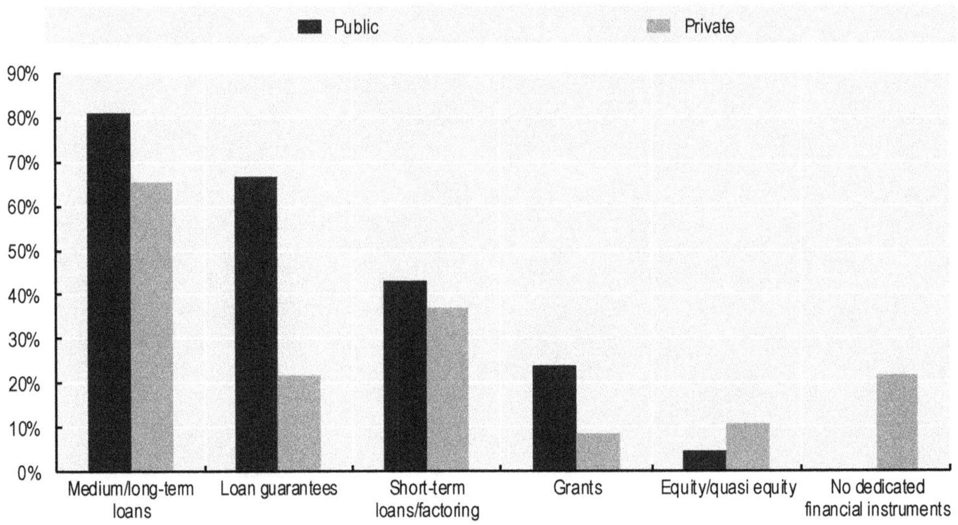

Source: (OECD, 2023[6]).

StatLink https://stat.link/4vq876

Data requirements have emerged as an important obstacle for financial institutions and SMEs to seize sustainable finance opportunities

FIs increasingly need data on clients' sustainability performance, but SMEs have limited capacity to respond

Financial institutions increasingly need and seek out granular data on their clients' sustainability performance in order to manage risks, develop financing instruments and meet reporting requirements (Box 2.3).

Box 2.3. What drives banks to collect sustainability-related data on SMEs?

Managing risks: FIs are increasingly taking into account the potential impacts of physical, transition and systemic risks stemming from climate change biodiversity loss and other environmental degradation in their SME-related assets and liabilities. The range of impacts is wide, from material damage related to increasingly severe weather events, which can impact the value of the FIs' assets, to the risks posed by the green transition itself, including regulatory, technology, market and reputation-related risks. In the latest OECD survey, over 50% of private FIs stated that they have integrated climate considerations in risk management policies, and 78% stated that climate related risks are regularly evaluated at executive/board level meetings (OECD, 2023[6]). Comprehensive assessment of FIs' exposure to climate and nature-related risks requires access to relevant data on the exposure of individual clients, including SMEs (OECD, 2023[6]).

Devising financing instruments: The net-zero and nature-positive transition of FIs also entails opportunities to develop new tailored financing products that can meet the transition-related financing and investment needs of SMEs. However, green and sustainability-linked financing instruments relate financing conditions with sustainability criteria or key performance indicators (KPIs), which means that they require some form of data collection on sustainability performance of clients. SMEs' more limited knowledge, capacities and resources to collect and report on such data makes them less able to tap into available sustainable finance instruments. In turn, FIs are less inclined to developed tailored sustainable financing instruments for SME clients, because, in the absence of relevant client data, they can be labelled as engaging in "greenwashing."

Meeting reporting requirements: In a growing number of OECD and non-OECD countries, financial institutions are subject to sustainability reporting requirements (see section *Data requirements have emerged as an important obstacle for financial institutions and SMEs to seize sustainable finance opportunities*). While these requirements often exempt non-listed SMEs, which account for the majority of enterprises in the economy, the reporting burden is increasingly transmitted to SMEs by the reporting entities, including FI, which have to disclose not only their direct environmental performance but also the performance of their clients (e.g. in the case of carbon emissions, FIs in many jurisdictions have to report on the so-called Scope 3 emissions which include the emissions of their supply chain as well as the financed emissions of their clients).

Source: (TCFD, 2017[53]) (TNFD, 2023[54])

Current regulations allow FIs and other reporting entities to use alternative methods of calculating the environmental performance of their financed portfolios. For example, in the case of carbon emissions, many entities use the method of the Partnership for Carbon Accounting (PCAF) which uses sector-based weights to estimate the carbon footprint of the SME portfolio without necessarily requiring any additional data from SME clients.

However, FIs also face challenges when they try to use alternative approaches that do not require collection of data from SME clients. These types of top-down approaches, which use sector-level data to estimate firm-level footprints, do not deliver sufficiently granular information to support decision-making. Where artificial intelligence is used, transparency presents an issue. FIs, therefore, have an incentive and do seek out sustainability related data from their SME clients to fulfil their various operational needs.

Survey results confirm that the lack of granular data on SME sustainability performance represents a critical challenge for most FIs. For example, around 85% of the surveyed public and private FIs in OECD countries cited the lack of data on SME climate performance as a barrier to the integration of climate considerations in SME operations (Figure 2.4). Most FIs also cited data challenges as the most important barriers to the development of net-zero targets and transition plans, reporting on financed emissions and taking overall action on climate change at an institutional level (OECD, 2023[6]).

Figure 2.4. Lack of granular data on SME climate performance is a challenge for most banks

What are the key challenges you face in integrating climate change considerations in financing/investment decisions regarding SME clients? (% of respondents)

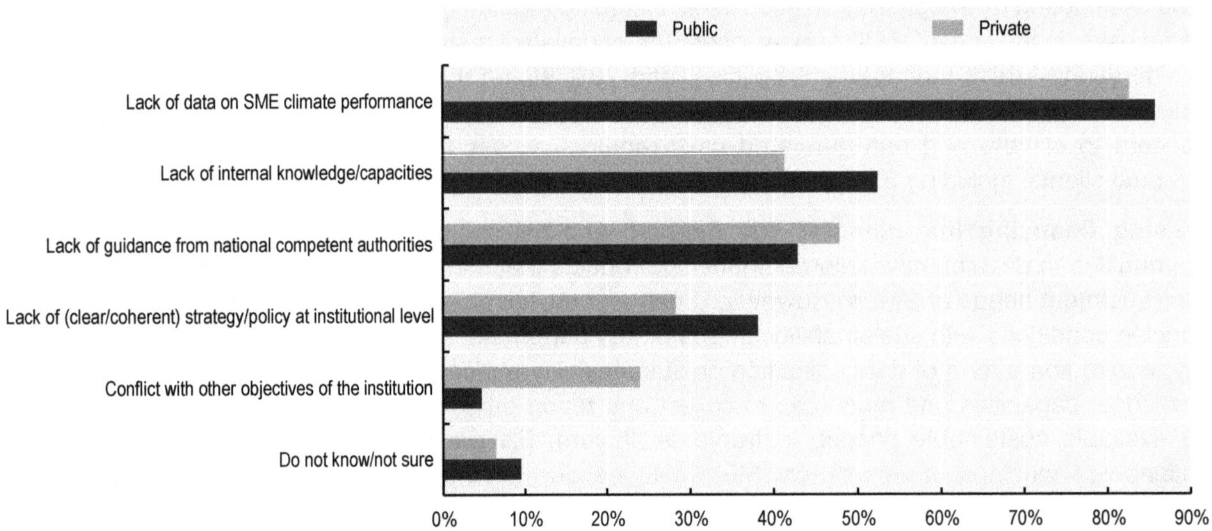

Source: (OECD, 2023[6]).

StatLink https://stat.link/ac6mrz

Currently most FIs ask for some type of sustainability-related data from their SME clients (Figure 2.5). These data can be collected through surveys or other means before the provision of financing and afterward, during the monitoring phase. The types of data requested can differ considerably across institutions as well as depending on the sector and size of the enterprise, the type of investment, the type of instrument used (e.g. asset-backed; sustainability-linked etc). Also, while some FIs use pre-defined frameworks to define the data requirements (e.g. EU green checker; ESG ratings), others are using or defining their own assessment/reporting framework (OECD, 2023[6]).

Figure 2.5. Most FIs ask for sustainability-related data from their SME clients

How is sustainability-related data obtained for small and medium-sized (SME) clients for the purposes of financing/investment decisions? (% of respondents)

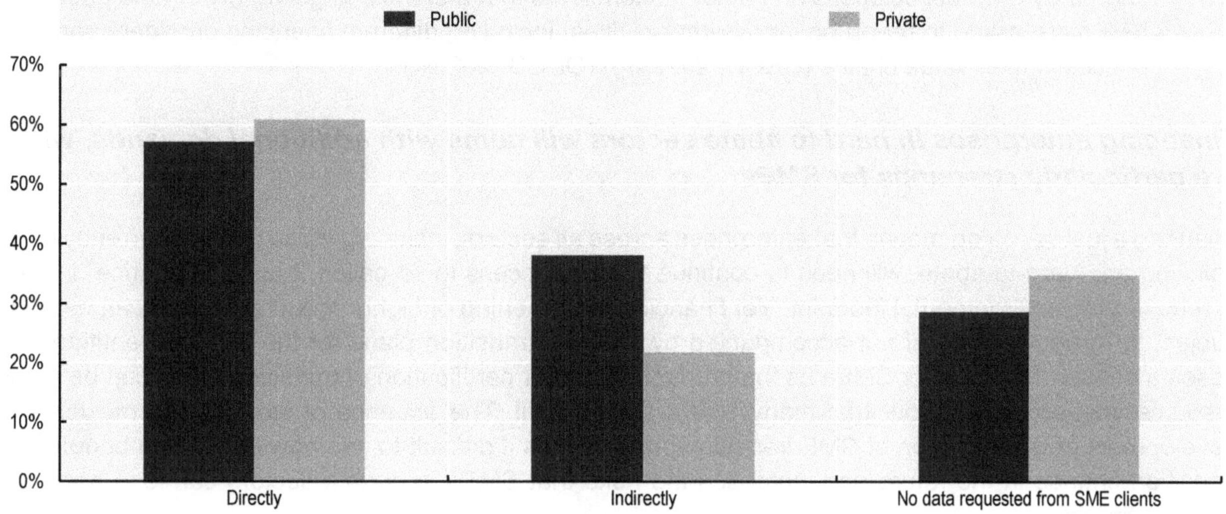

Source: (OECD, 2023[6]).

StatLink https://stat.link/8u10rl

There is currently no common approach in terms of the types of data asked from SME clients across institutions. Some examples cited in the 2023 OECD survey include data on GHG emissions; certificates/labels (e.g. energy performance, ISO on sustainability /waste management/water management etc.); ESG ratings (if any); ESG/sustainability strategy/commitments, audited integrated reporting, etc. During the monitoring or post-repayment stage, the data requirements can vary even further, with some FIs just asking for the same data as those requested prior to the provision of the financing and others asking only for data to verify the purpose of the financed activity. Some FIs also ask for proof of the achieved commitments or KPIs (e.g. energy savings), but this can vary from monitoring KPIs to only qualitative response to a questionnaire without further verification (OECD, 2023[6]) .

This current state of play presents many challenges for SMEs:

- SMEs have more limited capacities to measure and report on their sustainability performance compared to large enterprises. SMEs are generally not required to report on their non-financial performance; in some countries only listed SMEs will have to provide such disclosure. Likewise, few ESG rating providers assess SMEs specifically, and SMEs are underrepresented in ratings among the major ratings providers (OECD, 2020[55]). And although voluntary reporting, certifications and other means of communicating SMEs' environmental performance are on the rise, they are still employed by relatively few SMEs due to the associated costs. For example, despite representing over 99% of all businesses in OECD countries, only 10-15% of companies using the GRI Sustainability reporting standards are SMEs (ESG Investor, 2021[56]).
- Relatedly, there are concerns about the quality and consistency of the data produced by SME clients for the purposes of aggregation and reporting for large enterprises, which can be a disincentive for the provision of financing for SMEs. Sustainability data and ratings rely mainly on data that is self-reported or proxy data that is not verified or audited, and this can raise questions about the objectivity, comparability and reliability of these data with largely negative implications for SMEs. In the current context, the quality of these data reflects to some degree the capacities of

companies to adequately measure and report on their environmental performance and greening actions, and this likely disadvantages SMEs relative to large enterprises (OECD, 2022[35]).

- The lack of a standardised framework for data requirement compounds the above challenges and further adds to the burden on SMEs. Results from the OECD survey confirm anecdotal evidence shared by SME associations and other stakeholders that there is a large variety of data points that SMEs are asked to report on for different entities, including different financing providers and large entities in their value chains (OECD, 2022[57])) (OECD, 2023[6]).

Financing enterprises in hard to abate sectors will come with additional demands, which are particularly strenuous for SMEs

Ensuring a just transition means that enterprises across all sectors, including those that are currently highly polluting and hard-to-abate, will need to continue to have access to so-called "transition finance" in order to reduce their environmental footprint. Yet financing the greening of highly polluting sectors can easily be subject to "greenwashing" if not accompanied by credible transition plans for the financed entities. This poses a critical challenge for SMEs as the production and/or certification of transition plans can be a very resource intensive endeavour that many SMEs cannot fulfil. The absence of simplified frameworks for development and verification of SME transition plans makes it difficult to see how SMEs can benefit from transition finance in the future and increases the risks that SMEs in certain sectors can lose access to external finance.

Implications for SME access to finance

The sections above highlight that the shift of the financial sector toward more sustainable investments, while generally a very welcome development, also raises concerns about SMEs' access to finance. Data-related challenges, complexity and costs related to development of transition plans, and demonstrating improvements in sustainability performance, mean that SMEs may not be able to meet the emerging requirements that FIs will need to introduce to meet their own operational and reporting needs. This has implications for regulators, policy makers and other national and international public entities and calls for the development of effective solutions to help SMEs not only to navigate but also benefit from this evolution in the financial sector (see more in *section Creating a supportive ecosystem to help SMEs navigate the transition*).

Limited SME demand for sustainable finance poses an important challenge to further market development

In addition to the above-mentioned constraints to the provision of sustainable finance for SMEs, policy makers, public and private FIs, and other ecosystem actors need to tackle the challenge of SMEs' limited demand for sustainable finance, which reflects awareness, knowledge and resource barriers.

Information and awareness related barriers are high among SMEs

A lack of information and awareness of opportunities, environmental regulations and support options can constitute a significant barrier for greening efforts by SMEs and entrepreneurs. They may lack knowledge of current and upcoming policy requirements, possibilities and opportunities to reduce resource use and available financial or advisory support measures to assist them. Lack of awareness and information represent a common barrier for SMEs across different policy areas, but receives particular emphasis in the environmental domain, in part because of its perceived technical and economic complexity. For instance, SMEs are often unaware of many financially attractive opportunities for environmental improvement. There is a widespread misperception that protecting the environment is associated with technical complexity, burdens and costs (OECD, 2018[58]).

Even when well-informed, often owner–managers of small firms are 'struggling to bridge the gap between their environmental attitudes (aspirations) and their environmental behaviour (practices). While for many SMEs the business case for investing in the transition is clear, which makes them reactive to information on opportunities and obligations, for some (and potentially large) groups of SMEs, the business case may be less clear-cut. In this case, actions devoted to improve access to information may not be sufficient to change practices and incite investment.

SMEs also face high technical, market and regulatory uncertainty

Technical uncertainty often arises from questions about the technical feasibility of adopting new innovations and solutions, as well as their potential implications. SMEs often do not have technical expertise and have questions about the functionality, usefulness, or quality of new innovations for the performance of their own business. This uncertainty leads to an under-investment by SMEs.

Market uncertainty is frequently identified as one of the main barriers to greening in surveys of SMEs and entrepreneurs. SMEs often view environmental measures as reducing profits while simultaneously presenting uncertain market benefits even if there is considerable evidence to the contrary. For many SMEs, greening will likely have a net cost, which leads them to view "greening" with scepticism. In Korea, for example, 60% of SMEs and entrepreneurs consider that the net-zero transition would negatively impact their competitiveness over the near term, and 15% consider it even a threat to their existence (Korea Chamber of Commerce and Industry, 2021[14]). In the UK, about 30% of SMEs have cited feasibility as their top constraint to green investment, while in Canada SMEs cite their perceived inability to profitably provide affordable green products, services or processes as one of their top three obstacles for greening (British Business Bank, 2021[59]; Business Development Bank of Canada, 2021[60]). This obstacle is typically greater for SMEs than for large firms. It also represents a major hurdle for eco-entrepreneurs, since they typically need to build a market for a product that does not yet exist.

Policy and regulatory uncertainty can also be an obstacle to greening since policy volatility can contribute to market uncertainty. This is particularly true for innovation and entrepreneurship. Moreover, while regulation is considered a powerful driver for environmental innovation, environmental regulation is often more arduous for SMEs than for larger firms (Brammer, Hoejmose and Marchant, 2012[61]) since they have fewer resources to dedicate to navigating a complicated regulatory system that may require certifications and compliance inspections. For resource efficiency actions, complexity of administrative procedures is the most cited difficulty for European SMEs (34%) (European Commission, 2021[62]).

Capacity and resource constraints affect SME demand for sustainable investment and finance

SMEs willing and capable of adopting sustainable practices and seizing green business opportunities generally face skill deficits, size-related resource and technology constraints, and difficulties in obtaining government support (OECD, 2018[58]).

Even when SMEs are aware of the potential of better environmental performance to improve their competitiveness, a lack of appropriate skills and expertise commonly prevents these enterprises from acting upon win-win opportunities. In a 2023 survey, 58% of SMEs globally identified skills and knowledge as a barrier for taking action on climate (SME Climate Hub, 2023[3]). Managerial constraints have also been shown to limit SMEs' ability to implement solutions, with stronger green management being linked to more drastic cuts to greenhouse gas emissions (De Haas et al., 2021[63]).

SMEs also face technological and resource constraints as a result of their size. For instance, SMEs may be less able to access environmental technologies than large firms due to pre-existing challenges in finding capital or due to the economies of scale needed to realise the environmental benefits of the solution. In a meta-analysis of the 50 most cited articles related to sustainability barriers for SMEs, resource-based barriers (lack of resources, high initial capital costs and lack of expertise) were found to be the most important (Álvarez Jaramillo, Zartha Sossa and Orozco Mendoza, 2019[64]).

Finally, SMEs face constraints in obtaining government support. Government agencies increasingly need data as a means of proving a programme's effectiveness and showing progress towards environmental goals. As elaborated in previous sections, data provision is a challenge for resource-constrained SMEs. Additionally, the administrative costs of applying for and obtaining government support remain relatively fixed across firm size, hence affecting SMEs disproportionately. These challenges limit SMEs' utilisation of government support and thus lead to an under-investment in sustainable technologies.

SMEs need to interact with a wider range of actors in the sustainable finance ecosystem

SMEs have to navigate an increasingly complex sustainable finance ecosystem with a growing number of actors. In addition to the traditional players including public and private financial institutions, accountants, policy makers, regulators and others, SMEs also need to interact with many ESG intermediaries including Fintech companies and other service providers that can enable them to measure and report on their sustainability performance as well as take actions to improve it. SMEs may also need to interact with various verification bodies to ensure that their reporting or transition plans are credible and aligned with the Paris Agreement and other relevant global benchmarks. This can also temper their demand for sustainable finance and investment.

Implications for SME sustainable finance

SMEs' limited demand for sustainable investment and the related finance has several critical implications:

- SMEs need a stronger business case and external support to boost their investments in sustainability and seek the related financing;
- In the absence of SME demand, public and private FIs have limited incentives to develop tailored financing solutions for financing SMEs' net-zero and other investment needs;
- If they do not invest in improving their sustainability performance or can demonstrate credible transition plans, SMEs risk losing access to finance even for other investment needs as elaborated in the previous section.

A clear and transparent regulatory and policy framework is critical to limit regulatory and policy uncertainty and strengthen the business case for investing in net zero and greening. Financial and non-financial support aimed at strengthening SMEs' awareness and capacities and incentives to invest in the green transition will also be critical going forward. Different actors in the sustainable finance ecosystem - both public and private - need to be mobilised in this effort (see section *Conclusion and policy implications*).

Creating a supportive ecosystem to help SMEs navigate the transition

Creating a supportive ecosystem is critical to the green transition of a broad and diverse population of SMEs. To increase SME demand for sustainable finance and to address the above-mentioned constraints, regulatory frameworks must provide a stable and clear path for transitioning. These frameworks should take into consideration the capacity of SMEs while being comprehensive enough to allow financial institutions to reward those undergoing the transition.

Regulatory and policy approaches

Clear, transparent and predictable regulatory and policy framework

Clear, transparent and predictable regulatory and policy framework is critical to strengthening the case for SME investment in greening. As noted above, SMEs' demand for sustainable investments is constrained by the uncertain returns stemming in part from regulatory uncertainty. Governments must, therefore, ensure that they set a clear economy-wide transition path and a coherent regulatory and policy framework to support the private sector's sustainable investments.

Comprehensive regulatory framework (e.g. carbon pricing; non-financial disclosure, etc) will also provide banks greater incentives to price in climate- and nature-related risks into their operations, with impact on financing decisions and financing conditions. The latter implies that FIs will be able to increasingly offer better financing conditions for enterprises with better financial performance. Currently, by most accounts, the premia for better environmental performance are relatively small i.e. FIs can only offer small discounts for financing of SMEs that have a better financial performance. A more comprehensive regulatory approach that incentivises the internalisation of environmental externalities and pricing of environment-related physical transition and systemic risk can foster better pricing of financing products. A clear and comprehensive regulatory framework also provides incentives for SMEs to invest in greening and helps to address the demand-side constraints to the growth of sustainable finance.

Governments should also take the SME dimension into consideration when designing regulations and policies. As elaborated in the previous sections, SMEs do not have the same resources and capacities as large enterprises to address regulatory requirements, particularly complex requirements such as non-financial disclosure in line with various existing national and international reporting standards. This does not have to mean necessarily exemption of SMEs from regulations; in fact, exemptions may produce unintended consequences, such as creating a threshold or barrier for firm growth (OECD, 2021[65]). Moreover, as discussed above, even if exempted, SMEs may be indirectly impacted by the requirements imposed on larger entities. Consideration of the SME dimension can, for example, include the introduction of regulatory requirements that are proportional to firm size and thus entail considerable simplification and lower resource intensity for smaller enterprises (OECD, 2022[35]). When determining what policy intervention to use, governments should consider the impact of the policy, the relevance of SMEs to the goals of the policy, and what subgroups of SMEs (sector, age, geographic location, etc.) are most likely to be affected (OECD, 2021[65]).

Many countries have begun introducing a variety of mechanisms to better account for SMEs, including: collecting granular data on key features and behaviours of various types of SMEs, undertaking ex post evaluations to assess the effectiveness of policies and programmes for specific populations of businesses, creating dedicated institutions to coordinate functions, incorporating the use of SME threshold testing to gauge the relevance of a policy to SMEs, and strengthening consultation processes to include voices that are less heard (OECD, 2021[65]). The different approaches and mechanisms to include the SME dimension need to be adapted to fit the countries' specific institutional set-up (OECD, 2023[4]).

Sustainability reporting regulations

Many current and emerging regulations, notably regulations on sustainability disclosure, have been designed with large enterprises in mind and have largely exempted non-listed SMEs which account for the vast majority of SMEs. However, as elaborated above, SME are indirectly impacted by these regulations via the financing channel and/or their participation in the value chains. This means that reporting entities, including financial institutions, have to request a certain set of data points from their SME clients and translate them into relevant metrics to meet their own comprehensive reporting requirements. As noted, in the recently implemented survey by the OECD, some FIs use already existing frameworks for obtaining such data from SME clients, while others rely on their own assessments and methodologies. This creates a plethora of different approaches and data points that are being sought from SMEs, which further compounds the burden on these entities with limited capacities to measure and report on their sustainability performance.

The development of simplified reporting frameworks for SMEs can help take into account their relatively more limited capacities for measurement and reporting compared to large firms, as can the promotion of interoperability of these frameworks. Likewise, dialogue to explore how these requirements could be balanced or offset by using estimates can contribute to minimising the burden for both SMEs and financial institutions.

Some initiatives are already being put in place to address these challenges. The European Commission in 2023 introduced the SME Relief Package, which notes the difficulties SMEs have in accessing sustainable finance and commits to limiting disclosure requirements from trickling down through value chains and to adapting the Green Asset Ratio to improve incentives for SME financing (EU Commission, 2023[66]). Likewise, the European Financial Reporting Advisory Group (EFRAG), the EU advisory body that developed the European Sustainability Reporting Standards (ESRS), has been mandated to develop voluntary reporting standards for non-listed SMEs that can provide a common framework that FIs and SMEs can refer to. The IFRS is also developing guidance for SMEs (Box 2.3). The OECD Platform on Financing SMEs for Sustainability is also working to support this global effort for the development of a simplified SME reporting framework for FIs.

Box 2.3. Selected initiatives to limit the sustainability reporting burden on SMEs

IFRS

The **International Financial Reporting Standards** (IFRS) Foundation, which developed the International Sustainability Standards Board (ISSB) standards, has taken an initiative to streamline the ISSB standards for non-public SMEs. Compared to the full ISSB, these new accounting standards omit topics not relevant to SMEs, simplify the principles for recognising and measuring assets/liabilities/income/expenses, and require fewer disclosures. To ease readability, the streamlined offering is written in a clear, easily translatable language and some accounting choices are restricted to provide a simpler methodology. The initiative also limits the frequency of revisions to ISSB (once every 3 years) to further reduce the reporting burden for small businesses.

EFRAG

The **European Financial Reporting Advisory Group** (EFRAG) provides technical advice for the adoption of the European Sustainability Reporting Standards (ESRS) for listed SMEs. Their focus is to remove the reporting requirements that they deem are irrelevant to SMEs or are disproportionately burdensome. SMEs under the revised standards would have simplified disclosures for reporting on the roles/responsibilities of management as well as for sustainability impacts, risks and opportunities.

EFRAG has also begun to develop a Voluntary Sustainability Reporting Standard (VSRS) to be used by unlisted SMEs not covered under ESRS. Through VSRS, EFRAG aims to facilitate SMEs' access to sustainable finance without substantially increasing the reporting burden for SMEs.

Source: (IFRS, 2023[67]), (Deloitte, 2023[68]), (EFRAG, 2022[69]), (EFRAG, 2022[70])

Transition finance frameworks

Current reporting frameworks focus strongly on sustainable or sustainability-aligned activities which creates limited incentives for FIs to invest in brown activities or hard-to-abate activities, even when entities have developed credible transition plans. This excludes entities that are responsible for a high proportion of emissions and crucial to decarbonization efforts (OECD, Forthcoming[25]).

Transition finance frameworks exist to facilitate the phased transition plans of brown and hard to abate firms. Currently there exists no internationally recognized agreements on transition finance but various governments have established their own initiatives to foster the participation finance of market players (OECD, Forthcoming[25]).

Transition finance is reserved for firms that can develop and prove the credibility of their transition plans (e.g. through relevant independent verifications), creating a barrier for SMEs with lower reporting capacity and limited financial resources. Simplified frameworks for SMEs should be developed, and non-financial support be given to aid SMEs in developing transition plans. Financial institutions engaging in transition finance should apply the principle of proportionality when requesting transition-related information from SMEs (OECD, Forthcoming[25]).

Frameworks for inclusion of biodiversity and nature-related risks and opportunities in non-financial reporting

Going beyond measures related to carbon neutrality and GHG emissions, public and private actors are increasingly incorporating concepts of biodiversity as they look to develop holistic measures of environmental performance. The inclusion of biodiversity impacts and exposure to nature-related risks in disclosure and other regulatory requirements for FIs and large enterprises also poses challenges for SMEs. Currently reporting frameworks are varied in methodology due to geographic factors and interrelatedness, heightening the complexity of establishing biodiversity-related dependencies and impacts. SMEs often lack a comprehensive understanding of how their activities impact their ecosystems, along with information about how climate change affects the ecosystems they depend upon; they may thus lack the capacity to develop sustainable land/ocean/forestry practices in line with emerging frameworks.

Efforts are also being taken to increase the ease of reporting on biodiversity related impacts and risks. The Taskforce for Nature-related Financial Disclosures (TNFD) is a market-led taskforce of financial institutions that aims to develop a risk management and reporting framework that captures nature-related risks. TFND does not aim to create new standards for biodiversity but instead aims to create an integrated framework that aligns disclosures, provides flexibility in reporting depending on the capacity of the organisation, encourages easy adoption of natural related disclosures and overtime provides a structured path to increasing disclosure ambitions (TNFD, 2023[54]). As these frameworks become standardised and nature-related disclosures become mandatory, action is needed to ensure that SMEs are not overburdened by additional reporting standards.

On the regulatory side, governments are beginning to mandate the disclosure of biodiversity impacts and the exposure of firms to nature-related risks, many of which are based on the TNFD framework. The European Sustainability Reporting Standards (ESRS), for example has two modules dedicated to biodiversity and nature related risks: "Water and Marine Resources" and "Biodiversity and Ecosystems". Under both these modules entities are required to report their respective impact, mitigation efforts and material risks associated with the entity's activity (OECD, 2023[34]). As mentioned in Box 2.3, EFRAG is working to streamline ESRS for the use of SMEs, although this does not currently include changes to the two aforementioned modules (EFRAG, 2022[69]). Indonesia also has established in its reporting obligations that entities disclose all conservation activities and report on their exposure to biodiversity related impacts (Indonesia Financial Services Authority, 2017[71]).

Given the complexity of understanding and measuring nature-related risks and impacts, standard setters and regulators need to make sure that simplified measurement and reporting frameworks are in places. Different public and private actors should also provide tools, training and other capacity building support to help SMEs understand their dependency and impact on biodiversity and ecosystem services.

Public support to mobilise sustainable finance for SMEs

SME access to sustainable finance is subject to considerable supply-side constraints that reflect not only traditional challenges in the provision of SME financing (asymmetric information, high cost relative to the size of loan, limited collateral, etc.) but also specific challenges related to the needs of sustainable finance instruments, most notably the measurement, monitoring and reporting on their sustainability performance. As elaborated in the section *Data requirements have emerged as an important obstacle for financial institutions and SMEs to seize sustainable finance opportunities*, in the absence of public support to mobilise financing from private FIs, SMEs will have limited access to tailored financing solutions for the green transition and may even lose access to finance altogether. Financing support can take many forms.

Direct financing

Public lending schemes for SMEs are the most used direct financing instrument by public institutions. Direct lending is provided through specialised public banks that are focused on SME finance (e.g. the British Business Bank, the Business Development Bank of Canada, Bpifrance and the Industrial Bank of Korea) or through government-sponsored entities that can provide lending to SMEs (e.g. the US Business Administration). It can take the form of direct issuing of SME loans or it can entail the provision of credit lines for on-lending through private financial institutions (e.g. microloans). These lending schemes can be designed to target specific types of investments, including investments for greening or scaling up green solutions. As discussed above, lending to SMEs can be extended through a range of different instruments including concessional loans, bridge loans, revolving credit, etc. Public FIs can also channel financing obtained through the issue of green bonds to SMEs through various forms of credit.

Non-debt financing for SMEs, such as equity, can also be used by governments to mobilise finance to small business, particularly for new, innovative and fast-growing companies with a higher risk profile. These entrepreneurs and SMEs need substantial funds to finance green projects with high growth prospects, but their future earnings are often difficult to forecast and thus they are unlikely to be able to obtain bank credit. These financing constraints can be especially severe in the case of start-ups or small businesses whose business model relies on intangibles (e.g. green intellectual capital), which, despite their contribution to firm profitability and competitive advantage (Chen and Chang, 2011[72]), are difficult to use as collateral in traditional debt relations (OECD, 2022[73]) (OECD, 2015[46]).

Non-debt financing can also take the form of grants. Grants can be used to support eco-entrepreneurs that are seeking to develop and grow their innovative green ideas. They are particularly well suited to support technologies that are further away from the commercialisation stage. They can also be used to incentivise eco-adoption of greening technologies that can have broader environmental and social benefits.

Hybrid financing instruments are gaining increased attention in the post-COVID period as a means of recapitalising the SME sector. A 2021 study in the EU, recommended the use of a hybrid capital instrument, ideally guaranteed by an EU entity, which delivers equity accounting treatment as well as tax deductibility to mobilise SME sustainable finance. This kind of instrument could provide the scale to deliver cost-efficient capital that would not require relinquishing control of the company, which is a major concern for many SMEs (AFME, 2021[74]). Other hybrid instruments, such as convertible loans (i.e. loans are converted to equity once specific stipulations in the loan agreement are met), can also be used to support the financing of SMEs' green transition without further raising the debt burden on SMEs.

Mobilising private financing

Public credit guarantee schemes (PCGSs) are the most common instrument for mobilising debt financing for SMEs, and they have considerable potential to mobilise finance for sustainable investment as well as to reduce the cost of capital of green projects. Credit guarantees are especially instrumental in offsetting the informational asymmetries between borrowers and lenders as they absorb the risk of lending to SMEs. Financial institutions have higher incentives to provide the financing the company needs, as the risk of non-repayment in the case the company fails, is shared between the financing bank, the PCGs and the state. Although the coverage of credit guarantees varies largely among countries, in the European Union, for example, most of the credit guarantee coverages ranges from 60% to 80% (AECM, 2022[75]).

Credit guarantees that incorporate climate objectives are increasingly used around the world as a mechanism to mobilise sustainable and green finance for SMEs (Box 2.4). Credit guarantees can be an effective way to channel finance to eco-adopters considering the large upfront costs they face when they undertake sustainable investments. Similarly, credit guarantees can be useful to reduce the private sector's risk of investments to eco-innovators. Although these types of enterprises rely mainly on equity instruments to finance their operations, they also benefit from hybrid instruments and as such, can benefit from green credit guarantees.

Private financial institutions, in turn, can rely on a range of sustainable or green financing instruments to finance SMEs' sustainable investments. As noted above, financial institutions currently finance SME net-zero investments mainly through medium and long-term loans as well as short-term loans and factoring. Likewise, many FIs provide this financing through tailored instruments labelled as green, sustainable, or ESG-linked (OECD, 2023[6]).

Box 2.4. Examples of credit guarantee schemes aimed at mobilising green finance for SMEs

Green credit guarantees

The Sustainability Portfolio Guarantee Product, implemented by the **EIF** under the InvestEU programme, strives to enhance access to debt finance for SMEs investing in the EU's green and sustainable transformation. In comparison to the market's standard products, the EIF Sustainability Guarantee offers preferential conditions to financial intermediaries, such as a high guarantee coverage rate of up to 70% and a maximum transaction amount of 7.5 million when private financial intermediaries finance SMEs. Eligible to apply for the guarantees are "Sustainable Enterprises" (e.g. those working with clean-tech related technology or recipients of an eco-label from an EU labelling scheme) or "Green Investments" (such as SME's investment in energy efficiency or sustainable use of materials).

The €500 million Growth and Sustainability Loan Scheme operated by the **Strategic Banking Cooperation of Ireland** (**SBCI**) provides longer-term lending to SMEs. The Scheme targets a minimum of 30% of the lending volume towards environmental sustainability purposes with the aim of encouraging SMEs to take positive actions in support of the climate change agenda. In addition, up to 70% of lending will be for strategic investments with a view to increasing productivity and competitiveness and thus underpinning future business sustainability and growth.

In **Finland**, Finnvera, in collaboration with the European Investment Fund (EIF), offers direct financing for sustainability in the form of a Climate and Environmental Loan product aimed at supporting Finnish companies engaged in advancing renewable energy sources, energy efficiency, sustainable materials usage and the transition to a circular or low-emission economy. This initiative encompasses various sectors, including renewable energy, green and energy-efficient certified commercial buildings, zero- and low-emission mobility infrastructure, Green ICT investments, waste management, and circular economy business models. The scheme provides favourable loan terms, with amounts ranging from EUR 150 000 to EUR 2 million per financing project. The loan does not require collateral and the EIF provides a 60% guarantee.

Similarly, the French national promotional bank, **Bpifrance,** offers Green Guarantees as part of their Climate Plan. The Green Guarantees are provided for individual business projects as well as in the form of portfolio guarantees, e.g. to reduce environmental impacts and improve energy performance of

SMEs. The Green Guarantees cover 80% of the loan amount, up to a maximum risk commitment of 1.5 million Euros.

In **Portugal,** the government, through the Banco Portgues de Fomento, has allocated EUR 100 million for Linha de Credito para a Descarbonizacao e Economia Circular (Line of Credit for Decarbonization and Circular Economy). Through this scheme, SMEs can apply for financing backed by guarantees to invest in projects aimed at improving energy efficiency or incorporating circular economy concepts (e.g. upgrading equipment, processes for resource optimization, etc.). Guarantees cover 80% of outstanding capital up to a maximum amount of 2,000,000 Euros per company.

In **Romania,** the National Credit Guarantee Fund for Small and Medium Enterprises (FNGCIMM) provides guarantees for SMEs in the construction sector for projects related to energy efficiency, accessing green energy or aligning with environmental objectives. Guarantees cover 90% of outstanding loan amounts with a maximum of 5 million Romanian Leu for working capital financing and a maximum of 10 million Leu for investment loan guarantees.

In June 2021, the **Government of Sweden** launched a special credit guarantee for green investments. The programme will facilitate loan offerings to companies that contribute to reaching the goals of the environmental objectives system and climate policy framework. To qualify for the guarantee scheme, the company needs to its contribution to environmental objectives in line with the EC's Green Taxonomy.

In **Bulgaria, the Energy Efficiency and Renewable Sources Fund** (EERSF) includes a credit guarantee facility and a consulting company offering technical assistance to SME. The Fund also directly finances or co-finances projects in energy efficiency.

In **Korea**, **the Government,** in conjunction with **the Korea Energy Agency**, **Korea Credit Guarantee Fund and the Korea Technology Finance Corporation**, launched the Green Guarantee Program for SMEs that operate in the New and Renewable Power Generation sector or in the New and Renewable Energy Industry. The Program aims to provide liquidity support and incentivise capital expenditures in green facilities and technologies by guaranteeing up to 95% of the loan amount.

In **Mexico, the FIRA** (Fideicomisos Instituidos en la Relación con la Agricultura) promotes financing by granting loans and providing guarantees and technical assistance to SMEs that contribute to the sustainability of Mexico's agricultural sector.

Source: (AECM, 2023[76]) (EIF, 2023[77]) (SBCI, 2022[78]), (Finnvera, 2023[79]), (Bpifrance, 2023[80]), (Banco Portugues de Fomento, 2023[81]), (FNGCIMM, 2022[82]), (Swedish MInistry of Finance, 2021[83]), (Energy Efficiency and Renewable Sources Fund, 2004[84]), (ALIDE, 2017[85]), (AECM, 2022[86]).

Public institutions also have an important role to play in supporting the **development of green capital markets** and facilitating SMEs' participation in them. Bonds typically have to be of a relatively large size to be attractive for institutional investors, which is challenging for small-scale projects and issuers. This can result in these projects being inaccessible to large investors, resulting in higher cost of financing. Governments can support better access to capital markets through the aggregation of bonds, which in turn can be done through warehousing, standardisation of contracts or issuance of green covered bonds. Countries can also allow for issuance of small or "mini bonds" by unlisted SMEs (European Commission, 2016[87]). Many EU countries have created platforms or allow for the issuance of mini bonds including the UK (London Stock Exchange), Italy, Germany, Nordic countries (Nordic ABM), France, Spain, etc.

Non-financial support for SMEs

Public FIs and other public institutions, private banks and non-governmental initiatives also have a pivotal role to play in providing non-financial support for SMEs and entrepreneurs. Non-financial services, in the form of training and advice, consultancy and education, are crucial as part of the policy mix. They can help SMEs and entrepreneurs strengthen their ability to understand the steps needed to green their businesses and help them allocate financial resources appropriately.

Public FIs, as well as private financial institutions, are increasingly providing sustainability-related technical support, practical tools and education to entrepreneurs and SMEs in order to incentivise their net-zero transition. A number of governments and public FIs have established online hubs with tools and resources that can help SMEs to understand, measure and mitigate their carbon footprint. They also provide SMEs with data and information on the financial and other support they can tap into when taking their actions toward improved sustainability (Box 2.5).

Box 2.5. Examples of sustainability-related non-financial support provided to SMEs

Canada: The Business Development Bank of Canada (BDC) provides numerous forms of non-financial support to help SMEs. Their Climate Action Centre provides guidance on decarbonisation for SMEs based on data provided on their industry, size and operations. The Centre hosts and actively updates a list of active government grants, tax credits and loan programs to support the environmental initiatives of Canadian SMEs. BDC also offers technical assistance to help SMEs obtain B-Corp certification, with a benchmark tool on B-Corp eligibility that firms can use to gauge their alignment to social/environmental objectives. BDC is in the process of developing a carbon calculator which will help SMEs monitor and report on their environmental impact.

Denmark: The Danish Business Authority in collaboration with the Danish Energy Agency have launched a digital carbon footprint calculator (the Climate Compass), which is targeted at SMEs. With the Climate Compass, SMEs can access a free, authoritative tool to calculate their emissions in compliance with the GHG-protocol that is continuously updated by the Danish authorities with the newest available data.

France: Bpifrance and the French Agency for Ecological Transition, ADEME, implemented the Decarbonisation Accelerator, aimed at supporting French SMEs and midcaps in their green transition. The programme, spanning 2 years, involves an intensive 30-day individual support phase in which a firm-specific diagnosis, decarbonisation strategy and deployment plan are developed. The initiative provides 8 days of seminars offering key insights into low-carbon transitions, toolkits and case studies. Knowledge exchange is fostered through meetings with experts, peer-to-peer interactions and preferential access to Bpifrance and ADEME services. Bpifrance and ADEME additionally provide a climatometer- a free tool which allows SMEs to calculate their environmental footprint. SMEs obtain an individual diagnosis assessing environmental impacts and recommendations for climate actions they can take.

UK: The British Business Bank has established a demand development function that seeks to provide data, information and instruments that are impactful for SMEs and can incentivise their green actions. The BBB also has an online Finance Hub to direct SMEs to digital resources and information on these topics including information on digital carbon calculators, environmental initiatives and financing tools for sustainability.

Hungary: The European Investment Bank (EIB) and Magyar Fejlesztési Bank (MFB) developed co-operation in 2021 to help MFB's advisory unit provide advisory services to Hungarian project promoters. MFB's advisory unit will also focus on supporting the recovery and green investment activities of key economic players such as SMEs.

Greece: The Hellenic Development Bank has recently launched their ESG Tracker, an online platform that captures the progress of businesses in meeting ESG criteria. The program is freely accessible and provides firms with a real-time self-assessment and a tool to report on their sustainability progress. The platform aligns itself with international indicators from the Global Reporting Initiative, Sustainability Accounting Standards Board, Task Force on Climate Related Disclosures, and the Climate Disclosure Project as well as national standards used by the Athens Stock Exchange.

The European Commission's Covenant of Companies for Climate and Energy (CCCE) is an initiative to support SMEs in **Croatia, Finland, Italy, the Netherlands** and **Poland** with free technical assistance in energy auditing, types of financing mechanisms and available technologies to mitigate their environmental footprint.

As part of InvestEU, the **European Investment Fund (EIF)** has developed the Sustainability Guarantee Tool. This tool allows FIs and firms to assess the climate impact of their projects and their eligibility for the EIF's InvestEU Sustainability Portfolio Guarantee Product. The reports generated by the tool can be used to satisfy specific reporting requirements to the credit institutions under the Sustainability Guarantee Portfolio Product.

Source: (BDC, 2023[88]) (BDC, 2023[89]), (State of Green, 2022[90]), (Bpifrance, 2020[91]), (BBB, 2019[92]), (BBB, 2018[93]), (EIB, 2021[94]), (European Commission, 2022[95]), (EIF, 2023[77]), (EIF, 2023[96]), (Hellenic Development Bank, 2023[97])

In the OECD survey of FIs, a large share noted that they currently provide a range of non-financial support services to SME clients, including workshops, one-to-one consulting services, online and in-person training and capacity building, online tools, peer learning etc. (Figure 2.6).

Figure 2.6. Most FIs provide some type of non-financial support to SME clients

What type of non-financial support does your institution offer to SMEs to build their capacity to measure, report and take action on climate change and net zero? (% of respondents)

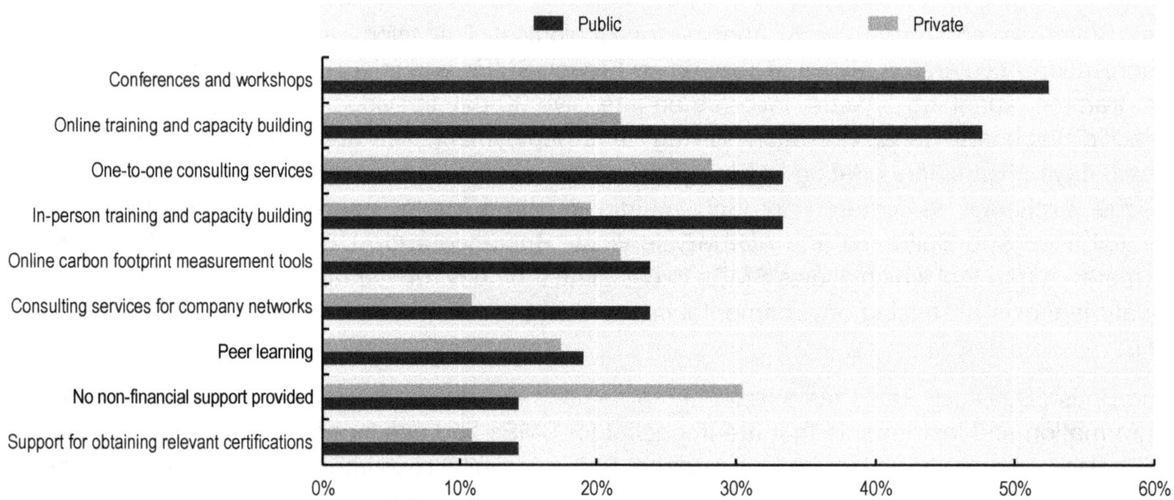

Source: (OECD, 2023[6]).

StatLink https://stat.link/ua49vq

International efforts

In addition, international institutions are stepping up initiatives to foster sustainable finance for SMEs (Box 2.6). The OECD Platform on Financing SMEs for Sustainability, launched in November 2021, contributes to efforts to reduce the barriers to the demand and supply of sustainable finance for SMEs. By convening key stakeholders from the SME sustainable finance ecosystem (public and private financial institutions, SME associations, policy makers, etc.), the Platform fosters knowledge sharing and policy dialogue whilst also advancing the data and analytical work on SME sustainable finance in order to accelerate SMEs' net-zero transition. The Platform works to develop and share recommendations and best practices, as well as promote and coordinate research to further obtain comparable information on SME access to sustainable finance (OECD, 2021[98]). The Platform builds upon the work of the Committee on SMEs and Entrepreneurship and complements other relevant OECD work and guidance, including on sustainable finance and investment, transition finance, corporate governance and others.

Box 2.6. Selected examples of international initiatives to support access to and uptake of SME sustainable finance

The **Executive Agency for Small and Medium-sized (EASME)** created by the European Commission aims to help create a more competitive and resource-efficient European economy based on knowledge transfer and innovation. The EASME manage the Sustainable Industry Low Carbon Scheme and is part of the EU programme for the Environment and Climate Action, the European Maritime and Fisheries Fund and the legacy of the Intelligent Energy Europe programme and the Eco-innovation initiative.

The **Asia-Pacific Economic Cooperation (APEC)** established a working group that developed a 2021–2024 strategic plan for SMEs' development in the Asia-Pacific region. As its key objective the working group highlights SMEs' access to global value chains, finance and alternative financial solutions. To foster SMEs' competitiveness and access to international markets, they promote green awareness among businesses and support green SMEs. Moreover, in September 2022 the APEC's Ministers responsible for SMEs urged APEC member states to accelerate SMEs' access to sustainable finance.

In Latin America, the **Green Finance Latin-American Platform** has been developed to support national development banks and private financial institutions to share knowledge on green finance. As of 2023, it has 12 initiatives in partnership with the Inter-American Development Bank to promote sustainable instruments including on Financing the Circular Economy on SMEs.

The working group on **Innovation of the Pacific Alliance** has created the programme on Innovation for Sustainability with the objective to help entrepreneurs in eco-innovation to grow and develop. The Programme has also the objective to help SMEs be competitive by implementing sustainable practices.

The **G20** launched the Sustainable Finance Working Group (SFWG) that focuses on several areas related to sustainable finance, including greening the banking system; greening bond markets; greening institutional investment; risk analysis; and measuring progress. In September 2023, the SFWG met under the Indian G20 Presidency and provided recommendations in the following key areas: mechanisms for mobilisation of resources for climate finance; measures for catalysing the development and deployment of green and low-carbon technologies; improving nature-related data and reporting and overcoming data-related barriers to climate investments.

The **European Commission's** Platform on Sustainable Finance provides recommendations around the usability of the EU Taxonomy and other sustainable finance frameworks. These recommendations include usability considerations for SMEs and entrepreneurs, with the goal of ensuring that SMEs have equitable access to sustainable finance.

The **European Association of Guarantee Institutions (AECM)** Working Group on Sustainability helps to foster knowledge exchange and coordination among its members in the area of guarantees to support access to sustainable finance.

Source: (APEC, 2022[99]), (Green Finance Latin American Platform, 2023[100]), (Cisneros, 2019[101]), (G20 Indonesia, 2022[102]), (EU Commission, 2020[103]), (AECM, 2022[104]).

Furthermore, in the context of the work of the CSMEE, with input from the Platform, a dedicated principle on SME access to sustainable finance is included in the 2022 Updated G20 OECD High-Level Principles on SME Financing, which formed the basis of the OECD Recommendation on SME Financing, adopted in June 2023 (OECD, 2022[5]) (OECD, 2023[105]) This update contributes to shaping SME sustainable finance policies within the G20 and OECD.

Private sector initiatives to drive SME sustainability

Private actors can play a key role for SME sustainability transition. The large financing gap cannot be filled by the public sector alone, which means that private financial institutions, Fintechs, ESG intermediaries, such as rating agencies, accountants and other relevant stakeholders all need to contribute to creating a conducive ecosystem that provides the right information, incentives and conditions to foster SME investment in greening and their uptake of relevant financing instruments to meet these investment needs (Box 2.7).

Box 2.7. Examples of private sector initiatives to drive SME sustainability

Bankers for Net Zero is the **UK** chapter of the Net Zero Banking Alliance, an initiative of global banks who aim to lower the emissions of their portfolio and reach net zero by 2050. Bankers for Net Zero seeks to decarbonize their portfolios in ways that do not generate an administrative burden for SMEs through the creation of a simplified reporting framework. This framework utilises open banking and accounting data models to both improve SMEs' access to sustainability reporting and the trust, reliability and standardisation of sustainability reports. In 2023, Bankers for Net Zero was also invited to convene an SME advisory group for the UK Transition Plan Taskforce (TPT) to consider proportionate sustainability reporting and transition planning for SMEs and provide recommendations to the TPT.

The SME Climate Hub is an initiative between the We Mean Business Coalition, a collection of leading climate oriented non-profit organizations, and the Exponential Roadmap Initiative, an initiative signed by 21 major multinationals and partners with the World Wildlife Fund. Its key objective is to mainstream climate action to SMEs. The hub offers practical tools for SMEs such as a Business Carbon Calculator as well as educational resources on creating credible transition plans and accessing sustainable finance. The SME Climate Hub recently launched a web-based reporting tool that facilitates climate-related data reporting by SMEs. The reporting tool is aligned with the Carbon Disclosure Project (CDP) and has three main components: reporting on annual GHG emissions, listing actions taken to reduce business and value chain emissions, and monitoring on progress so far.

Corporations supporting financing of SMEs in their supply chains. Supply chain financing is a set of financial instruments that financial institutions are using to bolster SMEs' working capital and fuel their financing needs as they transition. In recent years, large corporates have also been stepping up efforts to support SMEs in their supply chains to access financing and invest in improving their sustainability performance. Supply chain financing works by providing SMEs with green guarantees from business partners and commercial banks. These green guarantees improve SMEs credit ratings, incentivising the transition and offsetting the administrative cost to SMEs of transitioning.

The **European Banking Federation's (EBF)** Chief Sustainability Officers Roundtable convenes member CSOs with the aim to explore how the banking sector can collectively contribute to the European Union's sustainable transition. By facilitating high-level dialogue, the Roundtable aims to inform and enhance the sustainability actions of its 30 members.

Source: (Bankers for Net Zero, 2022[106]), (SME Climate Hub, 2023[107]), (McKinsey, 2020[108]), (SME Finance Forum, 2021[109]), (EBF, 2022[110]), (SME Climate Hub, 2023[111])

Conclusions and policy implications

The public and private sector both have an important role to play in fostering the provision and uptake of sustainable finance for SMEs. Given the challenges that SMEs face in investing in greening and measuring and reporting on their sustainability performance, and the risks for SMEs' continued access to external finance, a supportive ecosystem needs to be put in place to help SMEs to navigate this important transition. Critical considerations include:

- **Understand SMEs' diverse needs and pathways to net zero and nature positive**. SMEs are composed of a diverse set of enterprises ranging from microenterprises with fewer than 10 employees to mid-sized firms with hundreds of employees that may also be part of large and complex global value chains. These enterprises have very diverse levels of understanding of the sustainability transition and diverse starting points in the journey. They also have different awareness and capacities to take the steps they need to improve their sustainability performance as well as different levels of resources to put into the transition and the related measurement and reporting of their sustainability performance. Public institutions need to have a good understanding of SMEs' diverse net-zero pathways and needs in order to devise tailored solutions.
- **Devise policies and regulations that take into consideration the impact on SMEs**. SMEs have more limited capacity and resources to devote to regulatory and policy compliance compared to large enterprises. Providing due consideration to SMEs in regulation and policy making may entail, for example, applying proportionality in the development of requirements to meet the regulatory and policy needs without putting an excessive burden on SMEs. This can apply for example to mandatory or voluntary non-financial disclosure requirements.
- **Strengthen the transparency and interoperability of sustainability-related data, definitions and standards**. Lack of interoperability magnifies the burden on SMEs that have to respond to different data requirements or meet different criteria to access financing or value chains across different institutions and jurisdictions.
- **Ensure that policy and regulatory frameworks support sustainable investments by SMEs and provision of finance by FIs**. Regulatory stability helps reduce uncertainty and incentivises SMEs' investments in greening. The regulatory environment also plays a role in spurring FIs to integrate comprehensively climate- and nature-related considerations and risks into their operations. This can, in turn, create broader incentives for SME greening and allocation of financing to activities that are green/sustainable or brown activities that are backed by credible transition plans.
- **Provide financial support for SME sustainability activities and investments**. SMEs face traditional constraints in accessing external finance, and additional challenges in tapping into sustainable finance. Financial support can entail direct financing from public entities through loans, equity, grants, or indirect support through guarantees and other instruments that can crowd in private financing for SME clients. Fostering innovation in the financial system and markets is also critical to enable digital financial solutions to play a role in broadening SMEs' access to sustainable finance. Fostering SME participation in green financial markets is also important.
- **Provide non-financial support for SMEs to foster their access to and uptake of sustainable finance**. Non-financial support is critical to address awareness-, knowledge-, and resource gaps that SMEs face in embarking and advancing on the journey to net zero and nature positive, and in seeking out sustainable finance. It is also critical in helping SMEs to be able to measure and report on their progress on this journey.
- **Foster the sustainable finance ecosystem for SMEs by promoting dialogue and knowledge-sharing among the diverse actors**. Many different actors have to be mobilised to support SMEs' transition to sustainability, including regulators, policy makers, standard setters, public and private financial institutions, ESG intermediaries, accountants, providers of digital financial and non-

financial solutions, and many others. Fostering regular dialogue, knowledge-sharing and partnerships among these different entities can help generate and disseminate relevant solutions to accelerate the transition. The OECD Platform on Financing SMEs for Sustainability will continue to support this endeavour through its analytical work, data collection, and knowledge-sharing activities. It will also support efforts to build consensus around the types of data that FIs should seek from SMEs to minimise their compliance burden.

References

AECM (2023), *AECM members' sustainable products.* [76]

AECM (2022), "AECM Activitiy Report", https://aecm.eu/wp-content/uploads/2023/07/AECM-Annual-Activity-Report-2022.pdf. [104]

AECM (2022), "AECM member's Guarantee Products for Sustainability", https://eur02.safelinks.protection.outlook.com/?url=https%3A%2F%2Fwww.flipsnack.com%2Faecmeurope%2Faecm-members-sustainable-products.html&data=05%7C01%7CMiriam.KOREEN%40oecd.org%7C738d5ca5018c449ff04d08dbda29ba12%7Cac41c7d41f61460db0f4fc925a2b471c%7C0%7C1. [86]

AECM (2022), *AECM Statistical Yearbook 2022*, https://www.flipsnack.com/aecmeurope/202305_aecm-statistical-yearbook-2022.html. [75]

AFME (2021), *Introducing a New Hybrid Recapitalisation Instrument for Smaller EU Corporates*, https://www.afme.eu/Portals/0/AFME_COVID-19Recap2021_09.pdf?utm_campaign=2298240_Recap%20Second%20Report&utm_medium=email&utm_source=Association%20for%20Financial%20Markets%20in%20Europe&dm_t=0,0,0,0,0 (accessed on 9 August 2022). [74]

ALIDE (2017), "Fideicomisos instituidos en relación con la Agricultura (FIRA)", https://www.alide.org.pe/wp-content/uploads/2019/06/Bank-of-the-Year-2019-Eng-June-25.pdf. [85]

Álvarez Jaramillo, J., J. Zartha Sossa and G. Orozco Mendoza (2019), "Barriers to sustainability for small and medium enterprises in the framework of sustainable development—Literature review", *Business Strategy and the Environment*, Vol. 28/4, https://doi.org/10.1002/bse.2261. [64]

APEC (2022), "28th APEC Small and Medium Enterprises Ministerial Meeting - Phuket, Thailand - STATEMENT OF THE CHAIR", https://www.meti.go.jp/press/2022/09/20220912004/20220912004-2.pdf. [99]

APEC (2020), "Small and Medium Enterprises Working Group Strategic Plan 2021 – 2024", https://www.apec.org/docs/default-source/Groups/SMEWG/20_smewg50_030_r.pdf?la=en&hash=C68CF6917E54734C055F9CA8891173558669AC36. [121]

ASEAN (2019), *Green Financing Instruments Guide*, https://www.climatebonds.net/files/reports/asean_green_fin_istruments_cbi_012019_0.pdf. [40]

Banco Portugues de Fomento (2023), "Line of Credit for Decarbonization and Circular Economy", https://www.bpfomento.pt/pt/catalogo/linha-de-credito-para-a-descarbonizacao-e-economia-circular/. [81]

Bankers for Net Zero (2022), "SMEs risk losing access to funding in the race to Net Zero", https://www.bankersfornetzero.co.uk/2022/11/07/smes-access-to-funding/. [106]

BBB (2019), "Small Business Finance Markets Report", https://www.british-business-bank.co.uk/wp-content/uploads/2019/02/British_Business_Bank_Small-Business-Finance-Report-2019_v3.pdf. [92]

BBB (2018), "British Business Bank appoints its first Chief Marketing Officer to head new Demand Development Unit", https://www.british-business-bank.co.uk/press-release/british-business-bank-appoints-its-first-chief-marketing-officer-to-head-new-demand-development-unit/. [93]

BDC (2023), "Climate Action Centre", https://www.bdc.ca/en/articles-tools/sustainability/climate-action-centre. [88]

BDC (2023), "We're a B Corp", https://www.bdc.ca/en/about/b-corp. [89]

bnamericas (2022), *Colombia launches green taxonomy plan*, https://www.bnamericas.com/en/news/colombia-launches-green-taxonomy-plan. [19]

BNP Paribas (2021), *The path to ESG: no turning back for asset owners and managers*, https://www.theia.org/sites/default/files/2021-09/The%20ESG%20Global%20Survey%202021.pdf. [37]

Bpifrance (2023), *Catalogue des offres - transition ecologique et energetique*, https://www.bpifrance.fr/catalogue-offres/transition-ecologique-et-energetique. [80]

Bpifrance (2020), "Plan Climat : Bpifrance et la Banque des Territoires lancent un plan de 40", https://bigmedia.bpifrance.fr/news/plan-climat-bpifrance-et-la-banque-des-territoires-lancent-un-plan-de-40-milliards-deuros. [91]

Brammer, S., S. Hoejmose and K. Marchant (2012), "Environmental Management in SMEs in the UK: Practices, Pressures and Perceived Benefits", *Business Strategy and the Environment*, Vol. 21/7, https://doi.org/10.1002/bse.717. [61]

British Business Bank (2021), *Smaller businesses and the transition to net zero*, https://www.british-business-bank.co.uk/wp-content/uploads/2021/10/J0026_Net_Zero_Report_AW.pdf (accessed on 11 March 2022). [59]

British Chambers of Commerce (2021), *Net Zero and Covid-19 Reopening Survey*, https://www.britishchambers.org.uk/page/o2-bcc-survey-results. [13]

Busch, Bauer and Orlitzky (2016), *Sustainable Development and Financial Markets: Old Paths and New Avenues*, https://www.researchgate.net/publication/276369500_Sustainable_Development_and_Financial_Markets_Old_Paths_and_New_Avenues. [32]

Busch, T., R. Bauer and M. Orlitzky (2016), *Sustainable Development and Financial Markets: Old Paths and New Avenues*, https://journals.sagepub.com/doi/pdf/10.1177/0007650315570701. [31]

Business Development Bank of Canada (2021), *How Canadian Entrepreneurs Are Taking on the Environmental Challenge—Study | BDC.ca*, https://www.bdc.ca/en/about/analysis-research/transformation-in-progress (accessed on 11 March 2022). [60]

Canada, G. (2023), "Taxonomy Roadmap Report", https://www.canada.ca/en/department-finance/programs/financial-sector-policy/sustainable-finance/sustainable-finance-action-council/taxonomy-roadmap-report.html#part-two. [26]

Carbon Trust (2013), *Low carbon entrepreneurs: the new engines of growth*, https://www.carbontrust.com/resources/low-carbon-entrepreneurs-the-new-engines-of-growth. [12]

Chen, Y. and C. Chang (2011), *Enhance environmental commitments and green intangible assets toward green competitive advantages: an analysis of structural equation modeling (SEM)*, https://link.springer.com/article/10.1007/s11135-011-9535-9. [72]

Cisneros, N. (2019), "Crecimiento verde en la Alianza del Pacífico", https://wedocs.unep.org/bitstream/handle/20.500.11822/28679/Alianza-Crecimiento-verde.pdf?sequence=1. [101]

Cuerva, M., Á. Triguero-Cano and D. Córcoles (2014), "Drivers of green and non-green innovation: empirical evidence in Low-Tech SMEs", *Journal of Cleaner Production*, Vol. 68, pp. 104-113, https://doi.org/10.1016/J.JCLEPRO.2013.10.049. [113]

De Haas, R. et al. (2021), "Managerial and Financial Barriers to the Net-Zero Transition", *Discussion papers*, Centre for Economic Policy Research, https://cepr.org/active/publications/discussion_papers/dp.php?dpno=15886 (accessed on 18 July 2021). [63]

Deloitte (2023), *IFRS for Small and Medium-Sized Entities (IFRS for SMEs)*, https://www.iasplus.com/en/standards/other/ifrs-for-smes. [68]

EBF (2022), "CSO Banking Sustainability Efforts", https://www.ebf.eu/financing-growth/cso-banking-sustainability-efforts/. [110]

Edelman (2022), *Edelman Trust Barometer 2022*, https://www.edelman.com/sites/g/files/aatuss191/files/2022-01/2022%20Edelman%20Trust%20Barometer%20FINAL_Jan25.pdf (accessed on 27 July 2022). [38]

EFRAG (2022), *EU Voluntary Sustainability Reporting Standard for non-listed SMEs that are outside the scope of CSRD – Issue Paper*, https://www.efrag.org/Assets/Download?assetUrl=%2Fsites%2Fwebpublishing%2FMeeting%20Documents%2F2211041503270617%2F04-01%20Issue%20Paper%20-%20Approach%20to%20EU%20Voluntary%20Reporting%20Standard%20for%20SMEs%20outside%20the%20scope%20of%20CSRD%20and%20A. [70]

EFRAG (2022), *SME standards: approach and methodology*, https://efrag.org/Assets/Download?assetUrl=%2Fsites%2Fwebpublishing%2FMeeting%20Documents%2F2212120938015426%2F03-01%20SME%20standards%20approach%20and%20methodology.pdf. [69]

EIB (2021), , https://ec.europa.eu/commission/presscorner/detail/en/IP_21_7064. [94]

EIF (2023), "Guarantee Products", https://www.eif.org/InvestEU/guarantee_products/index.htm. [77]

EIF (2023), "Sustainability Guarantee Fund", https://sustainabilityguarantee.eif.org/. [96]

Energy Efficiency and Renewable Sources Fund (2004), "Energy Efficiency and Renewable Sources Fund", https://www.bgeef.com/en/about-us/. [84]

ESG Investor (2021), *SMEs and the Future of European Sustainability Reporting Rules*, https://www.esginvestor.net/smes-and-the-future-of-european-sustainability-reporting-rules/ (accessed on 14 August 2023). [56]

ETLA (2015), *From Cleantech to Cleanweb – The Finnish Cleantech Space in Transition*, https://www.etla.fi/wp-content/uploads/ETLA-Raportit-Reports-43.pdf. [11]

EU Commission (2023), "Championing Europe's SMEs: Commission provides new relief to boost the competitiveness and resilience of SMEs", https://ec.europa.eu/commission/presscorner/detail/en/ip_23_4409. [122]

EU Commission (2023), "SME Relief Package", https://single-market-economy.ec.europa.eu/system/files/2023-09/COM_2023_535_1_EN_ACT_part1_v12.pdf. [66]

EU Commission (2020), "Platform on Sustainable Finance", https://finance.ec.europa.eu/sustainable-finance/overview-sustainable-finance/platform-sustainable-finance_en. [103]

EU Parliament (2022), "Sustainable economy: Parliament adopts new reporting rules for multinationals", https://www.europarl.europa.eu/news/en/press-room/20221107IPR49611/sustainable-economy-parliament-adopts-new-reporting-rules-for-multinationals. [115]

European Commission (2023), *EU taxonomy for sustainable activities: What the EU is doing to create an EU-wide classification system for sustainable activities*, https://finance.ec.europa.eu/sustainable-finance/tools-and-standards/eu-taxonomy-sustainable-activities_en. [17]

European Commission (2022), "Launch of the first Covenant of Companies call for technical assistance", https://ec.europa.eu/info/news/launch-first-covenant-companies-call-technical-assistance-2022-jun-15_en. [95]

European Commission (2021), *Flash Eurobarometer 498, SMEs, green markets and resource efficiency*, https://data.europa.eu/data/datasets/s2287_fl498_eng?locale=en. [62]

European Commission (2017), *Defining "green" in the context of green finance*, https://ec.europa.eu/environment/enveco/sustainable_finance/pdf/studies/Defining%20Green%20in%20green%20finance%20-%20final%20report%20published%20on%20eu%20website.pdf. [41]

European Commission (2016), *Study on the potential of green bond finance for resource-efficient investments*, https://ec.europa.eu/environment/enveco/pdf/potential-green-bond.pdf (accessed on 5 August 2022). [87]

European Parliamentary Research Service (2021), *Green and Sustainable Finance*, https://www.europarl.europa.eu/RegData/etudes/BRIE/2021/679081/EPRS_BRI(2021)679081_EN.pdf. [42]

Eurosif (2016), *European SRI Study*, https://www.eurosif.org/news/eurosif-report-2016/. [30]

FCA (2022), *Mini-bonds*, https://www.fca.org.uk/consumers/mini-bonds (accessed on 8 August 2022). [43]

Finnvera (2023), , https://www.finnvera.fi/eng/financing/loans/climate-and-environmental-loan. [123]

Finnvera (2023), , https://www.finnvera.fi/eng/financing/loans/climate-and-environmental-loan. [79]

FNGCIMM (2022), "GARANT CONSTRUCT - SME INVEST PLUS COMPONENT", https://www.fngcimm.ro/garant-construct-componenta-imm-invest-plus. [82]

G20 Indonesia (2022), "Indonesia encouraged the acessibility and affordability of sustainable finance instruments - 3rd SFGW meeting", https://g20sfwg.org/news/indonesia-encouraged-the-accessibility-and-affordability-of-sustainable-finance-instruments-at-the-3rd-sfwg-meeting. [102]

GhanaWeb (2022), , https://www.ghanaweb.com/GhanaHomePage/NewsArchive/Soci-t-G-n-rale-Burkina-Faso-African-Guarantee-Fund-ease-access-to-financing-for-Burkinabe-SMEs-1536785. [120]

Global Sustainable Investment Alliance (2020), *Global Sustainable Investment Review*, http://www.gsi-alliance.org/wp-content/uploads/2021/08/GSIR-20201.pdf. [36]

Gobierno de México (2023), *Sustainable Taxonomy of Mexico*, https://www.gob.mx/cms/uploads/attachment/file/809773/Taxonom_a_Sostenible_de_M_xico_.pdf. [27]

Green Finance Institute (2023), , https://www.greenfinanceinstitute.co.uk/programmes/uk-green-taxonomy-gtag/. [22]

Green Finance Latin American Platform (2023), "Our Inititiaves Dropdown", https://greenfinancelac.org. [100]

Hellenic Development Bank (2023), "ESG Tracker", https://hdb.gr/esg-tracker-by-hdb/. [97]

Ho, V. (2020), "Non-Financial Reporting & Corporate Governance: Explaining American Divergence & Its Implications for Disclosure Reform", *Accounting, Economics, and Law: A Convivium*, https://doi.org/10.1515/ael-2018-0043. [124]

IBK (2023), *Sustainability Report 2023*, https://global.ibk.co.kr/en/investor/SustainabilityReport. [20]

IFRS (2023), "IASB amends the IFRS for SMEs Accounting Standard related to international tax reform", https://www.ifrs.org/news-and-events/news/2023/09/iasb-amends-the-ifrs-for-smes-accounting-standard-itr/. [67]

Indonesia Financial Services Authority (2017), *Application of Sustainable Finance To Financial Services Institutions, Issuer and Publicly Listed Companies*, https://www.ifc.org/wps/wcm/connect/ bab66a7c-9dc2-412f-81f6-f83f94d79660/Indonesia+OJK+Sustainable+Finance+Regulation_English.pdf?MOD=AJPERES&CVID=lVXU.Oy. [71]

ITC (2021), *SME Competitivness Outlook 2021: Empowering the Green Recovery*. [8]

KFW (2022), *Klimaschutzoffensive für Unternehmen*, https://www.kfw.de/s/deiBCGcA (accessed on 26 September 2022). [44]

Kim, S. et al. (2022), "ESG Lending", https://papers.ssrn.com/sol3/papers.cfm?abstract_id=3865147. [49]

Korea Chamber of Commerce and Industry (2021), *Website*. [14]

Lexology (2022), "The Korean Green Taxonomy and Its Implications", https://www.lexology.com/library/detail.aspx?g=861eba8d-0fdd-44d8-af20-2dc26ce55fbc. [24]

Lin, L. (2022), *Venture Capital in the Rise of Sustainable Investment*, https://link.springer.com/article/10.1007/s40804-021-00238-8#Fn2. [52]

McDaniels, J. and N. Robins (2017), *MOBILIZING SUSTAINABLE FINANCE FOR SMALL AND MEDIUM SIZED ENTERPRISES*, https://www.cbd.int/financial/2017docs/unep-smefinance2017.pdf. [45]

McKinsey (2020), "Supply-chain finance: A case of convergent evolution?", https://www.mckinsey.com/~/media/mckinsey/industries/financial%20services/our%20insights/accelerating%20winds%20of%20change%20in%20global%20payments/chapter-3-supply-chain-finance-a-case-of-convergent-evolution.pdf. [108]

Modern Mining (2022), *National Treasury launches the Green Finance Taxonomy Paper*, https://www.crown.co.za/modern-mining/insights/20404-national-treasury-launches-the-greenfinance-taxonomy-paper. [21]

Natixis (2021), *Sustainable Taxonomy development worldwide: a standard-setting race between competing jurisdictions*, https://gsh.cib.natixis.com/our-center-of-expertise/articles/sustainable-taxonomy-development-worldwide-a-standard-setting-race-between-competing-jurisdictions. [23]

OECD (2023), *2022 Updated G20/OECD High Level Principles on SME FInancing*, https://www.oecd.org/cfe/smes/2022-Update-OECD-G20-HLP-on-SME-Financing.pdf. [105]

OECD (2023), *Assessing biodiversity-related financial risks : Navigating the landscape of existing approaches | OECD Environment Policy Papers | OECD iLibrary*, https://doi.org/10.1787/23097841 (accessed on 2 August 2023). [34]

OECD (2023), *Assessing greenhouse gas emissions and energy consumption in SMEs: Towards a pilot dashboard of SME greening and green entrepreneurship indicators*, https://www.oecd-ilibrary.org/environment/assessing-greenhouse-gas-emissions-and-energy-consumption-in-smes_ac8e6450-en;jsessionid=hXk9cJQk0B7u_-cYU4fFqBkgn3uQrThkXphqB2ee.ip-10-240-5-34. [1]

OECD (2023), *Declaration on Enhancing SMEs and Entrepreneurship Policies for Greater Resilience and Successful Green and Digital Transitions*, https://legalinstruments.oecd.org/en/instruments/OECD-LEGAL-0497. [7]

OECD (2023), *Financing SMEs for Sustainability: Financial Institution Strategies and Approaches*. [6]

OECD (2023), "Inclusive Forum on Climate Mitigation Approaches", https://www.oecd.org/climate-change/inclusive-forum-on-carbon-mitigation-approaches/. [116]

OECD (2023), *OECD Platform on FInancing SMEs for Sustainability*, https://www.oecd.org/cfe/smes/financing-smes-sustainability.htm. [15]

OECD (2023), "OECD SME & Entrepreneurship Ministerial Meeting: Managing Shocks and Transitions Future-Proofing SME and Entrepreneurship Policies", https://www.oecd.org/cfe/smes/key-issues-paper-oecd-sme-and-entrepreneurship-ministerial-meeting-2023.pdf. [4]

OECD (2022), *Financing SMEs and Entrepreneurs 2022: An OECD Scoreboard*, OECD Publishing, Paris, https://doi.org/10.1787/e9073a0f-en. [10]

OECD (2022), *Financing SMEs for sustainability: Drivers, Constraints and Policies | en | OECD*, https://www.oecd.org/publications/financing-smes-for-sustainability-a5e94d92-en.htm (accessed on 2 August 2023). [35]

OECD (2022), "Financing SMEs for sustainability: Drivers, Constraints and Policies", *OECD SME and Entrepreneurship Papers*, No. 35, OECD Publishing, Paris, https://doi.org/10.1787/a5e94d92-en. [2]

OECD (2022), *OECD Guidance on Transition Finance: Ensuring Credibility of Corporate Climate Transition Plans*, Green Finance and Investment, OECD Publishing, Paris, https://doi.org/10.1787/7c68a1ee-en. [33]

OECD (2022), *OECD Recommendation on SME and Entrepreneurship Policy*, https://www.oecd.org/cfe/smes/oecdrecommendationonsmeandentrepreneurshippolicy/. [5]

OECD (2022), "Recommendation of the Council on SME and Entrepreneurship Policy", https://legalinstruments.oecd.org/en/instruments/OECD-LEGAL-0473. [119]

OECD (2022), *Secured lending for SMEs: Making effective use of registries and intangibles - A case study approach*, https://www.oecd.org/publications/secured-lending-for-smes-cf451ee7-en.htm. [73]

OECD (2022), *Summary of the Annual Conference of the OECD Platform on Financing SMEs for Sustainability 2022*, https://www.oecd.org/cfe/smes/oecdplatformonfinancingsmesforsustainability-annualconference.htm. [57]

OECD (2021), "Financing SMEs for Sustainability", https://www.oecd.org/cfe/smes/financing-smes-sustainability.htm. [98]

OECD (2021), "No net zero without SMEs: Exploring the key issues for greening SMEs and green entrepreneurship", *OECD SME and Entrepreneurship Papers*, No. 30, OECD Publishing, Paris, https://doi.org/10.1787/bab63915-en. [9]

OECD (2021), "The SME Test: Taking SMEs and Entrepreneurs into account when regulating", https://www.oecd.org/gov/regulatory-policy/the-sme-test.pdf. [65]

OECD (2020), *Building back better: A sustainable, resilient recovery after COVID-19*, OECD, https://www.oecd.org/coronavirus/policy-responses/building-back-better-a-sustainable-resilient-recovery-after-covid-19-52b869f5/. [118]

OECD (2020), "COVID –19 and the low-carbon transition. Impacts and possible policy responses", https://read.oecd-ilibrary.org/view/?ref=134_134752-qmhlk04mue&title=COVID%e2%80%9319-and-the-low-carbon-transition-Impacts-and-possible-policy-responses. [117]

OECD (2020), *Developing Sustainable Finance Definitions and Taxonomies*, Green Finance and Investment, OECD Publishing, Paris, https://doi.org/10.1787/134a2dbe-en. [16]

OECD (2020), *ESG Investing and the Climate Transition: Market Practices, Issues and Policy Considerations*, https://www.oecd.org/finance/ESG-investing-and-climate-transition-market-practices-issues-and-policy-considerations.pdf (accessed on 27 February 2022). [28]

OECD (2020), *ESG Investing: Practices, Progress and Challenges*, http://www.oecd.org/finance/ESG-Investing-Practices-Progress-Challenges.pdf. [55]

OECD (2020), *Sustainable and Resilient Finance: OECD Business and Finance Outlook*. [29]

OECD (2018), *Environmental Policy Toolkit for SME Greening in EU Eastern Partnership Countries*, OECD Green Growth Studies, OECD Publishing, Paris, https://doi.org/10.1787/9789264293199-en. [58]

OECD (2015), "New Approaches to SME and Entrepreneurship Financing: Broadening the Range of Instruments 2", https://www.oecd.org/cfe/smes/New-Approaches-SME-full-report.pdf (accessed on 27 September 2021). [46]

OECD (Forthcoming), *Transition Finance Policy Note*. [25]

Pinget IREGE, A. and R. Bocquet (2014), *Barriers to Environmental Innovation in SMEs: Empirical Evidence from French Firms*, https://www.strategie-aims.com/events/conferences/24-xxiiieme-conference-de-l-aims/communications/3151-barriers-to-environmental-innovation-in-smes-empirical-evidence-from-french-firms-les-barrieres-a-l-innovation-environnementale-des-pme-elements-empiriq (accessed on 2 July 2019). [112]

Reuters (2022), *Explainer: What is the EU's sustainable finance taxonomy?*, https://www.reuters.com/business/sustainable-business/what-is-eus-sustainable-financetaxonomy-2022-02-03/. [18]

SBCI (2022), "Energy Efficiency Loan Scheme - A low-cost scheme designed to support eligible SMEs including primary producers, investing in the energy", https://sbci.gov.ie/products/energy-efficiency-loan-scheme-eels. [78]

SME Climate Hub (2023), "About Us - SME Climate Hub", https://smeclimatehub.org/about-us/#:~:text=The%20SME%20Climate%20Hub%20is,resilient%20businesses%20for%20the%20future. [107]

SME Climate Hub (2023), "New reporting tool and guidelines are now available on the SME Climate Hub", https://smeclimatehub.org/new-reporting-tool-and-guidelines-are-now-available-on-the-sme-climate-hub/. [111]

SME Climate Hub (2023), *SME Climate Hub Survey 2023*, https://smeclimatehub.org/wp-content/uploads/2023/02/SME-Climate-Hub-Survey-2023.pdf (accessed on 31 July 2023). [3]

SME Finance Forum (2021), "Greening SME Finance through a Sustainable Supply Chain", https://www.smefinanceforum.org/post/greening-sme-finance-through-a-sustainable-supply-chain. [109]

SME guidance for business growth (2022), *Investors more likely to back start-ups with strong sustainability credentials*, https://www.smeweb.com/2022/04/27/investors-more-likely-to-back-start-ups-with-strong-sustainability-credentials/. [39]

State of Green (2022), "The Climate Compass", https://stateofgreen.com/en/solutions/the-climate-compass-climatecompass-dk/. [90]

Sustainalytics (2022), *Sustainability Linked Loans: Helping build Sustainability Linked Loan Programs*, https://www.sustainalytics.com/corporate-solutions/sustainable-finance-and-lending/sustainability-linked-loans. [47]

Swedish MInistry of Finance (2021), *Sweden's recovery plan*, https://www.regeringen.se/rapporter/2021/05/sveriges-aterhamtningsplan/. [83]

TCFD (2017), *Recommendations of the Task Force on Climate Related Financial Disclosures*, https://assets.bbhub.io/company/sites/60/2021/10/FINAL-2017-TCFD-Report.pdf. [53]

The Montreal Group (2016), *Development Banks' Best Practices on Green Financing for MSMEs*, https://themontrealgroup.org/article/development-banks-best-practices-on-green-financing-for-msmes/. [48]

TNFD (2023), *The TNFD Nature-Related Risk and Opportunity Management and Disclosure Framework*, https://framework.tnfd.global/wp-content/uploads/2023/03/23-23882-TNFD_v0.4_Integrated_Framework_v6-1.pdf. [54]

US Department of Energy (2021), *Green Revolving Funds*, https://betterbuildingssolutioncenter.energy.gov/toolkits/green-revolving-funds. [50]

WBG (2023), *Carbon Pricing Dashboard*, https://carbonpricingdashboard.worldbank.org/map_data. [114]

World Bank (2021), *Greening public credit guarantee schemes for net zero*, https://blogs.worldbank.org/psd/greening-public-credit-guarantee-schemes-net-zero. [51]

Note

[1] https://www.oecd.org/cfe/smes/financing-smes-sustainability.htm

Country snapshots

3. Australia

Key facts on SME financing

According to the Australian Bureau of Statistics (ABS), there were 2,565,367 small and medium-sized enterprises (SMEs) in Australia in 2021-22. SMEs account for 99.8% of all enterprises in Australia and employed more than 8.1 million people in 2021-22, which equates to around 66% of employment in the private sector.

The Australian economy has shown resilience to global headwinds, supported by a post-pandemic rebound in household spending, strong employment growth and a rise in wages. According to economic forecasts produced by the Australian Department of the Treasury, most recently reported in the 2023-24 Budget in May 2023, real GDP growth is expected to slow to 1½% in 2023-24, and then strengthen to 2¼% in 2024–25. This near-term outlook for Australia is unchanged from the October Budget.

Interest rates for both SMEs and large businesses have returned to pre-pandemic levels. SME interest rates in Australia have increased from 3.10% in 2021 to 5.48% in 2022. The interest rate spread between SME loans and large enterprise loans, which remained elevated at above 160 basis points since 2012, declined to 99 basis points in 2022. The low spread between interest rates for large and small businesses mainly reflects the fact that a high share of SME credit was fixed at low interest rates during the pandemic and some of these loans are yet to roll off onto higher interest rates.

New lending to SMEs increased from AUD 104.4 billion in 2021 to AUD 116.1 billion in 2022, mostly driven by lending to medium businesses. In 2021-22, the share of SME outstanding loans stood at 45.1% of total outstanding business loans. Growth in new lending to SMEs was strong in the first half of 2022, however, slowed down significantly since October 2022 given higher borrowing costs and a weaker appetite for new finance.

The total amount of venture capital invested by registered Early Stage Venture Capital Limited Partnerships (ESVCLPs) and Venture Capital Limited Partnerships (VCLPs) increased in 2019-20 by 54.6%, totalling AUD 1.5 billion, decreased in 2020-21 by 8.0% to AUD 1.4 billion, before rising to a high of AUD 2.1 billion in 2021-22, an increase of 48.4%. In 2021-2022, Australia saw a record surge in venture capital investment driven by an increased number of mega deals (AUD 50 million and above). This momentum did not carry forward into the second half of 2022 with both the number of deals and average deal size declining sharply – especially in later-stage funding rounds. Despite this downturn investment levels continue to exceed those observed pre-Covid, helped in part by a rise in deal size at the pre-seed and seed stage.

Leasing and hire purchase volumes dropped by 13.4% through the year to AUD 8.9 billion in 2022, this compares to an increase of 4.8% in 2020 and a decrease of 1.9% in 2021.

The number of bankruptcies per 10,000 businesses fell from 53 in 2012 to 29 in 2019, then continued to decrease during the pandemic in response to COVID-19 related policies before reaching its historical low of 15 in 2021-22. In March 2020, the Australian Government announced a series of temporary changes to bankruptcy law to protect otherwise viable businesses from bankruptcy. These measures expired on 31

December 2020. Permanent reforms, including a new formal debt restructuring process and a simplified liquidation pathway, came into effect on 1 January 2021, which are available to incorporated businesses with liabilities of less than AUD 1 million.

The Australian Government has a comprehensive SME agenda aimed at promoting growth, employment and opportunities across the economy. Its policies for promoting SMEs focus on improving the operating environment for businesses, increasing incentives for investment, and enhancing rewards and opportunities for private endeavours. Policies aiming to increase long-term opportunities for SMEs include taxation and business incentives, export financing, and small business assistance.

Table 3.1. Scoreboard for Australia

Indicator	Unit	2007	2008	2009	2010	2011	2012	2013	2014	2015	2016	2017	2018	2019	2020	2021	2022
Debt																	
Outstanding business loans, SMEs	AUD billion	189	204.6	204.7	225.2	235.9	239.9	243.1	251.4	261.5	271.4	281.4	283.7	426.6	421.3	436	476.2
Outstanding business loans, total	AUD billion	629	690.8	653.3	636.4	665.5	685.7	694.5	723.5	764.1	800.4	820.1	861.3	873.0	877.6	941.3	1056
Share of SME outstanding loans	% of total outstanding business loans	30.0	29.62	31.33	35.38	35.46	35.00	35.01	34.75	34.22	33.91	34.31	32.94	48.86	48.01	46.33	45.09
New business lending, total	AUD billion	375	336.1	265.5	265.8	310.7	273.8	292.4	360.5	391.7	341.8	346.0	346.9	..	517.3	426.8	612.9
New business lending, SMEs	AUD billion	77.5	79.9	69.6	82.5	81.6	73.7	79.1	85.4	91.2	86.7	79.7	76.7	..	80	104.4	116.1
Share of new SME lending	% of total new lending	20.7	23.77	26.20	31.04	26.25	26.91	27.06	23.69	23.27	25.37	23.03	22.11	..	15.50	24.46	18.94
Non-performing loans, total	% of all business loans	0.50	2.07	3.27	3.55	3.16	2.68	2.03	1.39	1.01	1.13	0.78	0.81	0.92	1.08	0.98	0.90
Interest rate, SMEs	%	8.66	8.04	7.60	8.40	8.02	7.13	6.54	6.27	5.63	5.36	5.28	5.33	4.18	3.40	3.10	5.48
Interest rate, large firms	%	7.95	6.34	5.94	7.02	6.74	5.50	4.77	4.60	3.90	3.49	3.43	3.72	2.48	1.63	1.50	4.50
Interest rate spread	% points	0.71	1.70	1.66	1.38	1.28	1.62	1.77	1.67	1.73	1.86	1.85	1.61	1.70	1.77	1.60	0.99
Non-bank finance																	
Venture and growth capital	AUD billion	516	373	259	126	451	250	234	293	554	909	947	1 190	1 032	1 596	1 469	2 179
Venture and growth capital (growth rate)	%, Year-on-year growth rate		-27.7	-30.6	-51.3	257.9	-44.6	-6.40	25.21	89.08	64.08	4.18	25.66	-13.3	54.65	-7.96	48.33
Leasing and hire purchases	AUD billion	9.25	9.28	6.73	6.55	6.90	8.75	7.34	8.77	9.86	8.89	10.14	9.71	10.04	10.53	10.33	8.95
Factoring and invoicing	AUD billion	54.8	64.99	63.10	58.66	61.42	63.36	63.27	62.39	64.40	..	..	..	..	..	..	..
Other indicators																	
Payment delays, B2B	Number of days	..	..	..	..	22	20	20	15	13	14	12	11	10	11	11	..
Bankruptcies, Unincorporated	Number	5045	4 427	4 426	5 616	5 266	5 858	4 761	4 007	4 088	4 350	4 168	4 291	3815	3 353	2 265	2 321

Bankruptcies, Unincorporated	Per 10 000 enterprises	42	36	36	45	43	50	42	35	34	36	34	36	26	23	24	16
Bankruptcies, Corporates	Number	7 489	9 067	9 465	9 605	10439	10583	10854	8 822	10093	8 511	7 819	8 052	8 324	4 943	4 511	4 912
Bankruptcies, Corporates	Per 10 000 companies	48	55	56	54	57	55	54	41	45	36	31	31	30	17	16	14
Bankruptcies, Total	Per 10 000 businesses	45	47	47	50	51	53	49	39	41	36	32	32	29	19	18	15
Invoice payment days, average	Number of days	53	56	54	53	54	53	54	53	47	..	..	..	..	..	..	..
Outstanding business credit, Unincorporated business	AUD billion	111	117	119	122	125	131	136	142	150	157	164	165	244	246	266	281
Outstanding business credit, Private trading corporations	AUD billion	500	555	514	500	514	524	531	556	592	626	636	663	619	621	664	688

Note: Data from 2019 onwards in the indicators of outstanding stock of loans and new lending are collected using a revised SME definition, so caution is necessary when conducting any comparison across time.
Source: See Table 3.4.

The full country profile is available at: https://doi.org/10.1787/fa521246-en.

4. Austria

Key facts on SME financing

As in many EU countries, SMEs contribute substantially to Austria's economy. In 2021, 99.8% of all firms were SMEs, employing approximately 66% of the labour force. The capital structure of SMEs in Austria is traditionally biased towards debt financing, and limitations on access to risk-finance are still apparent. Bank lending is therefore an important factor affecting the availability of external financing for SMEs. However, access to finance is generally not a major concern for Austrian SMEs.

In 2022, the outstanding business loans amounted to EUR 201.4 billion, which is an increase of around 9% compared to 2021. These are the holdings of non-financial corporations in Austria, according to the monetary statistics. In the Granular Credit Data Collection (GKE), conducted by the Austrian Central Bank (OeNB), Austrian credit institutions reported a total utilization to businesses of EUR 199.5 billion as of 31 December 2022. Of this, EUR 92.3 billion was awarded to the SME segment in Austria: EUR 28.8 billion to micro-enterprises, EUR 30.2 billion to small companies and EUR 33.3 billion to medium-sized companies.

In the case of non-financial corporations, EUR 4.28 billion were flagged as non-performing. This resulted in a nonperforming loans (NPL) ratio of 2.14%, which is almost the same as the year before (2.15%). EUR 3.05 billion were reported as non-performing in the SME sub-segment. This resulted in an NPL ratio for SMEs of 3.31%. In 2021, the NPL ratio for SMEs was slightly lower registering 3.09%.

The share of SMEs' new business lending was smaller than in previous years, with almost 12%. Interest rates have increased quite significantly, with an average interest rate of 2.08% in 2022 for loans up to EUR 1 million, compared to 1.63% in 2021. In 2022, interest rates for larger firms with loans over EUR 1 million were lower compared to SME interest rates at 1.82% but have also increased compared to 2021 when the interest rates for large firms were 1.34%.

When it comes to non-bank finance, venture capital declined by 65% compared to 2021. On the other hand, leasing and hire purchases as well as factoring and invoicing both showed a steady upward trend since 2014. Leasing and hire purchases increased almost 9%, factoring and invoicing by almost 18%.

Payment delays increased slightly in the B2B sphere, from 12 days in 2021 to 14 days in 2022. However, in the B2C sphere there was an improvement, with a 6-day payment gap in 2022, compared to 10 days in 2021. Bankruptcies have reached pre-crisis levels, with around 10 bankruptcies per 1 000 firms. Overall, there were 4 913 bankruptcies in 2022, an increase of almost 60% compared to the previous two years, which were exceptional and cannot be seen as representative. The 2022 figure is closer to the figures registered prior to the pandemic. Of the 4 913 companies that went bankrupt, 4 903 were SMEs, which also corresponds to the share of SMEs in the national economy.

Table 4.1. Scoreboard for Austria

Indicator	Unit	2010	2011	2012	2013	2014	2015	2016	2017	2018	2019	2020	2021	2022
Debt														
Outstanding business loans, total	EUR billion	135.5	138.8	140.4	140.3	136.6	137.2	135.6	143.8	153.0	162.9	169.8	184.5	20.,4
New business loans, total (flows)	EUR million	74 896	73 041	80 867	73 460	73 126	61 711	55 543	64 418	64 438	71266	60096	61035	62139
New business loans, SMEs (flows)	EUR million	9 414	9 476	9 347	8 884	8 237	8 116	7 499	8 304	8 182	8 639	9214	8 282	7283
Share of new SME loans	% of total business loans	12.57	12.97	11.56	12.09	11.26	13.15	13.50	12.89	12.70	12.12	15.33	13.57	11.72
short-term loans, SMEs (flow)	EUR million	5 139	4 944	4 901	4 536	4 016	3 345	3 010	2 539	1 998	1 969	1640	1691	1464
long-term loans, SMEs (flow)	EUR million	4 275	4 532	4 446	4 348	4 221	4 771	4 489	5 765	6 184	6 670	7574	6591	5819
Share of short-term SME lending	in %	54.59	52.17	52.43	51.06	48.76	41.21	40.14	30.58	24.42	22.79	17.80	20.42	20.10
Government loan guarantees, SMEs	EUR million	173	143	158	167	172	204	192	279	301	366	4898*	2115*	344
Government guaranteed loans, SMEs	EUR million	226	185	207	211	225	258	282	414	395	568	5508*	2492*	514
Government direct loans, SMEs	EUR million	607	633	539	594	490	543	454	744	690	749	793	874	700
Interest rate, SME, loans up to EUR 1m	in %	2.43	2.92	2.46	2.28	2.27	2.02	1.92	1.80	1.82	1.80	1.59	1.63	2.08
Interest rate, large firms, loans over EUR 1m	in %	1.96	2.55	1.98	1.77	1.74	1.61	1.54	1.45	1.38	1.32	1.36	1.34	1.82
Interest rate spread	in %	0.47	0.37	0.48	0.51	0.53	0.41	0.38	0.35	0.44	0.48	0.23	0.29	0.26
Non-performing loans, total	In %	..	2.71	2.81	2.87	3.74	3.39	2.67	2.37	1.88	1.77	1.58	1.46	1.39
Non-bank Finance														
Venture and growth capital (seed, start-up, later stage)	EUR million	43	97	44	59	60	112	57	108	86	81	105	701	182
Venture and growth capital (growth capital)	EUR million	34	118	29	26	45	85	29	179	49	88	146	156	117
Venture and growth capital (total)	EUR million	77	215	73	85	105	197	85	287	135	169	251	857	299
Venture and growth capital (growth rate)	In %	-31.5	177.61	-66.3	17.76	22.56	87.97	-56.6	235.47	-53	24.98	49.11	240.86	-65.12
Other														
Payment delays, B2B	Days	11	12	11	12	13	4	4	2	1	1	14	12	14
Payment delays, B2C	Days	11	11	9	9	9	1	4	1	1	5	9	10	6
Bankruptcies, total	Number	6 657	6 194	6 266	5 626	5 600	5 422	5 534	5 318	5 224	5235	3106	3076	4913
Bankruptcies, per 1 000 firms	Number	18	17	17	15	15	11	12	11	11	11	7	6	10

* Note: this temporary increase is related to COVID-19 crisis response measures.

The full country profile is available at: https://doi.org/10.1787/fa521246-en.

5. Belgium

Key facts on SME financing

In 2022, SMEs dominated the business enterprise landscape in Belgium, accounting for 99.8% of all firms.

The outstanding stock of SME loans was stable on an annual basis (+0.9%) compared with an increase of 4.5% the previous year. This relative stability can be explained by the global economic context and the significant support measures taken by the Belgian government in the context of the COVID-19 crisis.

SME interest rates increased significantly to 2.06% in 2022. The interest rate spread between loans charged to large enterprises and loans charged to SMEs remains virtually unchanged at 15 basis points.

Survey data illustrates that lending conditions eased between 2013 and the end of 2015 and remained relatively stable until the end of 2018. A deterioration of credit conditions for SMEs has been reported since the fourth quarter of 2018, and the latest figures from third quarter 2023 confirm this trend.

After a fall in leasing volumes of -8.14% in 2020, this activity recovered in 2021 and 2022 with an annual growth rate of 13% and 13.9% respectively. High inflation, which pushed up asset prices, and the announcement of a number of tax changes for vehicles supported this strong growth in 2022.

The factoring business has also expanded significantly over the last two years, with annual growth rates of 21.6% in 2021 and 25% in 2022. This increase can be attributed to the potential decline in factoring experienced in 2020 as a result of the COVID-19 pandemic, followed by robust developments in the last two years.

The amount of venture and growth capital investments fluctuates considerably due to the small number of deals conducted annually. After nearly doubling from 2020 to 2021, these investments decreased by 26.1% in 2022, totaling EUR 1.1 billion.

After a steady decline from 2016 to 2020, average payment delays for business-to-business transactions rose to 11 days in 2022. This is slightly below the annual average of 12.7% for the reference period (2009-2022).

The number of registered bankruptcies increased to 9 265 (+42%) in 2022. This increase can be explained by the end of various support measures for businesses taken in the context of the COVID-19 crisis, including the end of the moratorium on bankruptcies. However, the total number of bankruptcies remains lower than the number recorded in 2019 (10 598).

Policy initiatives to ease SMEs' access to finance have been taken at both the federal and regional levels. In 2021 and 2022, policy measures were primarily aimed at protecting healthy businesses in the context of COVID-19 and the energy crises resulting from the Russo-Ukrainian conflict.

For example, the 'Overbruggingslening' aims to support Flemish companies, including those in agriculture, horticulture, fisheries, and aquaculture, that have acute liquidity needs due to the war in Ukraine, rising energy costs, and the overall increase in price levels. The terms of this loan include a minimum loan amount of EUR 10 000 and a maximum amount of EUR 2 million.

Another case in point is the "Fonds de transition" programme, which started in September 2022. The objective of the programme is to finance SMEs in Brussels that need to transform their business models and production lines in order to meet regional and European environmental and climate objectives. The financing terms include amounts ranging from EUR 80 000 to EUR 1.5 million through loans, bank co-financing, quasi-equity debt or minority equity stakes in companies.

The Chèque-Entreprise Relance par le numérique or Business Voucher Digital Recovery programme in Wallonia started in November 2022 and is set to end on 31 August 2023. The objective of the programme is to help SMEs boost their digitalization, online activities, and cybersecurity. Public intervention amounts to 90% of the amounts concerned with variable ceilings for each phase, for a total subsidy of EUR 15 000.

In light of escalating energy prices and their subsequent effect on production costs and professional expenses, the Federal Government has launched the 'Droit Passerelle Energie' initiative to support self-employed workers, helpers, and assisting spouses who opt to pause or terminate their independent activity due to diminished profitability. This scheme offers an allowance for a duration of up to 12 months and maintains healthcare and disability benefits for up to 4 quarters without needing contributions.

Table 5.1. Scoreboard for Belgium

Indicator	Unit	2007	2008	2009	2010	2011	2012	2013	2014	2015	2016	2017	2018	2019	2020	2021	2022
Debt																	
Outstanding business loans, SMEs	EUR billion	82.8	89.1	88.9	93.9	100.0	109.6	109.5	100.7	104.4	108.0	115.7	123.9	130.9	133.8	138.0*	*
Outstanding business loans, total	EUR billion	134.2	149.4	141.8	150.6	153.7	167.6	162.0	151.7	164.6	163.4	173.6	184.1	193.0	200.0	201.8*	*
Share of SME outstanding loans	% of total outstanding business loans	61.72	59.62	62.73	62.35	65.07	65.43	67.60	66.39	63.44	66.12	66.66	67.31	67.8	68.39	68.41*	*
Outstanding short-term loans, SME	EUR billion	37.4	40.4	34.1	35.4	36.5	34.5	33.8	31.4	30.9	32.0	33.6	36.7	36.7	34.7	35.1*	*
Outstanding long-term loans, SME	EUR billion	59.7	66.1	72.2	77.2	79.3	82.5	83.9	80.3	84.8	90.8	97.8	103.4	109.6	115.5	124.4*	*
Share of short-term lending, total	% of total business lending	45.14	45.31	38.37	37.71	36.46	31.45	30.90	31.13	29.58	29.62	29.05	29.60	28.07	25.39	25.44*	*
Government loan guarantees, SMEs	EUR million	..	156.5	411.9	553.9	317.5	266.0	480.2	265.6	448.2	398.3	458.4	612.2	520	777	1 021.5	569.4
Government guaranteed loans, SMEs	EUR million	..	312.7	832.7	888.4	561.7	484.3	826.1	476.7	805.6	735.9	828.3	1130.3	993	1 318	2 086.6	1 106
Direct government loans, SMEs	EUR million	..	113.7	142.2	141.9	148.3	170.5	235.6	..	..	..	..	..	..	..	..	..
Interest rate, SMEs	%	5.45	5.70	3.01	2.51	2.88	2.32	2.06	2.09	1.83	1.72	1.66	1.60	1.58	1.55	1.57	2.06
Interest rate, large firms	%	4.72	5.05	2.09	1.70	2.22	1.74	1.76	1.77	1.60	1.34	1.40	1.35	1.31	1.40	1.44	1.91
Interest rate spread	% points	0.73	0.65	0.92	0.81	0.66	0.58	0.30	0.32	0.23	0.38	0.26	0.25	0.27	0.15	0.13	0.15

Collateral, SMEs	% of SMEs needing collateral to obtain bank lending	..	..	..	74.30	71.90	78.60	..	..	..	..	..	..	..	..	..	..
Percentage of SME loan applications	SME loan applications/ total number of SMEs	..	..	22.22	26.46	30.20	29.33	29.36	39.33	36.61	36.71	37.18	35.38	33.87	33.07	35.09	33.21
Rejection rate	(SME loans authorised/ requested)	..	..	0.52	5.13	6.44	10.40	10.91	5.88	5.71	6.13	5.07	2.75	3.39	7.62	5.59	6,77
Utilisation rate	SME loans used/ authorised	77.80	79.05	80.69	80.07	80.16	77.45	77.79	79.76	79.62	80.01	79.86	80.39	80.64	80.58	80.09	*
Non-bank finance																	
Venture and growth capital	EUR million	306	385.20	463.93	269.97	291.14	350.79	2451.09	457.12	449.78	691.92	562.91	546.84	853.72	737.14	1526.14	1127.24
Venture and growth capital (growth rate)	%, year-on-year growth rate		26%	20%	-42%	8%	20%	-9%	43%	-2%	54%	-19%	-3%	56%	-14%	107%	-26%
Leasing and hire purchases	EUR million	4406	4856	3756	4005	4439	4450	4121.7	4357	4800	6010	5800	668.4	6382	5863	6628	7549
Factoring and invoicing	EUR million	19.2	22.5	23.9	32.2	36.9	42.4	47.7	55.4	61.2	62.8	69.6	76.3	84.8	81.7	99.4	124.2
Other indicators																	
Payment delays, B2B	Number of days	..	..	17	17	15	19	18	19	13	10	8	9	7	3	12	11
Bankruptcies, total	Number	7 680	8 476	9 420	9 570	10 224	10 587	11 740	10 736	9 762	9 170	9 968	9 878	10 598	7 203	6533	9265
Bankruptcies, total (growth rate)	%, year-on-year growth rate	..	10.36	11.14	1.59	6.83	3.55	10.89	-8.55	-9.07	-6.06	8.77	-0.90	7.29	-32.03	-9.30	41.82
Bankruptcies, SMEs	Number	7 679	8 476	9 418	9 570	10222	10583	11 739	10736	9 760	9 168	9 967	9 878	10596	7 197	6 532	9 265
Bankruptcies, SMEs (growth rate)	%, year-on-year growth rate		10.39	11.21	1.44	6.94	3.45	10.96	-8.62	-8.90	-6.11	8.77	-0.75	7.17	-32.09	-9.24	41.84

Note: * Data were compiled before for the last trimester /December. As these data will not be published before a reform of these statistics, the data used for 2021 correspond to the last available month (November 2021).

6. Brazil

Key facts on SME financing

Micro and small enterprises (MSEs) form an essential part of the Brazilian economy, accounting for 93.7% of all legally constituted companies (20.3 million) according to the Enterprise Map as of December 2023.

The reference interest rate of *Banco Central do Brasil* (Special Clearance and Escrow System - SELIC) has gradually declined, from 14.15% per annum in December 2015 to 2.0% in January 2021. The previous period of a rate hike (from 7.25% in March 2013 to 14.25% in September 2016) led to high-interest rates on loans for large corporate borrowers (14.8%) and SMEs (30.6%), leading to a shrinking demand for new SME loans. Interest rates have increased more for micro-enterprises and SMEs than for large businesses. However, this trend was reversed when the Central Bank decreased its rate at the end of 2016, thus decreasing interest rates for SMEs. Since January 2021, the reference interest rate increased substantially, returning to the standard seen previously in 2016, reaching 13.75% in August 2022 and being adjusted to 12.25% in the second semester of 2023, which impacted SME loans.

The stock of SME loans fell in 2015 and new lending to SMEs declined in 2014 and 2015. Both observations contrast with lending to large businesses, where the outstanding stock of loans, as well as new lending, was up in 2014 and 2015. A sharp rise in both new lending and outstanding stock of loans was observed in 2020 due to measures adopted in the context of the COVID-19 pandemic (especially through programmes such as Pronampe and PEAC). The level of lending (stock and flows) was maintained in 2021 and 2022, reflecting an increase in the share of SME loans over total loans.

Since 2008, large companies have received a larger share of business loans than SMEs. The government has taken on a more active role in this area, often with the aim of providing financial services to small businesses excluded from traditional financial institutions. Developments include a micro-credit programme, a quota to use 2% of demand deposits of the National Financial System to finance loans to low-income individuals and micro-entrepreneurs, and a strong increase in the number of agencies where financial services are provided.

In the area of equity finance, the regulatory framework for angel investors was revised in 2016 and further adjusted in 2017, removing some long-standing barriers for investors in SME markets, in particular by offering more legal protection in the case of company closures, more flexibility in the type of investment and more information sharing between recipients and investors. In addition, new regulations concerning investment-based crowdfunding and Fintech were introduced in 2017 and 2018, fostering financing digital companies and more competitive market.

In October 2023, the Brazilian government created a Ministry for Entrepreneurship, Micro and Small Enterprises, highlighting the importance of SMEs in the Brazilian agenda.

Table 6.1. Scoreboard for Brazil

Indicator	Unit	2007	2008	2009	2010	2011	2012	2013	2014	2015	2016	2017	2018	2019	2020	2021	2022
Debt																	
Outstanding business loans, SMEs	BRL billion	251	332	365	448	533	609	666	711	682	566	488	497	533	700	821	938
Outstanding business loans, total	BRL billion	501	682	775	930	1 107	1 279	1 460	1 623	1 734	1 565	1 436	1 441	1 427	1 754	1 923	2 101
Share of SME outstanding loans	% of total outstanding business loans	50.08	48.61	47.10	48.15	48.15	47.62	45.65	43.78	39.36	36.13	33.97	34.48	37.36	39.93	42.67	44.66
New business lending, total	BRL billion						1 240	1 267	1 266	1 281	800	777	921	1 055	1 317	1 487	1 729
New business lending, SMEs	BRL billion						786	783	782	727	381	367	415	484	579	592	694
Share of new SME lending	% of total business lending						63.43	61.78	61.75	56.79	47.62	47.26	45.07	45.92	43.96	39.83	40.11
Outstanding short-term loans, SMEs	BRL billion	89	98	90	107	136	146	150	145	133	110	103	111	117	94	130	134
Outstanding long-term loans, SMEs	BRL billion	147	198	232	292	369	459	515	564	548	456	385	386	416	606	690	805
Share of short-term SME lending	%	37.69	33.04	28.08	26.83	26.94	24.20	22.51	20.50	19.49	19.41	21.09	22.31	21.88	13.48	15.89	14.31
Government guaranteed loans, SMEs	BRL billion	40	46	93	51	705	810	705	2 777	3 420	3 793	3 022	484	294	44 062	60 420	79 028
Direct government loans, SMEs	BRL billion	17	24	26	27	31	35	36	43	46	39	33	26	20	22	20	22
Non-performing loans, total	% of all business loans	1.54	1.55	2.67	1.84	2.02	2.22	1.84	1.88	2.39	3.15	2.99	2.45	2.08	1.20	1.34	1.64
Non-performing loans, SMEs	% of SME loans	2.83	2.83	4.99	3.56	3.95	4.4	3.7	3.8	5.4	6.9	6.30	4.63	3.62	2.16	2.62	3.48
Interest rate, SMEs	%						19.7	23.8	25.3	35.0	34.5	26.5	22.4	24.6	11.6	17.9	23.7
Interest rate, large firms	%						10.2	13.8	14.4	17.5	18.8	14.3	11.0	8.7	6.2	10.6	16.1
Interest rate spread	% points						9.5	10.0	10.9	17.5	15.7	12.2	11.5	15.9	5.4	7.2	7.7

Note: Regarding the government guaranteed loans indicator, the 2020 figure considers two of the emergency credit programmes launched by the federal government in the context of the Covid-19 pandemic (National Program to Support Micro and Small Enterprises – Pronampe, and Emergency Employment Program – Pese). In both cases, relevant federal government guarantees are provided for loans.

The full country profile is available at: https://doi.org/10.1787/fa521246-en.

7. Canada

Key facts on SME financing

In 2022, Canadian small businesses establishments (1-99 employees) constituted 98% of all businesses. Small businesses employed 6.6 million individuals at the enterprise level, or 41.1% of the private sector labour force.

Supply-side survey data show that outstanding debt held by all businesses increased in 2022 to CAD 1 236 billion. Lending to small businesses increased to CAD 140.4 billion (from CAD 125.7 billion in 2021). As a result, small businesses' share of total outstanding business loans in 2022 was 11.4%.

Small business credit conditions tightened in 2022. The average interest rate charged to small businesses increased from 4.1% in 2021 to 6.2% in 2022, with an average business prime rate (the rate charged to the most creditworthy borrowers) of 4.1% (from 2.5% in 2021). The business risk premium (measured as the difference between the average small business interest rate and the business prime rate) stood at 2.1%, reflecting a tightening in access to financing for small businesses in Canada. Bank of Canada survey results indicate that lenders reported that overall business lending conditions tightened towards the end of the second half of 2022. Borrowers also reported tightening of credit conditions during the same period.

In 2022, the small business 90-day delinquency rate fell to 0.33% after reaching 0.66% in 2021 and 0.76% in 2020.

Total venture capital (VC) investment levels in Canada reached a peak of CAD 14.4 billion in 2021, followed by a decline to CAD 9.8 billion in 2022.

The Business Development Bank of Canada (BDC), a crown corporation with the mandate to support Canadian entrepreneurship, had CAD 47.8 billion in financing and investments, as of 31 March 2022, committed to 95 000 clients operating across Canada. As the most active VC investor in Canada, the BDC invests both directly into firms and indirectly through external VC funds, with the objective of making Canadian VC a financially viable and attractive asset class for private sector investors and institutional investors.

The Government of Canada has further supported the development Canada's VC ecosystem by convening public, private, and institutional sources of financing through its Venture Capital Action Plan (VCAP) and Venture Capital Catalyst Initiative (VCCI). Taken together, the Government of Canada has invested CAD 761 million, resulting in a combined total of over CAD 3 billion in capital raised from public and private sources to help Canadian companies start up and grow.

The Government of Canada has established a number of programmes to provide support targeted to entrepreneurs from underrepresented groups. The Government has made total investments of nearly CAD 7 billion in the Women Entrepreneurship Strategy (WES); of CAD 265 million in the Black Entrepreneurship Program (BEP); of CAD 38 million for Futurpreneur, a programme to support youth entrepreneurs; and of CAD 150 million for the Indigenous Growth Fund launched by the National Aboriginal Capital Corporations Association alongside with the BDC. The Aboriginal Entrepreneurship Programme also provides support to First Nations, Inuit and Métis Nation entrepreneurs by lowering the cost of business financing and offering business support services.

The Government of Canada launched Canada's Export Diversification Strategy in Fall of 2018. In total, the Export Diversification Strategy is a CAD 1.1 billion investment over six years, that aims to help Canadian businesses access new markets and increase Canada's overseas exports by 50% by 2025.

Table 7.1. Scoreboard for Canada

Indicator	Unit	2007	2008	2009	2010	2011	2012	2013	2014	2015	2016	2017	2018	2019	2020	2021	2022
								Debt									
Outstanding business loans, SMEs	CAD billion	83.4	83.4	86.4	85.7	90.1	87.7	92.2	93.5	97.4	99.6	104.1	105.7	109.8	117.9	127.5	140.4
Outstanding business loans, total	CAD billion	479.8	534.0	482.3	489.5	514.4	557.3	602.1	658.5	739.0	774.7	834.1	918.2	984.9	10007	1097	1236
Share of SME outstanding loans	% of total outstanding business loans	17.39	15.61	17.92	17.50	17.52	15.75	15.31	14.20	13.18	12.86	12.49	11.51	11.15	11.71	11.63	11.36
New business lending, total	CAD billion	..	..	..	..	126.2	141.6	151.0	168.7	188.4	204.0	233.9	269.7	285.7	287.7	317.8	361.3
New business lending, SMEs	CAD billion	..	..	..	..	20.2	21.7	22.8	23.2	24.0	22.8	25.2	27.2	26.8	26.7	28.9	31.1
Share of new SME lending	% of total new lending	..	..	..	..	15.99	15.30	15.10	13.74	12.73	11.16	10.78	10.08	9.39	9.30	9.11	8.60
Outstanding short-term loans, SMEs	CAD billion	15.1	..			6.9	..	..	15.6	..	..	24.2	..	..	15.6	..	..
Outstanding long-term loans, SMEs	CAD billion	21.1	..	..	..	12.8	..	..	12.4	..	..	32.4	..	..	23.8	..	..
Share of short-term SME lending	% of total SME lending	41.62	..	43.40	36.30	35.13	39.00	46.00	55.71	47.20	36.20	42.8	30.10	19.50	39.62	31.52	19.66
Government loan guarantees, SMEs	CAD billion	1.20	1.30	1.20	1.30	1.30	1.08	1.06	1.01	1.11	1.30	1.54	1.75	1.89	3.27	3.91	3.98
Direct government loans, SMEs	CAD billion	4.40	4.10	5.50	4.70	6.00	5.80	4.60	6.50	6.70	7.9	8.0	8.4	8.10	9.92	11.35	13.18
Interest rate, SMEs	%	7.50	..	6.20	5.80	5.30	5.40	5.60	5.10	5.10	5.30	5.20	5.70	5.30	4.80	4.09	6.21
Interest rate, large firms	%	6.10	..	3.10	2.60	3.00	3.00	3.00	3.00	2.80	2.70	2.90	3.64	3.60	2.77	2.45	4.11
Interest rate spread	% points	1.40	..	3.10	3.20	2.30	2.40	2.60	2.10	2.30	2.60	2.30	2.06	1.70	2.03	1.64	2.10
Collateral, SMEs	% of SMEs needing collateral to obtain bank lending	47.7	..	56.1	66.7	64.8	76.0	56.0	66.6	80.0	74.0	64.1	70.0	72.73	61.10	57.77	62.02
Percentage of SME loan applications	SME loan applications/ total number of SMEs	17.0	..	14.0	18.0	24.0	26.0	30.0	27.0	23.0	26.0	26.0	27.0	26.71	16.10	16.70	17.69
Rejection rate	Percentage of businesses' debt financing requests that were rejected.	..	..	..	9.0	8.0	7.0	9.0	12.8	7.0	9.0	9.5	9.0	8.3	8.4	5.5	7.1

The full country profile is available at: https://doi.org/10.1787/fa521246-en.

8. Chile

Key facts on SME financing

In general, as of September 2023, inflation has continued to fall, although it remains high, in a context where activity and demand have continued to advance in their adjustment process, cost pressures have been reduced and two-year inflation expectations stand at 3%.

From a subnational perspective, GDP grew in all regions, registering a rise of 2.4% for the country. It was estimated that in 2023 it would fall between -1.75% and -0.75% and increase between 2 and 3% in 2024. To a large extent, the downward correction for 2023 and 2024 responds to the new assumption for trend growth.

The Internal Revenue Service (SII) provides a size classification according to total annual sales of businesses. MSMEs concentrate 98.56% of companies according to SII records for the tax year 2021, excluding companies without information from the total universe of companies (i.e. excluding informal entities). MSMEs only accounted for 13.93% of total annual sales in UF.

According to the Quarterly Survey of Bank Credit Conditions of the Central Bank of Chile in Q4 2022, the conditions for the supply of credit to companies remain limited. The fraction of entities reporting more demanding loan standards for large firms and SMEs reached 39% and 36%, respectively, which is slightly lower than the figures reported during the previous quarter.

As in previous years, in 2022, Chile developed a solid economic relief plan through the so-called ‘Chile Apoya Plan”, an inclusive recovery plan including 25 measures to boost job creation, support smaller firms, and address the rise in the cost of living, among others.

In the case of smaller firms, support was channelled through Production Development Corporation (Corfo) and Technical Cooperation Service (Sercotec). These institutions sought to expand the coverage of support programmes for reactivation and the creation of special support instruments focused on tourism and culture sectors, with a special focus on gender parity and fostering cooperatives. The programmes allowed to assist more than 120 000 MSMEs and cooperatives from all regions of the country, for a total of USD 1 billion.

Additionally, for MSMEs a new stream to access credit guarantees was delivered by the creation of the Fogape Chile Apoya bill. Unlike the previous two Fogape bills (2020 and 2021), the state guarantee for loans is exclusively for MSMEs.

In 2021, the guarantee programmes granted by the Corfo, such as COBEX, Pro Inversión and FOGAIN, benefited almost 32,000 companies, reflecting an increase of 62.3% compared to the same period of 2021, granting more than 40,000 operations with Corfo Guarantees of more than USD 1.3 million. 89% of the guarantees were allocated to micro and small firms.

Venture capital funds, supported by Corfo programmes, continue to be an important source of financing for technology-based companies with high growth capacity. Although in 2020 there was a 14% drop in investments compared to 2019, mainly due to the effects of the pandemic, in 2021 and 2022, venture capital investment experienced a year-on-year growth of 30% and 23% respectively, growing from CLP 49 billion in investment in 2020 (about USD 63 million) to CLP 77 billion (about USD 89 million) in 2022.

In the case of non-bank financing, in 2022 the Corfo MiPymes Credit Programme allowed 82,000 companies to access financing through non-bank financial institutions, mobilising almost USD 255 million in credits, factoring and leasing.

In 2022, the Superintendence of Insolvency and Reentrepreneurship (Superir) worked on the modernisation project of regulation No. 20,720, with the aim of providing relief by reallocating resources and creating new procedures for micro and small enterprises in order to ease their experience.

Finally, the Commission for the Financial Market (CMF) has been leading the discussion of the Fintech bill. The bill was approved by the Congress in December 2022, and promulgated on January 2023. The Law establishes a flexible regulatory framework for a number of companies that offer financial services but are not currently regulated or supervised by the Financial Market Commission. These include crowdfunding platforms, financial transaction platforms and custodians, intermediation and order routing.

Additionally, a new framework is created for the development of a regulated Open Finance System, in which Chilean citizens and firms will be able to share, with prior consent, their financial information, with the aim of accessing better products and services.

Table 8.1. Scoreboard for Chile

Indicator	Unit	2007	2008	2009	2010	2011	2012	2013	2014	2015	2016	2017	2018	2019	2020	2021	2022
								Debt									
Outstanding business loans. SMEs	CLP billion	6.8	7.6	8.1	9.3	10.1	11.5	11.8	13.7	15.8	17.3	18.7	19.8	20.8	23. 9	25.3	25.8
Outstanding business loans. total	CLP billion	40.9	49.9	46.3	48.1	57.2	64.6	69.8	76.4	84.9	88.7	90.3	99.5	108.5	111. 8	125.9	133.9
Share of SME outstanding loans	% of total outstanding business loans	16.7	15.2	17.5	19.3	17.7	17.9	16.9	18.0	18.6	19.5	20.7	19.9	19.2	21.4	20.1	19.3
New business lending. total	CLP billion	..	..	..	53.3	58.0	58.0	58.1	63.9	67.8	67.4	67.7	71.4	77.1	70.8	70.4	85.8
New business lending. SMEs	CLP billion	..	..	..	2.6	3.1	3.8	3.8	4.4	5.1	5.1	5.6	5.63	5.8	8.7	6.5	4.2
Share of new SME lending	% of total new lending	..	..	..	4.9	5.3	6.5	6.6	6.8	7.5	7.6	8.2	7.8	7.5	12.3	9.2	4.9
Outstanding Short-term loans. SMEs	CLP billion	..	..	..	1.6	2.0	2.3	1.8	1.8	1.9	1.8	1.8	1.9	1.8	1.1	0.9	1.0
Outstanding Long-term loans. SMEs	CLP billion	..	..	..	1.0	1.1	1.5	2.0	2.5	3.2	3.3	3.8	3.8	4.0	7.6	5.6	3.2
Share of short-term SME lending	% of total SME lending	..	..	..	60.2	63.3	60.3	47.8	41.9	36.9	35.8	32.8	33.3	31.0	12.6	13.2	24.8
Government loan guarantees. SMEs	CLP billion	0.2	0.3	0.8	1.1	1.3	1.9	1.9	1.6	1.7	1.8	1.7	1.6	1.7	7.7	6.1	2.2
Government guaranteed loans. SME	CLP billion	0.3	0.5	1.3	1.8	2.0	2.9	3.1	2.3	2.4	2.6	2.6	2.5	2.6	10.3	8.4	3.4
Direct Government loans. SMEs	CLP billion	..	..	..	..	..	..	..	..	..	..	..	..	..	..	..	..
Non-performing loans. total	% of all business loans	...	...	2.5	2.2	2.1	2.2	2.4	2.6	2.4	2.1	2.3	2.5	2.4	2.1	1.9	4.4

Non-performing loans. SMEs	% of all SME loans	..	..	5.9	6.1	5.5	5.4	6.1	6.1	5.9	5.3	5.2	5.9	5.9	4.7	4.1	2.2
Interest rate. SMEs	%	..	..	..	..	..	..	11.8	10.3	9.3	9.3	8.4	8.3	7.7	5.4	6.4	11.2
Interest rate. large firms	%	..	..	..	..	..	..	4.7	4.0	3.8	4.0	3.7	3.8	3.7	3.1	2.9	7.2
Interest rate spread	% points	..	..	..	..	..	..	7.1	6.3	5.5	5.3	4.7	4.5	4.0	2.3	3.6	4.0
Collateral. SMEs	% of SMEs needing collateral to obtain bank lending	44.0	..	49.8	..	..	..	72.8	..	68.1	..	59.9	..	..	..	..	..
Percentage of SME loan applications	SME loan applications/ total number of SMEs	32.9	..	32.4	..	..	..	26.4	..	24.6	..	26.2	..	..	..	..	..
Rejection rate	1-(SME loans authorised/ requested)	41.4	..	15.0	..	..	..	12.3	..	14.7	..	9.4	..	..	..	..	..
Utilization rate	SME loans used/ authorised	86.6	..	91.0	..	..	..	87.9	..	96.7	..	89.3	..	..	..	..	..
Non-bank finance																	
Venture and growth capital	CLP billion	0.02	0.02	0.02	0.02	0.03	0.04	0.03	0.04	0.03	0.05	0.02	0.04	0.05	0.04	0.06	0.07
Venture and growth capital (growth rate)	%. Year-on-year growth rate	..	-27.8	15.3	22.0	25.1	27.0	-28.5	40.1	-19.6	-100	-45.3	79	18.3	-12.0	29.6	22.5
Leasing and hire purchases	CLP billion	3.0	3.6	3.5	3.8	4.5	5.0	5.6	6.2	6.6	6.7	7.8	8.2	8.7	8.4	8.8	8.8
Factoring and invoicing	CLP billion	2.0	2.0	1.4	1.9	2.4	2.6	2.6	2.6	2.8	3.0	3.8	4.4	4.7	4.4	4.7	5.6
Other indicators																	
Payment delays. B2B	Number of days	..	..	..	75.8	74.9	56.7	52.7	55.2	58.0	54.9	56.0	51.8	60.5	53.8	48.5	47.5
Bankruptcies. SMEs	Number	122	127	125	136	146	146	164	6	154	295	285	397	368	368	354	314
Bankruptcies. SMEs (growth rate)	% year-on-year growth rate	..	4.1	-1.6	8.8	7.4	0.0	12.3	-96.3	2 467	91.6	-3.4	39.0	15.36	0.00	-3.8	-11.3

The full country profile is available at: https://doi.org/10.1787/fa521246-en.

9. Colombia

Key facts on SME financing

Access to finance is one of the main elements for strengthening and keeping entrepreneurships and micro, small and medium-sized enterprises (MSMEs) growing, allowing them to invest in order to increase their productivity, competitiveness and consolidation in the market. In times of economic distress, obstacles to access formal financing sources, significantly limit MSMEs' ability to invest in upgrading their operations or in innovation, as they are required to have liquidity buffers to face economic uncertainty.

In 2022, for example, there were a range of factors that led to economic uncertainty becoming a global challenge for enterprises. The large-scale aggression of Russia against Ukraine, global inflation, major economic slowdowns, the lack of raw materials, an energy crisis, and a rise in interest rates have made the economic outlook tense. As a result of this, markets suffered high volatility.

In Colombia, uncertainty was felt in spite of relatively good internal economic performance compared to other countries in the region. On the one hand, the rise in interest rates and high inflation during the year has been a source of concern, and on the other hand, relative uncertainty could have emerged as a result of the change of government. Notwithstanding, GDP grew by 7.3% in 2022, and 310 000 new enterprises were established, which represents 1% more than in 2021. Of the newly established businesses, 62.5% are enterprises led by women (Confecámaras, 2023[1]).

The results of the Entrepreneurial opinion survey, conducted by Fedesarrollo, demonstrated that trust by traders increased and reached 22.6% in December 2022 due to greater optimism about the current situation, in comparison with 19.2% in November of the same year. However, it is important to note that this percentage is below the 41.3% recorded in the same period in 2021 (Fedesarrollo, 2022[2]).

The entrepreneurial opinion survey also provides information regarding the main sources of finance used by MSMEs. Findings show that 50.6% of micro-enterprises indicated their own resources as the most important source of finance, 39% mention profit reinvestment, 23.9% choose traditional bank loans. Nevertheless, promoting financial inclusion and bridging the gap in access to finance as a mechanism to reduce business informality in Colombia continues to be an internal challenge.

In relation to the destination of credit resources, the majority of SMEs in the three main sectors (manufacturing, services, and trade) used credit resources to finance working capital. The second most frequent use of resources was the consolidation of liabilities, and the third use was the purchase or lease of machinery. Particularly, this last use was evident in companies in the industrial sector.

On the other hand, despite the lack of sources to accurately calculate business informality[1], estimates show that the percentage of informal businesses in Colombia is high. According to data reported in the Household Survey, it is estimated that over 57.6% of businesses are informal, with the percentage even higher in rural regions at 84.7%, correlating with limited access to financing. In the country, only 15.8% of microenterprises have access to credit products, 63.6% for small enterprises, and 77% for medium-sized enterprises (Banca de Oportunidades, 2023[3]).

Table 9.1. Scoreboard for Colombia

Indicator	Unit	2007	2008	2009	2010	2011	2012	2013	2014	2015	2016	2017	2018	2019	2020	2021	2022
Debt																	
Outstanding business loans, SMEs	COP billion	25.6	28.6	26.6	29.1	40	46.8	51.6	55.2	58.2	62.1	64.9	68.5	63.9	68.0	77.6	83.01
Outstanding business loans, total	COP billion	78.4	94.7	95.9	113.8	134.8	152.8	171.3	197.2	226.3	243.2	251.8	253.6	261.2	272.4	294.8	345.04
Share of SME outstanding loans	% of total outstanding business loans	32.7	30.2	27.7	25.6	29.7	30.6	30.1	28.0	25.7	25.5	25.8	27.0	24.48	25	26.3	24.1
New business lending, total	COP billion	67.7	76.0	77.2	79.0	77.7	95.4	104	117	118	117	153	160.1	118.6	112.5	138.7	146
New business lending, SMEs	COP billion	13.2	13.5	15.22	16.91	21.09	23.53	23.57	24.69	25.53	25.3	34.11	35.48	29.68	25.44	29.4	39.07
Share of new SME lending	% of total new lending	19.50	17.76	19.71	21.39	27.13	24.67	22.65	21.10	21.70	21.57	22.25	22.05	25.03	22.6	21.2	26.8
Outstanding short-term loans, SMEs	COP billion	4.98	7.52	6.14	6.41	10	11.55	12.36	12.93	13.8	13.59	14.44	12.86	11.39	11.26	13.28	16.2
Outstanding long-term loans, SMEs	COP billion	20.63	21.07	20.44	22.71	29.97	35.22	39.24	42.3	44.37	48.5	50.44	55.63	52.62	56.77	64.3	66.7
Share of short-term SME lending	% of total SME lending	19.45	26.30	23.10	22.01	25.02	24.70	23.95	23.41	23.72	21.89	22.26	18.78	17.69	16.6	17.1	19.6
Government loan guarantees, SMEs	COP billion	0.56	1.39	1.82	1.94	5.46	6.19	7.14	7.51	7.72	10.52	11.53	9.40	11.48	15.20	18.1	17.2
Government guaranteed loans, SMEs	COP billion	2.23	2.59	2.98	3.16	7.26	9.12	10.81	11.96	12.69	15.37	16.51	15.22	16.27	23.66	27.1	26.9
Non-performing loans, total	% of all business loans	0.95	1.27	1.59	1.07	1.00	1.03	1.08	1.33	1.34	1.51	2.36	2.61	2.51	3.1	2.4	1.6
Non-performing loans, SMEs	% of all SME loans	2.52	3.66	5.05	3.68	1.76	1.81	1.99	2.45	2.25	3.12	3.71	3.84	3.44	3.6	3.3	2.6
Interest rate, SMEs	%	20.09	23.13	20.43	18.66	14.34	14.68	13.24	13.54	14.69	16.87	15.37	13.03	13.34	12.3	12.4	21.8
Interest rate, large firms	%	12.61	14.74	9.41	7.16	8.90	8.61	7.54	8.02	8.66	11.02	9.16	6.32	6.05	5.3	5.2	13.9
Interest rate spread	% points	5.13	5.43	5.45	5.06	5.64	6.24	5.77	6.02	6.92	7.20	6.21	6.71	7.30	7.0	7.1	7.9
Collateral, SMEs	% of SMEs needing collateral to obtain bank lending	79.25	87.54	86.28	87.31	90.04	90.12	90.02	89.30	91.04	91.71	92.15	91.75	91.92	93.3	93.3	91.7
Percentage of SME loan applications	SME loan applications/ total number of SMEs	49	53	44.6	49.6	47	44	43.3	39.6	42.6	34	40	40	25	35	27.7	
Rejection rate	1-(SME loans authorised/ requested)	2	4	9	5	3	4	7	3	7.5	4	8	7	26	30	29.2	
Utilisation rate	SME loans used/ authorised	98	96	91	95	97	96	93	97	92.5	96	92	93	88	70	..	
Non-bank finance																	
Venture and growth capital	COP billion	..	..	..	..	..	..	..	..	1.83	2.91	4.23	5.61	5.70	..	..	..

Venture and growth capital (growth rate)	%, Year-on-year growth rate	..	..	..	..	..	..	..	..	..	59 .3	45 .5	32.69	1.57	..	..	..
Leasing and hire purchases	COP billion	..	..	..	..	..	..	..	..	33.34	39.45	41.98	50.17	..	..	..	..
Factoring and invoice discounting	COP billion	5.77	6.04	7.15	7.01	12.85	10.55	17.56	23.75	31.47	25.77	25.53	26.58	..	23	28.8	..
Other indicators																	
Payment delays, B2B	Number of days	49	50	61	62	59	55	56	65	66	85	95	101	80.01	..	..	..
Bankruptcies, SMEs	Number	..	1	12	18	40	59	76	83	85	131	193	443	608	661	691	..
Bankruptcies, SMEs (growth rate)	%, Year-on-year growth rate	..	..	1100	50	122.2	47.50	28.81	9.21	2.41	54.12	47.33	129.5	37.25	8.72	4.54	..

Note

1. Formalisation is a mean for companies to be economically, environmentally and socially included in the markets, increase productivity rates, access the financial system, and become sustainable. Although a percentage of companies in Colombia are not completely formal, there are several in the transition to formality.

The full country profile is available at: https://doi.org/10.1787/fa521246-en.

10. Czech Republic

Key facts on SME financing

In 2021, there were roughly 1.23 million active enterprises in the Czech Republic. 99.86% of these firms were SMEs with less than 250 employees each. Micro-firms dominated the business landscape, comprising 96 % of all SMEs in 2022. The total number of SME employees decreased by 36 000 in 2020 compared to 2019 and remained constant in 2021. Given the situation caused by the coronavirus epidemic, this decrease can be considered moderate.

In 2022, SME investment was assessed as favorable for established companies due to high bank liquidity. Banking and non-banking institutions, private individuals, venture capital funds offer a wide portfolio of financial products. However, between 2021 and 2022, there was a sharp decline in new business loans. Interest rates for SMEs increased by 113% in 2022 compared to 2021 in reaction to high inflation and the unstable geopolitical and economic situation.

SMEs are very vulnerable, especially in terms of financing, and have a higher perception of financial risk due to more frequent rejections of loan applications. Although, the situation in this area was improving until 2021, it reversed in 2022 in reaction to the geopolitical and economic turmoil. The 2022 SAFE Survey by ECB states that the share of SMEs in the Czech Republic, which mention the access to finance as being no obstacle, decreased from 47% in 2021 to 37% in 2022. In terms of access to common methods of financing, the Czech Republic is above average in several indicators showing the quality of SMEs' access to finance. The most important direct sources of external financing for SMEs are credit lines or overdrafts (49%), bank loans (40%) and leasing (48%). So far, venture capital financing is relevant for only 2% of companies. In terms of the use of financing, between 2020 and 2022, investment in the development of new products or services has slightly decreased (from 25% to 22%). Most sources of finance are intended to finance either fixed investments or inventories and working capital. The share of companies that have stated that costs for materials and energy have increased rose dramatically from 2020 to 2022 (from 30% to 88%).

Alternative sources of financing include venture capital, angel investments, bond issuance, crowdfunding and state support. The Czech Republic is characterised by a weaker investment environment, which undermines the establishment of new companies and the financing of new SME projects. While crowdfunding has become a popular tool for obtaining the necessary financial resources, capital financing was underdeveloped compared to similarly sized EU economies for a long time. There was a lack of willingness to invest in the early stages of business development (pre-seed, seed, start-up and later stage venture). Investments in these entities are high risk for investors and banks, mainly due to the absence of relevant corporate history, lack of collateral or lack of information to assess their credit risk or valuation of their intangible assets. The situation changed drastically after three venture capital funds with public investments were established, and the venture capital supply in the Czech market is comparable to that of the other similarly sized EU economies. Venture capital and growth capital investments peaked in 2021, reaching EUR 751 million. In 2022, there was a drop of 63%, which may be due in part to incomplete data. The market for angel investments is barely visible and fragmented. However, the situation for innovators in the idea or start-up phase is still complicated. Consequently, the Czech government plans to establish another 3 pre-seed and spin-off co-investment funds in 2023.

The SMEs Support Strategy in the Czech Republic for the period 2021-2027 (SME 2021+) aims to increase the productivity and competitiveness of SMEs, and, at the same time, to strengthen their international position, inter alia in the field of research and innovation or the use of advanced technologies and skills. The Strategy represents the key strategic document for the preparation of the European Union (EU) cohesion policies over the 2021–27 programming period in the area of enterprise development. This includes the Operational Programme Technologies and Applications for Competitiveness (OP TAC), with a total allocation of CZK 81.5 billion. In 2021, the National Recovery Plan (NRP) was established, drawing its sources from the Recovery and Resilience Facility and offering CZK 191 billion to finance post-pandemic recovery. Government support for SMEs and entrepreneurs primarily consists of measures in the areas of investment and operational financing, export support, support of the energy sector, development of entrepreneurial skills and financial literacy of entrepreneurs, technical education and research, and development and innovation.

There are several financing tools, such as government loan guarantees (National Development Bank – former Czech-Moravian Guarantee and Development Bank), financing and insuring schemes for exporting SMEs (Czech Export Bank and Export Guarantee and Insurance Corporation) and government loans (EXPANZE). Most common are, however, direct grants. These are awarded from calls launched by OP TAC and NRP.

Table 10.1. Scoreboard for the Czech Republic

Indicator	Unit	2008	2009	2010	2011	2012	2013	2014	2015	2016	2017	2018	2019	2020	2021	2022
								Debt								
Outstanding business loans, SMEs	CZK billion	555.03	527.55	550.08	587.91	589.68	610.79	621.39	652.59	702.81	725.63	762.99	794.7	829.8	837.16	879.41
Outstanding business loans, total	CZK billion	850.76	784.07	783.54	831.21	840.59	871.58	890.23	935.36	994.86	1036.1	1097.4	1133.1	1135.1	1199.8	1244.5
Share of SME outstanding loans	% of total outstanding business loans	65.24	67.28	70.20	70.73	70.15	70.08	69.80	69.77	70.64	70.03	69.53	70.14	73.10	69.7	70.6
New business lending, total	CZK billion	866.11	780.87	667.98	599.09	694.94	500.50	544.73	607.59	510.58	457.94	461.84	521.11	590.21	715.8	470
New business lending, SMEs	CZK billion	207.24	147.74	123.40	124.12	129.83	86.66	97.76	118.28	100.46	101.24	97.92	92.27	119.82	87.3	70.1
Share of new SME lending	% of total new lending	23.93	18.92	18.47	20.72	18.68	17.31	17.95	19.46	19.68	22.11	21.20	17.71	20.30	12.2	14.9
Outstanding short-term loans, SMEs	CZK million	..	..	73 626	72 433	77 853	45 531	40 360	41 742	36 974	33 918	29 835	22 107	20 917	18 246	11 747
Outstanding long-term loans, SMEs	CZK million	..	..	49 772	51 684	51 977	41 129	57 404	76 475	63 490	67 325	68 090	70 166	98 904	69 105	58 348
Share of short-term SME lending	% of total SME lending	..	..	59.67	58.36	59.97	52.54	41.28	35.31	58.2	50.3	43.8	31.5	21.15	26.4	20.3
Government loan guarantees, SMEs	CZK million	3 529	6 369	6 593	472	1 534	3 251	4 010	6 913	3 530	4 014	6 485	9 786	22 423	9 676	14 005
Government guaranteed loans, SMEs	CZK million	5 094	9 550	10 070	630	2 215	4 616	5 771	9 947	5 055	5 758	9 287	13 534	30 431	13 876	19 562
Direct government loans, SMEs	CZK million	286	209	629	1 090	782	101	86	65	7	291	1 440	2 407	2 627	3 979	2 964

Non-performing loans, total	CZK million	35 340	61 904	70 166	67 876	61 480	62 032	58 694	52 677	50 307	43 225	38 596	35 871	46 615	45 599	42 103
Interest rate, SMEs	%	5.57	4.64	4.01	3.73	3.48	3.13	3.76	2.70	2.50	2.50	3.14	3.80	3.26	3.23	6.93
Interest rate, large firms	%	4.84	3.46	3.34	2.63	2.43	1.89	2.00	1.80	1.80	1.90	2.62	3.10	2.13	2.12	7.69
Interest rate spread	% points	0.73	1.18	0.67	1.10	1.05	1.24	1.76	0.90	0.70	0.60	0.52	0.70	1.13	1.11	-0.76
Non-bank finance																
Venture and growth capital	EUR million	104.0	219.7	153.8	18.3	9.5	23.3	34.6	12.4	9.4	16.3	18.7	149.8	41.7	750.7	277.4
Venture and growth capital (growth rate)	%, Year-on-year growth rate	..	111.2	-30.0	-88.1	-48.1	145.4	48.3	-64.0	-24.6	73.9	14.8	800.1	-73.83	1 697	-63
Leasing and hire purchases	CZK billion	25.7	26.9	27.3	30.4	32.9	35.4	40	50.1	49.3	55.1	56.7	57.8	53.6	65.3	69.2
Factoring and invoice discounting	CZK billion	134	99.7	111.9	128.2	130.6	145.4	163.9	136.9	131	156.3	174.3	184	183	234.4	285.9
Other indicators																
Payment delays, B2B	Number of days	18.00	19.00	14.00	14.00	15.00	14.00	14.00	14.00	19.00	16.00	38	24	39.00	48	43
Bankruptcies, SMEs	Number	758	1 114	1 739	2 590	3 843	6 052	9 101	9 077	8 040	7 202	6 052	8 521	7 911	7 052	5 835
Bankruptcies, SMEs (growth rate)	%, Year-on-year growth rate		47	56.1	49	48.4	57.5	50.4	-0.26	-11.4	-10.4	-16	40.8	-7.16	-10.86	-17.26

The full country profile is available at: https://doi.org/10.1787/fa521246-en.

11. Denmark

Key facts on SME financing

In 2021, not counting non-employer enterprises, SMEs accounted for 98.7% of all enterprises and 38.7% of all full-time employees in Denmark.

New lending to SMEs from financial institutions increased from DKK 50 billion to 57 billion between 2021 and 2022, representing a 14% increase. The 2022 level was slightly higher than the average in the period 2014-2022. The share of new SME lending compared to total new lending was 7.35% in 2022, which is below the average of 10.43% in the period 2014-2022.

Interest rates for SMEs as well as for large firms had been steadily declining since 2008 until a few years back. The interest rates for SMEs have been increasing each year since 2019 from 1.85% to 2.72% in 2022, resulting in a widening interest rate spread. The 2022 interest rate spread reached 1.16 percentage-points, up from 0.78 percentage-points in 2019 ascribed to a slight increase each year.

Venture and growth capital financing from Danish private equity firms increased in 2021 and 2022 and reached a record high level of EUR 1224 million in 2022. The overall increase results from an increase in growth capital as venture investments experienced a 52% decrease from the high level of 2021 to 2022. The 2022 levels of venture and growth capital were significantly higher than any year between 2010 and 2020.

Average payment delays increased over the last 3 years and stood at their highest level for the period 2014-2022, at 14 days in 2022. The number of bankruptcies among SMEs increased from 1 768 in 2021 to 2 351 in 2022, explained in part by the phasing out of the COVID-19 support schemes.

In 2022, government loan guarantees decreased from DKK 2.260 billion in 2021 to 1 542 million, and government guaranteed loans decreased from DKK 2.478 billion in 2021 to 1.780 billion in 2022.

On 1 January 2023 the Export and Investment Fund of Denmark (EIFO) was established through a merger of three previous state funds: The Growth Fund, Denmark's Green Investment Fund and EKF Denmark's Export Credit Agency. EIFO provides a single point of access for Danish companies requiring government financing and aims to improve growth in a green way.

Table 11.1. Scoreboard for Denmark

Indicator	Unit	2007	2008	2009	2010	2011	2012	2013	2014	2015	2016	2017	2018	2019	2020	2021	2022
Debt																	
Outstanding business loans, total	DKK billion	732	809	814	812	809	830	860	914	940	989	1 033	1 080	1 126	1 168	1302	1442
New business lending, total	DKK billion	332	385	318	313	292	241	303	474	519	508	521	570	597	505	517	780
New business lending, SMEs	DKK billion	41	35	28	35	34	39	37	55	73	51	52	49	68	56	50	57
Share of new SME lending	% of total new lending	12.29	9.15	8.96	11.21	11.70	16.25	12.07	11.51	14.10	10.12	10.08	8.60	11.36	11.08	9.73	7.49
New short-term loans, SMEs	DKK billion	26	26	22	23	24	20	22	34	35	31	29	27	24	26	25	39
New long-term loans, SMEs	DKK billion	14	9	6	23	10	19	15	21	38	21	23	22	44	30	25	19
Share of short-term SME lending	% of total SME lending	64.70	74.57	78.79	50.00	70.53	51.49	60.25	62.38	48.48	60.00	55.63	55.09	35.66	46.04	50.20	67.25
Government loan guarantees, SMEs	DKK million	210	178	209	769	1 192	1 222	783	658	668	620	514	529	512	7972	2260	1542
Government guaranteed loans, SMEs	DKK million	..	..	..	..	17	61	286	746	1 076	1 257	1 377	1 225	1 246	2 934	2478	1780
Interest rate, SMEs	%	5.97	6.59	5.33	4.39	4.38	3.91	3.78	3.44	2.99	2.74	2.36	2.27	1.85	1.93	2.02	2.72
Interest rate, large firms	%	5.23	5.68	3.63	2.49	2.40	2.14	1.73	1.65	1.53	1.34	1.23	0.98	1.07	1.03	0.90	1.56
Interest rate spread	% points	0.75	0.91	1.70	1.90	1.97	1.77	2.04	1.79	1.45	1.40	1.12	1.29	0.78	0.90	1.11	1.16
Non-bank finance																	
Venture and growth capital	EUR million	263	205	159	280	186	270	241	230	339	554	532	699	475	424	1076	1224
Venture and growth capital (growth rate)	%. Year-on-year growth rate	..	-22.34	-22.45	76.57	-33.49	45.13	-10.81	-4.73	47.66	63.33	-4.03	31.47	-32.03	-10.90	150.3	12,4
Other indicators																	
Payment delays, B2B	Number of days	7.2	6.1	12.0	12.0	13.0	12.0	10.0	9.0	4.0	4.0	2.0	3.0	3.0	14.0	11	14
Bankruptcies, SMEs	Number	..	..	2 563	2 583	1 938	1 958	1 698	1 328	1 584	1 853	1 888	2 013	2 153	1 841	1768	2351
Bankruptcies, SMEs (growth rate)	%. Year-on-year growth rate	..	..	..	0.78	-24.97	1.03	-13.28	-21.79	19.28	16.98	1.89	6.62	6.95	-14.49	-3.97	32.98

The full country profile is available at: https://doi.org/10.1787/fa521246-en.

12. Estonia

Key facts on SME financing

In 2021, Estonian SMEs employed 81% of the workforce. In 2020 they accounted for 80.5% of total value added, and in 2021 for 82.1% of total value added. In 2021, 94% of all enterprises were micro-enterprises, i.e. companies with less than 10 employees. Micro-enterprises employed 31.7% of the workforce and accounted for 31.5% of total value added in 2021.

Since 2021, outstanding business loans to SMEs have been increasing after a previous decline. During the COVID-19 crisis, SME outstanding loans declined despite the provision of cheap guarantees and direct loans from the government. This can be explained by the increase in SME interest rates in 2020, as well as the provision of public support through non-debt channels such as employment support and the deferral of taxes and instalments. Furthermore, under the Estonian corporate income tax system all reinvested profits are tax-free. Thus, companies have a strong incentive to re-invest their profits, which may be an explanation for the low demand for loans. Loans under EUR 1 million, which are used as a proxy to describe SME loans, may have become unreliable to depict SME activities. This is because the high inflation rates in recent years may have pushed SMEs to contract larger loans.

The base interest rate on SME loans (up to EUR 1 million) decreased steadily from 4% in 2012 to slightly below 3% in 2016. Since then, interest rates have been increasing, reaching 3.28% in 2018 and 4.08% in 2020. Interest rates had a slight decrease in 2021, at 3.75%, but reached 4.08% in 2022. For larger loans, the interest rate also moved upward to 3.44% in 2022. In 2020, the interest rate spread reached a high for the last decade at 1.31%, but decreased to 0.65% in 2022.

Venture and growth capital have been growing steadily in recent years but had a rapid growth in 2021. Estonia has a well-developed start-up community that has good potential for raising venture capital. In 2021 companies raised EUR 962 million, a 112% year-on-year growth rate. In 2022 companies raised EUR 1 302 million, a 35% year-on-year growth.

Leasing and hire purchases turnover declined sharply during the COVID-19 crisis in 2020 but increased again reaching EUR 805 million in 2022.

Table 12.1. Scoreboard for Estonia

Indicator	Unit	2007	2008	2009	2010	2011	2012	2013	2014	2015	2016	2017	2018	2019	2020	2021	2022
Debt																	
Outstanding business loans, SMEs	EUR billion	2.44	2.49	2.13	1.90	1.68	1.61	1.65	1.70	1.67	1.71	1.81	1.70	1.56	1.508	1.660	1.681
Outstanding business loans, total	EUR billion	6.80	7.20	6.86	6.46	5.95	6.15	6.25	6.44	6.80	7.34	6.93	7.17	7.18	7.518	8.175	8.987

Indicator	Unit	2007	2008	2009	2010	2011	2012	2013	2014	2015	2016	2017	2018	2019	2020	2021	2022
Share of SME outstanding loans	% of total outstanding business loans	35.83	34.55	31.01	29.37	28.28	26.24	26.45	26.40	24.56	23.23	26.1	23.7	21.7	20.06	20.31	18.70
New business lending, total	EUR billion	8.55	7.31	4.46	4.26	5.06	5.61	6.17	6.41	6.68	6.99	7.19	7.92	8.15	7.368	8.810	9.576
New business lending, SMEs	EUR billion	3.60	3.52	2.13	1.87	1.96	2.12	2.37	2.46	2.25	2.37	2.55	2.63	2.91	2.587	3.010	2.650
Share of new SME lending	% of total new lending	42.09	48.21	47.70	43.82	38.63	37.80	38.43	38.42	33.73	33.84	35.5	33.26	35.65	35.11	34.17	27.67
Short-term loans, SMEs	EUR million	480.5	475.1	377.1	317.8	325.9	302.3	317.4	333.4	300.8	314.8	320.1	299	263	199	187	211
Long-term loans, SMEs	EUR billion	1.96	2.01	1.75	1.58	1.36	1.31	1.34	1.37	1.37	1.39	1.49	1.40	1.30	1.308	1.473	1.469
Share of short-term SME lending	% of total SME lending	19.73	19.09	17.74	16.76	19.39	18.74	19.20	19.62	18.00	18.46	17.7	17.63	16.86	13.22	11.25	12.57
Government loan guarantees, SMEs	EUR million	15	23	52	66	53	60	52	66	66	93	61	72	75	112.60	94.0	100.56
Government guaranteed loans, SMEs	EUR million	27	39	86	122	116	122	100	111	112	171	100	118	145	188.13	140.10	153.72
Direct Government loans,SMEs	EUR million														85.1	10	3.79
Non-performing loans, total	% of all business loans	0.61	3.71	8.76	8.53	5.91	3.79	2.01	1.97	1.56	1.62	1.35	0.81	0.70	0.59	0.29	0.23
Non-performing loans, SMEs	% of all SME loans	0.95	3.59	7.36	8.17	6.31	5.18	3.27	2.96	2.79	2.88	1.94	1.99	2.19	2.09	0.84	0.56
Interest rate, SMEs	%	6.11	6.71	5.34	5.06	4.92	4.02	3.41	3.36	3.04	2.96	2.99	3.28	3.85	4.08	3.75	4.08
Interest rate, large firms	%	5.68	6.13	4.21	3.90	3.76	3.05	2.86	2.68	2.05	2.08	2.12	2.13	2.56	2.77	2.81	3.44
Interest rate spread	% points	0.43	0.58	1.14	1.16	1.16	0.98	0.56	0.68	0.99	0.88	0.87	1.15	1.29	1.31	0.93	0.65
Non-bank finance																	
Venture and growth capital	EUR million	..	4.74	4.51	17.8	5.53	16.6	10.9	68.7	96. 6	105.7	272.6	329	364	453	962	1302
Venture and growth capital (growth rate)	%, Year-on-year growth rate	..	..	- 5.00	293.7	- 68.8	200.2	- 34.3	530	40.6	9.4	157.9	19.3	-19	71.9	112.48	35.38
Leasing and hire purchases	EUR million	891.2	709.6	222.8	281.3	519.4	649.6	545.7	537.2	543	676	718	811	729	545	775	805
Factoring and invoicing	EUR billion	1.29	1.41	0.99	0.91	1.13	1.92	1.98	2.09	2.239	2.09	2.29	3 034	3451	2582	2989	3756
Other indicators																	
Payment delays, B2B	Number of days	9	8.1	12.7	12.8	10.2	10.1	9.4	7	6.9	6	5.5	..	6.4	..	...	..
Bankruptcies, SMEs	Number	202	423	1055	1028	623	495	459	428	376	335	343	273	271	341	103	98
Bankruptcies, SMEs (growth rate)	%, Year-on-year growth rate	..	109.4	149.4	- 2.56	- 39.4	- 20.5	- 7.27	- 6.75	- 12.1	- 10.9	2.39	-20.4	-1	25.8	-69.79	-4.85

The full country profile is available at: https://doi.org/10.1787/fa521246-en.

13. Finland

Key facts on SME financing

The Finnish economy had seen five years of continuous growth before the COVID-19 pandemic. The COVID-19 pandemic and the uncertainty in the global economy resulted in a recession in Finland as GDP declined 2.9% in 2020. The growth rate has gradually recovered since, at 3.0% in 2021 and 2.1% in 2022.

Due to the economic downturn caused by the pandemic, the Finnish Government supported companies in 2021 with EUR one billion in direct support (grants), a loan scheme of EUR 258 million and a guarantee scheme of EUR 301 million. Of all direct support paid due to the COVID-19 pandemic, 71% went to service sectors. By size category, EUR 297 million of support was paid to micro-enterprises, EUR 524 million to small enterprises, EUR 138 million to medium-sized enterprises and EUR 41 million to large enterprises. A total of 37,921 companies received some type of support due to the pandemic in the year 2021.

A total of 57,970 companies received COVID-19 subsidies in 2020 and 2021, to which EUR 2,278.9 million were paid, i.e. approximately 39,300 euros per recipient. There were a total of 59 016 companies that received some kind of COVID-19 support in 2020 and 2021 (including loans and guarantees). If we add to this figure the non-employers, the number of companies that received some kind of COVID-19 support comes to about 106,100 companies.

For the first months of 2022, the outlook for SMEs had clearly improved after the pandemic, and economic expectations rose strongly. However, the situation changed rapidly as, following Russia's invasion of Ukraine, the prospects for investment and private consumption weakened due to prolonged and accelerated price increases, decreases in foreign trade, and increased uncertainty. The exceptional situation is directly reflected in the outlook for small and medium-sized enterprises for short-term economic development. As a result, expectations fell sharply.

SMEs are expected to significantly reduce their investments in the near future. With the exception of manufacturing, in all main industries, there is a larger share of companies reducing rather than increasing their investments. The weak development of investment expectations is linked to the exceptionally high uncertainty about the continuation of the war, the rise in interest rates and the rate of economic growth. Even though GDP growth was 2.1% in 2022, the growth rate was 3.0% in 2021.

The outstanding business loans reached a record-high level in 2022 (in total EUR 100 billion). The new business lending was also a record-high, totalling EUR 45 billion. The volume of new lending to SMEs, however, decreased in 2022 in comparison to the years 2016 – 2020. The SMEs received around EUR 8 billion in new loans in year 2022 (the figure was EUR 9.8 billion in 2020 and EUR 8.1 billion in 2021). The share of new SME lending was 17.9%, the lowest level since year 2010 (15.6%).

The average interest rate for SMEs was 3.17% in 2022 (2.02% in 2020). The average interest rate charged from large companies was instead 1.88% in 2022, in comparison to 1.19% in 2021. The interest rate for large companies was at higher level last time in 2014 (1.96%). The credit spread between small and large business loans indicates a tightening of credit terms for SMEs compared to large enterprises. The interest rate spread was 1.29% in 2022, 0.94% in 2021 while it was 0.66% in 2020.

The structure of corporate finance is changing very slowly. Bank-centricity is still common in the financing of SMEs, although it has decreased. Public actors like Business Finland and ELY centers have maintained their position as the most important options for bank loans together with Finnvera. Especially, growth-oriented companies applied for funding from Business Finland and venture capitalists (SME-barometer 2/2022[1]).pl

Average B2B payment delays surged to 17 days in 2020. There was a significant increase in payment delays following the COVID-19 pandemic and during the economic downturn in Finland. Since the harsh first COVID year of 2020 the situation has improved significantly, with payment delays falling to 10 days in 2022. However, payment periods are still twice as long as they were in 2015 -2018.

The number of bankruptcies decreased markedly by 19% in 2020 from the previous year. Part of the decline is explained by the temporary amendment of the bankruptcy law (1 May 2020), which prevented bankruptcies of those enterprises whose financial difficulties would most likely be temporary due to the COVID-19 pandemic restrictions. In 2022, the number of bankruptcies has returned to the pre- COVID-19 pandemic level, totalling 2 666.

Finnish startups have once again raised a record amount of funding. The amount invested increased by almost half a billion from the previous year, totalling EUR 1.8 billion in 2022. The amount of funding raised by Finnish startups has increased tenfold in the last ten years. There have been especially great leaps in the last four years, and the long-term development has also been positive.

Table 13.1. Scoreboard for Finland

Indicator	Unit	2007	2008	2009	2010	2011	2012	2013	2014	2015	2016	2017	2018	2019	2020	2021	2022
									Debt								
Outstanding business loans, total	EUR billion	48.4	57.6	54.1	56.5	60.4	63.3	66.7	68.4	72.5	76.0	79.3	85.3	91.0	96.9	94.1	100.1
New business lending, total	EUR billion	42.7	54.4	50.9	54.4	37.4	34.9	39.5	35.5	34.6	35.9	36.4	35.2	35.6	41.4	40.3	45.2
New business lending, SMEs	EUR billion	11.6	11.9	9.9	8.3	7.9	7.7	7.3	6.7	8.1	8.6	8.9	9.1	8.7	9.7	8.08	8.09
Share of new SME lending	% of total new lending	27.11	21.85	19.56	15.25	21.11	22.23	18.55	18.99	23.37	23.87	24.54	25.85	24.39	23.63	20.06	17.9
Short-term loans, SMEs	EUR million	..	..	..	839	1615	1613	1312	1149	1301	1361	1374	1359	1124	1414	1117	1383
Long-term loans, SMEs	EUR million	..	..	..	3 314	6 287	6136	6018	5583	6789	7219	7561	7747	7566	8249	6971	6710
Share of short-term SME lending	% of total SME lending	..	..	..	20.20	20.44	20.82	17.90	17.07	16.08	15.86	15.38	14.92	12.93	14.63	13.81	17.09
Government loan guarantees, SMEs	EUR million	389	414	426	393	450	383	351	440	496	563	535	549	598	1100	839	702
Direct government loans, SMEs	EUR million	371	453	521	378	358	283	274	283	351	259	224	194	183	105	148	119
Non-performing loans, total	% of all business loans	..	..	..	..	..	..	..	..	1.96	1.47	1.27	3.72	3.75	3.91	2.08	1.79
Non-performing loans, total (amount)	EUR million	..	..	..	..	..	..	..	..	1 423	1 119	994	3 170	3416	3785	1955	1788
Interest rate, SMEs	%	5.39	5.58	3.02	2.66	3.23	2.86	2.81	2.74	2.39	2.23	2.14	2.21	2.13	2.02	2.13	3.17
Interest rate, large firms	%	4.83	5.08	2.24	1.93	2.59	2.07	1.91	1.92	1.46	1.33	1.35	1.24	1.33	1.33	1.19	1.88
Interest rate spread	% points	0.56	0.50	0.78	0.73	0.64	0.79	0.90	0.82	0.93	0.90	0.79	0.97	0.80	0.66	0.94	1.29

Collateral, SMEs	% of SMEs needing collateral to obtain bank lending	..	..	..	33	34	36	42	41	38	36	33	31	30	30	37	41
Percentage of SME loan applications	SME loan applications/ total number of SMEs	..	..	13.85	18.42	20.79	21.50	21.85	27.70	21.97	23.89	19.99	20.35	21.31	18.96	20.75	18.7
Rejection rate	1-(SME loans authorised/ requested)	..	..	6.98	4.92	3.12	8.08	7.06	6.71	6.24	5.59	6.76	4.15	6.11	8.74	7.77	8.46
Non-bank finance																	
Venture and growth capital	EUR million	189	218	146	351	148	185	173	168	190	219	203	338	678	714	1034	1186
Venture and growth capital (growth rate)	%, year-on-year growth rate	..	15.34	-33.0	140.4	-57.8	25.0	-6.49	-2.89	13.10	15.26	-7.31	66.50	70.35	5.31	44.82	14.7
Leasing and hire purchases	EUR million	..	..	1 067	1 361	1 658	1 765	1 658	1 858	..	..	..	..	..	..	..	..
Other indicators																	
Payment delays, B2B	Number of days	6	5	7	7	7	7	6	6	5	5	5	5	2	17	11	10
Bankruptcies, SMEs	Number	2 254	2 612	3 275	2 864	2 947	2 961	3 131	2 986	2 574	2 408	2 168	2 546	2623	2135	2473	2656
Bankruptcies, SMEs (growth rate)	%, year-on-year growth rate	..	15.9	25.4	-12.5	2.9	0.5	5.7	-4.6	-13.8	-6.4	-9.97	17.44	3.02	-18.6	15.8	7.39

Note

1. The SME Barometer is published twice a year by the Federation of Finnish Enterprises, Finnvera and the Ministry of Economic Affairs and Employment.

The full country profile is available at: https://doi.org/10.1787/fa521246-en.

14. France

Key facts on SME financing

France has approximately 4.2 million small and medium-sized enterprises (SMEs), which account for 99.9% of the total business population. The total number of firms has increased by 7.7% between 2020 and 2022.

The stock of outstanding business loans to SMEs soared in 2020 by 28%, partly due to the Government loan guarantees scheme as a response to the pandemic crisis. The stock of outstanding business loans to SMEs stabilised at 348 558 million in 2022, an increase of 32% relative to 2019. As a result, the share of SME outstanding loans in total business loans has risen slightly, exceeding the pre-crisis average by 1.3 percentage points.

In recent years, SME demand for short-term loans has fluctuated significantly. The pandemic crisis fuelled SME demand for short-term credit with the stock of SMEs short-term outstanding loans increasing by 125% year on year in 2020 and the share of SME short-term loans in total business loans rising by 72%. The trend shifted in 2021 as SMEs started repaying their short-term loans. By 2022, the share of SME short-term loans dropped to 9.3% due to SMEs' preference for long-term credit.

Interest rates for SMEs and large companies increased in 2021 and 2022 after a major drop in 2020, but stabilised in 2022 above the pre-crisis level. The interest rate gap between SMEs and large companies widened in 2022. Access to financing for SMEs has become slightly more difficult, as indicated by the rising rejection rate exceeding pre-crisis levels.

In 2022, private equity investments declined by 9%, following an exceptional year in 2021. Nonetheless, the number of companies funded through private equity rose significantly, marking a 14.5% increase compared to 2021 and exceeding the average level observed between 2012 and 2021. Investments in venture and growth capital (EUR 5.1 billion invested, +11% vs. 2021) and expansion capital (EUR 5.4 billion invested, +3% vs. 2021) are on the rise. The sub-total of venture capital, growth capital and expansion capital investments has grown 4.4 times in 10 years.

Crowdfunding continues to grow, despite macro-economic, geopolitical and health-related turbulence. Since 2015, the annual volume of equity crowdfunding provided through the platforms grew by a multiple of 14. Crowdfunding platforms benefit from a specific regulatory framework since 2014 which enables them to operate without a minimum amount of equity.

Factoring volumes increased by 15.5% in 2022, as did the number of ongoing operations (+ 7.9%). Activity development has been important since the pandemic crisis, with a 30% increase of volumes compared to 2020.

The plan *France 2030* seeks to position France as a leader in innovation in key sectors. Following a decrease in investments in 2020, it recovered in 2021. Investments in digital, healthcare and consumer goods account for 73% of total investment.

In 2020, the French government initiated a EUR 100 billion recovery plan ('France Relance'). Stemming from COVID-19 crisis responses, this plan, grounded in three pillars (environment, competitiveness, and cohesion), seeks to overhaul the economy and generate new employment opportunities. Additionally, the French government has introduced measures to address inflation and high energy costs, including energy assistance programmes such as capping electricity prices.

The financial stability of French companies was impacted by both the COVID-19 crisis and the rise in gas and electricity prices. Strengthening the balance sheet was a critical concern to safeguard the investment capacity of SMEs and mitigate the risk of insolvency. Credit mediation and loan programmes remained crucial in supporting SMEs.

Table 14.1. Scoreboard for France

Indicator	Unit	2010	2011	2012	2013	2014	2015	2016	2017	2018	2019	2020	2021	2022
Debt														
Outstanding business loans, SMEs	EUR Billion	199 413	209 955	213 698	216 199	219 231	224 487	232 926	243 431	253 324	263 367	336 197	337 906	348 558
Outstanding business loans, total	EUR Billion	974 427	1 012 699	1 010 201	1 026 553	1 037 246	1 080 039	1 131 846	1 196 423	1 263 254	1 342 067	1 514 613	1 541 624	1 666 273
Share of SME outstanding loans	% of total outstanding business loans	20.5	20.7	21.2	21.1	21.1	20.8	20.6	20.3	20.1	19.6	22.2	21.9	20.9
New business lending, total	EUR Billion	9 052	34 600	7 752	1 565	18 942	35 009	43 799	56 141	58 737	51 560	141 309	43 683	91 896
Outstanding short-term loans, SMEs	EUR Billion	38 066	40 268	41 045	42 738	43 219	43 444	43 805	44 640	44 776	44 351	99 496	57 444	28 560
Outstanding long-term loans, SMEs	EUR Billion	134 211	142 457	146 236	146 049	148 620	152 314	158 883	166 645	175 189	184 879	198 717	243 500	279 925
Share of short-term SME lending	% of total SME lending	22.1	22.0	21.9	22.6	22.5	22.2	21.6	21.1	20.4	19.3	33.4	19.1	9.3
Government loan guarantees, SMEs	EUR Billion	5 326	4 231	4 157	4 394	4 783	4 984	5 229	5 103	5 095	4 805	5 873	5 315	6 366
Government guaranteed loans, SMEs	EUR Billion	11 883	9 826	8 465	8 925	7 800	8 000	8 400	8 900	8 700	8 500	116 800	21 000	13 810
Non-performing loans, total	% of all business loans	4.6	4.0	4.1	4.3	4.1	4.0	3.9	3.6	3.3	2.5	2.2	1.9	1.8
Interest rate, SMEs	%	2.5	3.1	2.4	2.2	2.1	1.8	1.5	1.4	1.5	1.4	1.0	1.3	1.9
Interest rate, large firms	%	1.6	2.2	1.7	1.5	1.3	1.2	1.1	1.1	1.0	0.9	0.7	1.1	1.3
Interest rate spread	% points	0.9	0.9	0.7	0.7	0.8	0.6	0.4	0.3	0.4	0.5	0.3	0.2	0.6
Collateral, SMEs	% of SMEs needing collateral to obtain bank lending			94	8.5	7.3	6.3	5.2	4.3	4.2	3.8	3.6	2.8	4.8

Percentage of SME loan applications	SME loan applications/ total number of SMEs			38.4	35.6	35.7	37.9	37.9	37.2	36.7	36.3	39.3	31.7	33.4
Rejection rate	1-(SME loans authorised/ requested)			11.12	8.00	6.61	7.55	6.21	5.14	4.36	2.55	2.38	4.18	8.91
Utilisation rate	SME loans used/ authorised	86.4	87.0	87.6	87.3	87.5	87.2	87.0	86.8	86.8	87.0	88.7	89.1	88.5

The full country profile is available at: https://doi.org/10.1787/fa521246-en.

15. Georgia

Key facts on SME financing

As of June 2023, 99.7% of active enterprises in Georgia were SMEs[1]. In 2022 SMEs accounted for 60.1% of business sector employment, 34.5% of business sector turnover and 51.4% of output in the business sector.

In recent years, credit to SMEs rose significantly, amounting to a staggering 412.5% increase from GEL 1 400 million in 2010 to GEL 7 174 million in 2022.[2] Throughout this period, total business loans grew by more than 261%, and the proportion of SME loans as a percentage of total business loans grew from 33.8% to 48%. In 2021 and 2022, credit to SMEs increased by 15.2% and 7.5%, while total business loans increased by 11.1% in 2021 and decreased by 0.1% in 2022. Accordingly, the share of SME loans in business loans increased to 44.53% in 2021 and to 47.94% in 2022.

The average interest rate charged to SMEs in Georgia is high by OECD standards, but it has significantly declined over the last decade, from 17.5% in 2010 to 9.3% in 2020. Because of financial tightening interest rates rose to 9.9% in 2021 and 11% in 2022. Also from 2018, the interest rate spread has shown a declining trend. The interest rate spread was 0.76 percentage points in 2021 and 0.14 percentage points in 2022.

In 2022, the overall volume of non-performing SME loans amounted to GEL 659 million (a decrease of 12% with respect to 2021). Despite a significant decrease in non-performing loans, the amount is still higher than it was before the pandemic. The share of non-performing SMEs loans is now at 5.3% (1.2 p.p. decrease from the last year).

The government of Georgia has prioritised SME development as the main source of private sector growth, job creation and innovation. For instance, the Innovation and Entrepreneurship Policy is one of the successful reforms the Georgian Government has conducted. Through budgetary support, in 2014, the Ministry of Economy and Sustainable Development of Georgia established two sister agencies, Georgia's Innovation and Technology Agency (GITA) and Enterprise Georgia, with the main objective of promoting SME development and strengthening SME competitiveness. Both agencies provide financial support to SMEs, as well as a broader range of services that includes access to special infrastructure, mentoring, training and various advisory services. In addition to the establishment of these two agencies, the Government of Georgia has introduced several private sector development programmes, which include financial and technical assistance components to support SMEs at different stages of development.

Table 15.1. Scoreboard for Georgia

Indicators	Units	2009	2010	2011	2012	2013	2014	2015	2016	2017	2018	2019	2020	2021	2022
Debt															
Business loans, SME	GEL million	..	1 400	1 548	1 738	2 051	2 422	3 621	3 992	5 176	6 620	8 121	9 987	11 501	12 364
Business loans, total	GEL million	3 097	4 145	4 821	5 344	6 080	7 268	9 575	10 500	12 000	14 687	19 070	23 042	25 828	25 791
Business loans, SMEs	% of total business loans	..	33.8%	32%	32%	33.7%	33.3%	38%	38%	43.1%	45.1%	42.6%	43.0%	44.5%	47.9%
Non-Performing Loans, total	GEL million	926	784	666	810	791	988	1 202	1 380	1 337	1 480	1 414	3 203	2 255	1 838
Non-performing loans, SMEs	GEL million	..	145	134	111	102	101	161	206	221	407	400	974	749	659
Non-performing loans, total	% of all business loans	..	16.1%	11%	12%	10.7%	10.6%	9.8%	10.1%	7.7%	6.6%	4.9%	8.4%	5.2%	4.1%
Non-performing loans, SMEs	% of total SME loans	..	10.3%	8.7%	6.4%	5.0%	4.2%	4.4%	5.2%	4.3%	6.1%	4.9%	9.8%	6.5%	5.3%
Interest rate, SME	%	..	17.5%	16%	15%	12.9%	11.6%	13%	10.2%	10.4%	10.5%	9.9%	9.3%	9.9%	11%
Interest rate, large firms	%	..	14.9%	15%	13%	11.4%	10.2%	10%	9.6%	9.3%	9.3%	8.7%	8.4%	9.1%	10.8%
Interest rate spread		..	2.6%	1.0%	2.3%	1.5%	1.4%	2.4%	0.6%	1.0%	1.2%	1.2%	0.9%	0.9%	0.8%
Collateral, SMEs	%	..	..	..	..	95.6	..	..	..	..	..	..	..	..	..
Rejection rate	%	..	..	..	..	4.6	..	..	..	..	..	..	..	..	..
Utilization rate	%	..	..	..	..	95.4	..	..	..	..	..	..	..	..	..
Other indicators															
Procedures of enterprises' liquidation (incl. bankruptcy)	Number	52	2 094	3 176	2 524	1 775	1 785	1 560	229	293	153	208	147	..	..
Procedures of enterprises' liquidation (incl. bankruptcy)	Year-on-year growth rate (%)	-14.75	3 927	51.67	-20.5	-29.68	0.56	-12.6	-85.3	28	-47.78	35.95	-29.33	..	..

Notes

1. According to the methodology introduced by the Georgian National Statistics Office in 2016 to gather statistics on the country's SMEs and in pursuant of the National Strategy of SME development.

2. Figures are inflation-adjusted, with 2010 as the base year.

The full country profile is available at: https://doi.org/10.1787/fa521246-en.

16. Germany

Policy developments

German SMEs have felt the burden of the pandemic, but generally they have come through the crisis years with few bruises. Rapid adjustments to business models and, above all, strong growth in digital sales of products and services have often proved to be lifesaver and prevented worse outcomes (KfW, 2021[4]).

Despite all the coronavirus worries, 2021 was a very good year for SMEs. Seemingly unimpressed by the pandemic, sales and employment returned and employment returned to pre-crisis levels.

At the start of 2022, businesses confronted the current crisis on a solid foundation (KfW, 2022[5]). Even as the burdens from the pandemic are easing, the economic situation has worsened as a consequence of Russia's war of aggression against Ukraine. The escalation of the conflict has led to enormous uncertainty.

The impact of the war, in combination with directly and indirectly perceivable consequences of sanctions (such as loss of export markets, energy price increases, rising inflation, supply chain disruptions and production losses), has been afflicting many businesses (KfW, 2022[5]). Despite all stress factors, the damage to SMEs is still moderate.

However, the economic outlook for 2024 is muted, prospects for investment and turnover are dim and, not least, businesses are feeling the implications of tighter monetary policy (KfW, 2023[6]).

It became apparent already at the end of the last year that the situation in the credit market was becoming more difficult for businesses. They reported that banks were taking an increasingly restrictive position in loan negotiations (KfW, 2023[6]).

To some extent, this reflects the now higher interest rate environment, which companies might perceive as more restrictive lending. But banks are also applying more conservative lending criteria, reflecting the current economic uncertainty. There is, however, no sign of a credit crunch, and banks have sufficient surplus capital and enough lending capacity to finance German SMEs.

The task now is to support SMEs in the transformation to more sustainability and climate protection, which requires massive investments in the decarbonisation of our economy. For this purpose, the differentiated range of funding from the ERP Special Fund is available and is constantly being further developed.

Programmes

Credit-based financing for start-ups, succession, growth, innovation and digitalisation in the sustainable transformation

The ERP Special Fund [ERP: European Recovery Program] provides a differentiated and well-established system of promotional loan instruments for different start-up phases. The KfW promotional loans have been established on the market for several decades and are available with attractive conditions for financing investments, including investments in climate-neutral and digital transformation. The German government supports SMEs with its credit-based ERP funding instruments, which are open to all business sectors. These programmes are passed on to the final borrowers by the Kreditanstalt für Wiederaufbau (KfW), the Federal Promotional Bank, via the house banks (private banks, cooperative banks savings banks). Various programmes cover the investment and working capital needs of newly established and established SMEs (up to 500 million euros turnover).

In order to provide SMEs with the best possible support in the period after the Corona pandemic and in the transformation to a sustainable and digital economy, the promotional programmes for small and medium-sized enterprises were restructured at the beginning of 2022:

The ERP Start-Up Loan-StartGeld (ERP-Gründerkredit-StartGeld) is available for start-ups, freelancers and small businesses that have been active on the market for less than five years and require little start-up capital.

Small and medium-sized enterprises ERP-SME-Promotional-Loan (ERP-Förderkredit KMU) and larger SMEs KfW-Promotional-Loan-For-Large-Mid-Sized Companies (KfW-Förderkredit großer Mittelstand) now each have their own promotional programme for financing projects as well as start-ups and company takeovers. The improved conditions of the ERP and KfW promotional loan programmes allow SMEs to finance their projects at favourable and attractive conditions. Young enterprises and those in regional assisted areas continue to receive particularly strong support.

For companies affected by Russia's attack on Ukraine or the sanctions against Russia and Belarus, the KfW Special Programme UBR (Ukraine, Belarus, Russia) 2022 (KfW-Sonderprogramm UBR) 2022 was available until 31 December 2023.

Innovation and digitization support in Germany include the ERP-Digitisation-and-Innovation-Loan (ERP-Digitalisierungs- und Innovationskredit) and the ERP-Mezzanine for Innovation (ERP-Mezzanine für Innovationen).

The KfW-Loan-for-Growth[1] (KfW-Kredit für Wachstum), which supports larger projects in the area of innovation and digitalisation, including investments and working capital.

The KfW-Syndicated-Loan-Sustainable-Transformation (KfW-Konsortialkredit Nachhaltige Transformation) offers larger companies flexible financing for ambitious, sustainable and transformative measures that meet the technical criteria of the EU taxonomy.

Equity and venture capital financing

INVEST grant for venture capital

INVEST is a funding programme of the Federal Ministry for Economic Affairs and Climate protection. It was launched in 2013 and further developed in 2017 and 2023 to support private investors who want to invest in young and innovative companies. Under this programme, business angels who invest in innovative start-ups receive an acquisition grant of 25% of the investment amount. The investor must provide at least EUR 10 000 to the company. A maximum of EUR 100 000 in acquisition grants is approved per investor. In addition, natural persons can receive a lump-sum tax compensation with the exit grant amounting to 25 % of the profit made from the sale of his/her shares supported with the acquisition grant. The exit grant is limited to 25% of the investment amount of the INVEST shares, and the shares must be held for at least three years.

KfW Capital

As 100% subsidiary of KfW Group, KfW Capital invests in German and European venture capital and venture debt funds since its establishment in October 2018, thereby strengthening the funds' capital base. The aim of KfW Capital is to improve access to capital for innovative technology-oriented growth companies in Germany through financially strong funds. KfW Capital has doubled the annual amount of funding to EUR 400 million from 2021 onwards. Funding takes place particularly as part of the ERP-VC Fund Investments programme as well as of the ERP/Future Fund Growth Facility as a module of the 'Zukunftsfonds' (Future Fund).

ERP-Financing-Instruments in cooperation with the European Investment Fund (EIF)

ERP Special Fund and EIF have been cooperating very successfully in the field of equity and mezzanine financing for nearly twenty years. This makes an important contribution to ensuring that innovative start-ups in Germany have access to capital. The financing instruments include, amongst others, the ERP/EIF Venture Capital Fund of Funds with a total fund volume of EUR 3.7 billion.

Zukunftsfonds (Future Fund)

The 'Zukunftsfonds', set up by the Federal Government in 2021, is providing EUR 10 billion until the end of 2030 for a venture capital fund for forward-looking technologies ('Future Fund') at the KfW to foster the German venture capital market. Factoring in the contributions from private together with public-sector partners, the Future Fund, with financial contributions from the ERP Special Fund, aims to mobilise at least EUR 30 billion in start-up funding. The overarching principle of the Future Fund is to broaden the German VC market, requiring a substantial private-sector investment contribution, also for the sake of market principles and in compliance with European competition and state aid rules. The new fund addresses various development phases of start-up financing – with a special focus on start-ups going through the capital-intensive scale-up phase – with a set of closely interlinked modules, comprising both a qualitative and quantitative expansion of existing instruments as well as the development of new modules to increase start-up funding. Within the Future Fund, the ERP/Future Fund Growth Facility, with a total of EUR 2.5 billion, as well as the GFF-EIF Growth Facility, with a volume of up to EUR 3.5 billion, increase fund volumes and facilitate larger financing rounds for the period up to 2030. In 2023 the European Tech Champions Initiative has been launched with a total fund size of up to EUR 3.75 billion to tackle the European scale-up gap; Germany is contributing EUR 1 billion alongside the EIB-Group and several contribution Member States. A fund of funds for growth capital (Growth Fund for Germany) aims in particular to mobilise capital of institutional investors for start-ups. The KfW programme Venture Tech Growth Financing (VTGF) was expanded in 2022 with a volume of up to EUR 1.3 billion to strengthen the area of venture debt in Germany. The DeepTech & Climate Fund (up to EUR 1 billion) directly invests into deep tech and climate tech start-ups together with private investors. Since 2023 it has invested in several start-ups.

With the launch of the EUR 1 billion fund-of-funds "Wachstumsfonds Deutschland", a key module of the Future Fund to provide institutional investors with attractive investment opportunities in the Venture Capital asset class has been realized. It is funded primarily by private resources. Besides the Federal Government and KfW Capital as anchor investors, the fund has more than 20 major institutional investors including insurers, superannuation funds, foundations, asset managers and large family offices. The Wachstumsfonds Deutschland invests in German and international VC funds. This will significantly improve access to urgently needed growth capital for start-ups and innovative technology firms while strengthening Europe and Germany as an innovation location.

Further instruments and components of the Future Fund have been implemented throughout the year 2023, e.g. improving the access to venture capital for female founders and investors with the Emerging Manager Facility. Under this programme, KfW Capital is investing in smaller private venture capital (VC) funds managed by women or gender-diverse teams. These teams are often very young first-time entrants to the VC market ("emerging managers". Overall, EUR 200 million is available from the Future Fund for the new programme until 2030.

Furthermore, HTGF Growth Facility with a volume of EUR 660 million will be launched as a co-investment fund to provide additional growth capital to particularly promising companies in the investment portfolio of the HTGF Seed Funds (HTGF I to IV), and RegioInnoGrowth will address start-ups and SMEs which are typically not addressed by venture capital funds.

High-Tech Gründerfonds (HTGF)

The High-Tech Gründerfonds (HTGF) is an early-phase funding programme for highly innovative and technology-oriented companies whose operative business activities started less than three years ago. To be eligible for financing, projects must have shown promising research findings, be based on innovative technology, and the market situation for the product must be bright. In addition to providing capital, the fund ensures that the management of young start-ups receives the necessary help and support. An initial funding amount of up to EUR 1 million is provided, with a total of up to EUR 4 million usually being available per company. In February 2023 the fourth fund, HTGF IV, with a volume of EUR 493.8 million was closed.

Mikromezzaninfonds # Micro-Mezzanine Fund

The Micro-Mezzanine Fund was launched in 2013 and provides dormant equity of up to EUR 50 000 for small companies and business starters and of up to EUR 150 000 for companies within the special target group. The fund's special target group are companies that provide training, are operated by women or people with a migrant background, or were founded by persons who were formerly unemployed. Social enterprises operating commercially are also eligible to apply for financing on the terms of the special target group, as are companies with a focus on environmentally-compatible production.

Note

1.This programme is to be renamed "KfW -Syndicated-Loan-Innovation and Digitalisation" in the near future.

The full country profile is available at: https://doi.org/10.1787/fa521246-en.

17. Greece

Key facts on SME financing

During 2021 and 2022, economic activity rebounded significantly, covering most of the lost ground from the pandemic shock. Real GDP increased by 8.4% in 2021 after shrinking by around 9% in 2020. This strong growth trend continued in 2022 during which real GDP grew by 5.9%. This is mainly due to private consumption, a significant increase in investments and the recovery of tourism. The uptick in investments in 2022 is related to a significant increase in new business lending, which almost doubled in 2022 after a decade of relatively low volume and a decrease of 26.8% in 2021 vis-à-vis 2020. Still, new lending to SMEs grew proportionally less, by 35%, compared to an impressive 87% increase in new loans for all firms' sizes. As a result, the share of SMEs in new loans dropped to 20.5%, down from 28.3% in 2021.

However, despite the economic recovery and the increase in new lending, outstanding credit to all businesses in 2022 remains below the level of 2020. Nonetheless, in 2020 the decline in the outstanding stock of SME loans was driven by a significant removal of non-performing loans (NPLs) from Greek banks' balance sheets (from 36.1% of total loans in 2019 to 28.5% of total loans in 2020) through the introduction in late 2019 of the "Hercules" asset-protection scheme.

As a result of ECB monetary policy tightening, interest rates for both SMEs and large firms increased in 2022, after a downward trend that lasted for nine years. Interest rates climbed to 4.28% for large firms and to 3.23% for SMEs. The spread between the two decreased marginally by 0.05 but remains above 1% for the third year in a row.

Credit conditions tightened significantly, and access to finance continues to be a central problem for Greek SMEs, according to the most recent ECB Survey on Access to Finance of Enterprises (SAFE), which documents increased collateral requirements for more firms and an increase in loan rejection rate for Greek SMEs in 2022.

The percentage of SME non-performing loans was 9.18% in 2022 and has declined for the eighth year in a row since 2016 when it reached 43.2%. This decline is explained by public programmes such as the Hercules Programme that assists commercial banks in securitising and removing NPLs from their balance sheets. Accordingly, 5.63% of all business loans were non-performing in Greece in 2022.

In 2022, alternative sources of finance were in a small decline in Greece and remained at low volumes in general. Venture capital financing amounted to EUR 325 million, which represented a decrease of 35% compared to 2021. It should be noted though, that 2021 was an exceptional year with EUR 500 million of total volume in funding, and that the equity finance ecosystem in Greece exhibits a general growth trend since it started from a relative low volume. This positive trend is evident if we take in to account the 2020 funding volume, which was merely EUR 150 million, but nevertheless constitutes a quadrupling from the 2016 volume of EUR 38 million. Factoring increased significantly to EUR 2.98 billion compared to EUR 2.37 billion in 2021. Leasing and hire purchase activities increased slightly, reaching EUR 2.7 billion compared to EUR 2.5 billion in 2017.

As a response to the COVID-19 pandemic, the Greek government put in place several measures to tackle the impact of the crisis on SMEs. One of the measures in place was the "COVID-19 Guarantee Fund".

During the first cycle, the guarantee rate was set at 80% per loan, while the maximum guarantee was set at 40% for a loan portfolio to SMEs and 30% for a loan portfolio to large companies, while at the third cycle the cap rate for micro enterprises loan portfolio was set at 60%. The total Fund resources reached EUR 2 million. In the second cycle of the Fund the provision of the guarantee paid by the companies is fully subsidised. 75% to 90% of the new loans of the second cycle of the Guarantee Fund are addressed with priority to MSMEs. As a result, the Fund reached an amortised amount of EUR 6.4 million by the end of 2022, during an operation period of two years.

Table 17.1. Scoreboard for Greece

Indicator	Unit	2007	2008	2009	2010	2011	2012	2013	2014	2015	2016	2017	2018	2019	2020	2021	2022
Debt																	
Outstanding business loans, SMEs	EUR billion	..	..	..	44.9	41.6	39.1	48.1	48.1	46.9	48.4	44.7	41.1	35.2	32.0	25.5	..
Outstanding business loans, total	EUR billion	102	124	124	117	113	101	97	95	89	88	82	76.4	67.3	66.6	57.9	64
Share of SME outstanding loans	% of total outstanding business loans	..	..	..	38.5	36.8	38.8	49.7	50.6	52.6	55.3	54.4	53.8	52.3	48.1	43.99	..
New business lending, total	EUR billion	..	36.5	36.3	20.7	29.4	21.8	24.3	14.9	6.9	5.8	7.3	11.4	7.9	16.2	11.85	22.19
New business lending, SMEs	EUR billion	..	12.5	13.0	4.4	5.2	4.1	3.7	2.3	3.2	2.8	3.1	3.3	3.2	6.0	3.4	4.54
Share of new SME lending	% of total new lending	..	34.2	35.6	21.4	17.8	18.9	15.0	15.6	17.0	18.4	15.5	10.18	16.05	31.8	28.39	20.46
Outstanding short-term loans, SMEs	EUR billion	..	..	..	..	..	..	..	18.1	17.6	18.8	17.0	15.1	13.4	9.5	6.93	..
Outstanding long-term loans, SMEs	EUR billion	..	..	..	..	..	..	..	30.1	29.3	29.6	27.7	25.9	21.7	22.5	18.56	..
Share of short-term SME lending	% of total SME lending	..	..	..	..	..	..	..	37.6	37.6	38.9	38.0	58.4	61.6	42.3	37.37	..
Government loan guarantees, SMEs	EUR billion	..	..	..	..	..	..	0.37	0.31	0.24	0.56	1.08	1.2	1.3	3.9	3.97	4.05
Non-performing loans, total	% of all business loans	4.60	4.30	6.70	8.70	14.2	23.4	31.8	29.4	31.0	30.3	30.5	28.6	25.5	19.1	8.8	5.63
Non-performing loans, SMEs	% of all SME loans	..	..	..	..	..	..	..	41.2	44.1	43.2	42.5	38.1	36.1	28.5	16.4	9.18
Interest rate, SMEs	%	6.57	6.82	4.62	5.53	6.77	6.87	6.51	5.80	5.38	5.32	4.91	4.66	4.31	3.9	3.79	4.28
Interest rate, large firms	%	5.32	5.71	3.52	4.27	5.74	5.92	5.77	5.55	4.82	4.61	4.20	3.81	3.64	2.8	2.7	3.23
Interest rate spread	% points	1.25	1.11	1.10	1.26	1.03	0.95	0.74	0.25	0.56	0.71	0.71	0.85	0.67	1.1	1.09	1.05
Collateral, SMEs	% of SMEs needing collateral to obtain bank lending	..	..	51.4	40.5	49.4	46.7	45.9	46.2	49.2	39.8	25.7	20.7	18.5	18.4	13.72	28.5
Percentage of SME loan applications	SME loan applications/ total number of SMEs	..	..	37.9	39.6	30.8	29.9	21.4	25.5	18.8	21.5	17.5	23.0	23.9	31.3	21.93	23.23
Rejection rate	1- (SME loans authorised/ requested)	..	..	25.8	24.5	33.8	28.3	26.0	21.5	19.9	18.2	16.2	20.5	11.4	12.3	10.35	14.96

Utilisation rate	SME loans used/ authorised	..	..	..	..	..	..	..	..	..	..	..	..	..	..	..	..
Non-bank finance																	
Venture and growth capital	EUR million	19.0	32.7	16.7	25.0	10.1	..	4.8	12.6	36.8	38.0	44.5	84.1	147.1	150	500	325
Venture and growth capital (growth rate)	%, Year-on-year growth rate	..	72	-49	50	-60	..	..	160	193	3	17	88.8	74.87	1.99	233.3	-35
Leasing and hire purchases	EUR billion	7.28	7.87	7.50	7.28	6.85	6.22	3.36	4.08	4.72	4.40	4.25	3.96	3.39	3.32	2.52	2.69
Factoring and invoice discounting	EUR billion	1.28	1.73	1.77	1.73	1.49	1.53	1.41	1.69	1.69	1.72	1.74	1.93	1.96	1.89	2.37	2.98
Other indicators																	
Payment delays, B2B	Number of days	..	25	34	30	35	40	43	41	36	47	47.	33	17	..	50	36
Bankruptcies, SMEs	Number	513	359	355	355	445	415	392	330	189	108	123	114	63	57	53	..
Bankruptcies, SMEs (growth rate)	%, Year-on-year growth rate	..	-30	-1	0	25	-7	-6	-16	-43	-43	14	-7	-23.2	-9.52	-7.02	..

The full country profile is available at: https://doi.org/10.1787/fa521246-en.

18. Hungary

Key facts on SME financing

According to the preliminary data of the Hungarian Central Statistical Office, at the end of 2021, 892 106 enterprises operated in Hungary, 99,89% of which (891 137 enterprises) qualified as SMEs. Hungarian SMEs make up 75% of total employment and generated 61% of value added.

The COVID-19 pandemic in early 2020 created a protracted international crisis situation, which had an impact on the Hungarian economic ecosystem.

The rapid economic growth after the coronavirus crisis ended with a sharp downturn. In February of 2022, the large-scale aggression of Russia against Ukraine escalated in the region's vicinity, causing another crisis for the Hungarian economy. As a result of the war, SMEs have to deal with drastically increased energy costs, shortages of basic and raw materials, rising transport costs, regulatory changes, and value chain disruptions. The energy bill increased from EUR 6.8 billion to EUR 16.6 billion.

In 2022, even under such unforeseen circumstances, the level of employment activity and the dynamics of the economy were maintained. The unemployment rate fell to 3.6% compared to 6.2% in the EU. Peak employment was registered in September, with 4.7 million: people employed, which represented an increase of 60,000 people compared to the same period in the previous year and exceeds the employment level in 2019 before the outbreak of COVID.

The gross investment rate of non-financial corporations, which is the gross fixed capital formation divided by gross value added in 2021 and 2022 was between 33% and 35% respectively, which is high compared to the values of other EU member states. In 2022, a record amount of EUR 7 billion of foreign capital (FDI) flowed into the country, and it was expected to reach up to EUR 10 billion in 2023.

Despite all the negative effects that were caused by Russia's aggression against Ukraine, the energy crisis and the significant increase of inflation, not experienced for decades, the Hungarian GDP grew by 4.6% in 2022. This value equates to growth 1.2 percentage points higher than the EU average.

Growth was supported by strong performance in the construction sector, expanding retail sales and the strong performance of the majority of service sectors.

The stock of foreign direct investment capital in Hungary peaked according to the Global Innovation Index Report. The net FDI inflows in ratio of the GDP increased to 61% by the end of 2022, which is a strong value in the European Union.

The 14% annual growth rate of Hungarian banks' outstanding corporate loans was the fourth highest when compared to other EU countries. Based on preliminary data, outstanding loans to the micro, small and medium-sized enterprise segment expanded by 13% year on year, with significant continued support from the Széchenyi Card Programme (SCP). The average interest rate on market-based corporate loans was generally in line with the rise in interest rates. In 2022 the interest rate was 10.99% for SMEs and 11.18% for large firms.

A rise in demand for foreign currency loans as well as for short-term loans was seen in this period.

Central banks reacted to the high inflation caused by the war with high interest rates, which had a negative impact on corporate lending. The high interest rates dried up credit markets and justified targeted, stimulative lending by the state. The Government's Széchenyi Card Programme MAX+ and the Baross Gábor Loan Programme supported the SME sector's access to credit financing through state-subsidised loan and guarantee schemes. The state-subsidised loan schemes are typically available at an annual interest rate of 5-6%, while market loans can have interest rates of up to 20%. As part of the fight against soaring interest rates and energy prices, the Government introduced an interest freeze on retail loans, which could help more than 60 000 SMEs. The interest freeze was implemented on November 2022 until December 2023.

Overall, the data suggests a mixed picture for the private equity and venture capital market in Hungary. While there was a decline in the total number of companies receiving investments (from 255 in 2021 to 198 in 2022), there was a significant increase in the total investment amount (from EUR 174.5 million in 2021 to EUR 220.1 million in 2022). The substantial increase in total investment suggests that despite the decrease in the number of companies, there was a focus on backing high-potential companies and making larger investments. This is especially notable in the buyout category, where the investment amount increased significantly from EUR 18.129 million in 2021 to EUR 63.076 million in 2022.

The growth in start-up investments and VC-backed growth capital also indicates continued interest in supporting early-stage and scaling companies in Hungary. This suggests that investors and venture capitalists are still optimistic about the potential for growth and innovation within the start-up ecosystem. Additionally, the decrease in the number of companies receiving investments could be reflective of a more selective investment approach or consolidation within the market.

A decrease in new funds raised may indicate a potential slowdown in private equity and venture capital activity within the country. It could suggest a decrease in investor confidence or reduced interest in funding startups and growth-stage companies.

The National Capital Holding was registered in November 2022 and started its operations on 1 January 2023. It oversees the operation of the Holding's funds: the MFB Invest Zrt., the EXIM Invest Zrt. and their subsidiaries and implements new economic stimulative programmes such as the Baross Gábor Capital Programme.

Table 18.1. Scoreboard for Hungary

Indicator	Unit	2007	2008	2009	2010	2011	2012	2013	2014	2015	2016	2017	2018	2019	2020	2021	2022
					Debt												
Outstanding business loans, SMEs	HUF Billion	5 280	5 823	5 379	4 783	4 797	5 014	5 064	4 831	4 942	4 411	4 674	4 691	5 122	5 626	6 199	7 175
Outstanding business loans, total	HUF Billion	8 466	9 613	8 959	8 770	8 825	7 892	7 648	7 761	7 355	7 073	7 545	8 562	8 715	9 836	10 853	12 540
Share of SME outstanding loans	% of total outstanding business loans	62.36	60.58	60.05	54.54	54.36	63.53	66.21	62.25	67.20	62.37	59.31	54.7	58.77	57.2	57.12	57.22
New business lending, SMEs	HUF Billion	3 851	4 384	3 660	3 531	3 585	3 870	4 662	4 302	3 665	4 187	4 443	3 743	4 670	4 738	5 569	5 430
Short-term loans, SMEs	HUF Billion	2 473	2 966	2 832	2 775	2 767	3 052	2 654	2 570	2 424	2 708	2 727	2 002	2 417	2 113	2 509	2 313
Long-term loans, SMEs	HUF Billion	1 377	1 418	828	756	818	818	2 008	1 732	1 241	1 478	1 274	1 741	2 252	2 624	3 059	3 117

Share of short-term SME lending	% of total SME lending	64.23	67.66	77.37	78.59	77.18	78.86	56.93	59.75	66.14	64.69	68.16	53.48	51.77	44.61	45.06	42.60
Government loan guarantees, SMEs	HUF Billion	308.8	352.1	409.2	377.1	343.4	251.9	350.0	346.2	348.7	469.3	525.7	725.5	707.1	1 193	1 413	*1 526*
Government guaranteed loans, SMEs	HUF Billion	381.4	436.4	600.3	472.0	437.2	314.8	458.0	433.8	429.4	568.6	731.0	894.2	934.8	1 561	1 726	*1 908*
Non-performing loans, total (amount)	HUF Billion	..	..	..	832	1 155	1 272	1 124	961	697	577	526	472	334	336	355	316
Non-performing loans, total	% of all business loans	3.10	4.70	10.10	12.8	17.4	17.7	16.1	13.7	9.6	5.4	3.3	5.5	3.83	3.42	3.6	3.96
Non-performing loans, SMEs	% of all SME loans		5.40	8.90	12.8	15.9	20.5	18.6	20.7	13.7	6.3	4.4	3.5	6.18	1.39	1.14	1.6
Interest rate, SMEs	%	10.19	11.25	12.31	8.99	9.38	9.7	7.4	5.1	4.7	4.2	3.3	2.44	2.97	1.88	3.53	10.99
Interest rate, large firms	%	8.97	10.28	11.07	..	..	8.9	5.9	4.1	2.4	2.8	1.8	2.0	1.3	1.58	2.77	11.18
Interest rate spread	% points	1.22	0.97	1.24	..	..	0.80	1.50	1.00	2.30	1.40	1.50	0.44	1.67	0.30	0.76	-0.19
Collateral, SMEs	% of SMEs needing collateral to obtain bank lending	..	..	..	..	..	..	..	71	64.5	60.1	53.4	..	..	..	..	..
Rejection rate	1-(SME loans authorised/ requested)	..	..	..	..	..	..	68.8	67	84.4	74.46	53.65	77.79	82.11	67.88	7.70	72.51
Utilisation rate	SME loans used/ authorised	..	..	..	..	..	..	81.5	..	..	..	..	..	..	..	..	..
Non-bank finance																	
Venture and growth capital	HUF Billion	3.95	13.78	0.72	6.98	11.31	19.36	15.88	18.76	27.74	12.1	11.47	28.66	28.8	45.84	46.84	36.48
Venture and growth capital (growth rate)	%, Year-on-year growth rate	..	249.00	-94.8	869.72	61.96	71.22	-18	18.13	47.89	-56.5	-4.97	149.88	..	..	..	..
Leasing and hire purchases	HUF Billion	..	..	..	..	..	..	..	..	..	490. 5	483.26	538.4	677.45	734.32	749.76	845.75
Factoring and invoicing	HUF Billion	..	..	..	..	..	..	..	..	..	46.47	107.85	66.72	55.21	41.45	32.36	49.34
Other indicators																	
Payment delays, B2B	Number of days	16	19	19	15	22	20	..	17	17	4	-1	5	1	18	5	11
Bankruptcies, total	Number	153	168	212	232	279	301	376	644	488	377	322	401	370	225	228	384
Bankruptcies, total (growth rate)	%, Year-on-year growth rate	..	10.35	25.65	9.5	20.4	7.9	24.7	71.3	-24.2	-22.9	-14.4	24.34	-8	-39	1.15	69

The full country profile is available at: https://doi.org/10.1787/fa521246-en.

19. Ireland

Key facts on SME financing

SMEs accounted for 99.8% of all active enterprises in Ireland in 2021. They also accounted for 60.1% of total persons employed. Over half of all SMEs (55.9%) in the Irish business economy in 2020 were in the services sector.

Total SME bank debt has fallen from EUR 60 billion in 2010 to EUR 18.4 billion in 2022. Much of the decline can be attributed to SMEs' deleveraging real estate-related debt since the great financial crisis (GFC).

Gross new lending to core SMEs (all non-financial and non-property related sectors) was EUR 3 billion in 2022. This reflected a year-on-year increase of EUR 102 million, marking the largest year-on-year increase in almost three years. Survey data from the SME Credit Demand Survey show that SMEs in Ireland are choosing to access bank credit less. For 79% of SMEs, having sufficient internal funds was the reason for not seeking credit.

Loan approval rates are broadly unchanged, with 90% of all applications for the period April – September 2022 (excluding "still pending") either being fully or partially approved.

The interest rate on new SME loan drawdowns increased by 112 basis points over the quarter and now stands at 5.23%. Rates on new SME loans increased across all sectors over the quarter and over the year to Q4 2022.

The Government of Ireland has implemented a range of measures to assist SMEs, including primary producers, in dealing with the rising costs of energy, together with an increased inflationary environment, as a consequence of the conflict in Ukraine. In January 2023, the Ukraine Credit Guarantee Scheme worth EUR 1.2 billion was launched. This is aimed at providing low-cost working capital to SMEs, primary producers, and small mid-caps, and is available through a growing number of lenders which include banks and credit unions. In September, the EUR 500 million Growth and Sustainability Loan Scheme was launched, with the aim of providing longer-term lending. Loans under these schemes are currently available through two of the main banks, with other lenders expected to take part in the scheme. Prior to that, in July 2022, the SME Energy Efficiency Loan Scheme (EELS) was launched under the Climate Action Plan. Its purpose is to assist SMEs, including primary producers, to invest in the energy efficiency of their enterprises. This scheme will close for applications at the end of 2023. The Government introduced a Temporary Business Energy Support Scheme in 2023 to assist businesses with the increase in cost of their electricity bills. The Government also introduced the Business Users Support Scheme for Kerosene for businesses that were impacted by the increased cost of Kerosene during 2022.

Since commencement of its lending in March 2015, Ireland's national promotional bank, the Strategic Banking Corporation of Ireland (SBCI) is working closely with the Department of Enterprise, Trade and Employment, the Department of Agriculture, Food and the Marine and the Department of Finance in the design of and implementation of a number of credit-related support and investment schemes, such as;

- Credit Guarantee Scheme;

- Brexit Loan Scheme;
- Brexit Impact Loan Scheme;
- the COVID-19 Working Capital Scheme;
- the COVID-19 Credit Guarantee Scheme;
- the Future Growth Loan Scheme;
- SME Energy Efficiency Loan Scheme
- Ukraine Credit Guarantee Scheme;
- Growth and Sustainability Loan Scheme.

Currently, the last three schemes listed above are open for loan applications.

The overriding objective of these schemes is to provide flexible funding for those firms that require it. More details on these schemes are provided in the full country profile.

Credit Review was established in 2010 and continues to be crucial to assist SMEs and farm borrowers who have been refused bank credit, including an SBCI product. It helps SMEs who have had an application for credit of up to EUR 3 million declined or reduced by the participating banks, and who feel that they have a viable business proposition. This is a strictly confidential process between the business, Credit Review, and the bank.

Table 19.1. Scoreboard for Ireland

Indicator	Unit	2007	2008	2009	2010	2011	2012	2013	2014	2015	2016	2017	2018	2019	2020	2021	2022
Debt																	
Outstanding business loans, SMEs	EUR Billion	..	..	..	27.1	27.34	25.7	24.52	21.4	19.31	16.11	15.82	15.06	14.25	12.79	12.66	12.54
Outstanding business loans, total	EUR Billion	56.08	59.57	52.5	42.42	40.31	38.06	36.65	31.79	29.82	28	27.74	29.55	28.80	25.58	24.63	25.24
Share of SME outstanding loans	% of total outstanding	..	..	..	63.89	67.82	67.51	66.89	67.32	64.78	57.54	57.04	50.96	49.47	50.02	51.43	49.67
New business lending, SMEs	EUR Million	..	..	..	2 284	2 211	1 990	1 905	2 401	2 646	3 235	3 682	3 468	3618	2914	2905	3007
Outstanding short-term loans, SMEs	EUR Billion	17.26	15.02	10.93	6.05	3.81	3.06	3.02	2.39	1.79	2.03	2.52	2.45	2.52	2.43	4.78	4.36
Outstanding long-term loans, SMEs	EUR Billion	2.12	1.93	1.34	0.93	0.58	0.54	0.6	0.78	1.09	1	0.73	0.81	0.69	0.46	7.88	6.97
Share of short-term SME lending	% of total SME lending	89%	88%	89%	86%	87%	85%	83%	75%	61%	67%	77%	75%	80%	84%	38%	39%
Non-performing loans, total	% of all business loans	..	..	..	..							14	7.4	4.7	5.4	6.9	6.5
Non-performing loans, SMEs	% of all SME loans	..	..	..	..	..	41	41	27	26	18.7	22.6	11.1	6.8	8	9.8	8.1
Interest rate, SMEs	%	6.23	6.67	3.98	3.88	4.68	4.34	4.3	4.78	4.77	4.65	4.28	4.3	4.2	4.17	3.88	4.2
Interest rate, large firms	%	5.95	6.19	3.22	2.86	3.33	2.81	2.76	2.96	2.37	2.18	2.24	2.15	2.47	2.23	1.99	3.29
Interest rate spread	% points	0.28	0.5	0.76	1.03	1.36	1.54	1.6	1.8	2.63	2.25	1.98	2.21	1.75	1.94	1.89	0.91
Collateral, SMEs	% of SMEs needing collateral	..	..	..	..	..	..	..	41	40	46	41	39	42	34	42	53

Percentage of SME loan applications	SME loan applications/ total SMEs	..	..	..	..	36	39	36	31	30	23	21	20	20	18	17	17
Rejection rate	1-(SME loans authorised/ requested)	..	..	..	..	30	24	20	14	15	16	15	14	14	15	9	10
Utilisation rate	SME loans used/ authorised	..	..	..	..	..	..	81	82	84	75	75	83	76	..	..	..
Non-bank finance																	
Venture and growth capital	EUR Million	226	243	288	310	274	269	285	401	522	888	994	738	820	925	1330	1331
Venture and growth capital (growth rate)	%, Year-on-year growth rate	..	7.53	18.61	7.67	-11.5	-2	5.95	40.65	30.3	70.1	11.92	-25.7	11.1	12.8	44	0
Other indicators																	
Bankruptcies, SMEs	Number	344	613	1 245	1 386	1 410	1 317	1 119	1 007	816	642	720	543	678	492	345	462
Bankruptcies, SMEs (growth rate)	%, Year-on-year growth rate	..	78.2	103.1	11.33	1.73	-6.6	-15	-10	-19	-21.3	12.15	-24.6	24.86	-27.4	-29.9	33.91

The full country profile is available at: https://doi.org/10.1787/fa521246-en.

20. Israel

Key facts on SME financing

As of 2022, there were 660 000 businesses in Israel, 99.5% of which were SMEs (i.e., companies employing up to 100 workers). In an average year, 55 000-60 000 businesses are created and about 40 000 closed down formally, with another 5 000-10 000 becoming 'silent' businesses, waiting for economic or personal development. In 2021, 64 825 new companies were established and 40 192 were closed. Removal of government support measures might result in many enterprises shutting down in the post-crisis period. In 2022 the record was broken with 71 006 new businesses according to the Central Bureau of Statistic.

SME and entrepreneurship policies in Israel are primarily designed by the Ministry of Economy and Industry and implemented by the Israel Innovation Authority (IIA) and the Small and Medium Business Agency (SMBA). While the IIA (formerly known as the Chief Science Office) focuses on leading technology-based start-ups and SMEs, the SMBA caters to all SMEs in Israel's main economic sectors through business management training and coaching, subsidized access to finance (for example, through the national loan guarantee program) and the work of the business development centres (MAOF centres).

Table 20.1. Scoreboard for Israel

Indicator	Unit	2007	2008	2009	2010	2011	2012	2013	2014	2015	2016	2017	2018	2019	2020	2021	2022
								Debt									
Outstanding business loans, SMEs	NIS billion	169.3	171.2	161.6	173.8	177.7	187.0	186.7	211.9	244.6	259.6	266.1	281.8	273.7	280.1	314.2	344.6
Outstanding business loans, total	NIS billion	413.9	460.9	425.2	438.9	458.6	450.4	445.7	447.9	415.6	435.5	444.4	476.9	488.2	512.36	591.9	696.9
Share of SME outstanding loans	% of total outstanding business loans	40.9	37.14	38.01	39.6	38.75	41.52	41.89	47.31	58.86	59.61	59.88	59.1	56.07	54.67	53.09	49.45
Government loan guarantees, SMEs	NIS million	27	17	121	164	116	116	215	232	257	184	144	166	220	4 170	365	119
Government guaranteed loans, SMEs	NIS million	170	109	757	1 028	890	1 057	1 951	2 112	2 340	1 838	1 618	1 618	1 887	21 951	2,634	918
Non-performing loans, total	% of all business loans	..	..	..	..	..	..	..	..	2.77	2.18	1.57	1.25	1.55	1.76	1.23	0.83
Non-performing loans, SMEs	% of all SME loans	..	..	..	..	..	..	..	..	2.13	1.77	1.5	1.31	1.52	1.77	1.35	1.03

Interest rate, SMEs	%	..	..	..	..	..	..	..	..	3.96	3.83	4.02	4.06	4.02	3.81	3.67	4.8
Interest rate, large firms	%	..	..	..	..	..	..	..	..	2.95	2.97	3.05	2.98	2.88	2.45	2.54	3.86
Interest rate spread	% points	..	..	..	..	..	..	..	..	1.02	0.86	0.97	1.08	1.14	1.36	1.13	0.94
Non-bank finance																	
Venture and growth capital	USD billion	1.76	2.08	1.12	1.22	2.08	1.88	2.95	3.77	4.75	5.10	4.86	6.35	8.30	10.40	25.60	15.74
Venture and growth capital (growth rate)	%, year-on-year growth rate	..	18.0	-46.1	8.8	70.3	-9.5	28.0	41.8	26.4	12.2	7.3	30.7	30.7	32.3	146.2	-38.5
Other indicators																	
Payment delays, B2B	Number of days	..	..	..	..	..	..	..	..	..	57.2	53	28	28	..	..	..
Bankruptcies, SMEs	Number	..	..	2 061	2 834	3 737	5 000	5 610	5 322	5 175	7 900	..	..	..	..	..	..
Bankruptcies, SMEs (growth rate)	%, year-on-year growth rate	..	..	..	37.51	31.86	33.8	12.2	-5.13	-2.76	52.66	..	..	..	..	..	..

The full country profile is available at: https://doi.org/10.1787/fa521246-en.

21. Italy

Key facts on SME financing

Small and medium-sized enterprises (SMEs) form the backbone of the business community, accounting for a large share of value added and employment.

The Italian economy experienced a more subdued expansion in 2022 after the sharp recovery of the previous year, which made up for two-thirds of the exceptional contraction that occurred during the pandemic. GDP growth was weighed down by heightened uncertainty following the large-scale aggression of Russia against Ukraine, rising energy and food prices, and the shift towards tighter monetary policy.

Weak cyclical conditions swiftly affected credit markets: lending to SMEs came to a halt and eventually declined at a sustained pace, ending a period of expansion fuelled by support measures adopted during the pandemic. In early 2023, loans to large enterprises also began to contract slightly.

After remaining broadly relaxed during the pandemic, credit supply policies gradually tightened, partly as a result of banks' higher perceived risk. Business borrowing rates rose, reflecting the process of monetary policy normalisation; however, collateral requirements remained stable and low by historical standards.

Credit quality remained good. The ratio of SME new non-performing loans to outstanding loans stood at a historically low level. The stock of non-performing exposures continued to decline, also as a result of the still high volume of disposals.

Equity financing for SMEs soared in the early-stage segment reached an unprecedented peak since 2007, also thanks to a very active institutional entity investing in young companies with high growth prospects. Conversely, after the upsurge recorded in 2021, expansion capital declined for both SMEs and large companies alike.

Business-to-business payment delays reached a 15-year low in 2022, after falling well below pre-pandemic levels in the previous year. The widespread decline of the indicator was more pronounced for micro firms than for SMEs and large enterprises.

After the increase observed in 2021, judicial liquidations started to fall again, well below the pre-pandemic values, partly thanks to firm support measures and economic recovery. The Business Crisis and Insolvency Code finally entered into force in July 2022, with the aim of better tackling corporate crises.

Financial support measures, introduced or stepped up in recent years, continued to help firms cope with the heightened uncertainty surrounding the macroeconomic developments.

Credit guarantee schemes, which have traditionally played a key role in facilitating SME access to finance, were strengthened during the pandemic. The preferential programme for the granting of public guarantees by the Central Guarantee Fund and SACE was extended several times.

In application of the European Commission's Temporary Crisis Framework for State aid measures in support of the economy following Russia's war against Ukraine, further measures were introduced to address firms' liquidity needs, including a new regulation on public guarantees until the end of 2022, providing for the granting of the Central Guarantee Fund and SACE guarantees to companies hit by a contraction of activity due to the consequences of the war, and an increase in the coverage of the Fund's guarantees for financing aimed at improving the efficiency or diversification of energy production or consumption.

Table 21.1. Scoreboard for Italy

Indicator	Unit	2007	2008	2009	2010	2011	2012	2013	2014	2015	2016	2017	2018	2019	2020	2021	2022
								Debt									
Outstanding business loans, SMEs	EUR billion	187	191	193	210	206	204	196	192	188	175	169	166	160	166	165	162
Outstanding business loans, total	EUR billion	998	1067	1057	1122	1134	1118	1061	1026	1016	984	959	960	931	984	992	983
Share of SME outstanding loans	% of total business loans	18.7	17.9	18.3	18.7	18.2	18.2	18.5	18.7	18.5	17.8	17.7	17.3	17.2	16.9	16.7	16.4
Short-term loans SMEs	EUR billion	59	56	52	50	48	47	42	39	35	31	28	27	26	19	17	17
Long-term loans SMEs	EUR billion	115	120	125	136	133	128	122	115	112	103	101	100	97	112	114	110
Total short and long-term loans, SMEs	EUR billion	174	177	177	186	181	175	164	154	147	134	129	127	123	131	132	127
Share of short-term loans, SMEs	% of total short and long-term SME loans	34.0	31.9	29.3	27.0	26.5	26.7	25.7	25.3	23.8	22.9	21.8	21.3	20.8	14.6	13.2	13.6
Direct government loans, SMEs	EUR million	337	373	255	276	273	252	390	597	392	418	431	439	633	1 338	3 186	1 658
Government guaranteed loans SMEs (CGF)	EUR million, flows	2 300	2 353	4 914	9 119	8 378	8 190	10 811	12 935	15 065	16 703	17 462	19 314	19 376	124 387	93 555	53 860
Government loan guarantees, SMEs (CGF)	EUR million, flows	1 146	1 160	2 756	5 225	4 435	4 036	6 414	8 392	10 216	11 570	12 260	13 731	13 342	105 921	67 642	42 136
Non-performing loans, SMEs	EUR million	..	22 864	27 949	35 221	38 025	43 792	48 358	53 704	56 181	54 937	50 594	47 337	45 713	42 736	40 436	40 509
Non-performing loans, SMEs	% of total SME loans	..	12.0	14.5	16.8	18.4	21.5	24.6	28.0	30.0	31.4	29.9	28.6	28.5	25.7	24.5	25.1
Interest rate, SMEs	%	6.3	6.7	3.8	4.0	5.2	6.0	5.7	4.8	4.2	3.5	3.3	3.4	3.4	2.3	2.8	5.3
Interest rate, large firms	%	5.7	5.7	2.4	2.4	3.6	4.0	3.8	2.9	2.2	2.1	2.1	2.1	1.7	1.5	1.6	3.3
Interest rate spread	%	0.6	1.0	1.4	1.6	1.6	2.0	2.0	1.9	1.9	1.4	1.2	1.3	1.7	0.8	1.2	2.0
Collateral, SMEs	%	54	54	52	53	55	54	56	56	57	58	58	57	57	53	52	52
Rejection rate	% of firms reporting that they had not obtained some or all of the credit requested	3.1	8.2	6.9	5.7	11.3	12.0	8.9	8.4	6.0	4.0	4.2	4.6	4.1	5.8	2.8	2.6
Utilisation rate	SME loans used / authorised	79.7	80.7	80.7	82.8	84.4	86.6	87.2	87.7	87.4	85.3	85.0	85.4	84.7	83.4	84.1	84.5
								Non-bank finance									
Venture capital investments (early stage), SMEs	EUR million	66	115	98	89	82	135	82	43	74	103	133	324	270	355	587	1179
Growth capital investments (expansion), SMEs	EUR million	295	440	260	263	500	504	438	230	170	155	161	125	143	133	325	204

Growth capital investments (expansion), total	EUR million	641	796	371	583	674	926	914	1179	333	710	337	816	896	354	858	483

The full country profile is available at: https://doi.org/10.1787/fa521246-en.

22. Japan

Key facts on SME financing

Japanese SMEs accounted for 99.7% of all businesses and employed 33 million individuals, approximately 69.7% of the private sector labour force in 2021.

Lending to SMEs declined continuously between 2007 and 2012, with a total decrease of 6.6% over that period. In 2013, the volume of outstanding SME loans shifted upward and has increased consistently since then: JPY 323.6 trillion in 2021 and JPY 335.9 trillion in 2022.

Average interest rates on new short-term loans in Japan have been very low and declined further between 2007 and 2022, falling from 1.64% to nearly a quarter of that amount (0.42%) because of the policy of monetary easing. Long-term interest rates on new loans followed a broadly similar pattern, more than halving from 1.73% in 2007 to 0.78% in 2022.

Japanese venture capital investments peaked at JPY 193 billion in FY2007, before decreasing by 29.5% and 36.0% in FY2008 and FY2009, respectively. After fluctuating for the following five years, the volume of VC investments started to increase in 2015. Since then, VC investments have been on a rapid rise, except for a sharp drop amid the disruption of the COVID-19 pandemic in 2020, and reached their highest value of JPY 341 billion in FY2021. The Government of Japan endeavours to increase the number and scale of startups.

Leasing volumes to SMEs plummeted in the aftermath of the global financial crisis, dropping by almost 40% between 2007 and 2009. Subsequently, with the recovery of domestic capital investment demand, the volumes have been on an upward trend and recovered to JPY 2.7 trillion in 2019. More recently, the amount of leasing decreased to JPY 2.1 trillion in 2021 and rose slightly to JPY 2.2 trillion in 2022.

SME bankruptcies, which account for more than 99% of all bankruptcies in Japan, decreased from 15,500 in 2008 to 6000 in 2021. With COVID-19 financing support measures, the number of SME bankruptcies was curbed at approximately 6,000 in 2021, the lowest level over the last 57 years, before experiencing an increase of 6.6% in 2022.

Total non-performing business loans have declined continuously since FY2013, after having experienced erratic movement over the FY2007-12 period. In FY2019, total NPLs decreased to JPY 10.3 trillion, followed by increases to JPY 11.5 trillion in FY2020 and 12.6 trillion in FY2021.

The Japanese Government offers financial support for SMEs in the form of credit guarantees and direct loans. In 2020, as a response to the COVID-19 crisis, government-affiliated and private financial institutions provided interest-free and unsecured loans. As of March 2022, the total amount of outstanding SME loans was approximately JPY 314 trillion (provided by domestically licensed banks and credit associations); the outstanding amount of the credit guarantee programme was JPY 41.9 trillion (covering 1.58 million SMEs); and the outstanding amount of the direct loan programme was JPY 29.8 trillion, (covering 1.33 million of Japan's 3.58 million SMEs).

While the Japanese economy continued to recover moderately from the COVID-19 crisis, its growth rate in FY2022 was 1.4%, affected by the global energy and food price hikes and the global economic slowdown. GDP growth is projected at 1.3% in FY2023 as of July 2023, attributed to a recovery in personal consumption, including service consumption, and an increase in corporate capital investment, although a slowdown in exports is expected to put downward pressure on the economy.

Table 22.1. Scoreboard for Japan

Indicator	Unit	2007	2008	2009	2010	2011	2012	2013	2014	2015	2016	2017	2018	2019	2020	2021	2022
Debt																	
Outstanding business loans, SMEs	JPY trillion	260.8	259.1	253.1	248.3	245.6	243.6	247.2	251.7	258.4	265.6	275.4	281.4	286.6	314.9	323.6	335.9
Outstanding business loans, total	JPY trillion	358.2	369.2	360.7	346.9	346.8	349.6	356.5	365.3	376.2	388.5	400.3	415.0	424.7	459.3	460.0	480.1
Share of SME outstanding loans	% of total outstanding business loans	72.81	70.18	70.17	71.58	70.82	69.68	69.34	68.90	68.69	68.37	68.80	67.81	67.48	68.56	70.35	69.96
Value of CGCs loan guarantees (Government loan guarantees, SMEs)	JPY trillion	29.4	33.9	35.9	35.1	34.4	32.1	29.8	27.7	25.8	23.9	22.2	21.08	20.8	40.5	41.9	40.4
Non-performing loans, total (amount)	JPY trillion	17.1	17.1	16.8	16.6	17.2	17.3	15.3	13.9	12.8	11.8	10.5	10.3	10.3	11.5	12.6	..
Non-performing loans, total	% of all business loans	4.77	4.63	4.66	4.79	4.96	4.95	4.29	3.81	3.40	3.04	2.62	2.48	2.43	2.50	2.74	..
Prime lending rate for short-term loans	%	1.88	1.68	1.48	1.48	1.48	1.48	1.48	1.48	1.48	1.48	1.48	1.48	1.48	1.48	1.48	1.48
Prime lending rate for long-term loans	%	2.30	2.40	1.65	1.60	1.40	1.20	1.20	1.10	1.10	0.95	1.00	1.00	1.05	1.00	1.10	1.40
New short-term interest rate (Not only for businesses)	%	1.64	1.53	1.23	1.10	1.04	1.02	0.91	0.88	0.80	0.67	0.61	0.60	0.60	0.47	0.44	0.42
New long-term interest rate (Not only for businesses)	%	1.73	1.67	1.46	1.29	1.21	1.16	1.10	1.00	0.94	0.80	0.80	0.76	0.72	0.76	0.73	0.78
Outstanding short-term interest rate (Not only for businesses)	%	1.67	1.49	1.26	1.19	1.10	1.03	0.88	0.85	0.78	0.62	0.58	0.60	0.60	0.48	0.46	0.44
Outstanding long-term interest rate (Not only for businesses)	%	2.05	1.99	1.76	1.65	1.54	1.42	1.30	1.19	1.10	0.97	0.90	0.85	0.85	0.78	0.76	0.75
Collateral, SMEs	% of SMEs needing collateral to obtain bank lending	..	..	..	..	..	..	..	..	..	..	..	29.4	28.2	26.8	26.0	..
Non-bank finance																	
Venture capital investments (all stages total)	JPY billion	193	136	87	113	124	102	181	117	130	152	197	277	289	224	341	..
Venture capital investments (all stages total)	%, year-on-year growth rate	..	-29.5	-36	29.89	9.73	-17.7	77.45	-35.4	11.11	16.92	29.61	40.61	4.33	22.49	52.23	..
Venture capital (seed and early stage)	% (share of all stages)	..	..	36.80	32.50	44.30	57.80	64.50	57.20	62.80	68.30	67.80	71.40	73.7	72.1.	70.0	..
Venture capital (expansion and later stage)	% (share of all stages)	..	..	63.20	67.50	55.70	42.20	35.50	42.80	37.20	31.70	32.20	28.60	26.3	27.9.	30.0	..

Leasing, SMEs	JPY billion	3 471	2 822	2 100	2 139	2 231	2 284	2 645	2 363	2 604	2 566	2 570	2664	2700	2329	2129	2230
Other indicators																	
Bankruptcies, SMEs	Thousands	14.0	15.5	15.4	13.2	12.7	12.1	10.8	9.7	8.8	8.4	8.4	8.2	8.4	7.8	6.0	6.4
Bankruptcies, SMEs	%, year-on-year growth rate	..	10.76	-0.82	-14	-4.22	-4.81	-10.2	-10.4	-9.43	-4.17	-0.50	-1.93	1.74	-7.27	-22.4	6.60
Bankruptcies, total	Thousands	14.1	15.6	15.5	13.3	12.7	12.1	10.9	9.7	8.8	8.4	8.4	8.2	8.4	7.8	6.0	6.4
Bankruptcies, total	%, year-on-year growth rate	..	11.04	-1.06	-14	-4.41	-4.79	-10.5	-10.3	-9.44	-4.15	-0.49	-2.02	1.80	-7.28	-22.4	6.60

The full country profile is available at: https://doi.org/10.1787/fa521246-en.

23. Kazakhstan

Key facts on SME financing

In 2022, SMEs made up 96.9% of all businesses in Kazakhstan. The share of people employed by SMEs was 45.8% of the total employed population. SMEs contributed 36.5% to the country's GDP that same year.

SME lending was on the rise in Kazakhstan since 2014 up to 2017. In 2017-2019 the SME loan portfolio was showing a negative trend. In 2022 the SME loan portfolio increased by 20.1%. At the same time, new lending to SMEs increased by 16.4% over the last year. Due to the fact that the portfolio of loans to SMEs increased, the share of loans to SMEs in the total portfolio of business loans also grew to 34.1%. The increase in lending dynamics is largely due to a significant improvement in the operating environment, relaxed quarantine restrictions, the offer of new products, and the development of digital channels and ecosystems.

Interest rates for SMEs have fluctuated over the last years, growing steadily from a record low of 11.5% in 2014 to 14% in 2016. In 2022, the rate was 17.2%, while that of large enterprises was 15.9%. This growth is due to the increase in the base rate by the National Bank of the Republic of Kazakhstan.

Among non-bank sources of finance, leasing has the largest market and is steadily growing. In 2021, leasing and hire purchases were almost 8 times higher than their 2010 level. The development of leasing and the growth of its indicators is due to several reasons. First, there is a growing need for industrial, transport and agricultural enterprises to update and expand the fleet of machinery and equipment. Second, many enterprises have problems providing collateral for loans from STB, while leasing companies are more flexible in their collateral policy. Third, the procedure for making lease payments is one of the biggest advantages of leasing. The agreement may optimally take into account the interests of all parties, since the size and period of payments are determined on the basis of a joint agreement.

Non-performing loans (NPL) with arrears of more than 90 days in banks' portfolio among both total loans and SME loans slightly increased in 2022 from 3.3% to 3.4%. Commercial banks fulfil requirements of the National Bank of Kazakhstan concerning maximum appropriate NPL level of no more than 10% of the total loan portfolio.

An important role in maintaining SMEs' access to lending is played by the state, which places funds in commercial banks to provide concessional lending to SMEs during shortages of liquidity in the market. The largest placement of state funds for SME lending took place in 2018. The main part of loans was allocated in 2014-2016 to support SMEs in the manufacturing industry at a rate of 6% per annum, which are issued by banks on a revolving basis.

Since 2010, the government, through "Damu" Entrepreneurship Development Fund, has provided subsidizing of interest rate expense and loan guarantees for SMEs under the "Business Roadmap" Programme. A new financial instrument in Kazakhstan, loan guarantees are becoming popular very quickly, escalating from just three guarantees in 2010 to 50 789 guarantees at the end of 2022.

Table 23.1. Scoreboard for Kazakhstan

Indicator	Unit	2007	2008	2009	2010	2011	2012	2013	2014	2015	2016	2017	2018	2019	2020	2021	2022
Debt																	
Outstanding business loans, SMEs	KZT billion	1 508	1 571	1 708	1 389	1 341	1 412	1 283	1 788	2 060	3 105	2 789	2 364	2 109	2 515	3 772	4 530
Outstanding business loans, total	KZT billion	5 220	5 605	5 879	5 892	6 849	7 534	8 110	8 532	9 027	9 234	8 568	8 348	7 771	7 742	8 857	9 637
Share of SME outstanding loans	% of total outstanding business loans	28.89	28.02	29.06	23.58	19.58	18.74	15.83	20.95	22.83	33.62	32.55	28.32	27.14	32.49	48.72	47.01
New business lending, total	KZT billion	7 764	5 373	3 742	3 291	4 795	5 774	6 109	8 044	7 345	7 724	7 615	9 412	9 720	9 757	12 345	12 713
New business lending, SMEs	KZT billion	1 870	1 273	753.1	690 .1	794 .5	1 050	889 .7	1 198	1 279	1 984	1 524	1 737	1 670	2 439	3 727	4 338
Share of new SME lending	% of total new lending	24.08	23.70	20.13	20.97	16.57	18.18	14.56	14.90	17.41	25.68	20.02	18.46	17.18	25.00	30.19	34.12
Short-term loans, SMEs	KZT billion	296	298	236	206	219	277	199	392	390	826	411	388	335	345	1 923	1 026
Long-term loans, SMEs	KZT billion	1 211 2	1 273	1 472	1 183	1 122	1 135	1 084	1 395	1 670	2 279	2 377	1 976	1 774	1 780	1 804	3 504
Share of short-term SME lending	% of total SME lending	19.66	18.96	13.82	14.83	16.34	19.64	15.51	21.95	18.93	26.60	14.75	16.43	15.87	16.25	51.60	23.65
Government loan guarantees, SMEs	KZT million	..	..	..	339	2 060	3 854	3 336	7 284	11 021	11 952	17 016	21 728	33 789	103 112	171 109	202 021
Government guaranteed loans, SMEs	KZT million	..	..	..	677	4 238	10 991	7 090	15 423	26 964	26 903	42 783	51 216	89 054	265 817	348 983	365 787
Direct government loans, SMEs	KZT billion	5.5	125.2	257.4	132.9	82.7	78.2	85.8	188.4	236.9	247.3	230.5	272.9	239.5	207 588	213 304	184 000
Non-performing loans, total	% of all business loans	..	..	..	..	..	29.80	31.15	23.55	7.95	6.72	9.31	7.38	8.13	7.55	3.30	3.40
Non-performing loans, SMEs	% of all SME loans	..	..	..	..	..	22.33	22.40	11.74	12.69	8.79	9.58	9.33	14.58	11.90	4.40	3.90
Interest rate, SMEs	%	14.28	15.67	14.01	13.34	12.49	12.10	12.46	11.48	12.95	14.01	13.66	12.71	12.66	12.72	12.92	17.20
Interest rate, large firms	%	12.77	14.88	14.04	12.72	11.08	10.58	10.07	10.01	13.47	14.49	12.39	11.22	11.32	11.17	11.99	15.88
Interest rate spread	% points	1.51	0.79	-0.03	0.62	1.41	1.52	2.39	1.47	-0.52	-0.48	1.27	1.49	1.34	1.54	0.93	1.32
Non-bank finance																	
Leasing and hire purchases	KZT billion	..	..	..	60.4	80.1	84.5	106.8	129.0	126.6	167.0	176.5	277.6	347.4	479.3	491.6	..
Factoring and invoicing	KZT million	..	..	..	..	..	7 889	15 125	33 160	37 655	..	..	..	..	..	..	..
Other indicators																	
Bankruptcies, total	Number	0	2	3	8	36	77	125	143	257	516	1 978	3 493	3 129	2 763	3 028	3 029
Bankruptcies, total (growth rate)	%, year-on-year growth rate	..	..	50.00	166.67	350.00	113.89	62.34	14.40	79.72	100.78	283.33	76.59	-10.42	-11.70	9.59	0.03

The full country profile is available at: https://doi.org/10.1787/fa521246-en.

24. Korea

Key facts on SME financing

In 2022, the Korean economy experienced weakened growth attributed to sluggish exports and external challenges despite improved domestic consumption. In 2023, the economic outlook predicted a continued slowdown due to global economic challenges, rising market interest rates, and the need for cautious macroeconomic policies and financial stability measures, especially concerning potential defaults in real estate and corporate debt.

In 2022, despite a sharp increase in benchmark interest rates, Korea witnessed a steady rise in corporate debt, with a surge in defaults in real estate portfolios and tightening conditions in the corporate bond and short-term funding markets.

In 2022, a rapid increase in the base interest rate led to a significant uptick in interest rates on loans to both large corporations and SMEs, widening the interest rate gap between them.

Venture investment reached a record KRW 7.68 trillion in 2021, experiencing a notable 78.4% year-on-year surge. However, in 2022, the impact of rising benchmark interest rates led to a contraction in the venture investment scale to KRW 6.76 trillion, representing an 11.9% decrease compared to the previous year, with early-stage companies being the only category to see an increase in investments.

Since 2015, Korea experienced a consistent decrease in the proportion of non-performing loans, with the non-performing loan ratio dropping from approximately 2.56% in 2015 to 0.68% in 2022.

The average payment delay for short-term SME loans decreased from 13.3 days in 2016 to a low of 7.4 days in 2018 but reversed from 2019 onwards, experiencing a continuous increase to 9.2 days in 2022.

Since April 2020, Korea has implemented the "Loan Maturity Extension and Repayment Deferral System" to aid SMEs facing temporary liquidity challenges due to COVID-19, offering support for maturity extension until September 2025 and repayment deferral until September 2023, with gradual repayment options until September 2028.

Additionally, special guarantee programmes for individuals with medium to low credit ratings and the Hope Loan Plus initiative aim to provide financial support to small businesses affected by the pandemic, offering loans and guarantees based on specific eligibility criteria and creditworthiness.

Table 24.1. Scoreboard for Korea

Indicators	Units	2009	2010	2011	2012	2013	2014	2015	2016	2017	2018	2019	2020	2021	2022
Debt finance															
Outstanding business loans, SMEs	KRW trillion	443	441	455	462	489	522	561	610	655	696	747	836	922	993
Outstanding business loans, total	KRW trillion	531	541	586	618	654	706	756	776	817	857	906	1 020	1 114	1 222
Share of SME outstanding loans	% of total business loans	83.5	81.5	77.7	74.7	74.7	74.0	74.2	78.6	80.2	81.2	82.4	82.0	82.8	81.3
Outstanding Short-term loans, total; loans for operation	KRW trillion	373	372	388	395	405	419	426	414	419	429	462	528	558	611
Outstanding Long-term loans, total; loans for equipment	KRW trillion	158	169	197	223	249	287	330	362	398	428	444	492	555	610
Share of short-term loans; loans for operation	KRW trillion	70.3	68.7	66.3	63.9	61.9	59.3	56.3	53.4	51.3	50.1	51.0	51.8	50.1	50.1
Government loan guarantees, SMEs	KRW trillion	56	56	55	57	59	60	61	63	66	67	69	80	85	87
Government guaranteed loans, SMEs	% of SME business loans	12.7	12.7	12.2	12.3	12.2	11.5	10.9	10.3	10.0	9.7	9.2	9.6	9.2	8.8
Direct government loans, SMEs	KRW billion	4 812	3 098	2 957	3 149	3 715	3 270	3 902	4 551	4 666	4 415	4 358	6 290	6 010	5 440
Non-performing loans, total	% of all business loans	1.6	2.6	1.73	1.66	2.39	2.09	2.56	2.06	1.76	1.88	1.45	1.17	0.91	0.68
Non-performing loans, SMEs	% of all SME loans	1.8	3.11	2.17	1.96	2.11	1.94	1.64	1.3	1.11	1.10	0.94	0.79	0.60	0.56
Interest rate, SMEs	%	6.18	6.52	6.36	5.93	5.11	4.69	3.95	3.63	3.62	3.82	3.71	3.06	2.92	4.13
Interest rate, large firms	%	5.62	5.98	5.81	5.50	4.87	4.51	3.79	3.40	3.31	3.45	3.38	2.83	2.74	3.84
Interest rate spread	%	0.56	0.54	0.55	0.43	0.24	0.18	0.16	0.24	0.31	0.37	0.33	0.23	0.19	0.29
Rejection rate	%, 1 – (SME loans authorised/ requested)	..	..	..	..	..	6.9	3.7	12.2	12.9	15.5	10.4	16.1	19.1	..
Non-bank finance															
Venture and growth capital	KRW billions	867	1 091	1 261	1 233	1 385	1 639	2 086	2 150	2 380	3 425	4 278	4 305	7 680	6 764
Venture and growth capital (growth rate)	%	19.7	25.8	15.6	-2.2	12.3	18.4	27.2	3.1	10.7	43.9	24.9	0.63	78.4	-11.9
Leasing and hire purchases	KRW trillions	14.4	20.4	21.6	20.6	22.6	25.5	28.3	29.5	32.9	34.7	36.1	39.0	39.3	42.5
Other indicators															
Payment delays, SMEs	Number of days past due date	9.9	12.1	11.7	9.1	9.7	10.0	9.2	13.3	8.9	7.4	8.4	8.5	8.6	9.2
Bankruptcies, total	Number	..	..	..	..	..	..	..	..	..	..	..	..	..	..
Bankruptcies, growth rate	Year-on-year growth rate, %	..	..	..	..	..	..	..	..	..	..	..	..	..	..

The full country profile is available at: https://doi.org/10.1787/fa521246-en.

25. Latvia

Key facts on SME financing

Latvia had been experiencing stable economic growth rates exceeding the EU average until the COVID-19 pandemic. From 2013 to 2019, GDP grew by 2.9% per year on average.

The COVID-19 pandemic has had a significant impact on economic development for the global economy and Latvia was not the exception. In 2020, GDP shrank by 2.3%. Nonetheless, the extensive government and EU funds support measures, as well as the improvement of the epidemiological situation in 2021, contributed to the recovery of Latvia's economy, and GDP grew by 4.3%.

The recovery of Latvia's economy from the COVID-19 pandemic crisis was interrupted by the large-scale aggression of Russia against Ukraine. On 24 February 2022, when Russia invaded Ukraine, the geopolitical situation and prospects for economic development deteriorated. Energy and food prices rose significantly, intensifying the inflation pressure at a time when the cost of living around the world had already skyrocketed as the world was recovering from the pandemic. The global economy was also affected by disruptions in raw material supply chains due to the war. In 2022, GDP grew by 2.8%, i.e. the lowest growth since 2017, excluding the drop of 2020 due to the COVID-19 pandemic. However, despite the war in Ukraine, the decline in GDP was smaller than predicted due to strong private consumption and export growth.

Further economic development in the medium term depends on the situation in the external environment and progress in reforms. The highest risk to the growth of Latvia is related to global economic development, in particular the geopolitical situation. Further development of the EU's economic performance is equally important. In the medium term, economic advantages of Latvia are mainly based on the achievement of macroeconomic stability, as a result of which Latvia's credit ratings have improved, as well as on the efficiency of planned aid programmes of the EU funds and on the improvements in the business environment. Latvia owes its economic competitiveness to technological factors, improvements in production efficiency, increased innovation, and to a lesser extent cheap labour and low resource prices. In the medium term, Latvia's growth rates may reach a 4-5% increase per year. If the war in Ukraine continues, the pace of economic recovery might be slower.

In Latvia, 99.8% of economically active merchants and commercial companies are SMEs, 91.1% of which are micro-enterprises.

In 2022, SMEs in Latvia continued their recovery, with SME value added growing by 7.9% and SME employment increasing by 1.7%. However, as value added growth is not adjusted for inflation, in the high-inflation environment of 2022, growth in real terms has been lower (SME value added growing by 6.7% and SME employment increasing by 0.7%).

As economic operators are experiencing the effects of the large-scale aggression of Russia against Ukraine, including supply chain disruptions, market shocks, uncertainty, and inflation, the government has developed solutions to overcome the crisis and stabilise the market by offering various financial instrument programmes.

Currently, state support programmes are introduced via the JSC Development Finance Institution Altum (henceforth – Altum), a state-owned development finance institution offering aid and financial tools to various target groups. Altum develops and implements state aid programmes to compensate for market shortcomings that cannot be resolved by private financial institutions.

Table 25.1. Scoreboard for Latvia

Indicator	Unit	2007	2008	2009	2010	2011	2012	2013	2014	2015	2016	2017	2018	2019	2020	2021	2022
Debt																	
Outstanding business loans, SMEs	EUR million	7 727	8 672	8 376	7 764	7 035	6 154	5 404	4 939	4 771	4 942	4 482	4 110	3 922	3 648	3 598	4 119
Outstanding business loans, total	EUR million	8 865	10 359	9 681	8 888	8 212	7 474	7 058	6 379	6 274	6 373	5 887	5 591	5 481	5 017	4 961	5 418
Share of SME outstanding loans	% of total outstanding business loans	87.16	83.71	86.52	87.34	85.67	82.34	76.57	77.43	76.05	77.55	76.1	73.52	71.57	72.71	72.52	76.03
New business lending, total	EUR million	..	..	..	..	1 708	1 914	1 965	1 268	1 346	1 795	1 347	1 312	1 558	1 650	1825	2533
New business lending, SMEs	EUR million	..	..	..	..	1 506	1 625	1 613	1 020	947	1 399	974	1 012	1 075	855	1113	1573
Share of new SME lending	% of total new lending	..	..	..	..	88.20	84.90	82.08	80.47	70.39	77.95	72.3	77.19	69.01	51.81	61.0	62.1
Outstanding short-term loans, SMEs	EUR million	2 653	3 203	3 262	3 009	2 682	2 349	1 852	1 570	1 672	1 371	1 287	1 229	1 179	975	764	968
Outstanding long-term loans, SMEs	EUR million	5 048	5 409	4 912	4 701	4 353	3 805	3 552	3 369	3 099	3 571	3 195	2 894	2 743	2 673	2834	3151
Share of short-term SME lending	% of total SME lending	34.4	37.2	39.9	39	38.1	38.2	34.3	31.8	35.1	27.7	28.7	29.8	30.1	26.7	21.2	23.5
Non-performing loans, total	% of all business loans	0.7	3.2	20.2	20.8	16.4	9.7	6.9	5.9	4.4	2.7	3.1	2.5	4.4	2.5	1.3	0.6
Non-performing loans, SMEs	% of all SME loans	0.8	3.7	22.4	23.4	18.8	11.7	8.4	7.2	5.7	3.3	3.8	3.3	3.8	2.3	1.8	0.9
Interest rate, SMEs	%	8.3	8.9	7.9	7.1	5.8	4.5	4.5	4.7	4.5	4.4	3.8	3.8	4.0	4.4	4.2	4.0
Interest rate, large firms	%	6.6	7.1	5.2	4.3	4	3.6	3.8	3.3	3.1	2.5	2.6	2.7	2.9	2.9	2.7	3.1
Interest rate spread	% points	1.7	1.8	2.7	2.8	1.8	0.9	0.7	1.4	1.4	1.9	1.2	1.1	1.1	1.5	1.5	0.85
Non-bank finance																	
Venture and growth capital	EUR million	..	..	..	..	..	..	..	37.95	51.98	79.37	101	118	157.5	147.6	211.6	117.9
Venture and growth capital (growth rate)	%, Year-on-year growth rate	..	..	..	..	..	..	..	..	36.97	52.69	27.76	16.45	33.38	-6.29	43.36	-44.29
Leasing and hire purchases	EUR million	1 576	1 594	1 145	841	810	867	875	864	932	939	1034	1102	1075	944.1	873.5	958.6

Indicator	Unit	2007	2008	2009	2010	2011	2012	2013	2014	2015	2016	2017	2018	2019	2020	2021	2022
Factoring and invoice discounting	EUR million	227.2	301.9	149.1	60.68	90.96	96.15	108	114.5	151.8	166	152.6	173.4	161.8	137	167.3	142.8
Other indicators																	
Bankruptcies, SMEs	Number	..	1 292	2 202	2 714	898	884	820	959	803	731	590	592	580	375	242	302
Bankruptcies, SMEs (growth rate)	%, Year-on-year growth rate	..	..	70.43	23.25	-66.91	-1.56	-7.24	16.95	-16.37	-8.85	-19.29	0.34	-2.03	-35.34	-35.47	24.79

Note: * The reduction of SME bankruptcies can be explained by the fact that due to the rapid spread of Covid-19, on 12 March 2020 the government had declared a state of emergency which lasted until 10 June 2020. On 9 November 2020 repeatedly the government had declared a state of emergency which lasted until 6 April 2021. During this period creditors were prohibited from submitting an application for insolvency proceedings of a legal person.

The full country profile is available at: https://doi.org/10.1787/fa521246-en.

26. Lithuania

Key facts on SME financing

Continued high inflation, tightening financing conditions and deteriorating trade prospects are slowing down Lithuania's economic growth. With high inflation constraining consumption both in Lithuania and in export markets, the number of Lithuanian firms facing insufficient demand rose slightly in 2022, mostly in the trade and industrial sectors.

SMEs account for 99.6% of all enterprises operating in Lithuania, the majority of them (84.6%) being micro-enterprises. Most SMEs (73.2%) have chosen the legal form of private limited liability company and are primarily engaged in wholesale or retail trade activities (more than one-fourth of all SMEs). The share of employees working in SMEs is around 70%, while the share of gross value added generated by SMEs is close to 56%.

In 2022, companies borrowed very actively, mainly because of high demand for working capital driven by higher prices of raw materials and intermediate goods. These conditions have led to NFCs' (non-financial corporations) significant short-term borrowing. However, the level of indebtedness of SMEs operating in Lithuania is relatively low and internal resources remain their main source of funding.

As a result of a decrease in demand for bank credit among large NFCs and structural changes in their loan portfolios, the share of SME loans over total business loans increased by 17 p.p. since 2019 and the level remained elevated in 2021 and 2022 (57% and 58.7% respectively).

In Lithuania, most NFC loans are granted at variable interest rates. Thus, rising key interest rates affect the majority of borrowers. However, the interest rate spread between small and large loans has been contracting since 2019, indicating that interest rate-related credit conditions began to be more accommodative to SMEs, and in 2022, the average interest rates of small loans were just 0.1 percentage points higher than for large ones. On the other hand, the surveys of commercial banks suggest that in 2022, lending standards to SMEs have tightened, although did not reach the levels of 2020. In Q1 2023, a decline in demand for corporate loans was identified by one-third of the surveyed banks.

In 2022, NFCs also borrowed extensively from each other. The peer-to-peer business loan portfolio increased by as much as 31.3% year-on-year and amounted to EUR 7 billion at the end of 2022. State aid measures and EU funds were also significant sources of finance, whereas venture capital investments have been steadily growing since 2016. In 2022, demand for alternative financing (e.g., private capital or risk funds, crowdfunding, etc.) was quite low.

The government supports SMEs by ensuring that they benefit from favourable conditions to obtain the necessary financing to start and develop their business. When a company does not have sufficient collateral, it can apply to the state-controlled enterprise UAB Investicijų ir verslo garantijos (INVEGA), which provides various options of loan guarantees, factoring, leasing and export credit repayments. INVEGA also provides an option for different preferential loans through alternative financing or crowdfunding and loans with preferential rates from the different Venture Capital funding services. In addition, municipalities provide different support schemes to SMEs; for example, when starting a business, entrepreneurs can expect support to cover their set-up costs, part of the interest payments, as well as other support. To reduce the impact of the crisis caused by the large-scale aggression of Russia against Ukraine, direct loans to business entities affected by the war have been introduced.

Table 26.1. Scoreboard for Lithuania

Indicator	Unit	2007	2008	2009	2010	2011	2012	2013	2014	2015	2016	2017	2018	2019	2020	2021	2022
									Debt								
Outstanding business loans, SMEs	EUR million	..	..	..	..	..	..	..	3 143	3 231	3 404	3 723	3 920	3 670	4 390	4 790	5 790
Outstanding business loans, total	EUR million	8 409	9 864	7 978	6 816	6 906	7 047	6 828	7 530	7 610	8 310	8 830	9 250	8 700	7 400	8 400	9 870
Share of SME outstanding loans	% of total outstanding business loans	..	..	..	..	..	..	..	41.74	42.44	40.91	42.13	42.38	42.18	59.41	57.02	58.66
New business lending, total	EUR million	10 420	6 395	2 084	2 764	3 761	4 560	4 745	4 799	3 994	3 966	4 836	4 442	3 777	3 000	4 803	5 326
New business lending, SMEs	EUR million	8 996	4 336	1 330	1 892	2 452	2 948	3 206	3 075	2 398	2 731	2 948	2 628	2 284	2 022	3 356	3 481
Share of new SME lending	% of total new lending	86.33	67.80	63.84	68.46	65.19	64.65	67.56	64.07	60.05	68.85	60.97	59.16	60.48	67.40	69.87	65.36
Share of short-term SME lending	% of total SME lending													22.44	22.45	19.87	19.15
Government guaranteed loans, SMEs	EUR million									148.4	218.8	241.6	224.5	188.7	257.7	315.8	356.8
Non-performing loans, total (NFCs)	% of all business loans	..	..	..	..	..	..	..	10.31	6.25	6.25	5.04	4.05	2.95	3.52	1.74	1.48
Non-performing loans, SMEs	% of all SME loans	..	..	..	..	..	..	..	17.54	14.11	11.18	8.59	6.60	4.83	4.88	2.16	1.87
Interest rate, SMEs	%	6.13	6.72	5.06	4.64	5.04	4.04	3.45	3.27	3.13	2.76	2.80	3.29	3.30	3.17	2.89	3.50
Interest rate, large firms	%	5.70	6.27	4.32	3.90	4.17	3.24	2.74	2.66	2.35	2.18	2.16	2.56	2.91	2.81	2.60	3.40
Interest rate spread	% points	0.43	0.45	0.74	0.74	0.87	0.80	0.71	0.61	0.78	0.58	0.64	0.73	0.39	0.36	0.29	0.10
Colalteral, SMEs	% of SMEs needing collateral to obtain bank lending							69.80	62.10	69.00	64.50	64.40	67.70	69.90	61.20	38.90	67.30
Percentage of SME loan applications	SME loan applications/ total number											36.33	27.10	27.70	26.72	41.67	42.12

	of SMEs																
Rejection rate	1-(SME loans authorised/ requested)	..	..	..	..	15.4	30.8	11.5	21.3	14.3	19.4	22.5	43.2	43.8	43.49	34.76	38.28
Non-bank finance																	
Venture and growth capital	EUR million												178	159	39	391	339
Venture and growth capital (growth rate)	%, Year-on-year growth rate													-10.7	-75.2	892.4	-13.3
Leasing and hire purchases	EUR million	..	..	..	1 756	1 547	1 452	1 527	1 521	1 660	2 111	2 463	2 950	3 000	2 810	3 000	3 410
Factoring and invoice discounting	EUR million	..	..	..	151	200	231	348	359	407	434	517	464	453	220	338	429
Other indicators																	
Payment delays, B2B	Number of days	..	..	..	..	..	..	..	..	..	..	3	3	2	16	12	12
Bankruptcies, SMEs	Number	606	957	1844	1637	1274	1401	1554	1686	1983	2741	2979	2091	1609	790	808	1193
Bankruptcies, SMEs (growth rate)	%, Year-on-year growth rate	..	57.9	92.7	-11.2	-22.2	10.0	10.9	8.5	17.6	38.2	8.7	-29.8	-23.1	-50.9	2.3	47.6

The full country profile is available at: https://doi.org/10.1787/fa521246-en.

27. Luxembourg

Key facts on SME financing

According to the latest available data, SMEs (firms that employ less than 250 employees) accounted for 99.5% of all non-financial firms in Luxembourg in 2020. SMEs employed approximately 66% of the labour force and generated 59% of the economy's total value added.

New loans to all enterprises continued to decrease in 2022, marking the lowest level since records began. New loans to SMEs also decreased in 2022, but at a slower pace than loans to all enterprises. The share of new lending to SMEs increased to 17.2%, surpassing the previous peak of 16.1% in 2011. It should be noted that, due to limited data availability, loans to SMEs are proxied by loans that amount to a maximum of EUR 1 million.

Interest rates experienced a sharp rise in the second half of 2022, a trend that continued into 2023. As of August 2023, the interest rate for SME loans reached 4.79%. For loans exceeding EUR 1 million, the interest rate was lower, at 2.81%.

Over the period 2007-2022, interest rates for SMEs remained consistently higher than those for large firms. In 2022, the interest rate for SMEs was 1.73%, compared to 1.47% for large firms. In absolute terms, this translates to a spread of 0.26 percentage points. In relative terms, interest paid by SMEs is approximately 17.9% higher than interest paid by large firms in 2022. The gap in interest rates between SMEs and large firms widened further in 2023. As of August 2023, SME loans had an interest rate of 4.79%, while large firms were charged a lower rate of 2.81%. This difference represents a 1.98 percentage point spread, meaning SMEs pay about 70% more in interest compared to large firms.

Alternative forms of financing, such as venture capital, may be important for SMEs seeking finance. In 2022, nearly EUR 225 million of venture capital was invested in Luxembourg's firms. The largest portion of all venture capital funding was invested in firms active in the financial and insurance industry (EUR 178 million).

In 2022, government-guaranteed loans reached EUR 157.7 million, showing a significant increase from EUR 112.3 million in 2021, EUR 128.7 million in 2020, and just EUR 14.8 million in 2019. This trend underscores the countercyclical nature of these loans and highlights the government's commitment to supporting SME financing during the COVID-19 pandemic.

The government has also emphasised innovation within SMEs. In 2022, SMEs accounted for 76% of Research, Development, and Innovation (RDI) projects financed by the Ministry of the Economy.

The number of bankruptcies among all firms in Luxembourg stood at 1011 cases in 2022, marking a 12.7% decrease from the 1158 reported in 2021.

Table 27.1. Scoreboard for Luxembourg

Indicator	Unit	2007	2008	2009	2010	2011	2012	2013	2014	2015	2016	2017	2018	2019	2020	2021	2022
Debt																	
New business lending, total	EUR million	113 817	181 792	166 287	111 898	111 568	105 854	100 444	92 349	83 076	87809	80 264	95 633	84 091	62 083	56 126	50 775
New business lending, SMEs	EUR million	12 800	14 555	14 754	15 441	17 979	15 593	13 713	10 765	10 142	9 395	9 698	10 440	10 184	8 682	9 336	8 760
Share of new SME lending	% of total new lending	11.25	8.01	8.87	13.80	16.11	14.73	13.65	11.66	12.21	10.70	12.08	10.92	12.11	13.98	16.63	17.25
Non-performing loans, total	% of all business loans	0.12	0.18	0.44	0.48	0.64	0.59	0.52	0.41	0.40	0.27	0.38	0.40	0.42	0.57	0.46	0.60
Government loan guarantees, SMEs	EUR million													8.7	72.0	41.1	130.5
Government guaranteed loans, SMEs	EUR million													14.8	128.7	112.3	157.7
Interest rate, SMEs	%	5.51	5.72	2.81	2.71	2.68	2.22	2.05	2.08	1.88	1.75	1.76	1.73	1.65	1.57	1.37	1.73
Interest rate, large firms	%	4.96	4.97	2.59	2.30	2.62	1.86	1.64	1.47	1.42	1.20	1.21	1.26	1.12	1.10	0.98	1.47
Interest rate spread	% points	0.54	0.75	0.21	0.41	0.06	0.35	0.41	0.62	0.46	0.55	0.55	0.47	0.53	0.47	0.40	0.26
Percentage of SME loan applications	SME loan applications/ total number of SMEs	..	..	..	..	18.20	..	25.80	16.40	23.00	26.15	18.93	32.28	27.02	22.68	27.77	17.20
Non-bank finance																	
Venture and growth capital	EUR thousand	103 343	298 650	49 021	132 917	281 484	86 212	31 090	128 472	144 368	196 346	59 145	113 098	173 872	199 386	72 608	225 269
Venture and growth capital (growth rate)	%, Year-on-year growth rate	..	188.99	-83.6	171.14	111.77	-69.4	-55.2	230.97	13.00	34.10	-69.9	91.22	53.74	14.67	-62.1	210.25
Factoring and invoice discounting	EUR million	..	..	349	321	180	299	407	339	..	..	..	..	..			
Other indicators																	
Bankruptcies, Total	Number	659	574	693	918	978	1 050	1 049	850	873	961	904	1 191	1 262	1 198	1 158	1 011
Bankruptcies, Total (growth rate)	%, Year-on-year growth rate	..	-12.90	20.73	32.47	6.54	7.36	-0.10	-18.97	2.71	10.08	-5.93	31.75	5.96	-5.07	-1.28	-12.69

The full country profile is available at: https://doi.org/10.1787/fa521246-en.

28. Malaysia

Key facts on SME financing

Over the years, there have been various initiatives implemented to enhance the MSME financing ecosystem in Malaysia. Access to finance is a critical enabler for MSMEs to start operations, invest and grow, withstand shocks, transition to the sustainable and digital economy and participate in the supply chains. In 2022, total financing outstanding and approvals to support MSME relief and recovery exceeded that of 2021. MSME outstanding loans stood at RM355 billion in 2022, compared to RM320 billion in 2021, while the share of MSME lending in proportion to business loans rose to reach 48% in 2022, from 45% in 2021. Banking institutions remain the main source of financing for MSMEs, providing more than 90% of total financing.

The financing ecosystem for MSMEs has been strengthened considerably over the years and continued to be enhanced amid the pandemic. The existence of a stronger and more effective ecosystem which played a pivotal role in providing critical financial support to MSMEs in distress was hugely instrumental in facilitating the recovery of the Malaysian MSME during these uncertain times.

While alternatives to traditional debt finance are particularly important for start-ups, high-growth and innovative MSMEs, the development of alternative financing techniques may be relevant to the broader population of MSMEs. Capital gaps exist also for firms seeking to implement important transitions in their activities, such as ownership and control changes, as well as for MSMEs seeking to leverage and improve their capital structures. Excessive reliance on debt financing compared to equity will lead to higher cost, as loans to indebted firms tend to have higher interest rates and increase the risk of financial distress and bankruptcy. Thus, the Government's decision to allocate more funds into alternative financing from the capital market and innovative platforms, such as equity crowdfunding (ECF), peer-to-peer (P2P), private equity and venture capital, will further support the financial needs and open opportunities for businesses, particularly MSMEs. Alternative fundraising avenues via ECF and P2P financing rose in 2022 and continued to support the funding needs of MSMEs, with a total of 7,218 MSMEs enabled to raise more than RM4.4 billion.

Malaysia's financial system is the outcome of continuous efforts and reforms over decades, core building blocks were established and have placed Malaysia's financial sector on a stronger footing, not only to withstand the shocks of the pandemic and natural disaster, but also to become a source of strength to cushion the impact to the economy which is highlighted in the Financial Sector Blueprint 2022 - 2026 and one of the key initiatives is the enhancements to the financing ecosystem for micro, small and medium enterprises (MSMEs). As Malaysia continue to build on these foundations, it is crucial that the Malaysian financial system keeps pace with emerging developments.

Looking ahead, various megatrends are expected to shape the future economic and financial landscape. The pandemic has accelerated certain developments – accentuating some pre-existing vulnerabilities while also giving rise to opportunities for reforms that are long overdue.

Table 28.1. Scoreboard for Malaysia

Indicator	Unit	2007	2008	2009	2010	2011	2012	2013	2014	2015	2016	2017	2018	2019	2020	2021	2022
Debt																	
Outstanding business loans, MSMEs	MYR billion	128.0	138.9	141.6	141.2	165.3	187.0	211.0	243.7	274.4	299.7	315.7	297.6	278.4	305.1	320.0	355.7
Outstanding business loans, total	MYR billion	290.7	328.3	343.1	375.3	422.0	461.6	499.8	545.9	588.1	615.9	623.8	658.9	675.0	680.6	713.1	748.5
Share of MSME outstanding loans	% of total outstanding business loans	44.03	42.30	41.28	37.61	39.17	40.52	42.22	44.64	46.66	48.66	50.60	45.17	41.24	44.82	44.87	47.51
New business lending, total	MYR billion	164.0	129.5	105.2	141.4	171.7	166.1	140.8	148.6	156.6	145.8	159.5	159.0	164.7	137.9	149.6	338.5
New business lending, MSMEs	MYR billion	63.2	58.9	50.9	62.2	75.2	82.9	78.3	77.7	72.0	74.6	70.7	69.6	71.2	66.8	72.3	155.0
Share of new MSME lending	% of total new lending	38.57	45.52	48.37	43.99	43.81	49.92	55.61	52.28	45.94	51.17	44.31	43.79	43.21	48.40	48.36	45.80
Share of short-term MSME loans outstanding	% of total MSME lending	..	..	..	..	..	..	..	..	..	..	..	..	..	..	23.30	23.83
Guarantee and Financing Schemes	No. of accounts (in thousands)	13.00	10.37	14.07	7.67	7.50	2.15	2.37	6.84	8.23	7.57	8.64	8.99	10.83	13.43	21.74	13.16
Guarantee and Financing Schemes	MYR million	4 567	3 014	3 112	2 495	2 861	1 066	1 546	3 175	3 356	4 224	3 380	3 682	3 968	5 922	6 078	3 549
Impaired financing, total (amount)	MYR billion	24.2	20.3	18.2	23.6	21.4	18.5	17.8	17.9	18.9	20.5	20.8	21.3	23.7	23.4	23.5	27.0
Impaired financing, total	% of all business loans	8.31	6.18	5.30	6.29	5.06	4.01	3.56	3.28	3.22	3.33	3.34	3.23	3.51	3.44	3.29	3.61
Impaired financing, MSMEs (amount)	MYR billion	12.1	9.9	8.9	10.6	9.6	8.6	8.2	8.6	8.9	8.9	10.1	10.2	10.3	9.8	10.1	12.8
Impaired financing, MSMEs	% of all MSME loans	9.44	7.12	6.28	7.50	5.78	4.58	3.89	3.51	3.24	2.96	3.19	3.43	3.70	3.21	3.14	3.60
Interest rate, MSMEs	%	6.06	6.39	5.50	5.69	5.74	5.72	5.53	5.77	5.99	6.01	5.82	6.06	6.05	4.91	4.68	4.98
Collateral, MSMEs	% of MSMEs accounts with newly approved loans with collateral pledged	..	..	..	..	..	..	..	..	..	..	..	..	..	..	54.49	49.68
Non-bank finance																	
Venture and growth capital	MYR million	479	477	597	453	253	230	264	318	365	569	418	613	566	334	1 063	1 275
Leasing and Factoring	MYR million	..	..	..	..	721	918	1 099	1 170	1 086	834	1 280	..	..	..	..	..

The full country profile is available at: https://doi.org/10.1787/fa521246-en.

29. Mexico

Key facts on SME financing

In Mexico, approximately 29.6% of the micro, small and medium-sized enterprises (MSMEs) had access to finance from any source between 2019 and 2021, according to the National Survey of Enterprise Financing (ENAFIN) 2021, conducted by the National Institute of Statistics and Geography (INEGI), which is representative of a sample framework of 266 270 MSMEs of 6 workers or more.

In 2022, the average interest rate for loans to MSMEs was 14.26%, which was 2.4 percentage points higher than the previous year, in line with the contractionary monetary policy stance of the Bank of Mexico, in the aftermath of its efforts to restrain inflationary pressures linked to the global macroeconomic conditions. Between the firms, the interest rate varied according to the amounts of the loans and the size of the borrowing company. For large companies, the average interest rate was approximately 10.68%, which means that the spread with MSMEs' loans is 3.58 percentage points (see Table 30.1).

The Mexican government has several funds that have been used to develop more specific programmes. For instance, amid the COVID-19 pandemic, the government implemented additional programmes to support SMEs in strategic sectors such as retail trade, manufacturing, lodging services, food and beverage preparation, restaurants, and the dough and tortilla industry, in order to contribute to economic reactivation.

Also, the institutional framework on the domestic financial market has allowed the entrance of several Fintech institutions, not only as payment aggregators but as non-banking lenders. According to Finnovista, there were 650 Fintech operating in the Mexican ecosystem at the end of 2022, 65% more than the number in 2019 (394 institutions). Also, 145 of these institutions in 2022 were in the lending segment, which represents an increase of 40.7% when compared to 2021 (103 institutions). This phenomenon has contributed to increasing competition and generating a market environment that eases access to funding. However, there is still room for these entities to improve the credit conditions for MSMEs, in particular in the offer of longer loan maturities and lower interest spreads.

Table 29.1. Scoreboard for Mexico

Indicator	Unit	2007	2008	2009	2010	2011	2012	2013	2014	2015	2016	2017	2018	2019	2020	2021	2022
Debt																	
Outstanding business loans, MSMEs	MXN billion	…	…	178.1	198.8	230.2	275.3	321.0	359.3	401.3	459.4	501.0	506.4	492.3	462.2	460.7	487.1
Outstanding business loans, total	MXN billion	…	…	890.7	968.4	1 135.2	1 219.4	1 336.7	1 445.3	1 681.5	2 386.8	2 835.7	3 106.0	3157.4	3 113	3 179.	3 540
Share of MSME outstanding loans	% of total outstanding business loans	…	…	20.0	20.5	20.3	22.6	24.0	24.9	23.9	19.2	17.7	16.3	15.6	14.8	14.5	13.8
New business lending, total	MXN billion	…	…	…	1 310.5	1 624.8	1 806.2	1 949.7	2 009.8	2 253.7	2 621.6	4 605.1	5 195.2	5 602	6 003.	5 723	10 795
New business lending, MSMEs	MXN billion	…	…	…	250.4	304.5	367.8	426.3	468.0	517.3	544.2	911.0	825.6	795.8	658.4	740.0	1 070
Share of new MSME lending	% of total new lending	…	…	…	19.1	18.7	20.4	21.9	23.3	23.0	20.8	19.8	15.9	14.2	11.0	12.9	9.9
Outstanding short-term loans, MSMEs	MXN billion	11.1	41.3	39.1	30.8	30.0	36.9	34.3	12.5	17.7	21.7	32.1	23.8	…	…	…	…
Outstanding long-term loans, MSMEs	MXN billion	10.8	22.4	38.5	36.6	44.2	60.1	80.9	89.0	90.1	107.1	99.1	115.3	…	…	…	…
Share of short-term MSME lending	% of total MSME lending	50.6	64.8	50.4	45.7	40.4	38.0	29.8	12.3	16.4	16.8	24.5	17.1	…	…	…	…
Government loan guarantees, MSMEs	MXN billion	0.8	1.1	1.9	2.3	3.0	3.0	3.7	4.3	3.2	2.7	1.9	4.0	0.8	1.4	…	…
Government guaranteed loans, SMEs	MXN billion	21.9	63.8	77.7	67.4	74.3	96.9	115.1	101.6	107.8	128.8	131.2	139.1	34.0	39.7	…	…
Direct government loans, SMEs	MXN billion	…	…	29.5	30.8	53.3	63.0	88.1	135.4	183.8	6.5	6.5	6.8	5.7	5.3	4.3	1.2
Non-performing loans, total	% of all business loans	…	…	2.0	1.9	2.2	2.0	3.5	3.1	2.6	1.8	1.7	1.7	1.8	1.9	1.7	2.0
Non-performing loans, MSMEs	% of MSME loans	…	…	4.6	4.5	4.2	3.8	3.9	4.3	4.0	4.1	4.5	5.0	5.8	5.9	4.6	3.8
Interest rate, MSMEs	%	19.9	16.2	12.1	11.9	11.4	11.2	9.9	9.2	9.1	11.0	17.0	17.7	13.9	11.7	..	..
Interest rate, large firms	%	7.4	8.0	8.1	7.9	7.7	7.6	6.6	6.0	6.0	8.1	10.6	11.8	8.3	6.3	..	..
Interest rate spread	% points	12.4	8.3	3.9	4.0	3.8	3.6	3.4	3.2	3.1	2.9	6.4	5.9	5.5	5.5	..	..
Non-bank finance																	
Venture and growth capital	USD billion	4.1	2.1	…	…	2.1	4.7	2.1	7.2	13.2	5.2	4.6	3.6	0.7	1.3	0.3	…
Venture and growth capital (growth rate)	%, Year-on-year growth rate	…	-49.6	…	…	…	128.1	-54.5	238.4	83.2	-60.9	-11.6	-21.8	-80.6	94.3	…	…

Note: Venture capital data were updated for previous years by AMEXCAP (association for the private equity industry in Mexico).

The full country profile is available at: https://doi.org/10.1787/fa521246-en.

30. The Netherlands

Key facts on SME financing

The Dutch economy recovered quickly after the initial effects of the COVID-19 crisis, however, in 2022 and 2023, SMEs were challenged by the consequences of the large-scale aggression of Russia against Ukraine and the widespread effect of inflation. Despite these challenges, the need for external financing from SMEs has gradually decreased during recent years. Some trends have continued with banks being still the main channel for SME financing, although their share is becoming relatively smaller compared to alternative sources of financing.

New lending by the three major banks to SMEs stood at approximately EUR 12.7 billion in 2022. The vast majority of SME loan is provided via the three major banks. This represents a strong decrease compared to 2021 and 2020, when it stood at EUR 15.5 billion in 2021 and EUR 18.1 billion in 2020. The total outstanding business loans to SMEs decreased slightly, from EUR 122.4 billion in 2021 to EUR 121.7 billion in 2022. It should be noted that not all banks active in the field of SME finance are taken into account by these figures[1].

Bank loans continue to be the main source of external financing for SMEs in the Netherlands, although alternative sources of finance are gaining more importance among SMEs. According to the latest Financing Monitor 47% of financing applications in 2022 were made at an alternative financier[2] or a combination of an alternative and a bank finance. Only 53% of the applications were made at a bank. Financing needs smaller than EUR 1 million are more often made by an alternative financier. Alternative financiers provide debt, equity or asset-based finance, for example leasing or crowdfunding.

Total venture and growth capital investments in the Netherlands have shown a strong decrease in 2022 compared to 2021, however, it should be noted that 2021 was an exceptional year with several very large funding rounds. In 2022, EUR 2565 million was invested compared to EUR 4397 million in 2021. Since 2016 venture and growth capital investments have shown a strong increase, as only EUR 727 million was invested in 2016. Despite the lower figure of venture and capital investments in 2022 compared to 2021 the number of investments, measured in number of deals, did increase from 345 in 2021 investments to 419 in 2022.

Investments to SMEs and innovative start-ups from regional development agencies and the national promotional institution (NPI), Invest-NL, has strongly increased with EUR 324 million invested in 2022 compared to EUR 119 million in 2021. In particular, more investments to later-stage ventures were made. This could be partially explained by the increase of investments made by the NPI Invest-NL, which was created in 2019 and whose aim is to help SMEs through financing or the development of a viable business case.

Investments via private equity have also shown a gradual increase in recent years with total investments exceeding the EUR 10 billion mark for the first time, a total investment of EUR 10,113 billion.

The number of bankruptcies increased in 2022 with a year-to-year increase of 21%, this amounted to 1854 bankruptcies. The total number of bankruptcies in 2020 was the lowest in two decades. The number of voluntary business terminations was higher with the highest level so far. In 2022, 47% more companies closed compared to 2021, although in 2021 the number of closures was relatively low.The crisis in Ukraine and the ensuing energy crisis has been a difficult challenge for Dutch SMEs with many being unable to (fully) calculate the increase of costs in their prices. Therefore, the Dutch government introduced a price cap for energy-intensive SMEs in 2022. SMEs with an energy bill of at least 7% of revenues are able to receive compensation for the increase in energy prices.

The Dutch government increased focus of its investments, focusing more on DeepTech. A specific DeepTech Fund was introduced with a focus on increasing the availability of scale-up finance. Furthermore, the Seed Capital scheme will focus increasingly on DeepTech funds, especially early stage funds.

Due to the increase of alternative financiers SMEs find it more difficult to acquire suitable financing. In a response the Dutch government has announced to develop a financing hub in order to support SMEs in their processes of acquiring external finance.

Table 30.1. Scoreboard for the Netherlands

Indicator	Unit	2007	2008	2009	2010	2011	2012	2013	2014	2015	2016	2017	2018	2019	2020	2021	2022
								Debt									
Outstanding business loans, SMEs	EUR billion	..	..	..	..	..	..	143.3	136.0	130.4	124.1	125.9	127.1	124.5	121.0	122.4	121.7
Outstanding business loans, total	EUR billion	258.0	304.8	313.5	313.9	342.1	349.1	346.5	330.5	370.2	349.1	328.3	325.3	320.5	308.9	311.6	322.9
Share of SME outstanding loans	% of total outstanding business loans	..	..	..	..	..	..	41.4	41.1	35.2	35.6	38.3	39.1	38.8	39.2	39.3	37.7
New business lending, total	EUR billion	..	..	..	123.0	124.9	110.0	97.3	83.7	146.7	122.7	129.8	130.6	122.8	119.4	144.9	146.3
New business lending, SMEs	EUR billion	..	..	..	10.2	19.5	18.7	18.8	18.0	18.2	16.0	20.9	18.2	17.06	18.1	15.5	12.7
Share of new SME lending	% of total new lending	..	..	..	8.3	15.6	17.0	19.3	21.5	12.4	13.0	16.1	13.9	13.8	15.2	10.7	8.66
Outstanding short-term loans, SMEs	EUR billion	..	..	..	..	..	..	30.1	26.8	23.1	19.8	17.9	16.6	15.2	11.5	10.4	10.8
Outstanding long-term loans, SMEs	EUR billion	..	..	..	..	..	..	113.3	108.2	107.3	104.3	107.9	110.0	109.3	109.4	98.8	110.8
Share of short-term SME lending	% of total SME lending	..	..	..	..	..	..	21.0	19.8	17.7	15.9	14.3	13.1	12.2	9.5	9.55	8.93
Government loan guarantees, SMEs	EUR million	..	400.0	370.0	945.0	1040.0	590.0	415.0	473.0	523.0	710.0	646.0	643.0	586	1485	618.1	348.3
Non-performing loans, SMEs	% of all SME loans	..	..	..	..	..	..	10.0	10.8	9.5	8.1	8.8	9.2	7.7	7.2	6	4.79
Interest rate, SMEs	%	5.4	5.7	4.5	6.0	6.4	5.1	4.3	4.1	4.4	3.7	2.9	4.1	3.7	3.3.	3.1	3.8
Interest rate, large firms	%	..	..	..	..	3.5	3.6	3.4	2.8	2.4	3.2	2.5	2.1	2.9	1.7	1.7	2.9
Interest rate spread	% points	..	..	..	..	2.9	1.5	0.9	1.3	2.0	0.5	0.4	2.0	0.8	1.6	1.4	0.9

Collateral, SMEs	% of SMEs needing collateral to obtain bank lending	..	..	47.0	45.0	44.0	47.0	50.0	43.0	29.0	34.0	40.0	59.0	55	54	41	50
Percentage of SME loan applications	SME loan applications/ total number of SMEs	..	..	29.0	22.0	18.0	22.0	21.0	21.0	16.0	14.0	18.0	12.8	11.4	10.4	8.5	7.9
Rejection rate	1-(SME loans authorised/ requested)	..	..	31.0	10.0	13.0	28.0	28.0	27.0	7.0	18.0	17.0	7,4	9,4	7,8	14,3	4,7
Utilisation rate	SME loans used/ authorised	..	..	72.0	75.0	70.0	50.0	54.0	44.0	89.0	73.0	83.0	84.0	84.0	79.0	77	91
Non-bank finance																	
Venture and growth capital	EUR million	498.0	691.0	526.5	291.2	612.8	417.5	398.6	681.1	788.3	727.7	930.2	1093	1224. 13	1704.66	4396.6	2565.2
Venture and growth capital (growth rate)	%, Year-on-year growth rate	..	38.7	-23.8	-44.7	110.4	-31.8	-4.53	70.86	15.7	-7.68	27.8	17.52	11.98	39.25	157.9	-41.6
Leasing and hire purchases[1]	% of SMEs	..	..	..	..	..	3888	4191	4292	5205	5551	5975	7150	7743	6631	6896	6916
Factoring and invoice discounting	% of SMEs	..	..	..	..	..	..	..	..	..	..	..	5816	6473	4815	5843	8037
Other indicators																	
Payment delays, B2B	Number of days	13.2	13.9	16.0	17.0	18.0	18.0	17.0	16.0	6.0	5.0	5.0	1.0	20.0	- 2.0	11	13
Bankruptcies, SMEs	Number	3 589	3 842	6 942	6 162	5741	6870	7825	5889	4485	3730	3018	2818	2986	2521	1440	1705
Bankruptcies, SMEs (growth rate)	%, Year-on-year growth rate	..	7.0	80.7	-11.2	-6.83	19.67	13.90	-24.74-	-23.84	-16.83	-19.09	-6.63	6.07	-15.66	-42.88	18.40

Notes

1. Not all Dutch banks are included in the DNB graph 5.14, only the three major banks.
2. All financiers except for banks are considered alternative financers.

The full country profile is available at: https://doi.org/10.1787/fa521246-en.

31. New Zealand

Key facts on SME financing

In 2019, New Zealand was ranked as the number one country in the world for ease of doing business as recognized by the World Bank. As a small open economy, with a population of 5 million, SMEs play a significant role in the New Zealand economy.

SMEs account for 98.8% of all New Zealand businesses. Additionally, Māori-led SMEs, who are indigenous in New Zealand and Treaty partners to the Crown, mostly fall into the sectors of agriculture, fisheries, or the technical and scientific space. In New Zealand, SMEs are defined as businesses with 0-49 employees.

Aligning with global economic inflationary trends, the New Zealand consumer price index peaked at 7.3% in June 2022. In addition, severe weather events have contributed to inflationary pressures. In January 2023, Auckland and surrounding areas experienced catastrophic flooding. In February 2023, Cyclone Gabrielle hit the Northern Island. Both events caused widespread damage to buildings, businesses, and infrastructure, with damage to farms and orchards likely to see loss of primary production beyond 2023.

In response to inflationary pressures, the Reserve Bank of New Zealand increased the official cash rate (OCR) from 0.25% in 2020 to 5.5% in 2023. As a result, interest rates for SMEs increased from 8.7% to 11.5% during 2022. Despite these changes, the stock of SME outstanding business loans increased from NZD 74.3 billion in 2021 to NZD 77.6 billion in 2022, although the share of SME outstanding business loans as a percentage of the total outstanding business loans fell from 60.3% in 2021 to 58.4% in 2022.

Other indicators show a slight increase in SME non-performing loans, from 0.6% in 2021 to 0.7% in 2022. Business-to-business late payments increased from 5.9 days in 2020 to 6.0 days in 2021. The annual number of bankruptcies continued a downward trend from 1863.0 in 2017 to 525.0 in 2022. The decrease in bankruptcies, while going against global trends, is also reflective of the various government policy responses to COVID-19 for SMEs referenced in the 2022 New Zealand profile.

In alternative financing, New Zealand early-stage capital markets saw a decline in capital from NZD 411.8 million in 2021 to NZD 329 million in 2022. A decrease in investment was also prevalent in the mature and later stage ventures.

As mentioned in the New Zealand profile of the 2022 edition of the SME Financing Scoreboard, to cushion the impact of COVID-19, the New Zealand Government had implemented various policies to support SMEs. Recent policy responses have included grants and financing for businesses that were impacted by the cyclone, as well as continuing some COVID-19 programmes with adjustments.

Table 31.1. Scoreboard for New Zealand

Indicator	Unit	2007	2008	2009	2010	2011	2012	2013	2014	2015	2016	2017	2018	2019	2020	2021	2022
Debt																	
Outstanding business loans, SMEs	NZD billion	..	..	31.6	32.4	32.1	30.9	32.4	34.2	36.5	60.4	64.6	68.2	72.6	70.8	74.3	77.6
Outstanding business loans, total	NZD billion	80.0	87.6	80.4	78.9	79.9	83.0	85.4	89.0	95.0	101.6	107.7	113.0	120.5	116.3	123.2	132.9
Share of SME outstanding loans	% of total outstanding business loans	..	..	39.3	41.1	40.2	37.2	37.9	38.4	38.4	59.4	60.0	60.4	60.2	60.9	60.3	58.4
Non-performing loans, total	% of all business loans	..	..	1.7	2.1	1.8	1.5	1.1	0.8	0.6	0.5	0.5	0.5	0.6	0.6	0.4	0.4
Non-performing loans, SMEs	% of all SME loans	..	..	2.7	2.9	2.8	2.7	2.4	1.6	0.7	1.1	0.9	0.6	0.7	1.0	0.6	0.7
Interest rate, SMEs	%	12.2	11.2	9.8	10.1	10.0	9.6	9.5	10.3	9.4	9.2	9.3	9.4	9.0	8.4	8.7	11.5
Interest rate, large firms	%	9.0	8.2	5.7	6.3	6.1	6.0	5.4	6.0	5.4	4.6	..	..	..	..		
Interest rate spread	% points	3.2	3.0	4.1	3.8	4.0	3.5	4.2	4.3	4.0	4.6	..	..	..	..		
Rejection rate	% (SME loans rejected/ requested)	6.9	11.6	18.4	20.9	11.4	14.6	9.4	8.4	10.6	4.8	11.7	9.0	9.9	15.1	14.1	13.3
Non-bank finance																	
Venture and growth capital (seed and early stage)	NZD million	29.5	32.6	43.2	53.1	34.8	29.9	53.1	56.4	61.2	69.0	87.0	111.3	128.7	158.0	257.6	186.6
Venture and growth capital (seed and early stage) (growth rate)	%, year-on-year growth rate	..	10.3	32.8	22.8	34.5	14.1	77.6	6.3	8.5	12.6	26.2	28.0	15.6	22.8	63.0	-27.6
Other indicators																	
Payment delays, B2B	number of days	..	..	..	..	15.7	13.5	12.7	10.4	7.1	5.9	5.8	5.9	6.6	5.9	6.0	..
Bankruptcies, total	number	3 585	2 504	2 564	3 054	2 714	2 417	2 188	1 921	1 979	1 996	1 863	1 486	1 319	1 102	782.0	525.0
Bankruptcies, total (growth rate)	%, year-on-year growth rate	..	-30.2	2.4	19.1	-11.1	-10.9	-9.5	-12.2	3.0	0.9	-6.7	-20.2	11.2	-16.5	29.0	32.9

The full country profile is available at: https://doi.org/10.1787/fa521246-en.

32. Norway

Key facts on SME financing

98% of all firms in Norway employ between 1 to 50 people. The SME definition in Norway differs from the definition in use in most EU countries. To contribute to cross-country comparison and make the Scoreboard indicators also relevant to Norway, Statistics Norway used firms with less than 250 as well as those with less than 50 employees to analyse the Norwegian SME population along the indicators covered in the OECD Scoreboard.

After three years of increase, the outstanding stock of SME loans fell in 2016 and 2017, then increased again from 2018 to 2022. The SME share of overall business lending in 2022 stood at the highest level at nearly 40%. The majority of SME lending in Norway is long-term, accounting for an average of over 80%.

Venture and growth capital investments followed almost the same trend as the SME loans. After three years of increase, the venture and growth capital investments fell in 2016 but increased again in 2017 and reached a milestone of over NOK 100 million in 2020.

Most of the equity investments for new enterprises, those founded within previous two years, are channelled to large enterprises. The proportion of venture and growth capital allocated to new SMEs has been within the range of 16% and 21% from 2016 to 2022.

The number of bankruptcies had the highest level in 2019 and the lowest level in 2021 during the 2013-2022 period. In 2019 and 2020, 2 105 and 2 093 bankruptcies were registered respectively, while the corresponding figure in 2021 was 1 449. The low number of bankruptcies in 2021 was likely a result of the government support for business that were implemented together with the temporary Reconstruction Act to remedy financial problems during the pandemic.

Table 32.1. Scoreboard for Norway

Indicator	Unit	2007	2008	2009	2010	2011	2012	2013	2014	2015	2016	2017	2018	2019	2020	2021	2022
Debt																	
Outstanding business loans, SMEs	NOK billion	359	451.1	416.4	433.8	454	452.8	433	474.9	550	530.3	509.3	561.5	618.3	652.3	678.3	773.2
Outstanding business loans, total	NOK billion	837.2	1 033	1 031	1 057	1 125	1 131	1 195	1 289	1 409	1 413	1 484	1 517	1 678	1 717	1 738	1 945
Share of SME outstanding loans	% of total outstanding business loans	42.88	43.65	40.40	41.03	40.35	40.04	36.23	36.84	39.04	37.54	34.33	37.01	36.84	38.00	39.02	39.76
Outstanding short-term loans, SMEs	NOK billion	69.15	83.9	69.9	72.95	75.9	85.43	81.13	90.5	100.2	85.30	87.06	100.6	107.2	89.04	102.2	149

Outstanding long-term loans, SMEs	NOK billion	289.8	367.2	346.5	360.1	378.1	367.4	351.9	384.4	449.8	445	422.3	460.9	511.1	563.2	576.2	624.2
Non-bank finance																	
Venture and growth capital	NOK billion	39.89	29.6	14.6	30.30	39.3	37.7	63.3	74.55	75.1	51.52	52.8	75.	99.4	102.4	102.1	131.2
Venture and growth capital	%, Year-on-year growth rate	..	-25.80	-50.75	107.9	29.56	-3.98	67.72	17.91	0.73	-31.40	2.54	42.00	32.50	3.07	-0.28	28.43
Other indicators																	
Bankruptcies, total	Number	952	1 427	2 059	1 804	1 725	1 525	1 774	1 829	1 794	1 781	1 843	2 067	2 105	2 093	1 449	1 713
Bankruptcies, total	%, Year-on-year growth rate	..	49.89	44.29	-12.38	-4.38	-11.59	16.33	3.10	-1.91	-0.72	3.48	12.15	1.84	-0.57	-30.77	18.22

The full country profile is available at: https://doi.org/10.1787/fa521246-en.

33. People's Republic of China

Key facts on SME financing

In China, SMEs play a key role in maintaining economic dynamism and boosting innovation and entrepreneurship. SMEs contribute approximately 50% of tax revenue, 60% of GDP, 70% of technological innovation, and 80% of urban employment. In 2022, there were about 52 million SMEs in China, and the number of newly registered enterprises reached an average of 23 800 per day.

Outstanding business loans for Micro and Small Enterprises (MSEs) increased to CNY 59.7 trillion in 2022, up 19.4% from 2021. The share of outstanding business loans for MSEs has been relatively stable for the past two years, at 46.52% in 2021 and 49.12% in 2022, respectively. The ratio of short-term loans to total loans for SMEs increased from 40.76% to 42.22% over 2020-21. This ratio increased to 43.1%, up 0.88 percentage points in 2022.

In 2022, interest rates for SMEs and large firms were 4.45% and 4.29%, down 0.07 and 0.24 percentage points, respectively, compared to 2021.The interest rate spread between SMEs and large enterprises was positive, and the difference rose from -0.01% to 0.16% in 2021-22 (the difference rose from -0.22% to -0.01% in 2020-21). In recent years, China has improved and implemented the policy of cutting taxes and fees on debt finance. In 2022, SMEs were on average charged 1.42% of the total value of bank loans in the form of extra loan fees, slightly down 0.39 percentage points with respect to the previous year. In 2022, the 1-year interest rate in the shadow banking sector[1] ranged from 11.78% - 13.11%, with a spread of about 7.3% - 8.7% compared to formal bank loans. In 2022, the shadow banking assets reached CNY 50.3 trillion, a significant decrease of CNY 3.29 trillion, and the ratio of shadow banking assets to GDP dropped to 41.6%, the lowest level since 2013.

In 2022, the rejection rate of SME loan applications was stable at around 3.61%, and the utilisation rate of SME bank loans has remained at a high rate of 87.69%. On average, 58.38% of SMEs tried to apply for a bank loan.

In 2022, SMEs obtained CNY 252.0 billion from STAR Market, CNY 179.6 billion from Shenzhen Venture Board, and CNY 16.38 billion from Beijing Stock Exchange, up by 24.22%, 21.78%, and 117.81% respectively, compared to the previous year. Venture capital, leasing and factoring, online lending and crowdfunding continue to remain important sources of SME financing.

In 2020, the ratio of non-performing loans to total MSE loans was 2.81%, down 0.28 percentage points from 2019. The bankruptcy rate for SMEs was 3.48% in 2022 according to survey data, up 6.42% from the previous year.

In 2022, the National Financing Guarantee Fund supported 45.6 million SMEs, totalling CNY 70.91 billion. The National SME Development Fund raised nearly CNY 90 billion and invested in more than 1 100 projects. Special funds for SME Development account for over CNY 5.65 billion in total. Rewards and subsidies to reduce financing guarantee fees account for about CNY 3 billion.

In 2022, the Chinese government has continued to alleviate financing difficulties and reduce costs for SMEs, including tax and fee reduction, subsidies, financing guarantees, expansion of financing channels, improving financial services, and enhancing the connection between industry and finance. China has carried out special projects to clear up arrears in payments to SMEs, focusing on the development of technology-based SMEs.

Table 33.1. Scoreboard for the People's Republic of China

Indicator	Unit	2007	2008	2009	2010	2011	2012	2013	2014	2015	2016	2017	2018	2019	2020	2021	2022
Debt																	
Outstanding business loans, SMEs	RMB billion			13616	17139	21168	25356	28585	33302	35300	40517	46477					
Outstanding business loans, total	RMB billion			24940	30292	35017	39283	44019	52162	53895	62578	71545	78728	86123	97307	107482	121547
Share of SME outstanding loans	% of total outstanding business loans			54.60	56.58	60.45	64.55	64.94	63.84	65.50	64.75	64.96					
Outstanding business loans, Small and Micro Enterprises	RMB billion											30743.7	33492.3	36900	42700	50000	59700
Share of outstanding loans, Small and Micro Enterprises	% of total outstanding business loans											42.97	42.54	42.85	43.88	46.52	49.12
New business lending, total	RMB billion																
Share of short-term loans, total	% of total business lending							42.12	43.12	42.4	40.35	38.06	35.77	34.35	32.86	30.61	29.6
Share of short-term SME lending	% of total SME lending							56.1	49.24	47.56	54.69	40.97	41.62	39.09	40.76	42.22	43.1
Direct government loans, SMEs	RMB billion				1222.6	1550	1813.4	2082.4	2470	2820							
Non-performing loans, total	% of all business loans			2.58	1.76	1.26	1.21	1.25	1.49	2.04	2.07	2.05	2.29	2.24	1.95		
Non-performing loans, SMEs	% of all SME loans			3.83	2.52	1.75	1.65	1.66	1.97	2.59	2.6	2.58					
Non-performing loans, Small and Micro Enterprises	%							2.01	2.2	2.74	2.68	2.74	3.16	3.09	2.81		
Interest rate, SMEs	%							8.39	7.51	5.23	4.77	5.78	5.17	4.86	4.84	4.52	4.45
Interest rate, large firms	%							7.72	7.47	5.26	4.89	5.4	5.07	5.11	5.06	4.53	4.29
Interest rate spread	% points							0.67	0.04	-0.03	-0.12	0.38	0.1	-0.25	-0.22	-0.01	0.16
Collateral, SMEs	% of SMEs needing collateral to obtain bank lending			50.55	51.64	51.59	52.98	54.52	54.76	55.67	52.05	50.28	50.18				
Collateral, Small and Micro Enterprises	% of Small and Micro Enterprises needing collateral to obtain bank lending							55.8	56.96	58	54.2	52.4	52.5	53.2	50.9		
Percentage of SME loan applications	SME loan applications / total number of SMEs									69.88	63.06	53.09	58.36	54.79	57.94	56.67	58.38
Rejection rate	1 – (SME loans							6.19	11.97	11.72	6.13	4.07	3.69	4.05	3.79	3.59	3.61

	authorised / requested)																
Utilisation rate	SME loans used / authorised							93.51	94.75	94.48	94.03	89.91	86.26	84.32	84.55	87.66	87.69
Non-bank finance																	
Venture and growth capital (stock)	RMB billion	111.3	145.6	160.5	240.7	319.8	331.3	263.9	293.3	336.1	376.5	411	476.9	563.6	627.2	728.3	
Venture and growth capital (growth rate, stock)	%, Year-on-year growth rate		30.80	10.26	49.93	32.88	3.59	-20.34	11.15	14.59	12.02	9.16	16.03	18.18	11.28	16.12	
Venture and growth capital (incremental)	RMB billion						25.11	27.90	37.44	46.56	50.55	84.53	52.72	86.68	63.6	101.1	
Venture and growth capital (growth rate, incremental)	%, Year-on-year growth rate							11.11	34.19	24.36	8.57	67.22	-37.63	64.42	-26.63	58.96	
Leasing and hire purchases	RMB billion	24	155	370	700	930	1550	2100	3200	4440	5330	6060	6650	6654	6504	6323	5850
Factoring and invoicing	EUR million		55 000	67 300	154 550	274 870	343 759	378 128	406 102	352 879	301 635	405 537	411 573	403 504	433 162	469 575	576 885
Other indicators																	
Payment delays, B2B	Number of days							95.91	72.31	64.44	65.21	44	38				
Bankruptcies, SMEs	%							7.57	7.24	5.46	4.73	3.7	2.85	3.09	4.06	3.27	3.48
Bankruptcies, SMEs (growth rate)	%, year-on-year growth rate								-4.36	24.59	13.37	21.78	-22.97	8.42	31.39	-19.46	6.42

Note

1. The shadow banking sector primarily encompasses special purpose vehicles (SPV), entrusted loans, trust loans, non-equity private funds, and online P2P lending institutions.

The full country profile is available at: https://doi.org/10.1787/fa521246-en.

34. Peru

Key facts on SME financing

In 2022, Peru's economy grew by 2.7%, primarily driven by private consumption, leading to the expansion of the commerce and services sectors. However, the country faced challenges such as increased financing costs, inflation and social unrest. In 2023, SMEs and entrepreneurs were projected to encounter similar challenges. The business environment could be further complicated by both social conflicts and climate-related issues.

SMEs play a major role in the Peruvian economy, contributing to over 30% of value added and approximately 7% to exports. They have a particularly strong presence in sectors such as commerce, services, and manufacturing. Regarding the business landscape, SMEs comprise 99.4% of all enterprises and contribute significantly to employment, accounting for 90.5% of private employment. This highlights the importance of supporting their growth, as they are considered drivers for the development of the Peruvian economy.

SMEs accounted for a significant share of all outstanding loans in 2022, reaching 30.9%, driven by an 8.9% increase in the number of formal enterprises accessing the formal financial system. Between 2010-2019, the share of all outstanding loans was around 25% on average, a figure that experienced a positive increasing of 7 p.p. Thus, since 2020, the share on average was 32%. It should be noted that there was also observed growth in the number of SMEs, expanding at an average annual rate of 12.3%, going from 1 780 thousand companies in 2020 to 2 246 thousand companies in 2022.

While banks remained the primary lenders, alternative financing options such as factoring and invoice discounting gained some attention, although fluctuations have been observed in their usage in recent years. Moreover, over-indebtedness is a concern, as the majority of SMEs rely on a single institution, and small business loans face higher interest rates, posing affordability challenges.

In 2022, the interest rate spread between large companies and SMEs in Peru was 19.9 percentage points. It is important to note that the interest rates for small business loans experienced an increase from 24.0% in December 2021 to 27.1% in December 2022. Therefore, this upward trend suggests that despite the narrowing spread, the cost of borrowing for these enterprises has increased.

The government of Peru has implemented several programmes to address financing constraints and support businesses during the COVID-19 pandemic. These programmes include Reactiva Perú, FAE-Mype, PAE-Mype, FAE-Agro, FAE-Turismo, Programa de Garantías COVID-19, and FAE-TEXCO. These initiatives aim to provide favourable financing conditions and ensure the continuity of resilient businesses across sectors.

Table 34.1. Scoreboard for Peru

Indicator	Unit	2010	2011	2012	2013	2014	2015	2016	2017	2018	2019	2020	2021	2022
Debt														
Outstanding business loans, SMEs. As of 30 June	PEN Billion	17.18	19.75	23.23	26.62	30.14	32.44	32.46	34.11	35.56	36.48	61.92	73.63	66.12
Outstanding business loans, total. As of 30 June	PEN Billion	65.99	75.04	81.49	97.20	112.21	127.37	130.02	134.62	147.30	149.53	189.21	223.05	213.76
Share of SME outstanding loans	% of total outstanding business loans	26.04	26.31	28.50	27.39	26.86	25.47	24.97	25.34	24.14	24.39	32.73	33.01	30.93
New business lending, total	PEN Billion				264 129	244 850	249 880	226 035	219 435	244 928	241 292	281 590	273 983	327 359
New business lending, SMEs	PEN Billion				241 949	224 537	228 624	207 603	201 133	225 421	222 626	263 860	248 707	293 979
Share of new SME lending	% of total new lending				91.6	91.7	91.5	91.8	91.7	92.0	92.3	93.7	90.77	89.80
Government loan guarantees, SMEs	PEN Billion	..	..	..	..	..	..	400	..	..	..	..		
Direct government loans, SMEs	PEN Billion	30.98	49.06	59.57	219.92	365.33	369.45	389.18	320.85	399.83	367.95	387.01	373.92	316.37
Non-performing loans, total	% of all business loans	2.20	1.78	1.65	1.96	2.14	2.37	2.46	3.33	3.40	3.15	2.93	3.48	5.00
Non-performing loans, SMEs	% of all SME loans	7.83	6.33	5.19	6.30	7.11	8.42	9.03	8.69	10.53	10.94	6.63	9.81	16.43
Interest rate, SMEs	%	27.63	27.09	25.96	24.66	23.41	25.59	26.37	26.57	26.31	25.28	20.23	24.03	27.05
Interest rate, large firms	%	4.98	6.03	6.60	6.49	6.37	6.29	6.86	6.75	6.00	5.93	4.39	3.80	7.20
Interest rate spread	% points	22.65	21.06	19.35	18.17	17.04	19.30	19.52	19.82	20.31	19.35	15.84	20.22	19.85
Percentage of SME loan applications	SME loan applications/ total number of SMEs	..	..	..	..	38.52	51.02	43.26	48.39		43.40			
Rejection rate	1-(SME loans authorised/ requested)	..	..	..	..	5.06	5.77	4.63	5.93		4.00			
Utilisation rate	SME loans used/ authorised	..	..	..	..	94.94	94.23	95.37	94.07		96.00			
Non-bank finance														
Leasing and hire purchases	PEN Billion	3 374	3 846	4 301	3 978	4 128	3 966	3 530	3 440	3 110	3 000	3 204	2 212	1 605
Factoring and invoice discounting	PEN Billion	768.98	754.27	719.99	779.45	809.13	819.41	835.50	833.89	1006.19	947.14	724.63	762.88	605.27
Other indicators														
Bankruptcies, all businesses	Number	162 948	168 261	233 287	152 758	225 384	242 842	259 443	362 091	199 303	183 442	859 595	247 397	218 568

Note: *Preliminary data.

The full country profile is available at: https://doi.org/10.1787/fa521246-en.

35. Poland

Key facts on SME financing

For the last three years, the Polish economy, as is the case with the European and global economy, has been strongly affected by the effects of the pandemic and the Russian aggression against Ukraine. Global turmoil and the energy crisis provoked by Russia have increased inflation around the world, especially in Europe, which had a significant impact on SMEs.

In 2021, there were 2 356 thousand non-financial enterprises in Poland, which is 4.2% more than the previous year, and 36.4% more compared to 2010. In 2021 SMEs made up 99.8% of all non-financial enterprises in Poland, numbering 2 352.2 thousand SMEs in total. As in previous years, non-financial enterprises are dominated by the presence of microenterprises, which were responsible for 97.1% share in the structure of the entire population in 2021. Among all size classes, the microenterprises recorded the greatest increase in the number of units in the years 2010–2021.

In 2022, the banking sector remained stable. As a result of the reforms implemented after the 2008-2009 global financial crisis, the Polish banking system has generally become more resilient to shocks, due to stronger capital and liquidity buffers. In 2022, a slight increase in debt was observed among both large companies and SMEs.

The stock of outstanding business loans and SME loans increased in 2022, which could be driven by an increase in credit demand. The share of non-performing loans (both total and SME) decreased slightly in 2022. The average interest rate, both for SMEs and large companies, increased in 2022. Similarly, the interest rate spread also rose to 1.23 percentage points.

According to PFR Ventures, the value of the venture capital market in 2022 was only slightly lower than the year before. Considering the global downward trend, this is a positive sign. The total number of transactions increased, but their average value fell from EUR 1.6 million in 2021 to EUR 1.4 million in 2022.

Despite the difficult business environment, the Warsaw Stock Exchange achieved stable financial results in 2022. The Warsaw Stock Exchange Capital Group generated PLN 389.3 million in revenue in 2022, which means a low, single-digit decrease (4.5%) compared to the record level from 2021. Last year, the Group recorded record shares in the profits of associates, which reached PLN 28.3 million and were 15.9% higher year-on-year.

In 2020, the government launched a number of tools to support domestic entrepreneurs. The "Anti-crisis Shield" included the so-called Financial Shields in the form of financial subsidies for SMEs and in the form of preferential financing for large companies, which were worth a combined total of PLN 71.37 billion (July 2021). Bank Gospodarstwa Krajowego provided support worth more than 240 billion (April 2023) –in the form of accessible guarantees. The Anti-crisis Shield also covered other measures such as social insurance exemptions, subsidies to the remuneration of employees and idle- time benefits. The government support under the Anti-crisis Shield had amounted in total to over PLN 236 billion as of July 2021. These measures have significantly mitigated the effects of the crisis in the non-financial corporate sector.

The measures on price mitigation taken so far have been addressed to a wide audience in order to remedy the situation on many levels. Measures to reduce the negative impact of high inflation include, among others:

- An anti-inflation shield that has reduced taxes on certain products, including energy;
- The Energy Shield, which introduced allowances and compensations for the purchase of energy raw materials for certain groups, including vulnerable entities;
- The Solidarity Shield, which set the maximum electricity prices, including for SMEs, PLN 785/MWh

Table 35.1. Scoreboard for Poland

Indicator	Unit	2008	2009	2010	2011	2012	2013	2014	2015	2016	2017	2018	2019	2020	2021	2022
							Debt									
Outstanding business loans, SMEs	PLN Billion	125.3	127.22	127.00	159.02	164.81	163.93	175.63	185.78	193.63	206.57	208.48	208.68	199.94	191.19	210.55
Outstanding business loans, total	PLN Billion	233.3	222.08	219.69	264.51	272.25	277.96	300.92	327.27	344.93	366.02	388.25	395.60	376.73	396.46	436.59
Share of SME outstanding loans	% of total outstanding business loans	53.72	57.29	57.81	60.12	60.54	58.97	58.36	56.77	56.14	56.44	53.70	52.75	53.07	48.22	48.23
Outstanding short-term loans, SMEs	PLN Billion	31.93	31.25	31.52	38.45	39.88	37.37	40.46	41.60	42.81	43.93	39.30	42.20	31.24	33.56	40.66
Outstanding long-term loans, SMEs	PLN Billion	90.18	93.24	93.73	116.22	122.23	123.43	130.25	138.33	145.05	156.36	161.89	158.13	160.56	148.83	160.80
Share of short-term SME lending	% of total SME lending	26.15	25.10	25.17	24.86	24.60	23.24	23.70	23.12	22.79	21.93	19.53	21.06	16.29	18.40	20.18
Government loan guarantees, SMEs	PLN Billion	..	..	..	..	..	7.00	9.65	8.90	9.36	9.91	10.17	11.56	23.58	34.17	37.82
Government guaranteed loans, SMEs	PLN Billion	..	..	..	..	..	12.24	17.43	15.86	16.43	17.80	18.17	20.71	33.70	46.24	51.81
Non-performing loans, total	% of all business loans	6.50	11.58	12.40	10.37	11.78	11.61	11.33	10.31	9.11	8.28	8.70	8.43	9.00	7.42	6.45
Non-performing loans, SMEs	% of all SME loans	7.46	13.35	14.59	12.33	13.06	12.99	12.75	12.29	10.97	10.04	11.32	11.16	12.18	10.93	9.70
Interest rate, SMEs	%	5.37	3.82	4.31	4.57	4.86	3.85	3.52	3.00	2.86	2.95	3.43	3.77	3.07	2.64	5.10
Interest rate, large firms	%	5.62	4.28	4.00	4.45	4.74	3.83	3.40	2.90	2.77	2.76	2.92	3.07	2.93	2.63	3.87
Interest rate spread	% points	-0.25	-0.46	0.31	0.12	0.12	0.02	0.12	0.10	0.09	0.19	0.51	0.70	0.14	0.01	1.23
Collateral, SMEs	% of SMEs needing collateral to obtain bank lending	..	..	..	..	..	..	..	..	38.92	30.33	..	..	..		

Percentage of SME loan applications	SME loan applications/ total number of SMEs	..	..	..	..	..	..	..	..	78.55	80.12	..	..	..		
Rejection rate	1-(SME loans authorised/ requested)	..	..	..	..	..	..	..	..	37.20	31.78	..	..	..		
Utilisation rate	SME loans used/ authorised	..	..	..	..	..	..	..	..	66.44	61.83	..	..	..		
								Non-bank finance								
Venture and growth capital	EUR Million	96.4	70.7	112.7	197.5	127.1	198.2	89.3	140.3	190.7	195.8	350.4	193.7	249,2	266.7	295.4
Venture and growth capital (growth rate)	%, Year-on-year growth rate	-34.65	-26.70	59.44	75.28	-35.62	55.93	-54.96	57.07	35.97	2.69	78.93	-44.72	21.72	7.04	10.75
Leasing and hire purchases	PLN Billion	24.09	21.43	23.92	27.79	26.90	30.42	34.29	37.83	51.01	58.19	66.44	61.49	50.19	71.68	68.41
Factoring and invoice discounting	PLN Billion	45.51	53.16	88.61	95.33	113.06	129.59	152.68	171.64	192.74	222.49	269.63	315.02	311.34	399.82	476.92

The full country profile is available at: https://doi.org/10.1787/fa521246-en.

36. Portugal

Key facts on SME financing

In 2021, SMEs comprised 99.9% of enterprises in Portugal, employed 71.5% of the labour force and were responsible for 56.8% of the turnover and 66.8% in total investment, including large and non-financial enterprises.

In 2021, the total stock of business loans increased 1% compared to 2020. In 2022, there was a decrease of -0.4% compared to 2021. In sum, in 2022, the share of SME outstanding business loans to total business loans stayed around 80% as has been the case for the last five years.

In 2021 and in 2022, short-term loans gradually increased, by 6.4% and 5.2%, respectively. On the other hand, long-term loans increased by 2.7% in 2021 and decreased 1.8% in 2022. The Portuguese financial system became restrictive concerning business loans to SMEs.

In 2020, the share of government-guaranteed loans in total SME loans had a steady acceleration, with an increase of 23.3%, demonstrating the sustained public efforts to support SME access to finance, during the COVID-19 crisis. In 2021, total government-guaranteed loans slightly increased to 3.2%, compared to 2020, and registered a decrease of -17.5% in 2022.

The average interest rate for SME loans decreased to 2.48% in 2020, marking the sixth consecutive year of decline. However, in 2021, it had a slight increase to 2.51%, and in 2022 an even larger increase to 3.18%, which reflects a setback in SME financing conditions.

Trends in venture capital have been uneven. Total venture capital investments in 2022 increased to EUR 72 million, a rise of 7.5% compared to 2021.

Late payments are still a problematic issue for Portuguese SMEs in both business-to-business (B2B) transactions and payments from public authorities, having been steadily decreasing in the last five years, with no relevant oscillations. In 2022, 41.8% of SMEs reported experiencing late payments. In addition, the time difference between agreed and actual payment is 13 days (increased by 1 day since 2021) in B2B transactions and 10 days (decreased by 12 days since 2021) for the public sector.

Concerning bankruptcies, 2020 closed with a decline of 2.3% compared to 2019, with 2 502 bankruptcies, despite the impact of the COVID-19 crisis on the economy. This decline can be explained in part by government measures that have allowed companies to avoid filing for bankruptcy during the COVID-19 crisis. In 2021, there was also a decrease, with 1 571 bankruptcies (-37.2%) and in 2022, there was again another decrease, with 1 309 bankruptcies (-16.6%).

The number of small and medium-sized businesses supported by the EIF's European Guarantee Fund have significantly increased year after year, from 12 000 in 2021 to 26 000 in 2022. The same strong results were achieved in terms of jobs supported, which increased from 188 000 in 2021 to 340 000 in 2022. This result is due to the large amounts signed in 2021 under the European Guarantee Fund. The EIF has provided support in Portugal under a wide range of programmes and mandates, such as COSME, *InnovFin,* and the Cultural and Creative Sectors Guarantee Facility. The EIF made five equity investments in 2022, committing EUR 123 million, which leveraged EUR 500 million of equity finance. These figures highlight the largest volumes ever committed by the EIF to Portuguese venture capital and private equity funds.

Table 36.1. Scoreboard for Portugal

Indicator	Unit	2007	2008	2009	2010	2011	2012	2013	2014	2015	2016	2017	2018	2019	2020	2021	2022
Debt																	
Outstanding business loans, SMEs	EUR billion			90.2	88.2	87.0	79.7	73.9	70.3	65.8	61.3	57.4	54.1	52.5	58.9	60.9	60.3
Outstanding business loans, total	EUR billion	102	115.8	117.8	114.6	113.8	105.3	99.3	86.5	82.2	77.3	73.1	69.5	67.0	73.9	75.6	75.3
Share of SME outstanding loans	% of total outstanding business loans			76.61	76.96	76.45	75.68	74.41	81.30	80.13	79.36	78.53	77.69	78.35	79.73	80.06	80.16
New business lending, total	EUR billion	64.3	61.8	46.3	45.6	45	45.6	49.1	41.2	33.8	29.8	28.8	31.6	32.7	33.5	20.8	22.0
New business lending, SMEs	EUR billion	28.9	26.4	23.1	9	14.2	12.5	11.9	11.9	11.9	11.3	10.9	11.2	11.8	11.8	7.6	7.4
Share of new SME lending	% of total new lending	44.9	42.7	49.9	19.7	31.6	27.5	24.1	28.7	35.2	37.8	37.7	35.5	36.1	35.2	36.5	33.7
Short-term loans, SMEs	EUR billion	..	..	24.7	22.7	21.3	15.3	13.4	11.5	9.5	9.5	8.9	7.3	6.5	8.1	8.7	9.1
Long-term loans, SMEs	EUR billion	..	..	65.6	65.5	65.7	64.4	60.5	58.7	56.3	51.9	48.5	46.8	46.0	50.8	52.1	51.1
Share of short-term SME lending	% of total SME lending	..	27.34	27.34	25.77	24.47	19.21	18.13	16.37	14.51	15.43	15.53	13.50	12.38	13.89	14.32	15.20
Government guaranteed loans, SMEs	EUR billion	..	..	5	6.8	6.1	6.0	5.8	5.5	5.6	5.7	6.1	6.2	6.3	13.6	14.0	11.5
Non-performing loans, total	% of all business loans	1.50	2.20	3.90	4.10	6.00	9.40	11.80	14.20	15.20	15.00	12.70	7.80	4.60	3.32	2.30	2.05
Non-performing loans, SMEs	% of all SME loans			4.67	5.00	7.33	11.76	14.82	16.50	17.89	17.62	14.65	8.83	5.15	3.87	2.66	2.43
Interest rate, SMEs	%	7.05	7.64	5.72	5.45	7.41	7.59	6.82	5.97	4.6	3.83	3.42	3.13	2.93	2.48	2.51	3.18
Interest rate, large firms	%	5.29	5.92	3.84	3.91	5.4	5.43	4.97	4.37	3.25	2.69	2.14	1.93	1.85	1.70	1.72	2.66
Interest rate spread	% points	1.76	1.72	1.87	2.25	2.01	2.16	1.85	1.60	1.35	1.14	1.28	1.20	1.08	0.78	0.80	0.52
Collateral, SMEs	% of SMEs needing collateral to obtain bank lending	..	..	76.25	81.16	82.63	82.15	83.09	80.14	81.84	79.60	80.98	83.13	86.95	89.88	89.60	88.73
Non-bank finance																	
Venture and growth capital	EUR million	129	92	70	74	26	53	106	106	102	18	29	30	69	42	67	72

Venture and growth capital (growth rate)	%, Year-on-year growth rate	..	-28.7	-23.9	5.7	-64.9	103.9	100.0	0.0	-3.8	-82.4	61.1	3.5	130.0	-39.1	55.8	7.5
Leasing and hire purchases	EUR million	..	..	53.24	52.42	3.442	3.037	2.666	2.425	2.345	2.295	2.175	2.204	1.879	1.866	467	497
Factoring and invoice discounting	EUR million	..	..	621	733	402	338	376	476	547	441	418	930	855	513	99	113
Other indicators																	
Payment delays, B2B	Number of days	40	33	35	37	41	40	35	33	21	20	20	12	18	12	12	13
Bankruptcies, SMEs	Number	2 612	3 528	3 815	4 091	4 746	6 688	6 030	4 019	4 714	3 620	3 099	2 694	2 560	2502	1571	1309
1309Bankruptcies, SMEs (growth rate)	%, Year-on-year growth rate	..	35.1	8.1	7.2	16.0	40.9	-9.8	-33.4	17.3	-23.2	-14.4	-13.1	-5.0	-2.3	-37.2	-16.7

The full country profile is available at: https://doi.org/10.1787/fa521246-en.

37. Serbia

Key facts on SME financing

SMEs dominate the Serbian business economy, accounting for 99% of all enterprises. In 2022, SMEs employed more than 64% of the labour force and accounted for 60% of total gross value added and for 65.6% of turnover. Sector-specific data indicates that most SMEs belong to the trade sector (22.9%), followed by the manufacturing sector (14.7%), professional, scientific and innovative activities (14%), and transportation and storage (9.8%).

According to the preliminary results from the 2022 SME lending conditions survey conducted by the National Bank of Serbia in 2023, the stock of SME loans in 2022 decreased by 6.6% year-on-year to EUR 8.5 billion (while compared to pre-crisis 2019, it represents an increase of 18.4%, which in absolute terms is an increase of EUR 1.3 billion). The decrease in 2022 compared to 2021 was partly due to the repayment of subsidized loans provided to SMEs aimed to support them during the COVID-19 crisis. The share of outstanding SME loans in total corporate loans decreased to 27.9% (from 33.2% in 2021). Long-term loans decreased as well and amounted to 86.0% of total SMEs loans.

New bank lending to SMEs in 2022 amounted EUR 5.2 billion (0.6% higher relative to 2021). The share of new SMEs loans among total corporate loans decreased by 2.4 percentage points to 34.7% in 2022.

Interest rates for SME loans in/or indexed to foreign currencies increased to 5.1% in 2022 (from 4.3% in 2021 and 3.8% in 2020). However, the interest rate spread between large companies and SMEs decreased to 1.9 percentage points (from 2.0 percentage points in 2021). On the Serbian dinar-denominated loans side, interest rates reached 6.7%, 1.8 percentage points higher compared to 2021 when it reached 4.9%, while the spread between large companies and SME decreased to 2.5 percentage points (from 2.8% in 2021).

The rejection rate (the percentage of SME loan applications that are rejected considering the total number of loans) was 16.6% in 2022 (20.5% in 2021), while the utilisation rate (the percentage of used SME loans among all SME loans that were approved) was 96.5% in 2022 (97.0% in 2021). At the same time, the share of SME loans requiring collateral (excluding bills of exchange) was 37.2% in 2022 (43.3% in 2021).

The share of NPLs in total SMEs loans slightly increased to 3.8% (compared to 3.5% in 2021), due to decreased stock of loans to SMEs. On the other hand, the NPLs of the whole corporate sector decreased to 1.9% in 2022 from 2.6% in 2021.

Table 37.1. Scoreboard for Serbia

Indicator	Unit	2010	2011	2012	2013	2014	2015	2016	2017	2018	2019	2020	2021	2022
							Debt							
Outstanding business loans, SMEs	EUR Million	4 202	4 320	4 352	4 061	4 779	5 340	5 552	5 802	6 488	7 140	8 194	9 043	8 450
Outstanding business loans, total	EUR Million	19 777	20 028	20 460	19 154	18 724	18 677	18 362	19 150	20 847	22 394	24 622	27 273	30 250
Share of SME outstanding loans	% of total outstanding business loans	21.25	21.57	21.27	21.20	25.52	28.59	30.24	30.30	31.12	32	33.28	33.16	27.93
New business lending, total	EUR Million	..	8 862	9 043	7 093	6 765	8 461	10 130	10 966	12 339	13 629	11 425	13 944	15 005
New business lending, SMEs	EUR Million	3 190	3 323	2 771	2 302	2 717	3 332	4 038	4 688	5 478	6 087	4 927	5 170	5 199
Share of new SME lending	% of total new lending	..	37.49	30.64	32.45	40.16	39.38	39.86	42.75	44.53	45	43.13	37.08	34.65
Outstanding short-term loans, SMEs	EUR Million	1 436	1 308	1 257	1 386	1 405	1 348	1 380	1 451	1 480	1 347	1 013	1 200	1 181
Outstanding long-term loans, SMEs	EUR Million	2 766	3 012	3 096	2 675	3 374	3 993	4 172	4 350	5 008	5 793	7 181	7 843	7 269
Share of short-term SME lending	% of total SME lending	34.17	30.28	28.87	34.13	29.40	25.24	24.86	25.01	22.81	19	12.36	13.27	13.98
Government subsidized loans, SMEs*	EUR Million	523	390	569	342	750	126	13	14	15	14	357	349	206
Non-performing loans, total	% of all business loans	20.70	22.33	19.19	24.52	24.64	21.71	17.22	10.41	5.05	3.17	2.82	2.64	1.94
Non-performing loans, SMEs	% of all SME loans	21.00	22.64	26.15	28.05	27.08	26.69	20.16	9.91	6.9	4.65	4.62	3.55	3.80
Interest rate, SMEs	%	10.06	9.72	8.15	8.03	7.25	6.31	5.69	4.58	4.23	3.98	3.70	4.27	5.06
Interest rate, large firms	%	7.36	7.88	6.60	6.34	5.18	3.87	3.13	2.78	2.30	2.56	2.09	2.26	3.12
Interest rate spread	% points	2.70	1.85	1.55	1.70	2.07	2.44	2.56	1.79	1.93	1.42	1.61	1.98	1.95
Collateral, SMEs	% of SMEs needing collateral to obtain bank lending	44.51	45.59	53.00	55.06	53.13	53.79	42.70	53.85	53.09	52.77	50.55	43.31	37.23
Percentage of SME loan applications	SME loan applications/ total number of SMEs	..	..	..	..	..	14.94	16.46	16.89	15.46				
Rejection rate	1 – (SME loans authorised/ requested)	27.13	15.77	32.02	32.18	25.15	24.52	28.18	28.32	17.09	6.51	19.27	20.46	16.55
Utilisation rate	SME loans used/ authorised	67.76	83.83	86.11	87.92	86.47	87.86	88.05	90.58	94.99	98.24	96.08	96.99	96.47

Note: *Stock of loans subsidized by the government realized through the bank as an agent.

The full country profile is available at: https://doi.org/10.1787/fa521246-en.

38. Slovak Republic

Key facts on SME financing

SMEs dominate the Slovak economy, accounting for 99.6% of the business population (excluding self-employed individuals). The number of SMEs increased by 3.9% in 2022, and micro-enterprises accounted for a considerable portion of this growth, growing by 4.2% year-on-year.

Although the interest rate increased in 2022, the volume of existing and new bank loans increased, year-on-year. The amount of outstanding business loans has been growing since 2013, increasing by 12.9% from EUR 17 344 million in 2021 to EUR 19 583 million in 2022. More than half of SMEs' outstanding business loans (62.46%) were long-term, while short-term loans accounted for 37.54% (EUR 7 451 million) of SMEs' outstanding business loans.

Favourable credit conditions and the availability of supporting financial instruments during COVID-19 increased interest in bank financing for all size categories of enterprises. In 2022, the volume of SMEs' new business lending increased year-on-year by 31.8% to EUR 5 720 million and the share of SMEs in the total volume of new lending increased by 4.1 percentage points to 43.13%.

The share of non-performing SME loans among all SME loans was higher (3.21%) than the share of non-performing loans among all business loans (2.73%) in 2022. In the year-on-year comparison, the share of SMEs' non-performing loans decreased by 0.65%.

Interest rates on SME loans fell from 3.8% in 2012 to 2.4 % in 2021. In 2022, the interest rate on SME slightly increased to 2.9% as the result of the change in policy interest rates set by European Central Bank (ECB) to help bring inflation back down.

After 2017's significant decline in the volume of venture and growth capital caused by the closure of funding support under the JEREMIE initiative for the 2007-2013 programming period, there has been a gradual recovery in the amount of venture capital investments. In 2022, the amount of venture capital investments increased year-on-year by 28.5 %, totalling EUR 36.05 million. The majority of investments were focused on established SMEs – to expand production capacities, to develop market potential or further development of products or services. Compared to SME bank financing, the amount of venture capital is still negligible.

The payment discipline of enterprises has improved. Average business-to-business (B2B) payment delays decreased by 7.7% year-on-year to 12 days in 2022.

Since 2020, the government has implemented several policies that seek to improve SMEs' access to finance and introduced new instruments to support SME financing during COVID-19. As the situation with COVID-19 improved throughout 2022, the volume of SME government loan guarantees, the guaranteed loans and SME government direct loans decreased significantly. The total volume of SME government loan guarantees decreased from EUR 293.5 million in 2021 to EUR 95.2 million in 2022. As a result of the decrease in government loan guarantees, there was also a significant decrease in the volume of guaranteed loans – from EUR 553.1 million in 2021 to EUR 360.6 million in 2022. The volume of SME government direct loans provided by the state banks and the Slovak Business Agency fell less rapidly in 2022 – by 12.7 % to EUR 186.5 million. In the context of mitigating the impact of the energy crisis the first support schemes have been launched in 2022 and will have a significant impact on SME subsidies in the following year.

Table 38.1. Scoreboard for the Slovak Republic

Indicator	Unit	2007	2008	2009	2010	2011	2012	2013	2014	2015	2016	2017	2018	2019	2020	2021	2022
								Debt									
Outstanding business loans, SMEs [1]	EUR billion	9.1	12.1	12	12	10.6	11	10.7	11.9	13.2	13.5	14.6	15.1	15.3	16.2	17.3	19.5
Outstanding business loans, SMEs [2]	EUR billion	..	..	..	..	..	5.9	6.7	6.9	7.4	8.7	8.9	9.2	9.7	10.7	11.9	14.1
Outstanding business loans, total	EUR billion	13.9	15.7	15.2	15.2	16.1	15.5	15.1	14.8	16.1	16.9	18.1	18.9	19.6	20.0	20.8	23.3
Share of SME outstanding loans [1]	% of total outstanding business loans	65.7	77.12	79.39	79.39	65.77	71.11	71.07	80.22	81.7	79.81	80.46	79.81	77.77	80.95	83.42	83.95
New business lending, total	EUR billion	8.49	9.44	7.56	9.12	10.69	11.69	11.88	12.5	11.78	8.67	9.50	10.72	9.31	11.26	11.12	13.26
New business lending, SMEs [2]	EUR billion	..	..	..	..	..	2.36	2.63	2.6	3.09	3.13	3.17	3.46	3.22	4.20	4.34	5.72
Share of new SME lending	% of total new lending	..	..	..	..	..	20.2	22.16	20.83	26.2	36.14	33.37	32.29	34.54	37.30	39.02	43.13
Outstanding short-term loans, SMEs	EUR million	4 609	4 797	4 981	4 987	4 188	4 481	4 532	5 385	5 766	5 394	5 695	5 683	5 926	6 547	6 445	7 451
Outstanding long-term loans, SMEs	EUR million	4 527	7 295	7 051	7 059	6 412	6 557	6 202	6 517	7 404	8 129	8 832	9 437	9 329	9 661	10 899	12 132
Share of short-term SME lending	% of total SME lending	50.45	39.67	41.4	41.4	39.51	40.6	42.22	45.24	43.78	39.89	39.21	37.59	38.84	40.39	37.16	38.05
Government loan guarantees, SMEs	EUR million	82	99	81	70	84	87	38	26	60	46	32	39	32	407	294	95
Government guaranteed loans, SMEs	EUR million	115	157	143	139	167	136	157	186	244	184	88	145	153	774	553	361
Direct government loans, SMEs	EUR million	117	160	139	146	168	209	152	159	172	177	120	132	204	245	213	186
Non-performing loans, total	% of all business loans	..	..	6.8	8.4	8.3	7.9	8.3	8.6	7.4	6.5	5	4.12	3.70	3.44	3.16	2.73
Non-performing loans, SMEs[2]	% of all SME loans	..	..	..	..	..	10.4	9.9	10.3	9	8.1	6.65	5.68	4.55	4.60	3.86	3.21
Interest rate, SMEs	%	5.5	4.6	3	3.2	3.2	3.8	3.6	3.8	3.4	3.1	3.0	3.0	2.9	2.6	2.4	2.92
Collateral, SMEs	% of SMEs needing collateral to obtain bank lending	100	100	100	100	100	100	100	100	100	100	100	100	100	100	100	100
Percentage of SME loan applications	SME loan applications/ total number of SMEs	..	..	..	..	17	..	16	..	23	18	22	17	22	28	23	21
Rejection rate	1-(SME loans authorised/ requested)	..	..	..	..	20	..	15	..	13	5	13	10	12	8	26	11
								Non-bank finance									
Venture and growth capital	EUR million	7	8	14.4	11.4	11.5	7	9	9	12.7	17.1	2.9	5.4	30,65	37.85	28.06	36.05
Venture and growth capital (growth rate)	%, year-on-year growth rate	..	14.3	80	-20.8	0.9	-39.1	28.6	-0.3	41.7	34.4	-83	85.57	467.6	23.49	-25,87	28.47

Indicator	Unit	2007	2008	2009	2010	2011	2012	2013	2014	2015	2016	2017	2018	2019	2020	2021	2022
Other indicators																	
Payment delays, B2B	Number of days	20	8	13	17	20	21	19	17	4	2	6	0	2	14	13	12
Bankruptcies, SMEs	Number	169	251	276	344	363	339	377	409	350	273	285	252	241	177	268	290
Bankruptcies, SMEs (growth rate)	%, year-on-year growth rate	..	48.5	10	24.6	5.5	-6.6	11.2	8.5	-14.4	-22	4.4	-11.6	-4.37	-26.6	51.41	8.21

Note: (1) SME loans classified according to the national/ EU definition of SMEs; (2) No EU definition used – SME loans classified based on banking standards.

The full country profile is available at: https://doi.org/10.1787/fa521246-en.

39. Slovenia

Key facts on SME financing

SMEs represent most business entities (99.8% of all of them), of which 90.8% are micro enterprises. In 2022, SMEs contributed 66.9% to the added value of the economy and employed 73.3% of all employees in Slovenia.

In Slovenia, the percentage of established female entrepreneurs has been increasing for three years in a row and reached 37% in 2022, thus above the average level European countries.

As a result of increased business uncertainty due to rise in input prices, uncertainty in supply chains, lower consumer demand, and tightening bank financing conditions including higher interest rates and other costs and conditions, companies were more concerned about the availability of finance. In 2023, access to finance became increasingly constrained.

Interest rates for SMEs declined in recent years, from 6% in 2011 to 2.5% in 2020. However, due to the rising inflationary pressure, the interest rates steadily increased in 2021-2022 period. For example, the monthly base interest rate in December 2022 was 0.8% and an annual base interest rate was 9.84%.

The government policy response has been primarily through the SID Bank and the Slovene Enterprise Fund. The SID bank, the national development bank, acts as a fund of funds manager for European cohesion funds (ERDF) and managed the EU funds directly or indirectly through the commercial banks or Slovene Enterprise Fund. It also implemented several loan funds. Additionally, the Slovene Enterprise Fund, acts as a public fund and a financial institution of Ministry of Economy, Tourism and Sports, offering favourable financial resources; grants (for innovative startups, for digital transformation of SMEs, etc.); seed capital; and microloans.

In addition to bank lending from commercial banks and the SID development bank, the government of the Republic of Slovenia has also implemented a range of measures to fill the gaps in SME access to finance and complement other financial measures. These policies include:

- Blended finance for innovative startups (EUR 2.1 million per year for 40 innovative startups). The government provide grants blended with mentoring and training.
- Blended finance for early-stage start-ups. The government provide seed capital in the form of convertible loans and equity capital blended with mentoring and training.

Table 39.1. Scoreboard for Slovenia

Indicator	Unit	2007	2008	2009	2010	2011	2012	2013	2014	2015	2016	2017	2018	2019	2020	2021	2022
Debt																	
Outstanding business loans, SMEs	EUR billion	7.30	8.12	7.86	9.67	9.79	9.53	5.70	4.31	4.12	4.35	4.61	4.71	4.80	4.74	4.94	5.57
Outstanding business loans, total	EUR billion	16.80	19.94	19.86	20.83	20.09	18.64	14.14	11.21	10.04	9.31	9.31	9.18	9.29	9.09	9.57	10.76
Share of SME outstanding loans	% of total outstanding business loans	43.45	40.71	39.59	46.43	48.75	51.14	40.29	38.47	41.01	46.79	49.52	51.33	51.69	52.13	51.62	51.75
New business lending, total	EUR billion				15.29	18.57	13.71	9.42	8.60	6.98	6.07	5.22	5.65	5.32	6.25	5.53	5.27
New business lending, SMEs	EUR billion				5.89	7.21	5.79	3.64	3.61	2.86	2.86	2.91	2.94	2.26	3.16	2.38	2.41
Share of new SME lending	% of total new lending				59.36	57.93	63.06	56.34	54.99	58.07	56.90	63.55	58.54	53.16	51.91	43.05	45.82
Outstanding short-term loans, SMEs	EUR billion	2.09	2.53	2.15	2.76	3.09	3.19	1.74	0.79	0.61	0.78	0.80	0.83	0.72	0.63	0.62	0.83
Outstanding long-term loans, SMEs	EUR billion	5.21	5.59	5.71	6.91	6.70	6.34	3.96	3.53	3.51	3.58	3.82	3.88	4.08	4.11	4.32	4.73
Share of short-term SME lending	% of total SME lending	28.62	31.19	27.33	28.54	31.55	33.47	30.51	18.22	14.70	17.87	17.26	17.72	14.94	13.37	12.55	14.96
Government loan guarantees, SMEs	EUR million	3.28	22.22	45.20	32.93	19.15	3.07	1012	552.1	0.00	520	710	0.00	0.00	155.9	12.86	-
Non-performing loans, total	% of all business loans	2.52	3.60	6.66	11.16	17.44	22.86	20.31	17.51	15.24	16.82	12.91	8.41	4.46	3.85	2.29	1.82
Non-performing loans, SMEs	% of SME loans	3.77	5.68	8.93	14.68	22.25	28.37	27.57	25.88	24.48	22.92	16.77	10.42	5.98	4.99	3.77	3.17
Interest rate, SMEs	%	7.07	7.46	6.95	5.82	6.01	5.89	5.84	5.19	3.73	3.00	2.77	2.60	2.48	2.53	2.3	2.82
Interest rate, large firms	%	5.55	6.07	4.61	5.02	5.17	4.87	4.52	4.19	2.92	2.19	2.26	2.05	1.64	1.79	1.52	1.92
Interest rate spread	% points	1.52	1.39	2.33	0.79	0.83	1.02	1.32	1.00	0.81	0.81	0.51	0.55	0.84	0.73	0.78	0.9

The full country profile is available at: https://doi.org/10.1787/fa521246-en.

40. Spain

Key facts on SME financing

In 2022, the GDP of the Spanish economy grew strongly, by 5.8%, reaching pre-pandemic levels in 2022 Q3. The economy showed a strong recovery during the first semester but decelerated afterwards as the reopening effects from the pandemic vanished and in the face of extraordinary events such as the large-scale aggression of Russia against Ukraine which exacerbated the rise in commodity prices. The rise in inflation was intense and persistent. After reaching a peak in the summer, the rate of headline consumer price variation began to decline, but core inflation remained high. The ECB's monetary policy tightening was sharp by historical standards, and financial conditions for companies became more restrictive.

The Survey on the Access to Finance of SMEs in the Euro Area (SAFE survey) reveals a deterioration in the perception of Spanish SMEs regarding the availability of bank credit since early 2022. Additionally, according to the SAFE survey, in 2022, there was an increase in the loan rejection rate to 6.39% (5.87% in the previous year). The demand for credit, proxied by loan applications, was also weak in this cycle, both due to the rise in interest rates and the deterioration of the macroeconomic environment and increased uncertainty.

In 2022, total outstanding business loans (excluding credit to sole proprietors) decreased slightly by 0.6% and reached EUR 470 billion, while outstanding SME loans experienced a greater decrease of 3.8%, to a total of EUR 228 billion. As a result, SME loans currently account for a share of 48.5% of total loans, 1.5 percentage points less than the previous year.

At the end of 2022, 4.21% of loans for productive activity in Spain were non-performing (NPLs), 0.8 pp lower than in December 2020. This decline – which was maintained during the first half of 2023- is mainly explained by a fall in non-performing assets of around 17% (numerator).

In this sense, the economic policy measures implemented during the pandemic have been important in maintaining the repayment capacity of debtors. In the case of companies, the operations guaranteed by the ICO have been important to expand credit under advantageous conditions, thus reducing impairments. On the other hand, the number of bankruptcies by non-financial corporations stood at 5 374 in 2022, which represents a rise of 21% compared to the previous year and an increase of 53% relative to 2020. This rise can largely be explained by recent reforms. First, the insolvency moratorium implemented to support businesses after the COVID-19 pandemic (in force since April 2020), ended on 30 June 2022). Secondly, the reform of the Spanish Bankruptcy Law entered into force on September 26, 2022, which enable a fresh start more appealing to sole proprietors and owners of small incorporated firms that had pledged personal guarantees to obtain funds for their businesses.

The volume of venture capital investment in Spain reached EUR 5.2 billion in 2022, which represents an increase of almost 20% compared to 2020.

Table 40.1. Scoreboard for Spain

Indicator	Unit	2007	2008	2009	2010	2011	2012	2013	2014	2015	2016	2017	2018	2019	2020	2021	2022
Debt																	
Outstanding business loans, SMEs	EUR billion	..	..	..	..	..	..	..	293	258	247	263	229	219	241	237	228
Outstanding business loans, total	EUR Billion)	893	952	915	896	840	708	609	545	518	493	477	446	435	471	473	470
Share of SME outstanding loans	% of total outstanding business loans	..	..	..	..	..	..	..	53.79	49.85	50.10	55.14	51.35	50.34	51.17	50.11	48.51
New business lending, total	EUR Billion)	991	929	868	665	527	485	393	357	393	323	339	347	348	357	299	359
New business lending, SMEs	EUR Billion	394	357	263	210	174	146	134	147	165	170	184	175	174	173	151	173
Share of new SME lending	% of total new lending	39.76	38.43	30.30	31.58	33.02	30.10	34.10	41.18	41.98	52.63	54.28	50.43	50	48.5	50.5	48.2
Outstanding short-term loans, SMEs	EUR	379	346	246	196	166	139	126	135	154	153	163	157	156	129	132	161
Outstanding long-term loans, SMEs	EUR	15	11	17	14	8	7	9	11	12	17	21	18	17	44	20	11
Share of short-term SME lending	% of total SME lending	96.19	96.92	93.54	93.33	95.40	95.21	93.33	92.47	92.77	90.00	88.59	89.71	90.2	74.6	86.8	93.6
Direct government loans, SMEs	EUR Million	10 592	13 127	20 825	24 929	27 674	53 519	63 110	56 160	51 369	46 047	41 234	37 728	32 676	30 774	27 883	24 942
Non-performing loans, total	% of all business loans	0.74	0.74	6.19	7.87	11.32	15.48	20.31	18.49	14.62	13.10	10.26	6.87	5.41	4.98	4.76	4.21
Interest rate, SMEs	%	5.96	5.51	3.63	3.78	4.95	4.91	4.79	3.86	3.01	2.44	2.15	1.89	1.71	1.71	1.56	3.44
Interest rate, large firms	%	5.33	4.30	2.16	2.57	3.36	2.61	2.69	1.99	1.97	1.56	1.56	1.69	1.15	1.39	1.04	3.23
Interest rate spread	% points	0.63	1.21	1.47	1.21	1.59	2.30	2.10	1.87	1.04	0.88	0.59	0.20	0.56	0.32	0.52	0.20
Collateral, SMEs	% of SMEs needing collateral to obtain bank lending	..	..	..	35.19	34.36	31.45	30.00	31.22	28.24	25.89	26.04	24.05	23.39	20.79	19.16	18.85
Percentage of SME loan applications	SME loan applications/ total number of SMEs	..	..	38.07	36.25	34.67	31.89	31.49	34.36	33.81	32.80	28.14	28.60	33.87	42.44	22.07	21.16
Rejection rate	1-(SME loans authorised/ requested)	..	..	22.74	15.87	12.83	18.47	12.85	9.77	7.87	6.95	4.75	5.95	4.38	3.85	5.87	6.39
Non-bank finance																	
Venture and growth capital	EUR Million	..	3 336	3 596	3 600	2 675	2 145	1 473	2 247	1 902	1 886	2 446	2 984	4 196	4 165	5 193	..
Venture and growth capital (growth rate)	%, Year-on-year growth rate	..	..	7.79	0.11	-25.7	-19.8	-31.3	52.5	-15.4	-0.8	29.7	22	40.6	-0.7	24.7	..
Other indicators																	
Payment delays, B2B	Number of days	5	3	13	10	4	8	8	15	12	7	5	2	0	3	2	..
Bankruptcies, SMEs	Number	894	2 550	4 463	4 187	4912	6627	7517	5096	3927	3305	3 310	3 346	3 744	3508	4437	5374

Indicator	Unit	2007	2008	2009	2010	2011	2012	2013	2014	2015	2016	2017	2018	2019	2020	2021	2022
Bankruptcies, SMEs (growth rate)	%, Year-on-year growth rate	..	185.2	75.02	-6.18	17.32	34.91	13.43	-32.2	-22.9	-15.8	0.15	-1.81	-11.9	-6.3	26.5	21.1

The full country profile is available at: https://doi.org/10.1787/fa521246-en.

41. Sweden

Key facts on SME financing

SMEs' dominance in the Swedish business landscape, with 99% representation, underscores their crucial role in the economy, but the contrasting value-added contributions between micro and large enterprises reveal an intricate economic structure where size matters significantly.

The 5% growth in SME debts and 7% increase in total business loans in 2021 signal a robust financing landscape, reflecting both the demands of SMEs and the broader economic momentum in Sweden.

The Swedish Central Bank's adjustments to the repo rate between 2018 and 2023, especially in the last two years, highlight a strategic alignment with macroeconomic conditions, aiming to maintain borrowing costs and economic stability amidst external shocks like the pandemic.

Due to a surge in inflation, the Central Bank raised the repo rate from 0.00% to 3.75% over the period between April 2022 and July 2023. These adjustments aimed to address the rapidly growing inflationary pressures in the economy.

The moderate decline in SME bankruptcies in 2020 and a sharp reduction in 2021, followed by a slight increase in 2022, illustrate the effectiveness of government interventions and the nuanced impact of the pandemic, reflecting both resilience and ongoing challenges.

The recent years emphasize the complex interplay of recovery from the pandemic, global conditions, and credit dynamics in Sweden, requiring continued adaptability, strategic planning, and support for sustained growth and stability in the SME sector.

The Swedish government's active interventions during the COVID-19 pandemic, evidenced by the moderate decline in SME bankruptcies and subsequent sharp reduction, signify a targeted and effective support strategy for the business sector. The Central Bank's adjustments to the repo rate and the overall lending environment suggest a conscious effort to manage economic stability, likely factoring in inflationary pressures in the broader macroeconomic context.

Table 41.1. Scoreboard for Sweden

Indicator	Unit	2008	2009	2010	2011	2012	2013	2014	2015	2016	2017	2018	2019	2020	2021	2022
								Debt								
Outstanding business loans, SMEs	SEK Billion	..	..	..	..	930	964	1 003	1 073	1 173	1 290	1 413	1514	1492	1564	..
Outstanding business loans, total	SEK Billion	..	..	..	..	2 683	2 722	2 812	2 901	2 962	3 189	3 831	3754	3868	4157	..
Share of SME outstanding loans	% of total outstanding business loans	..	..	..	..	34.66	35.39	35.67	36.99	39.60	40.46	36.89	40.33	38.57	37.63	..
Outstanding short-term loans, SMEs	SEK Billion	..	..	..	..	211	217	249	262	316	339	355	397	384	439	..
Outstanding long-term loans, SMEs	SEK Billion	..	..	..	..	719	747	754	811	857	951	1058	1177	1108	1125	..
Share of short-term SME lending	% of total SME lending	..	..	..	..	22.71	22.50	24.83	24.44	26.92	26.28	25.12	26.22	25.73	28.06	..
Direct government loans, SMEs	SEK Million	1 716	3 231	2 112	2 023	2 161	2 200	2 354	3 241	3 324	2 559	1 857	2292	3930	2513	2851
Non-performing loans, total	% of all business loans	0.46	0.83	0.78	0.65	0.70	0.61	1.24	1.17	1.04	1.12	0.49	0.58	0.51	0.42	0.30
Interest rate, SMEs	%	5.66	2.43	2.59	4.17	4.07	3.29	2.71	1.75	1.56	1.50	1.53	1.87	2.08	2.02	2.89
Interest rate, large firms	%	4.84	1.71	1.64	3.01	3.03	2.64	2.15	1.35	1.21	1.14	1.05	1.03	1.29	1.32	2.31
Interest rate spread	% points	0.82	0.72	0.95	1.16	1.04	0.65	0.56	0.40	0.34	0.37	0.48	0.84	0.79	0.70	0.58
								Non-bank finance								
Venture and growth capital	EUR Million	620.34	437.5	733. 5	443. 2	339.3	372.7	386.5	298.4	314	535.3	574.8	593.4	1 873.7	2 342.8	2 308.4
Venture and growth capital (growth rate)	%, Year-on-year growth rate	7.44	-29.47	67.66	-39.59	-23.44	9.84	3.72	-22.79	5.23	70.47	7.37	3.24	215.78	25.04	-1.47
								Other indicators								
Payment delays, B2B	Number of days	..	..	..	..	20.00	24.00	15.00	9.00	9.00	10.00	14	15	..	..	..
Bankruptcies, SMEs	Number	3 139	3 913	3 342	3 449	3 808	3 777	3 355	2 998	2 822	3 019	3 392	3 603	3 445	1 635	1 840
Bankruptcies, SMEs (growth rate)	%, Year-on-year growth rate	27.14	24.66	-14.59	3.20	10.41	-0.81	-11.17	-10.64	-5.87	6.98	12.36	6.22	-4.39	-52.54	12.54

The full country profile is available at: https://doi.org/10.1787/fa521246-en.

42. Switzerland

Key facts on SME financing

Only 0.3% of all Swiss enterprises are large, and SMEs continue to dominate the enterprise landscape, constituting 99.7% of all firms.

Switzerland exhibited a real GDP growth of 2.6% in 2022, compared with 5.4% the previous year (2021).

Total outstanding SME loans rose by 5.0% in 2022, reaching CHF 534 billion, an even higher growth rate compared to the 2021 figure of 4.4%. The most significant growth was recorded among micro enterprises with an increase of 6.4%. While small and medium-sized enterprises recorded a growth rate of 1.9% respectively 2.8%.

Over the 2007-2022 period, SME loans expanded by 65.4%, while overall corporate lending rose by 73.4%.

Lending standards remained broadly unchanged in 2022, with robust loan demand by firms throughout 2022, while demand for loans by households slowed slightly in the second half of 2022.

The average interest rate charged to SMEs increased since its low point of 1.74% in 2021 reaching 2.56% in 2022, while the interest rate spread between large and small companies decreased to its minimum since 2007 to 46 basis points.

In 2022, venture and growth capital investments experienced a 79.5% increase, driven mainly by a rise in growth capital, after the registered rise by 14.4% in 2021. These increases follow the sharp decrease of 89.3% in 2020 due to the COVID-19 pandemic.

Turning to the developments in online alternative finance, the volume of crowdfunding declined for the first time in 14-years as well as the number of active platforms, which fell from 37 to 35. The largest volume share within the various crowdfunding categories continues to come from crowdlending followed by crowdinvesting. The volume of crowd supporting/crowd donating has decreased compared to 2021.

Payment delays in the business-to-business sector remained substantially stable compared with 2021 dropping from 13 to 12 days in 2022. They are still higher than before the COVID-19 pandemic (8 days in 2019). The liquidity problems caused by the pandemic are still an effect.

In Switzerland, there are four guarantee cooperatives that help promising SMEs obtain bank loans of up to CHF 500 000. Loan guarantee volumes increased steadily over the 2007-2010 period, declined slightly in 2011, and continued to grow from 2012 to 2018. The Parliament amended the Federal Law on Financial Aid for Loan Guarantee Organisations: since 1 July 2019, the law allows for guarantees up to CHF 1 million (previously, the ceiling was CHF 500'000).

The Swiss Federal Council has adopted three measures in particular to support SME financing during and beyond the pandemic: bridging credits through a guarantee programme, credits through a guarantee programme specific for start-ups and a hardship support programme (mainly non-repayable contributions) for companies which were, due to the nature of their economic activities, particularly affected by the consequences of the COVID-19 crisis. These special COVID guaranteed credit programmes require full repayment of the credit in principle within eight years. At the end of 2023, approximately 13% of Swiss companies still benefit from these credits.

Table 42.1. Scoreboard for Switzerland

Indicator	Unit	2007	2008	2009	2010	2011	2012	2013	2014	2015	2016	2017	2018	2019	2020	2021	2022
	Debt																
Outstanding business loans, SMEs	CHF million	323 093	344 840	343 866	363 566	377 630	384 438	404 793	402 346	403 681	412 005	422 065	441 332	462 978	487 554	508 923	534 554
Outstanding business loans, total	CHF million	401 647	426 489	433 485	458 689	480 922	489 116	513 631	526 532	525 042	538 709	550 365	583 934	606 497	648 133	674 025	696 532
Share of SME outstanding loans	% of total outstanding business loans	80.4	80.9	79.3	79.3	78.5	78.6	78.8	76.4	76.9	76.5	76.7	75.6	76.3	75.2	75.5	76.7
Government loan guarantees, SMEs	CHF million	104	148	187	215	210	219	227	238	244	254	255	263	285	315	322	315
Interest rate, SMEs	%	..	..	2.21	2.11	2.08	2.01	1.99	2.05	2.07	2.04	2.09	1.96	1.83	1.76	1.74	2.56
Interest rate, large firms	%	..	..	1.35	1.23	1.16	1.11	1.16	1.16	1.30	1.25	1.30	1.33	1.30	1.29	1.15	2.10
Interest rate spread	% points	..	..	0.86	0.88	0.92	0.90	0.83	0.89	0.78	0.79	0.79	0.63	0.53	0.47	0.59	0.46
Collateral, SMEs	% of SMEs needing collateral to obtain bank lending	..	..	76.00	75.01	76.56	76.75	74.86	78.78	79.64	79.88	81.86	81.70	82.92	83.93	84.19	84.56
Utilisation rate	SME loans used/ authorised	71.0	70.0	71.0	70.0	69.0	71.0	72.0	72.0	71.8	71.7	70.6	70.3	70.1	71.5	71.3	71.8
	Non-bank finance																
Venture and growth capital	EUR million	319.8	300.9	308.5	330.1	227.6	245.8	216.8	237.2	394.3	452.4	1195.9	772.9	1 670	901.7	1032	1903.6
Venture and growth capital (growth rate)	%, Year-on-year growth rate	..	-5.91	2.53	7.00	-31.05	8.00	-11.80	9.41	66.23	14.73	164.35	-35.37	116.07	-46.01	14.45	79.48
	Other indicators																
Payment delays, B2B	Number of days	12	13	13	11	10	9	9	7	7	7	7	6	8	13	13	12
Bankruptcies, SMEs	Number	4 314	4 221	5 215	6 255	6 661	6 841	6 495	5 867	6 098	6 684	6 710	6 241	6 004	4897	5127	6799
Bankruptcies, SMEs (growth rate)	%, Year-on-year growth rate	..	-2.16	23.55	19.94	6.49	2.70	-5.06	-9.67	3.94	9.61	0.39	-6.99	-3.8	-18.44	4.78	32.61

The full country profile is available at: https://doi.org/10.1787/fa521246-en.

43. Thailand

Key facts on SME financing

In 2022, there were approximately 3.19 million SMEs in Thailand, which constituted 99.5% of all enterprises.

According to the criteria defined by the Ministry of Industry, SMEs are categorized by the number of employees and income. Meanwhile, for SME non-performing loans, the definition is based on credit line per bank not exceeding 500 million THB.

In 2022, outstanding SME loans were THB 3.387 trillion, representing 34.58% of all outstanding business loans, decreasing 4.4% in share of all outstanding loans from the previous year. Furthermore, SMEs are able to source funds from other financial institutions, the capital market, crowdfunding and venture capital.

Some SMEs still face problems, including collateral constraints and a lack of credit history, which limit their access to bank loans. Government policies have been put into place to address these constraints.

In 2022, SMEs' credit tended to contract mainly due to repayments on maturing soft loans. However, the BOT need to continue implementing debt restructuring measures with an emphasis on rolling out measures that would address debt problems of the vulnerable groups in a well targeted and sustainable manner.

For example, the Thai Credit Guarantee Corporation (TCG) provides credit guarantees for viable SMEs to ensure that SMEs with insufficient collateral have access to bank loans. In Thailand, credit guarantees are provided in the form of portfolio guarantees, which allow Financial Institutions (FIs) to select SMEs that are qualified as independently viable. As a result, the viability of each individual SME is determined by their own assessment and criteria.

Moreover, the Business Collateral Act B.E. 2558 (2015) simplified the process of security interest creation and expanded the types of collateral which SMEs can register and use to secure loans.

To proactively boost SMEs' financial access, the Bank of Thailand (BOT) has promoted innovative financial services and products for SMEs, such as digital personal loans and digital factoring. Furthermore, BOT has introduced infrastructure to support operational efficiency and a competitive environment in the financial sector, including a central web service to deal with double-financing for invoice finance. In addition, the government has launched and developed capacity-building programmes to enhance SMEs' competitiveness and access to finance.

During the COVID-19 pandemic, the BOT collaborated with the government in introducing financial and loan measures to support Thai people and businesses, particularly SMEs heavily affected by the crisis. These measures include loan payment holidays for all SMEs to reduce their financial burden and a soft loan facility to provide liquidity to severely affected SMEs. As part of the loan facility, the BOT also provided funding to financial institutions at low funding rate to channel liquidity to businesses in need.

Table 43.1. Scoreboard for Thailand

Indicator	Unit	2008	2009	2010	2011	2012	2013	2014	2015	2016	2017	2018	2019	2020	2021	2022
Outstanding business loans, SMEs	THB billion	2 753	2 565	2 749	3 145	3 481	3 968	4 266	4 511	4 574	4 703	4 893	4 877	3 214	3 385	3 387
Outstanding business loans, total	THB billion	5 117	4 863	5 298	6 080	6 515	7 189	7 495	7 583	7 950	8 123	8 344	8 884	8 756	9 358	9 793
Share of SME outstanding loans	% of total outstanding business loans	53.81	52.75	51.89	51.74	53.44	55.21	56.92	59.49	57.54	57.91	58.65	54.90	36.59	36.17	34.58
Government loan guarantee, SMEs	THB billion	..	..	73	113	180	244	270	309	331	353	373	388	451	626	651
Non-performing loans, total	% of all business loans	5.77	5.32	3.96	2.97	2.36	2.15	2.15	2.55	2.83	2.91	2.94	2.98	3.11	2.97	2.72
Non-performing loans, SMEs	% of all SME loans	..	7.11	5.38	3.97	3.46	3.29	3.11	4.04	5.29	5.5	6.02	6.10	6.83	6.96	6.68

Source: Bank of Thailand and Thai Credit Guarantee Corporation (Outstanding loans and non-performing loans include only Thai commercial banks, excluding specialized financial institutions).

The full country profile is available at: https://doi.org/10.1787/fa521246-en.

44. Türkiye

Key facts on SME financing

SME lending grew sharply, by 88.6%, in 2021-2022 period. In the same period, the share of outstanding SME loans in outstanding total business loans rose to 33.6%, below the Scoreboard median (47%).

Venture and private equity investments show an erratic pattern. In 2020, venture and private equity investments increased sharply by 506% from 2019. By 2021, these investments increased 225.96% year-on-year amounting to TRY 17.86 billion. That growth momentum continued into 2022. In 2022, new venture capital investments increased 47.07% year-on-year basis and exceeded TRY 17 billion marking a record high. Such impressive growth in the last years can be explained by the change of the legal framework in order to support entrepreneurship in Türkiye. Similarly, tax incentives for investors who invest in venture capital and private equity funds also supported the growth of the VC industry.

The share of non-performing loans (NPLs) for both total business loans and SME loans decreased significantly in 2022, to 2.18% and 2.81%, respectively. This was mostly the result of some temporary regulation changes in the definition of NPLs and of the increase in the total amount of SME loans.

The number of bankruptcies did not change much in 2021 and 2022. Company closures, including sole proprietorships, totalled 55 835 enterprises in 2022, lower than the figure in 2021.

In 2014, the government introduced a law regarding funds of funds, which enables the Ministry of Treasury and Finance (MoTF) to transfer capital to a fund of funds under certain conditions. In 2017, this law was changed to enable the MoTF to invest also in venture capital funds. The total amount of resources committed to the funds by the MoTF as of 3/6/2022 is TRY 3 billion, excluding fees and charges to be paid to the funds.

Moreover, a renewed Crowdfunding Communiqué has been prepared and issued in October 2021 in order to bring the debt-based crowdfunding model into the capital markets legislation, in addition to already existing equity-based crowdfunding model.

KOSGEB is the main body for executing SME policies in Türkiye. It provides 17 different support programmes and support for SMEs with considerable outreach throughout Türkiye.

Technology-oriented and industry-oriented supports are among KOSGEB's most prominent supports offered in recent years. KOSGEB has played an important role in the R&D, innovation and entrepreneurship ecosystem with technology-oriented support since its establishment. Products in medium-high and high technology areas and products that will contribute to the current account are localized and commercialized with these support programmes. Thanks to the incubation centers established by KOSGEB, it has pioneered the transformation of startups.

In 2022, KOSGEB launched the Living Cultural Heritage Business Support Programme to strengthen businesses operating in traditional, cultural and vanishing professions, to ensure that their experience is passed on to future generations and to revitalize traditional crafts.

The criteria used to identify SMEs in Türkiye have been updated with the SME Regulation published in the Official Gazette of Türkiye dated May 25, 2023. Under this Regulation, the SME definition has changed to include more enterprises within the scope of support. The annual turnover or annual balance sheet limit, which is one of the criteria for becoming an SME was increased from TRY 250 million to TRY 500 million.

Like most Mediterranean countries, Türkiye is highly vulnerable to the impacts of climate change. In recent decades, flooding, heatwaves, droughts, wildfires, landslides and extreme windstorms have affected the country with increasing frequency and intensity. To support Türkiye's climate action, "Türkiye Green Industry Project" was initiated in partnership with the World Bank which will provide USD 450 million of financing. With this project through KOSGEB, SMEs' renewable energy and green transformation investments will be supported and R&D projects aimed at circular economy and carbon emission reduction will be supported through TÜBİTAK.

Table 44.1. Scoreboard for Turkey

Indicator	Unit	2007	2008	2009	2010	2011	2012	2013	2014	2015	2016	2017	2018	2019	2020	2021	2022
Debt																	
Outstanding business loans, SMEs	TRY billion	76.5	84.6	83.3	125.5	162.8	199.7	271.4	333.3	388.7	420.5	513.2	611.3	615.3	848.8	1 074	2 026
Outstanding business loans, total	TRY billion	190.6	250.3	262.7	353.2	459.0	528.8	715.5	884.6	1 100	1 314	1 610	1 890	2 070	2 756	3 914	6 034
Share of SME outstanding loans	% of total outstanding business loans	40.14	33.80	31.70	35.52	35.47	37.77	37.94	37.67	35.34	32.00	31.88	32.34	29.72	30.8	27.44	33.59
Government loan guarantees, SMEs	TRY million	72.7	236	500.6	707.5	901.6	973.2	996.1	1 261	1 950	4 205	142 019	55 796	51 523	126 212 **	13 836	57 905.9
Government guaranteed loans, SMEs	TRY million	113.8	340.8	670.2	981.9	1 250	1 312	1 303	1 622	2 513	5 250	157 587	63 809	64 018	157 639 **	16 813	67 602.5
Direct government loans, SMEs	USD million	552	842	997	855	1 174	928	2 632	1 709	1 764	1 749	284.5.	457	200	1 878	1 766	674
Non-performing loans, total	% of all business loans	3.8	3.7	4.91	3.43	2.61	2.82	2.69	2.64	2.68	2.9	2.81	4.01	5.96	4.7	3.35	2.18
Non-performing loans, SMEs	% of all SME loans	3.62	4.79	7.64	4.49	3.1	3.17	3.12	3.27	3.92	4.9	4.71	6.69	9.21	6.4	5.25	2.81
Non-bank finance																	
Venture and growth capital*	TRY million	13.7	0.9	6.3	47.6	373.2	110.1	335.5	124.4	135.3	343.2	435.1	904	600	3640	11865	17450.6
Venture and growth capital (growth rate)*	%, year-on-year growth rate	..	-93.76	639.58	652.9	684.82	-70.5	204.78	-62.93	8.77	153.64	26.79	108	-33.55	506.2	225.96	47.07
Leasing and hire purchases	TRY billion	11.7	14.4	11.1	10.7	15.1	17.2	25.0	29.5	36.7	44.0	52.0	60.7	48.7	57.3	83.203	117.98
Factoring and invoice discounting	TRY billion	6.2	5.6	8.4	12.4	14.2	16.3	20.1	24.7	25.0	31.0	41.6	31.4	34.0	44.6	59.543	127.29
Other indicators																	
Bankruptcies, total	Number	52	47	50	68	72	141	69	99	108	222	130	105	97	68	108	109

Bankruptcies, (growth rate)	Total	%, year-on-year growth rate	..	-9.6	6.4	36.0	5.9	95.8	-51.1	43.5	9.1	105.6	-41.44	-19.23	-7.62	-29.8	58.8	0.9

Notes: * The data presented in this section do not refer to outstanding values but show the new investments each year.
** The data (2020) refer only to the data on the guarantees and loans used under the Treasury-Backed Guarantee System, which does not include the data that is related to KGF equity guarantees.

The full country profile is available at: https://doi.org/10.1787/fa521246-en.

45. Ukraine

Policy developments

Since the start of Russia's full-scale military invasion of Ukraine, Ukraine's economy has been operating in the face of unprecedented security challenges. The aggressor state has focused considerable efforts on the purposeful destruction of energy, transport and other critical infrastructure, production capacities of individual enterprises. Direct and indirect economic losses from destruction have already estimated by hundreds of billions of dollars and continue to grow daily.

The massive destruction, combined with other factors, such as a significant reduction in solvent demand in the domestic market, the destruction of logistics routes, the loss of traditional sales markets, deficiency or a significant increase in prices for some resources, the imbalance of the labor market due to large-scale internal migration led to the fact that many enterprises have significantly reduced their activities or even completely suspended their work. As a result, the fall of the economy in 2022 was 28.8%.

The logical consequence of the economic decline, the loss of Ukraine's access to international capital markets and an unprecedented increase in defense spending (defense spending in 2022 increased by more than 10 times) was the imbalance of the state budget (tax revenue in 2022 decreased by 14.2%, while costs increased by 81.4%) and an increase in public debt (in 2022 the state debt increased by 15 billion US dollars).

In such a difficult situation, the possibilities of the government and the central bank to improve the conditions for business financing are extremely limited. However, the Government takes anti-crisis measures aimed at minimizing the impact of the war on business, in particular, such as:

- implementation of a mild fiscal policy;
- extension and improvement of state programs that provide partial compensation of interest rate on loans and guarantees of government loans;
- implementation of programs of irrevocable financial support for business (providing grants);
- implementation of the state program of business relocation, which suffered from the war;
- cancellation of the need to obtain the vast majority of permits and licenses for doing business.

At the same time, the efforts of the National Bank are primarily aimed at:

- uninterrupted functioning of the financial system in conditions of war and cyber threats;
- preservation of liquidity of the banking sector, in particular through active refinancing of banks;
- maintaining control over inflationary processes;
- stabilisation of the exchange rate.

The increase in credit risks caused by hostilities led to tightening credit standards by financial institutions and reducing the demand for corporate lending. As a result, during the second half of 2022 and the first half of 2023, the corporate loan portfolio had a steady downward trend.

The situation with corporate lending improved slightly in the second half of 2023. Economic growth and higher business credit demand ensured the gradual growth of the corporate loan portfolio. This was also facilitated by a significant reduction in the NBU discount rate at the end of 2023 to 15%, while from June 2022 to July 2023 it was 25%.

The state program of preferential lending for business "Affordable loans 5-7-9%" continues to play a key role in lending of small and medium-sized businesses. Despite the fact that in some periods the activity under this program decreased significantly (in October 2022, the volume of gross debt within this program decreased for the first time since its introduction), even in such a situation it continued to be the main driver of corporate lending. As of 1.1.2024 since the beginning of a full-scale invasion within the framework of the state program "Affordable loans 5-7-9%", 44 142 loan agreements totaling UAH 177.2 billion have been concluded.

In turn, in 2023, government carried out a change in the design of the program, in particular, identified the following priority areas of financing such as business that creates the greatest added value (separate sectors of the processing industry), energy modernization projects, business in the areas of high military risk zone. Thus, this program of preferential lending remains not only a means of supporting and developing business, but also an instrument that contributes to a radical change in the structure of the economy as a whole.

Additionally, it can also be noted about the introduction and development of state programs of irrevocable financial assistance under the common name eRobota. Although the amount of assistance provided within the framework of this project is still not very significant (as of 1.1.2024, almost 11 000 grants were provided for the total amount of almost UAH 6 billion), but the implementation of this program contributes to improving the employment situation, reviving business activity, increases the survival of the most vulnerable small business, which is especially important in conditions of high cost of credit resources.

Like corporate lending, the retail loan portfolio also had a steady tendency to decline since the beginning of a full-scale invasion. The resumption and growth of retail lending began only in April 2023. Despite the long-term growth over several months (an average of 2.6% monthly), as of November 2023, loans for individuals are still a quarter lower than before a full-scale invasion.

One of the key factors that contributed to the stabilization of the situation of financing of medium and small businesses was the preservation of inflationary processes. The growth of consumer prices at the end of 2022 despite the full-scale war and high world inflation was moderate (the consumer price index increased by 26.6%) due to a set of crisis measures of the NBU and the government, as well as financial support of international partners. An important role in maintaining the control of inflationary processes was played by fixing the exchange rate. Maintaining exchange rate stability not only directly hindered the growth of the cost of goods and services, but also mitigated the fundamental price pressure, positively affecting the inflationary expectations of citizens and businesses.

The fall of Ukraine's economy in 2022 as a result of a full-scale invasion was the deepest in the modern history of Ukraine. However, the high ability of businesses and households to adapt, successful actions of the Ukrainian defense forces, receiving significant international assistance, as well as balanced state policy allowed to minimize this decline and move to the recovery of the economy and its growth in the shortest possible time.

Table 45.1. Scoreboard for the Ukraine

Indicator	Unit	2007	2008	2009	2010	2011	2012	2013	2014	2015	2016	2017	2018	2019	2020	2021	2022
Debt																	
Outstanding business loans, SMEs	UAH billion	..	..	..	..	..	..	..	..	..	..	443	445	432	451	468	455

Outstanding business loans, total	UAH billion	271	460	482	520	597	626	716	809	807	837	845	874	761	737	774	773
Share of SME outstanding loans	% of total outstanding business loans	..	..	..	..	..	..	..	..	..	..	52.42	50.86	56.77	61.23	60.41	58.83
New business lending, total	UAH billion	627	724	685	958	1 079	1 121	1 330	1 231	1 213	1 446	1 407	2 011	2408	2498	2794	2011
New business lending, SMEs	UAH billion	..	..	..	..	..	..	..	..	..	..	..	678	799	792	1124	728
Share of new SME lending	% of total new lending	..	..	..	..	..	..	..	..	..	..	..	33.74	33.18	31.68	40.22	36.19
Outstanding short-term loans, SMEs	UAH billion	..	..	..	..	..	..	..	..	..	..	200	215	213	243	274	262
Outstanding long-term loans, SMEs	UAH billion	..	..	..	..	..	..	..	..	..	..	243	230	218	208	194	193
Share of short-term SME lending	% of total SME lending	..	..	..	..	..	..	..	..	..	..	45.12	48.34	49.42	53.8	58.58	57.51
Government loan guarantees, SMEs	UAH billion	..	..	..	..	..	..	..	..	..	..	..	..	..	..	3.6	28.4
Government guaranteed loans, SMEs	Thousands issued	..	..	..	..	..	..	..	..	..	..	..	..	..	..	4.2	16.7
Interest rate, SMEs	%	..	..	..	..	..	..	..	..	..	..	..	17.35	17.51	13.84	11.59	15.14
Interest rate, large firms	%	..	..	..	..	..	..	..	..	..	..	..	15.52	14.09	8.68	7.39	13.76
Interest rate spread	%	..	..	..	..	..	..	..	..	..	..	..	1.82	3.42	5.16	4.21	1.37
Non-bank finance																	
Venture and growth capital	UAH billion	..	61.2	75.9	100.3	121.6	148.7	173.3	202.9	232.2	225.6	257.2	296.2	338.7	407.8	518.9	526.8
Venture and growth capital (growth rate)	%	..		24.01	32.22	21.20	22.34	16.51	17.07	14.43	-2.83	14.01	15.19	14.32	20.40	27.26	1.52
Leasing and hire purchases	UAH billion	12	8	2	3	9	9	25	6	5	10	13	22	26	26	40	12
Factoring and invoice discounting	UAH billion	0	1	2	6	7	12	10	24	17	17	31	48	56	85	72	47
Other indicators																	
Bankruptcies, all businesses	Number of subjects of entrepreneurial activity	..	..	..	..	..	9 540	7 168	6 098	6 292	6 007	4 920	4 075	3260	3173	3319	3404
Bankruptcies, all businesses (growth rate)	%	..	..	..	..	..	..	-24.86	-14.93	3.18	-4.53	-18.10	-17.17	-20.00	-2.7	4.60	2.56

The full country profile is available at: https://doi.org/10.1787/fa521246-en.

46. United Kingdom

Key facts on SME finance

The developments in SME finance markets in the United Kingdom in 2022 reflected the difficulties faced by the global economy. While the impact of the Covid-19 pandemic waned, major challenges emerged that affected the use of finance by SMEs. In particular, the large-scale aggression of Russia against Ukraine contributed to a sharp rise in input costs. This subsequently led to a large rise in the inflation rate which, in turn, resulted in the Bank of England raising the Bank Rate. The war also increased uncertainty about the outlook for the UK and other major economies.

Gross flows of bank lending (excluding overdrafts), the main component of SME finance markets, rose by 13% in 2022 to GBP 65.1 billion in nominal terms. This was the second-highest on record. The rise was largely driven by increased lending by challenger and specialist banks. However, gross repayments rose by 12% to GBP 73.6 billion, a record high. This led gross repayments to exceed gross lending for the second consecutive year. Consequently, net lending remained negative and widened to GBP 8.4 billion, the largest fall on record. The outstanding stock of bank lending fell but remained high at GBP 197 billion.

Among the commonly used forms of alternative finance, the use of asset finance and working capital products rose in 2022 while that of equity finance fell. Asset finance new business rose by 11% to GBP 22.5 billion, a new record high. This was in part due to pandemic-related disruption to supply chains easing for some sectors and SMEs needing to replace aging equipment. Among working capital products, invoice finance and asset-based lending rose by 30% to GBP 10.7 billion while overdrafts were up by 4% to GBP 6.1 billion. The rise in the use of working capital finance reflects that the higher input costs left many SMEs struggling to maintain cash flow. In contrast, the value of SME equity finance fell by 11% to GBP 16.7 billion and the number of announced deals was down by 7% to 2,702. The falls were due to concerns about potential over-valuations and a more challenging exit environment as well as higher interest rates making equity finance less attractive.

Similarly, the value of alternative finance lending from providers including marketplace, non-bank balance sheet and platform lenders is likely to have fallen in 2022. Around GBP 3.4 billion of SME business and property lending via such providers has been reported thus far, down from GBP 4.4 billion by those the British Business Bank has data for in 2021. The full results for 2022 of some providers are yet to be published but they are unlikely to change the picture significantly.

The UK government, the Department for Business and Trade as well as the British Business Bank will continue to work with a wide range of partners to support businesses across the UK as they look to invest and grow.

Table 46.1. Scoreboard for the United Kingdom

Indicator	Unit	2008	2009	2010	2011	2012	2013	2014	2015	2016	2017	2018	2019	2020	2021	2022
							Debt									
Outstanding business loans, SMEs	GBP billion	..	..	..	189	176	166	167	164	166	165	166	168	213	209	197
Outstanding business loans, total	GBP billion	..	..	..	504	472	448	435	430	449	466	477	490	530	526	540
Share of SME outstanding loans	% of total outstanding business loans	..	..	..	37.5	37.3	37.1	38.4	38.3	36.9	35.5	34.8	34.2	40.2	39.8	36.5
New business lending, total	GBP billion	..	..	..	..	146	163	190	205	234	259	273	259	329	241	277
New business lending, SMEs	GBP billion	..	..	..		38	43	53	58	59	57	58	57	105	58	65
Share of new SME lending	% of total new lending	..	..	..		26.1	26.4	28.2	28.2	25.3	22.2	21.2	22.0	31.9	23.9	23.5
Government loan guarantees, SMEs	GBP million	..	61	51	31	43	50	45	34	31	32	30	30	57 630	11 262	1 730
Government guaranteed loans, SMEs	GBP million	..	626	528	324	284	335	297	227	207	216	199	203	61 206	13 291	2 470
Direct government loans, SMEs	GBP million	..	..	..	..	0.8	60.6	70.6	61.9	82.6	106.9	85.4	89.8	126.4	134.7	121.5
Interest rate, SMEs	%	4.54	3.47	3.49	3.52	3.71	3.60	3.43	3.33	3.22	3.16	3.44	3.41	2.15	2.45	3.91
Interest rate, large firms / PNFCs *	%	3.49	2.35	2.10	2.25	2.41	2.20	2.45	2.11	2.60	2.43	2.70	2.64	1.87	2.12	3.23
Interest rate spread	% points	1.05	1.12	1.39	1.27	1.30	1.40	0.98	1.22	0.62	0.73	0.74	0.77	0.28	0.33	0.68
Collateral, SMEs	% of SMEs needing collateral to obtain bank lending	..	..	..	25	31	31	34	40	45	55	41	39	15	14	22
Percentage of SME loan applications	SME loan applications/ total number of SMEs	..	..	..	7	6	4	5	4	3	2	2	2	6	7	3
Rejection rate	1-(SME loans authorised/ requested)	..	..	..	..	31	32	23	18	19	20	24	25	16	15	45
							Non-bank finance									
Venture and growth capital	GBP billion	..	..	..	1.7	1.8	1.9	3.1	4.2	4.1	6.9	7.2	8.6	9.5	18.8	16.7
Venture and growth capital (growth rate)	%, Year-on-year growth rate	..	..	..		3	9	62	35	-2	68	4	19	10	98	-11
Leasing and hire purchases	GBP billion	..	..	..	12.0	12.8	13.5	14.8	16.3	17.0	19.3	19.8	20.6	16.3	20.3	22.5
Factoring and invoice discounting	GBP billion	..	8.5	8.6	9.2	9.6	9.8	10.6	10.6	10.8	11.8	12.0	11.8	7.8	8.2	10.7

Other indicators																
Bankruptcies, SMEs	Thousands	..	25.1	21.4	22.2	21.4	18.9	17.6	15.9	16.1	15.7	17.3	18.5	13.4	14.9	23.4
Bankruptcies, SMEs (growth rate)	%, Year-on-year growth rate	..	..	-14.7	3.7	-3.6	-11.7	-6.9	-9.7	1.3	-2.5	10.2	6.9	-27.6	11.2	57.0

Note: * Break in data series and definition from 2016.
Sources: Bank of England, British Business Bank, BVA BDRC SME Finance Monitor, Beauhurst, Financing and Leasing Association, UK Finance and the Insolvency Service.

The full country profile is available at: https://doi.org/10.1787/fa521246-en.

47. United States

Key facts on SME finance

The U.S. economy in 2022 continued to navigate an unprecedented global pandemic and weathered an additional price shock to energy and food caused by the large-scale aggression of Russia against Ukraine. Despite these and other challenges, the economy remained resilient with moderate output growth, strong employment growth, and inflation that peaked and then started to moderate late in the year.

The large-scale aggression of Russia against Ukraine in February created acute supply constraints on energy, food, and other commodities that raised inflation globally. In addition, in the first half of the year, COVID-19 continued to weigh on economies across the world, especially when its Omicron variant caused cases and fatalities to surge in the United States and abroad. Already grappling with transitory inflation after the height of the pandemic, the U.S. economy witnessed a four decades-high level of inflation, peaking at 9.1% in June of 2022.

2022 saw a pivot from many years of accommodative financial conditions. Monetary policy turned to fighting inflation and fiscal policy focused on strategies to complement that fight, while also working to guide the economy to stable and steady growth in 2022 and in the future. Even before the year began, government spending and deficits fell closer to pre-pandemic trends. As a result of the historic pace of U.S. economic and labour market recovery, the federal government spent about USD 1 trillion less on pandemic and economic support in 2022 than in 2021, slashing the U.S. federal budget in half. In March, the Federal Reserve began to reverse its asset purchase programme and started what became a swift series of interest rate hikes; stock markets and residential investment declined quickly. Faced with tightening monetary conditions, the U.S. economy showed signs of adjustment. GDP growth slowed, with a 6.5% increase in nominal GDP in the fourth quarter compared to 7.7% in the third quarter of 2022. Some measures of labour market tightness and inflation began to moderate, with inflation showing an easing at the end of the year.

Borrowing, including business loan originations and commercial and industry (C&I) loans, continued to grow at a slower pace in line with GDP, driven by an increase in consumer spending and companies increasing inventories. Tightening of lending conditions occurred gradually throughout the year and was most widely reported for premiums charged on riskier loans, costs of credit lines, and spreads of loan rates over the cost of funds. U.S. household and business indebtedness and debt servicing ability remained stable, with the effect of rising interest rates being offset by higher business earnings.

While some economic indicators exhibited a modest response to rising interest rates, labour conditions and consumer spending were less affected. The labour market was characterized by an unemployment rate near a historically low level, robust payroll gains, a high level of job vacancies, and elevated nominal wage growth. The civilian unemployment rate was a stable 3.5% as of December 2022, and a consistently large number of job openings implied a continual imbalance between labour supply and labour demand. Growth in consumer spending was stronger than expected and could be attributed to the strong labour market and households spending down excess savings accumulated during the pandemic.

Though SMEs reported progress in achieving post-pandemic operational recovery, they were less optimistic regarding future business conditions. The U.S. Census Small Business Pulse Survey indicated that most small businesses had either returned to normal operations or expected to return to normal operations within two to three months, with the fastest expected recoveries occurring in the utilities and finance and insurance industries. However, rising inflation and labour shortages following the pandemic hampered small business owners' expectations of better business conditions. According to the National Federation of Independent Businesses (NFIB), while SMEs recorded high levels of job openings, almost all of them reported few or no qualified candidates for the positions they were trying to fill. 75% of small business owners surveyed in the NFIB Optimism Index reported lower profit trends, most frequently attributed to a rise in the cost of materials. Nevertheless, 89% of owners reported that their credit needs were satisfied or that they were not interested in a loan.

Following record-breaking growth in 2021, venture capital deal value decreased each quarter in 2022 for a year-over-year decline of 28.8%. This reflects increasing interest rates, less attractive risk-return profiles, and therefore a relatively lower upside potential for venture capital asset classes compared to years prior. Late-stage deal value suffered the biggest hit of roughly 35%, while total angel and seed deal value actually increased.

Table 47.1. Scoreboard for the United States

Indicator	Unit	2008	2009	2010	2011	2012	2013	2014	2015	2016	2017	2018	2019	2020	2021	2022
									Debt							
Outstanding business loans, SMEs. As of 30 June	USD billion	616	604	569	530	523	519	524	534	551	589	626	638	887	800	
Outstanding business loans, total. As of 30 June	USD trillion	2.512	2.451	2.256	2.298	2.482	2.647	2.79	2.974	3.21	3.348	3.5	3.688	4.235	3.931	4.197
Share of SME outstanding loans	% of total outstanding business loans	24.53	24.65	25.22	23.05	21.06	19.60	18.80	17.94	17.17	17.58	17.88	17.30	20.95	20.34	
New business lending, SMEs	USD: Index	94.7	74.2	80.7	94.6	103.6	111.5	122.7	134.1	130.33	132.5	144.1	146.2	135.8	146.4	143.7
Government loan guarantees, SMEs	USD billion	71	73	77	84	88	93	98	101	106	113	120	122	639	453	179
Government guaranteed loans, SMEs	Number of loans (thousands)	388	385	366	354	337	323	316	313	316	321	326	322	5,389	6,445	1,425
Direct Government Loans, SMEs	USD billion													176	240	358
Non-performing loans, total	% of all business loans	1.88	3.91	3.46	2.01	1.34	1.00	0.80	0.87	1.57	1.34	1.03	1.11	1.24	1.09	1.06
Non-performing loans, SMEs	% of all SME loans	2.62	3.24	2.62	1.90	1.44	1.21	1.22	1.22	1.28	1.34	1.41	1.55	1.87	1.37	1.29
Interest rate, SMEs	%	6.32	4.1	4.33	4.22	4	3.74	3.59	3.53	3.63	4.28	5.04	5.27	3.29	3.13	4.37
Interest rate, all firms*	%	5.09	3.25	3.25	3.25	3.25	3.25	3.25	3.26	3.51	4.10	4.90	5.28	3.54	3.25	4.85
Collateral, SMEs	% of SMEs needing collateral to obtain bank lending	..	..	..	..	..	..	..	..	..	92.9	94.3	92.2	51.1		
Percentage of SME loan applications	Approved SME loan applications/	..	..	..	..	..	..	..	..	..	55.2	64.7	66.6	62.3	64.1	63.4

	total number received															
Rejection rate	1-(SME loans approved/ received)	..	..	..	..	..	..	..	..	..	35.3	33.4	37.7	35.9	36.6	
Utilisation rate	SME loans used/ authorised	..	..	..	..	..	..	..	..	..	37.8	37.6	31.9	33.3	33.2	
Non-Bank Finance																
Venture and growth capital	USD billion	37.2	27.7	31.9	45.3	41.6	49.7	74.1	86.7	84	89.9	145.7	150.3	170.9	346	246.28
Venture and growth capital (growth rate)	%, Year-on-year growth rate	-2.36	-25.54	15.16	42.01	-8.17	19.47	49.09	17.00	-3.11	7.02	62.07	3.16	13.71	102.46	-28.82
Leasing and hire purchases	USD billion	608.3	463.6	372.7	375.8	387	401.3	411.5	404.7	388	387.2	397.1	386.7	360.8	323.6	375.4
Factoring and invoice discounting	USD billion	109	96.5	103.6	114.5	84.5	91.3	106.5	103.6	97.5	94.8	95.7	91.3	69.9	102.8	109.8
Other Indicators																
Payment delays, B2B	Percent of Domestic Invoices Overdue	..	..	..	..	..		42.5	47.6	48.4	48.8	50	45.1	45.8	50	49
Bankruptcies, all businesses	Number (in thousand)	43.5	60.8	56.3	47.8	40.1	33.2	27.0	24.7	24.1	23.2	22.2	22.7	21.7	14.3	13.5
Bankruptcies, all businesses (growth rate)	%, Year-on-year growth rate	53.8	39.7	-7.5	-15.1	-16.2	-17.1	-18.8	-8.3	-2.5	-4.0	-4.0	2.46	-4.9	-33.8	-6.04

Note: Interest rates for all firms refer to the bank prime loan rate, which is the interest rate posted by the majority of the top 25 U.S. chartered commercial banks.

The full country profile is available at: https://doi.org/10.1787/fa521246-en.

Annex A. Methodology for producing the national Scoreboards

Financing SMEs and Entrepreneurs: An OECD Scoreboard provides a framework to monitor trends in SMEs' and entrepreneurs' access to finance and supports the formulation and evaluation of policies in this domain.

The individual country profiles present data for a number of core indicators, which measure trends in SME debt and equity financing, credit conditions, solvency and policy measures. The set of indicators and policy information provide governments and other stakeholders with a consistent framework to evaluate whether SME financing needs are being met, to support the design and evaluation of policy measures, and to monitor the implications of financial reforms on SME access to finance. Consistent time series for country data permit an analysis of national trends in participating countries. It is mainly by comparing trends that insights are drawn from the varying conditions in SME financing across countries. The focus on analysis of changes in variables, rather than on absolute levels, helps overcome existing limitations to cross-country comparability of the core indicators, due to differences in definitions and reporting practices.

This Annex describes the methodology for producing the national country profiles, discusses the use of proxies in case of data limitations or deviation from preferred definitions, and addresses the limits in cross-country comparability. It also provides recommendations for improving the collection of data on SME finance, including how to advance in the collection of disaggregated data.

Scoreboard indicators and their definitions

Core indicators

Trends in financing SMEs and entrepreneurs are monitored through 17 core indicators, which assess specific questions related to access to finance. These core indicators meet the following criteria:

- Usefulness: the indicators must be an appropriate instrument to measure how easy or difficult it is for SMEs and entrepreneurs to access finance and to help policy makers formulate or adjust their policies and programmes.
- Availability: the data for constructing the indicators should be readily available in order not to impose new burdens on governments or firms.
- Feasibility: if the information for constructing the indicator is not publicly available, it should be feasible to make it available at a modest cost, or to collect it during routine data exercises or surveys.
- Timeliness: the information should be collected in a timely manner so that the evolving conditions of SME access to finance can be monitored. Annual data may be more easily available, but should be complemented by quarterly data, when possible, to better capture variability in financing indicators and describe turning points.
- Comparability: the indicators should be relatively uniform across countries in terms of the population surveyed, content, method of data collection and periodicity or timeliness.

Data sources and preferred definitions

The data in the national Scoreboards are supplied by country experts with access to the information needed from a variety of supply-side and demand-side sources.

Most of the Scoreboard indicators are built on supply-side data, that is, data provided by financial institutions and other government agencies. There are several indicators which are based on demand-side surveys of SMEs. However, not all countries undertake such surveys. Use is made of quantitative demand-side data, as collected by SME surveys, to complement the picture and improve the interpretative power of the OECD Scoreboard. Whereas a plethora of qualitative SME surveys (i.e. opinion surveys) exist, quantitative demand-side surveys are less common. Experience shows that qualitative information based on opinion survey responses must be used cautiously. The broader perception of entrepreneurs about access to finance and credit conditions, emanating from such opinion surveys, has its own value though and complements the hard data provided in the quantitative analysis. Furthermore, the cross-country comparability of national surveys remains limited, as survey methodologies and the target population differ from country to country. Comparable demand-side surveys are undertaken on a regular basis by the European Central Bank and the European Commission, which provide an example of the benefits that can come from standardised definitions and methodology across countries when conducting demand-side surveys.

In order to monitor the core indicators, data are collected for 22 variables. Each variable has a preferred definition (see Table A..1.), intended to facilitate time consistency and comparability. In a number of cases, however, it is not possible for countries to adhere to the "preferred definition" of an indicator, due to data limitations or differences in reporting practices, and a proxy is used instead. For this reason, in each country profile, the data are accompanied by a detailed table of definitions and sources for each indicator. To ensure transparency of these limitations and assess how deviations affect comparability, attention is placed on the provision of more complete and detailed information with regard to the definitions and the sources of all indicators (both in the publication and in the metadata of the OECD online database on SME Financing).

Table A A.1. Preferred definitions for core indicators

Indicator	Definition/ Description	Sources
Outstanding business loans, SMEs	Bank and financial institution loans to SMEs, amount outstanding (stocks) at the end of period; by firm size using the national definition of SME or, if necessary, loan amounts less than EUR 1 million or an equivalent threshold that is deemed appropriate on a case-by-case basis	Supply-side data from financial institutions
Outstanding business loans, total	Bank and financial institution business loans to all non-financial enterprises, outstanding amounts (stocks)	Supply-side data
New business lending, total	Bank and financial institution business loans to all non-financial enterprises over an accounting period (i.e. one year), flows	Supply-side data
New business lending, SMEs	Bank and financial institution loans to SMEs over an accounting period (i.e. one year), flows; by firm size using the national definition of SME or, if necessary, loan amounts less than EUR 1 million or an equivalent threshold that is deemed appropriate on a case-by-case basis	Supply-side data
Short-term loans, SMEs	Loans equal to or less than one year; outstanding amounts or new loans	Supply-side data
Long-term loans, SMEs	Loans for more than one year; outstanding amounts or new loans	Supply-side data
Government loan guarantees, SMEs	Government guarantees available to banks and other financial institutions, stocks or flows	Supply-side data
Government guaranteed loans, SMEs	Loans guaranteed by government, stocks or flows	Supply-side data
Direct government loans, SMEs	Direct loans from government, stocks or flows	Supply-side data

Interest rate, SMEs	Average annual rates for new loans, base rate plus risk premium; for maturity less than one year; and amounts less than EUR 1 million	Supply-side data
Interest rate, large firms	Average annual rates for new loans, base rate for loans equal to or greater than EUR 1 million; for maturity less than one year	Supply-side data
Collateral, SMEs	Percentage of SMEs that were required to provide collateral on latest bank loan	Demand-side survey
Percentage of SME loan applications	SME loan applications divided by the total number of SMEs in the country, in %	Supply-side data or survey
Rejection rate	1-(SME loans authorised/ requested), in %	Supply-side survey
Utilisation rate	SME loans used/ authorised, in %	Supply-side survey
Venture and growth capital investments	Seed, start-up, early stage and expansion capital (excludes buyouts, turnarounds, replacements)	VC association (supply side)
Leasing and hire purchases	New production of hire purchases and leasing, which covers finance leases and operating leases of all asset types (automotive, equipment and real estate) and also includes the rental of cars, vans and trucks.	Business associations (supply side)
Factoring and invoice discounting	Factoring turnover volumes which includes invoice discounting, recourse factoring, non-recourse factoring, collections (domestic factoring), export factoring, import factoring and export invoice discounting (international factoring)	Business associations (supply side)
Non-performing loans, total	% of total business loans	Supply-side data
Non-performing loans, SMEs	% of total SME loans	Supply-side data
Payment delays, B2B	Average number of days delay beyond the contract period for the Business to Business segment (B2B)	Demand-side survey
Bankruptcies, SMEs	Number of enterprises ruled bankrupt; or number bankrupt per 10 000 or 1 000 SMEs	Administrative data

Share of SME loans in total business loans: This ratio captures the allocation of credit by firm size, that is, the relative importance of SME lending in the national credit market. The business loan data, which are used in the construction of several indicators in the Scoreboard, include overdrafts, lines of credit, short-term and long-term loans, regardless of whether they are performing or non-performing loans. In principle, this data does not include personal credit card debt and residential mortgages.

Share of SME new lending in total new business lending: This ratio equally captures the allocation of credit by firm size, but for new loans (flows). Flows, which are measured over an accounting period (i.e. one year), are expected to reflect short-term events and are therefore more volatile than stocks, which measure the value of an asset at a given point in time, and thus reflect latest flows, as well as values that may have cumulated over time, net of depreciation.

Share of short-term loans in SME loans: This ratio shows the debt structure of SMEs or whether loans are being used to fund current operations or investment and growth needs. However, caution should be used in interpreting this indicator, because it is affected by the composition of short-term loans versus long-term loans in the SME loan portfolio of banks. Indeed, the share of long-term loans could actually increase during a financial crisis, because it is easier for the banks to shut off short-term credit.

SME government loan guarantees, SME government guaranteed loans, SME direct government loans: These indicators show the extent of public support for the financing of SMEs in the form of direct funding or credit guarantees. By comparing government loan guarantees with guaranteed loans, information can be drawn on the take up of government programmes and on their leverage effect.

SME interest rates and interest rate spreads: These indicators describe the tightness of the market and the (positive or negative) correlation of interest rates with firm size.

Collateral required: This indicator also shows tightness of credit conditions. It is based on demand-side surveys where SMEs report if they have been explicitly required to provide collateral for their last loan. It is not available from supply-side sources, as banks do not generally divulge this information.

SME rejection rate: This indicator shows the degree to which SME credit demand is met. An increase in the ratio indicates a tightening in the credit market as more credit applications have been turned down. A limitation in this indicator is that it omits the impact of “discouraged” borrowers. However, discouragement and rejection seem to be closely correlated, as the number of discouraged borrowers tends to increase when credit conditions become tighter and a higher proportion of credit applications are refused.

SME utilisation rate: This ratio also captures credit conditions, and more precisely, the willingness of banks to provide credit, and is therefore sometimes used in addition to or instead of the rejection rate. An increase in this ratio indicates that a higher proportion of authorised credit is being used by entrepreneurs and SMEs, which usually occurs when credit conditions are tightening.

Venture capital and growth capital investments: This indicator shows the ability to access external equity in the form of seed, start-up, early-stage venture capital as well as expansion capital and is ideally broken down by the investment stage. It excludes buyouts, turnarounds and replacement capital, as these are directed at restructuring and generally concern larger enterprises.

Leasing and hire purchases: This indicator contains information on the use of leasing and hire purchases. New production of leasing includes finance leases and operating leases of all asset types (automotive, equipment and real estate) as well as the rental of cars, vans and trucks.

Factoring and invoice discounting provides information on factoring turnover volumes, including invoice discounting, recourse factoring, non-recourse factoring, collections (domestic factoring), export factoring, import factoring and export invoice discounting (international factoring).

SME non-performing loans/SME loans: This indicator provides information about the relative performance of SME loans in banks’ portfolio, that is, the riskiness implied by exposure to SME loans. It can be compared with the overall ratio of non-performing loans to all business loans to determine whether SMEs are more risky.

Payment delays: This indicator contributes to assess SME cash flow problems. Business-to-business (B2B) payment delays show supplier credit delays and how SMEs are coping with cash flow problems by delaying their payments and are more relevant to assess cash flow problems compared with business-to-consumer or business-to-government data.

SME bankruptcies or bankruptcies per 10 000 or per 1 000 SMEs: This indicator is a proxy for SME survival prospects. Abrupt changes in bankruptcy rates demonstrate how severely SMEs are affected by economic crises. However, the indicator likely underestimates the number of SME exits, as some SMEs close their business even when not being in financial difficulties. Bankruptcies per 10 000 or per 1 000 SMEs are the preferred measures because this indicator is not affected by the increase or decrease in the total number of enterprises in the economy. This indicator is also affected by important changes in bankruptcy procedures, which can stem from a response to global economic disruptions, such as the COVID-19 crisis. Changes in bankruptcy procedures can include raising the threshold limit of unpaid debt to initiate bankruptcy or changes in conditions to initiate bankruptcy procedures (e.g. request for restructuring before initiating procedure). In this context, a limitation is that the number of SMEs affected by the economic disruption could be underestimated, with many exiting the market without filing for bankruptcy.

Inflation-adjusted data

Differences in inflation levels across countries hamper comparability of trends over time. Considering this and since 2016, indicators in the trends chapter therefore have been adjusted for inflation when appropriate. For this purpose, the GDP deflator from the OECD Economic Outlook publication, deflating nominal values into real values, is used. The base year used is 2007 considering that the time series graphs found predominantly in Chapter 1 compare the median growth rate since 2008. This deflator is derived by dividing an index of GDP (measured in current prices) by a chain volume index of GDP. It is therefore a weighted average of the price indices of goods and services consumed by households; expenditure by government on goods, services and salaries; fixed capital assets; changes in inventories; and exports of goods and services minus imports of goods and services.[1] It is a very broad indicator of inflation and, given its comprehensiveness, it is thus suitable to deflate current price nominal data into a real terms prices basis for measures of national income, public expenditure and other economic variables with a focus beyond consumer items.

Inclusion of median values

In order to facilitate interpretation of the data, median values of core indicators are included when appropriate in Chapter 1 of this publication. This enables a better assessment of how participating countries are positioned in terms of the assessed core indicators on SME financing. Given the limited comparability of some indicators, this relative position needs to be interpreted carefully and within the country-specific context, however. Median values rather than average values are displayed because they are less sensitive to outliers in the data.

The Scoreboard provides the analysis of median values by grouping countries based on their income using the World Bank Country and Lending classification groups[2] or membership into supranational organisations, such as the European Union. Grouping countries based on their income is used considering that countries with similar levels of income can share economic characteristics, challenges and opportunities. This can include similar market maturity, market stability and associated risk, and similar dynamics in the demand and supply of finance for SMEs. Table A A.2 provides the grouping of the participating Scoreboard countries used to calculate the different medians. However, the analysis is made with caution as potential outliers can arise. In these cases, the Scoreboard provides detailed information and a potential explanation as to why the value in a specific country and indicator can stand apart.

Table A A.2. Scoreboard countries by groups

EU countries		Non-EU high-income countries	Upper-middle income countries
Austria	Lithuania	Australia	Brazil
Belgium	Luxembourg	Canada	China
Czech Republic	Netherlands	Chile	Colombia
Denmark	Poland	Israel	Georgia
Estonia	Portugal	Japan	Kazakhstan
Finland	Slovak Republic	Korea	Malaysia
France	Slovenia	New Zealand	Mexico
Germany	Spain	Norway	Peru
Greece	Sweden	Switzerland	Serbia
Hungary		United Kingdom	South Africa
Ireland		United States	Thailand
Italy			Turkey
Latvia			

SME target population

The SME target population of the Scoreboard consists of non-financial "employer" firms, that is, firms with at least one employee besides the owner/ manager, which operate a non-financial business. This is consistent with the methodology adopted by the OECD-Eurostat Entrepreneurship Indicators Programme to collect data about business demography. The target group excludes firms with no employees or self-employed individuals, which considerably reduces the number of firms that can be considered SMEs. For most of the countries in the report, data are available for this target population. However, not all countries collect data at the source and compile them in accordance with these criteria. Therefore, in a few cases data include financial firms and/or self-employed individuals. This is mostly the case in countries reporting financial indicators based on loan size, rather than the target population, or when sole proprietorships/ self-entrepreneurs cannot be distinguished from the SME population at the supply-side level of reporting.

Timeframe for data collection

The data in the present report cover the period 2007 to 2022, complemented by information available for 2023. Specific attention is placed on developments occurring in 2021, 2022 and the first half of 2023. In addition, information on government policies to ease SMEs' access to finance is also collected on a systematic basis.

Deviations from preferred definitions of indicators

Data limitations and country-level specific reporting practices imply that the national Scoreboards may deviate from the preferred definitions of some core indicators. Some of the main deviations in the definition of variables and data coverage are discussed below.

SME loans

The OECD Scoreboard aims to collect business loan data that include overdrafts, lines of credit, short-term loans, and long-term loans, regardless of whether they are performing or non-performing loans. Additionally, it aims to exclude personal credit card debt and residential mortgages. However, for some countries, significant deviations exist from this preferred SME loan definition. For instance, in some cases, credit card debt is included in SME loans, and it cannot be determined which part corresponds to consumer credit card debt and which part is business credit card debt. In other cases, lines of credit and overdrafts are excluded, while a number of other products are indeed included in SME loans, such as securitised loans, leasing and factoring.

In some countries, central banks do not require any reporting on SME lending. In these cases, the SME loans are estimated from SME financial statements available from tax authorities.

SME loans requested, authorised and used

The indicators on SME loans authorised and SME loans requested, which are used to calculate the rejection rate, are obtained from demand-side surveys. However, not all countries undertake such surveys, or, if they do, the results are not necessarily comparable. This also constitutes an area, where substantial data improvements could be made, such as enriching the analysis by the inclusion of an indicator on the level of discouragement to apply for a bank loan. To capture discouragement, this indicator should ideally be analysed in tandem with the number of loan applications. If both, loan applications and rejection rates decrease over the same period, this would suggest a higher level of discouragement. As presumably the least credit-worthy firms are deterred from applying for a loan, this could also be indicative of the average riskiness of SME lending.

Another potential improvement concerns the granularity and level of detail of the data; it might be possible to distinguish the rejection rate according to the type of loan (e.g. specific rejection rates on overdrafts, term loans, credit card loans and so on), to separate partial rejections from full rejections, including more analysis on the (likely) reason(s).

A similar problem holds true for the utilisation rate, which consists of SME loans used divided by SME loans authorised. A decline in this ratio suggests that the credit market is easing, or that banks have been providing more credit than has been used. Again, not every country has reliable survey data on the SME loans used and caution is warranted when making comparisons across countries.

Government loan guarantees and guaranteed loans

The report includes data on government loan guarantees and on the value of loans backed by government guarantees. Supply-side data are the best source of information on loan guarantees. There are many sources for such guarantees: local, regional or central governments. In some countries, an important volume of guarantees is also provided by mutual guarantee schemes. These are private schemes that typically benefit from public support, in the form of direct funding or counter-guarantees. However, the various loan guarantees schemes, public, private and mixed, are not always consolidated to obtain national figures. Therefore, the OECD Scoreboard reports mostly on government loan guarantees which are readily available at central government level. This is also a way to avoid the double-counting of guarantees that have multiple layers, given the existence of counter-guarantees at other levels (regional or supra-national). Still, cross-country differences exist in the degree to which the reported data include all government guarantee programmes, or only large ones.

In some cases, lack of awareness and reporting make it difficult to collect data on guaranteed SME loans. In fact, SMEs are not always aware that their loan is backed by a government guarantee and banks do not usually report this information. When these guaranteed SME loans are reported, they usually represent the full value of the loan and not the portion of the loan that is actually backed by a public institution guarantee. Nevertheless, this figure has a value of its own when compared to the total amount of SME loans outstanding. Also, it allows the calculation of the leverage effect of government guarantees to SMEs (ratio of guaranteed SME loans to corresponding government guarantees).

SME credit conditions

Significant differences exist across countries in the calculation for SME interest rates. While there is agreement that "fees" should be included in the "cost" of the SME loans, it appears to be particularly difficult to determine which "fees", among the various charges applied to firms, to include in the interest rates. In most cases, the interest rate charged on SME loans, net of any fee, is reported. The additional fees, however, represent a rather significant cost for SMEs that is not being captured by the current indicators built on supply-side data, particularly in the case of small SME loans. In this regard, demand-side surveys could be used to collect information on the total cost of funding.

Central banks usually do not collect key pieces of information on SME access to finance, such as the collateral required for SME loans. Banks consider this to be confidential information. A rough approximation can be obtained from demand-side information, that is, the percentage of SMEs required to provide collateral on new loans. This measure is currently used in the OECD Scoreboard, and more transparent reporting by banks on the terms of their SME lending is recommended to improve information on SME credit conditions.

Equity financing

The present report monitors external equity, that is, venture and growth capital. Venture capital is usually reported by stage of development: seed, start-up and early expansion capital. Later stage expansion capital, referred to as growth capital, is also reported. Buyouts, turnarounds and replacement capital are excluded from venture and growth capital. Country classification systems do not always break down private equity data into these categories and most do not break it down by firm size. Indeed, at present, the lack of a standard international definition of venture capital limits cross-country comparability. Also, venture capital data are sometimes collected by private venture capital associations, which rely on voluntary reporting and whose membership may be incomplete. There is a need for greater standardisation of venture capital data reporting, in terms of both the definition used for the different stages of investment, and the methodology employed to collect data[3].

Asset-based finance

Most of the indicators of the Scoreboard relate to bank finance, although in practice SMEs and entrepreneurs also rely on other financing options. Including statistics on the use of asset-based finance allows for a more complete overview of trends of access to finance for SMEs and entrepreneurs. Asset-based financing covers a variety of instruments whereby a firm obtains cash based on the value of a particular asset, rather than on credit standing. These instruments include asset-based lending, factoring, hire purchases and factoring.

Asset-based lending is any sort of lending secured by an asset (such as accounts receivable, inventory, real estate, equipment). As these loans are usually issued by banks, information on asset-based loans is already covered in the indicator on SME loans, and a separate indicator is not required. More detailed information on the composition of bank loans would, however, shed light on the importance of asset-based lending and what assets are most often used as a security.

The indicator on leasing covers either the new production (i.e. a flow indicator) of finance leases and operating leases of all asset types (automotive, equipment and real estate) and also includes the rental of cars, vans and trucks. Leasing is an agreement whereby the owner of an asset provides the right to use the asset for a specified period of time in exchange for a series of payments. Information on hire purchases, which are agreements where the purchaser agrees to pay for the goods in parts or percentages over a number of months and which is very similar to leasing is also covered. Factoring is a type of supplier financing where firms sell their credit-worthy accounts receivable at a discount and receive immediate cash. Data on factoring turnover volumes includes all turnover that is covered by invoice discounting, recourse factoring, non-recourse factoring, collections (domestic factoring), export factoring, import factoring and export invoice discounting (international factoring).

It is important to note that these data usually do not distinguish between SMEs and large corporations, and a breakdown of data according to the size of the lessees does not exist in most countries, although research indicates that leasing and other forms of asset-based finance are very often used by SMEs. Increasing the number of countries providing data and deriving information on the take-up of asset-based finance by firm size, either directly or through a proxy, constitutes an important avenue for future research.

Non-performing loans

There is also a great deal of latitude in how banks define non-performing loans. The generally accepted threshold of 90-day arrears, i.e. payments of interest and principal past due by 90 days or more, is indeed used by many of the Scoreboard countries, but not all. Even when this same threshold is adopted, there is a great deal of variation across countries in the measurement of SME non-performing loans. In some cases, these are measured as a percentage of the entire SME loan portfolio and in other cases they are not. In addition, it is common practice to classify loans that are unlikely to be repaid in full as non-performing, even when the threshold of 90-day arrears is not met. The circumstances under which loans are considered unlikely to be repaid, and hence deemed non-performing, vary substantially across countries and financial institutions. Caution is therefore warranted when interpreting this data.

When compared to the non-performing loans ratio of large firms, this indicator provides a good description of the performance of SME loans on a national level, irrespective of the particularity of the national definition. In addition, if the changes in the non-performing ratio are analysed over time, the indicator has value for cross-country comparisons.

Payment delays and bankruptcies

Payment delays and bankruptcy data are usually collected for all enterprises and not broken down by firm size. Since SMEs account for more than 97% of the enterprises in the participating countries, the national figures for payment delays and bankruptcy rates were used in this report. However, bankruptcies are hard to compare across countries because of different bankruptcy costs, legislation and behaviour in the face of bankruptcy. In some cases, bankruptcy procedures take a long time and so bankruptcies only show up in later periods rather than during the crisis period.

Payment delays are reported as delays beyond the contractual date on a B2B or on a broader B2B and B2C basis. Reporting of payment delays is important, given that it captures an additional source of cash flow constraints for SMEs. The reporting of both indicators and the comparison of B2B with B2C delays can also be used to uncover whether and how SMEs make use of such payment delays to resolve short-term cash flow issues in lieu of working capital credit facilities.

Differences in definitions of an SME

One of the biggest challenges to comparability is represented by existing differences in the statistical definition of an SME by banks and national organisations across countries. Greater harmonisation continues to prove difficult due to the different economic, social and political concerns of individual countries. In addition, within-country differences exist: some banks and financial institutions do not use their national statistical definitions for an SME but a different definition to collect data on SME financing.

In many cases, the national authorities collect loan data using the national or EU definition for an SME, based on firm size, usually the number of employees or the annual turnover (see Box A.A.1).

Box A A.1. What is an SME?

While there is no universal definition of an SME and several criteria can be used in the definition, SMEs are generally considered to be non-subsidiary firms which employ less than a given number of employees. This number of employees varies across countries. The most frequent upper limit designation of an SME is 250 employees, as in the European Union. However, some countries set the limit at 200, while the United States considers SMEs to include firms with fewer than 500 employees. Small firms are mostly considered to be firms with fewer than 50 employees while micro-enterprises have less than 10. Medium-sized firms have between 50 and 249 employees. Turnover and financial assets are also used to define SMEs: in the EU, the turnover of an SME cannot exceed EUR 50 million and the annual balance sheet should not exceed EUR 43 million. However, a change in this definition has recently been under discussion within the European Commission to raise the upper limit of balance sheet and turnover requirements to adjust for inflation, and to give greater recognition to the productivity gains of firms that have outgrown the definition, so-called mid-caps, and their role in the EU economy.

Source: OECD (2006), The SME Financing Gap (Vol. I): Theory and Evidence, OECD Publishing, Paris, SME Relief Package, (European Commission, 2023[1])

In other cases, the SME loan data are based not on firm size but rather on a proxy, that is, loan size.[4] However, the size of the SME loan can differ among countries and sometimes even among banks within the same country.

Several reasons are advanced for not compiling financial statistics based on firm size including:

- Banks do not collect data by firm size;
- It is too expensive to collect such data;

- Breaking down loan data by firm size would jeopardise confidentiality and are not gathered or communicated as a consequence.

Experience gained from the OECD Scoreboard suggests that loan data broken down by firm size are already in the financial system but are not extracted unless banks are under a regulatory obligation to provide them. Experience also suggests that the challenges mentioned above could be addressed quite easily. For instance, confidentiality requirements in theory could be met through the use of judicious sub-grouping. In this case, resolution of this issue could be found if national regulatory authorities were to make the provision of this information mandatory for banks.

Table A A.3. Difference between national statistical and financial definitions of SMEs

Country	National statistical definition of SMEs	Indicator	Definition of SMEs used
Australia	Size of firm: less than 200 employees	Business loans, SMEs	Firm size: turnover less than AUD 50 million
		Interest rate, SMEs	Firm size: turnover less than AUD 50 million
Austria	Size of firm: 1 – 249 employees	Business loans, SMEs	Loan size: amounts up to EUR 1 million
		Short- and long-term loans, SMEs	Loan size: amounts up to EUR 1 million
		Government loan guarantees and government guaranteed loans, SMEs	Firm size: enterprises with less than 250 employees
		Direct government loans, SMEs	Firm size: enterprises with less than 250 employees
		Rejection rate	Firm size: enterprises with less than 250 employees
		Interest rate, SMEs	Loan size: amounts up to EUR 1 million
Belgium	Size of firm: less than 250 employees	Business loans, SMEs	Firm size: enterprises with less than 250 employees
		SME loans authorised and used	Firm size: enterprises with less than 250 employees
		Interest rate, SMEs	Loan size: amounts up to EUR 1 million
Brazil	annual turnover of up to BRL 4.8 million	Outstanding business loans, SMEs	Loan size: amounts up to BRL 100 million
			Measured on a client-facility-month basis
Canada	Size of firm: 1-499 employees	Business loans, SMEs	Loan size: amounts up to CAD 1 million
		Short- and long-term loans, small businesses	Firm size: enterprises with 1-99 employees
		Government guaranteed loans, SMEs	Firm size: annual sales (turnover) lower than CAD 5 million
		Direct government loans, SMEs	Firm size: annual sales (turnover) less than CAD 25 million
		Risk premium for small businesses	Firm size: enterprises with 1-99 employees
		Loans authorised and requested, small businesses	Firm size: enterprises with 1-99 employees
		Collateral, small businesses	Firm size: enterprises with 1-99 employees
Chile	Annual sales of firm: up to UF	Business loans, SMEs	Loan size: amounts up to UF 18 000
		Short- and long-term loans, SMEs	Loan size: amounts up to UF 18 000

	100 000	Government guaranteed loans, SMEs	Firm size: annual sales up to UF 100 000 or annual exports up to UF 400 000
		Direct government loans, SMEs	Less than 12 hectares and capital up to UF 3 500
		Loans authorised and requested, SMEs	Firm size: annual sales up to UF 100 000
		Non-performing loans, SMEs	Loan size: amounts up to UF 18 000
		Short-term and long-term interest rate, SMEs	Loan size: amounts up to UF 18 000
		Payment delays, SMEs	Loan size: amounts up to UF 18 000
China	The definition of SMEs differs according to sector.		The definition of SMEs differs according to sector.
		Short- and long-term loans, SMEs	The definition of SMEs differs according to sector.
		Government loan guarantees, SMEs	The definition of SMEs differs according to sector.
		SME government direct loans	The definition of SMEs differs according to sector.
		Non-performing loans, SMEs	The definition of SMEs differs according to sector.
		SME loans requested, authorized and used	The definition of SMEs differs according to sector.
		interest rates, SMEs	The definition of SMEs differs according to sector.
		Collateral, SMEs	The definition of SMEs differs according to sector.
		Loan fees, SMEs	The definition of SMEs differs according to sector.
Colombia	Size of firm: less than 200 employees	Business loans, SMEs	Firm size: enterprises with less than 200 employees
		Non-performing loans, SMEs	Firm size: enterprises with less than 200 employees
		Government guaranteed loans, SMEs	Firm size: enterprises with less than 200 employees
		Interest rate, SMEs	Firm size: enterprises with less than 200 employees
		Collateral, SMEs	Firm size: enterprises with less than 200 employees
Czech Republic	Size of firm: less than 250 employees	Business loans, SMEs	Loan size: amount up to CZK 30 million
		(New business loans, SMEs – flows)	Loan size: amount up to CZK 30 million
		Business loans, SMEs	Firm size: up to 250 employees
		(Outstanding business loans, SMEs – stock)	
		Interest rate, SMEs	Loan size: amount up to CZK 30 million
Denmark	Size of firm: less than 250 employees	Business loans, SMEs	Loan size: amounts up to EUR 1 million
		Short- and long-term loans, SMEs	Loan size: amounts up to EUR 1 million
		Government loan guarantees, SMEs	Firm size: up to 250 employees
		Interest rate, SMEs	Loan size: amounts up to EUR 1 million
Estonia	Size of firm: less than 250 employees	Business loans, SMEs	Loan size: amounts up to EUR 1 million
		Government loan guarantees, SMEs	Loan size: amounts up to EUR 1 million
		Non-performing loans, SMEs	Loan size: amounts up to EUR 1 million
		Interest rate, SMEs	Loan size: amounts up to EUR 1 million
Finland	EU definition (less	Business loans, SMEs	Loan size: up to EUR 1 million

	than 250 employees and annual turnover below EUR 50 million and/ or balance sheet below EUR 43 million)	Short- and long-term loans, SMEs	Firm size: less than 250 employees
		Value of government guaranteed loans, SMEs	Firm size: less than 250 employees
		Loans authorised and requested, SMEs	Loan size: up to EUR 1 million
		Interest rate, SMEs	Loan size: up to EUR 1 million
		Collateral, SMEs	Firm size: less than 250 employees
France	EU definition (less than 250 employees and annual turnover below EUR 50 million and/ or balance sheet below EUR 43 million)	Business loans, SMEs	Firm size: number of employees (less than 250), turnover (less than EUR 50 million), total assets of legal units (less than EUR 43 million) and independent; bank must inform the Central Credit Register when it grants a loan of more than EUR 25 000
		Short- medium- and long-term loans	Firm size: number of employees (less than 250), turnover (less than EUR 50 million), total assets of legal units (less than EUR 43 million) and independent; bank must inform the Central Credit Register when it grants a loan of more than EUR 25 000
		Share of the outstanding loans of failing companies, SMEs except micro-enterprises	Firm size: number of employees (less than 250), turnover (less than EUR 50 million), total assets of legal units (less than EUR 43 million) and independent; bank must inform the Central Credit Register when it grants a loan of more than EUR 25 000
		Interest rate, SMEs	Loan size: less than EUR 1 million
		Bankruptcies, SMEs	Firm size: number of employees (less than 250), turnover (less than EUR 50 million), total assets of legal units (less than EUR 43 million) and independent
Georgia	Less than 100 employees and turnover below GEL 1.5 million	Business loans, SMEs	Less than 100 employees and turnover below GEL 1.5 million
		Non-performing loans, SMEs	
		Interest rate, SMEs	
		Collateral SMEs	
Greece	EU definition (less than 250 employees and annual turnover below EUR 50 million and/ or balance sheet below EUR 43 million)	Business loans, SMEs	Firm size: number of employees (less than 250 employees), turnover (less than EUR 50 million) and total assets (less than EUR 10 million)
		Interest rate, SMEs	Loan size: less than EUR 1 million
		Collateral, SMEs	Loan size: less than EUR 1 million
Hungary	EU definition (less than 250 employees and annual turnover below EUR 50 million and/ or balance sheet below EUR 43 million)	Business loans, SMEs	Firm size: number of employees (less than 250 employees), turnover (less than EUR 50 million) and total assets (less than EUR 10 million)
		Overdraft loans, SMEs	Firm size: number of employees (less than 250 employees), turnover (less than EUR 50 million) and total assets (less than EUR 10 million)

		Investment loans, SMEs	Firm size: number of employees (less than 250 employees), turnover (less than EUR 50 million) and total assets (less than EUR 10 million)
		Direct government loans, SMEs	Firm size: number of employees (less than 250 employees), turnover (less than EUR 50 million) and total assets (less than EUR 10 million)
		Government guaranteed loans, SMEs	Firm size: number of employees (less than 250 employees), turnover (less than EUR 50 million) and total assets (less than EUR 10 million)
		Non-performing loans, SMEs	Firm size: number of employees (less than 250 employees), turnover (less than EUR 50 million) and total assets (less than EUR 10 million)
		Average interest rate, SMEs	Loan size: amounts up to EUR 1 million
Ireland	EU definition (less than 250 employees and annual turnover below EUR 50 million and/ or balance sheet below EUR 43 million)	Business loans, SMEs	Firm size
		Short- and long-term loans, SMEs	Loan size: less than EUR 1 million
		Interest rates, SMEs	Loan size: less than EUR 1 million
Israel	Size of firm: less than 100 employees and annual turnover of up to NIS 100 million	Business loans, SMEs	Loan size: amounts of NIS differ depending on the bank
		Interest rate small firms and medium firms	Loan size: amounts of NIS differ depending on the bank
Indonesia	Maximum turnover of 50 billion rupiah or maximum assets (excluding building land asset) of 10 billion rupiah	Business loans, SMEs	Firm size: Maximum turnover of 50 billion rupiah
Italy	EU definition (less than 250 employees and annual turnover below EUR 50 million and/ or balance sheet below EUR 43 million)	Business loans, SMEs	Firm size: less than 20 workers
		Short- and long-term loans, SMEs	Firm size: less than 20 workers
		Government guaranteed loans, SMEs	Firm size: less than 250 employees
		Direct government loans, SMEs	Firm size: less than 250 employees
		Loans authorised and used, SMEs	Firm size: less than 20 workers
		Non-performing loans, SMEs	Firm size: less than 20 workers
		Interest rate, average SME rate	Firm size: less than 20 workers
		Collateral, SMEs	Firm size: less than 20 workers
		Venture and expansion capital, SMEs	Firm size: less than 250 employees
		Payment delays, SMEs	Firm size: turnover of up to EUR 50 million and less than 250 employees
Japan	Varies by sector	Business loans, SMEs	The definition of SMEs differs according to sector.
		Bankruptcies, SMEs	The definition of SMEs differs according to sector. Only enterprises with debts of at least JPY10 million are included.

Kazakhstan	Less than 250 employees in addition to an annual income criterium	Business loans, SMEs	Firm size: less than 250 employees and up to MCI 3 million or KZT 9.54 billion
Korea	Varies by sector	Business loans, SMEs	The definition of SMEs differs according to sector.
		Short- and long-term loans, SMEs	The definition of SMEs differs according to sector.
		Government loan guarantees, SMEs	The definition of SMEs differs according to sector.
		Direct government loans, SMEs	The definition of SMEs differs according to sector.
		Loans authorised and requested, SMEs	The definition of SMEs differs according to sector.
		Non-performing loans, SMEs	The definition of SMEs differs according to sector.
		Interest rate spread, SME and large firm rates	The definition of SMEs differs according to sector.
		Payment delays, SMEs	The definition of SMEs differs according to sector.
Latvia	EU definition (less than 250 employees and annual turnover below EUR 50 million and/ or balance sheet below EUR 43 million)	Interest rate, SMEs	Loan size: Loans of less than EUR 250000
Lithuania	EU definition (less than 250 employees and annual turnover below EUR 50 million and/ or balance sheet below EUR 43 million)	Business loans, SMEs	Firm size: Less than 250 employees and annual turnover below EUR 50 million
Luxembourg	EU definition (less than 250 employees and annual turnover below EUR 50 million and/ or balance sheet below EUR 43 million)	SME loans	Loan size: Loans of less than EUR 1 million
		SME interest rate	Loan size: Loans of less than EUR 1 million
Malaysia	Manufacturing sector: Sales turnover not exceeding RM 50 million or full-time employees not exceeding 200. Services and other	SME loans	Firm size: Sales turnover not exceeding RM 50 million or full-time employees not exceeding 200 for firms operating in the manufacturing sector and sales turnover not exceeding RM 20 million or full-time employees not exceeding 75 for firms operating in services and other sectors,

	sectors: Sales turnover not exceeding RM 20 million or full-time employees not exceeding 75.	SME short-term loans	Firm size: Sales turnover not exceeding RM 50 million or full-time employees not exceeding 200 for firms operating in the manufacturing sector and sales turnover not exceeding RM 20 million or full-time employees not exceeding 75 for firms operating in services and other sectors,
		SME long-term loans	Firm size: Sales turnover not exceeding RM 50 million or full-time employees not exceeding 200 for firms operating in the manufacturing sector and sales turnover not exceeding RM 20 million or full-time employees not exceeding 75 for firms operating in services and other sectors,
		SME non-performing loans	Firm size: Sales turnover not exceeding RM 50 million or full-time employees not exceeding 200 for firms operating in the manufacturing sector and sales turnover not exceeding RM 20 million or full-time employees not exceeding 75 for firms operating in services and other sectors,
		SME loans authorised	Firm size: Sales turnover not exceeding RM 50 million or full-time employees not exceeding 200 for firms operating in the manufacturing sector and sales turnover not exceeding RM 20 million or full-time employees not exceeding 75 for firms operating in services and other sectors,
		SME loans requested	Firm size: Sales turnover not exceeding RM 50 million or full-time employees not exceeding 200 for firms operating in the manufacturing sector and sales turnover not exceeding RM 20 million or full-time employees not exceeding 75 for firms operating in services and other sectors,
		SME interest rate	Firm size: Sales turnover not exceeding RM 50 million or full-time employees not exceeding 200 for firms operating in the manufacturing sector and sales turnover not exceeding RM 20 million or full-time employees not exceeding 75 for firms operating in services and other sectors,
Mexico	Firm size: up to 100 or 250 employees, depending on the sector	SME loans	The definition depends on the number of employees and the annual revenues of the borrower
		SME guaranteed loans/direct loans	Firm size: up to 100 or 250 employees, depending on the sector
		SME loans requested and authorized	Firm size: up to 100 or 250 employees, depending on the sector
		SME interest rate	Firm size: up to 100 or 250 employees, depending on the sector
The Netherlands	EU definition (less than 250	Business loans, SMEs	Loan size: up to EUR 1 million
		Short- and long-term loans, SMEs	Loan size: up to EUR 1 million

	employees and annual turnover below EUR 50 million and/ or balance sheet below EUR 43 million)	Government loan guarantees, SMEs	Firm size: up to 250 employees
		Loans authorised and requested, SMEs	Firm size: up to 250 employees
		Collateral, SMEs	Size of firm up to 50 employees
New Zealand	No unique national definition.	Interest rates, SMEs	Loan size: up to NZD 1 million
		Loan authorised, SMEs	Firm size: enterprises with 6-19 employees
		Loan requested, SMEs	Firm size: enterprises with 6-19 employees
Norway	EU definition (less than 250 employees and annual turnover below EUR 50 million and/ or balance sheet below EUR 43 million)	Business loans, SMEs	Firm size: less than 250 employees
		Venture Capital, SMEs	Firm size: less than 250 employees. Invested equity in the last two years.
		Bankruptcy, SMEs	Firm size: less than 250 employees, excludes non-employer firms and sole proprietorships.
Portugal	EU definition (less than 250 employees and annual turnover below EUR 50 million and/ or balance sheet below EUR 43 million)	Business loans, SMEs	Firm size: EU definition (less than 250 employees and annual turnover below EUR 50 million and/ or balance sheet below EUR 43 million, Com Recommendation 2003/361/EC)
		Short- and long-term loans, SMEs	Firm size: EU definition (less than 250 employees and annual turnover below EUR 50 million and/ or balance sheet below EUR 43 million, Com Recommendation 2003/361/EC)
		Government guaranteed loans, SMEs	Firm size: EU definition (less than 250 employees and annual turnover below EUR 50 million and/ or balance sheet below EUR 43 million, Com Recommendation 2003/361/EC)
		Loans authorised and requested, SMEs	Firm size: EU definition (less than 250 employees and annual turnover below EUR 50 million and/ or balance sheet below EUR 43 million, Com Recommendation 2003/361/EC)
		Non-performing loans, SMEs	Firm size: EU definition (less than 250 employees and annual turnover below EUR 50 million and/ or balance sheet below EUR 43 million, Com Recommendation 2003/361/EC)
		Interest rates, SMEs	Loan size: up to EUR 1 million (prior to 2010) and loans up to EUR 0.25 million (in 2010)

		Collateral, SMEs	Firm size: EU definition (less than 250 employees and annual turnover below EUR 50 million and/ or balance sheet below EUR 43 million, Com Recommendation 2003/361/EC)
Peru	SMEs are defined by annual turnover	Outstanding business loans, SMEs	Defined by annual sales of the borrower
Serbia	Up to 250 employees, turnover up to EUR 10 million, total assets up to EUR 5 million	Business loans, SMEs	Firm size, in accordance with national statistical definition.
		Interest rate, SMEs	Loan size: up to EUR 1 million.
Slovak Republic	EU definition (less than 250 employees and annual turnover below EUR 50 million and/ or balance sheet below EUR 43 million)	Business loans, SMEs	Firm size: less than 250 employees (including natural persons)
		Short- and long-term loans, SMEs	Firm size: less than 250 employees (including natural persons)
		Government loan guarantees, SMEs	Firm size: less than 250 employees (including natural persons)
		Government guaranteed loans, SMEs	Firm size: EU definition (less than 250 employees and annual turnover below EUR 50 million and/ or balance sheet below EUR 43 million, Com Recommendation 2003/361/EC)
		Direct government loans, SMEs	Firm size: less than 250 employees (including natural persons)
		Direct government loans, SMEs	Firm size: less than 250 employees (including natural persons)
		Collateral, SMEs	Firm size: EU definition (less than 250 employees and annual turnover below EUR 50 million and/ or balance sheet below EUR 43 million, Com Recommendation 2003/361/EC)
		Venture capital, SMEs	Firm size: EU definition (less than 250 employees and annual turnover below EUR 50 million and/ or balance sheet below EUR 43 million, Com Recommendation 2003/361/EC)
Slovenia	EU definition (less than 250 employees and annual turnover below EUR 50 million and/ or balance sheet below EUR 43 million)	Short- and long-term loans, SMEs	Firm size: less than or equal to 250 employees and asset value less than or equal to EUR 17.5 million.
		Direct government loans, SMEs	Firm size: less than or equal to 250 employees and asset value less than or equal to EUR 17.5 million.
		Interest rate, SMEs	Firm and loan size: enterprises with less than 250 employees and amounts less than EUR 1 million.
South Africa	SMEs are defined by annual turnover	Business loans, SMEs	Firm size: Businesses with turnover less than ZAR 400 million
		Non-performing loans	Firm size: Businesses with turnover less than ZAR 400 million where an exposure is overdue for more than 90 days
Spain	EU definition (less than 250	Business loans, SMEs	Loan size: less than EUR 1 million
		Short- and long-term loans, SMEs	Loan size: less than EUR 1 million

	employees and annual turnover below EUR 50 million and/ or balance sheet below EUR 43 million)	Government guaranteed loans, SMEs	Firm size: less than 250 employees
		Interest rate, SMEs	Loan size: less than EUR 1 million
		Venture capital, SMEs	Firm size: less than 250 employees
		Payment delays, SMEs	Firm size: EU definition
		Bankruptcies, SMEs	Firm size: EU definition
Sweden	EU definition (less than 250 employees and annual turnover below EUR 50 million and/ or balance sheet below EUR 43 million)	Business loans, SMEs	Firm size: 1-249 employees
		Short- and long-term loans, SMEs	Firm size: 1-249 employees
		Government guaranteed loans, SMEs	Firm size: 0-249 employees
		Government loan guarantees, SMEs	Firm size: 0-249 employees
		Direct government loans, SMEs	Firm size: 0-249 employees
		Loans authorised, SMEs	Firm size: 0-249 employees
		Interest rates, SMEs	Loan size: up to EUR 1 million
Switzerland	Size of firm: less than 250 employees	Business loans, SMEs	Firm size: less than 250 employees
		Government guaranteed loans, SMEs	Firm size: less than 250 employees
		Loans used, SMEs	Firm size: less than 250 employees
		Collateral, SMEs	Firm size: up to 249 employees
		Interest rates, SMEs	Loan size: less than CHF 1 million
Thailand	Number of employees and revenue according to the industry: firms in manufacturing less than 200 employees and revenue of less than THB 500 million Firms in services: Less than 100 employees and THB 300 in revenue.	Business loans, SMEs	Firm size: according to the sector, revenue and number of employees.
		Short- and long-term loans, SMEs	Firm size: according to the sector, revenue and number of employees
		Government guaranteed loans, SMEs	Firm size: according to the sector, revenue and number of employees
		Loans authorised and requested, SMEs	Firm size: according to the sector, revenue and number of employees
		Non-performing loans, SMEs	Firm size: according to the sector, revenue and number of employees
		Interest rate, SME average rate	Firm size: according to the sector, revenue and number of employees
		Payment delays, SMEs	The National definition of SMEs differs according to sector.
		Bankruptcies, SMEs	The National definition of SMEs differs according to sector.
Turkïye	Less than 250 employees and TRY 40 million in assets	Business loans, SMEs	Firm size: less than 250 employees
		SME non-performing loans	Firm size: less than 250 employees
Ukraine	Less than 250 employees and EUR 50 million in turnover	Business loans, SMEs	Firm size: Less than 250 employees and EUR 50 million in turnover
		Interest rates, SMEs	
United Kingdom	Size of firm: less than 250	Business lending, SMEs	Firm size: turnover of up to GBP 25 million
		Interest rates, SMEs	Firm size: turnover up to GBP 25 million

	employees	Collateral, SMEs	Firm size: less than 250 employees, including non-employer enterprises
United States	Size of firm: less than 500 employees	Business loans, SMEs	Loan size: up to USD 1 million.
		Short-term loans, SMEs	Loan size: up to USD 1 million.
		Interest rates, SMEs	Loan size up to USD 5 million
		Government guaranteed loans, SMEs	Varies by industry
		Collateral, SMEs	Loan size: up to USD 1 million

Impact of diversity in definitions

The many limitations in data collection above outlined limit the possibility to make cross-country comparisons using the raw data. However, it is possible to observe general trends for the indicators, both within and across countries, using growth rates. When analysing trends, the differences in the exact composition of the indicators are muted by the fact that the changes in the indicators over time are being examined instead of levels. Additionally, if the indicators are analysed as a set, it is possible to form an overview of the country trends in SME financing. It is precisely comparing trends that the Scoreboard sheds light on changing market conditions and policies for financing SMEs and entrepreneurs.

However, again, caution is required in cross-country comparisons, especially as concerns the use of flow variables and stock measures. Flows, which are measured over an accounting period (i.e. one year), capture changes of a given variables and are therefore more volatile than stocks, which measure levels, i.e. the value of an asset at a given point in time, and thus reflect latest flows, as well as values that may have cumulated over time, net of depreciation. The comparison of flows and stock measures can be particularly problematic when growth rates are considered. In fact, a negative growth rate of a flow variable can be compatible with a positive growth rate of the same variable measured in stocks. This would be the case if the stock variables increases over time but the absolute increase by which the stock variables grows becomes smaller. Similarly, a negative growth rate of a loan stock does not necessarily mean a decline in SME lending, but could be attributed to maturing loans exceeding the value of new loans granted. Such difficulties underline the importance of complementing stock data with flows of new loans.

Recommendations for data improvements

Standardised template

To enable more timely collection of data and better cross-country comparison in the future, it is necessary for countries to advance in the harmonisation of data content and in the standardisation of methods of data collection. The adoption of a standardised table for data collection and submission on SME finance has contributed to improve the process of data collection for the Scoreboard, while allowing for some customisation at the country level, and should thus be further pursued, as country coverage increases. The systematic use of the template is furthermore intended to facilitate the timely publication of the data on core indicators on the OECD.Stat website, from which it can then be customised, manipulated and downloaded.

The long-term objectives of timeliness, comparability, transparency and harmonisation of data should continue to be pursued actively by national authorities. To that end, national authorities should work with financial institutions to improve the collection of data on SME and entrepreneurship finance, by:

- Requiring financial institutions to use the national definition for an SME based on firm size.

- Requiring financial institutions to report on a timely basis to their regulatory authorities SME loans, interest rates, collateral requirements, by firm size and broken down into the appropriate size subcategories, as well as those SME loans which have government support.
- Working towards international harmonisation of data on non-performing loans.
- Encouraging international, regional and national authorities as well as business associations to work together to harmonise quantitative demand-side surveys in terms of survey population, questions asked and timeframes; encourage the competent organisations to undertake yearly surveys.
- Promoting the harmonisation of the definition of venture capital in terms of stages of development and the methodology employed to collect data.

Core indicators

Since the Scoreboard pilot exercise was launched in 2009-10, important progress has been made in terms of standardisation and comparability of information. As country coverage continues to increase, it is important for good practices in data collection and reporting to be shared among countries, but also for further advancement to be made in the harmonisation of core indicators. A number of areas can be identified to improve the monitoring over time of trends at the country level and across countries.

First, it is of paramount importance to improve reporting of SME loan variables. Key areas for refinement include:

- Separate reporting of financial information for non-employer and employer-firms, so as to harmonise the financial data with the SME definition employed in national statistics. The separation would also allow for a more in-depth evaluation of financing trends at the country level, distinguishing between funding that is directed to businesses that generate employment from that directed to self-employers, which may however represent an important share of the country's business activity.
- Collection of stock and flow data for SME loans. These two indicators are complementary and should be jointly analysed in order to draw a comprehensive picture of the evolution of the SME lending portfolio.
- Information on the composition of lending portfolios, broken down by different products (overdrafts/ lines of credit/ leases/ business mortgages or credit cards/ securitised loans). Greater granularity in the reporting of business loans would allow for the identification of the underlying elements of the SME business loan portfolio. This represents a necessary first step towards pursuing greater harmonisation in the definition of SME loans across countries, or, at least identifying a common "base composition" for more meaningful cross-country comparisons.

Second, it is also necessary to fill the gaps in available data and work towards more comprehensive information for other core indicators in the Scoreboard:

- Government guarantees: Provide consolidated figures, which take into account the entire range of public guarantee programmes, while excluding double counting related, for instance, to the counter-guarantee of the same lending portfolio. Include additional information on the scope and coverage of public guarantee schemes, in particular information on the volume of outstanding guarantees, the public contribution to the fund's capitalisation, and the value of the loans supported by public guarantees. The Scoreboard data should be complemented, in the policy section of country profiles, by the monitoring of the take-ups and phasing out of these guarantee schemes. Specify the figures that can be attributed to schemes in response to the COVID-19 crisis or the energy crisis (e.g. new government guarantee schemes, new lines of direct lending) in the reporting of Scoreboard indicators. In the context of specific measures on greening and digitalization, provide information on new or expanded government schemes, including information on eligibility criteria and duration, and if possible, amount of total funding allocated to those schemes. This information could also complement the work of the OECD Platform on Financing SMEs for Sustainability as well as the D4SME initiative. The new data and metadata would also contribute to enriching the SME Financing database in OECD.stat.

- Government guaranteed loans: Provide the corresponding loans backed by the reported government guarantees so as to allow for the calculation of a leverage ratio. Optimally, the guaranteed portions of these loans should be also reported.
- Non-performing loans (NPLs): Provide the NPL ratio for SME loans, together with the overall NPL ratio of the business loan portfolio or the NPL ratio for large firms. The latter would be used as a benchmark against which the performance and quality of the SME loan portfolio is measured.
- Asset-based finance: Obtain data broken down by firm size or a functioning proxy of firm size. Currently, business associations usually do not make the distinction according to the use of these instruments by firm size, which limits the understanding of the importance of these non-bank financial instruments for SMEs.
- SME loan fees: Provide information on the standard practice of the commercial banking sector with respect to loan fees charged to SME loans in addition to the interest rate, at a national level. If possible, use demand-side surveys to collect information on this indirect cost on SME lending.
- Collateral: Improve the description of what constitutes collateral and use demand-side survey information to compensate for lack of supply-side data on collateral.

Using complementary sources of information to enrich the core indicators

Many countries do not collect data on the uptake of the full range of financing instruments other than straight debt by SMEs, despite the increasing importance of these instruments. In recent years, more data from secondary sources such as research institutes and industry bodies, have been included in the Scoreboard for an increasing number of finance instruments such as leasing and hire purchases, factoring activities, and venture capital. Data on online alternative finance was one of the indicators that was outsourced from a dedicated research institute. However, more recently this information is proving more difficult to collect considering the growing complexity of the industry stemming from the increasing number of platforms and other actors and the different types of financing solutions that are provided to SMEs.

The OECD Secretariat will continue to enrich the core indicators with other complementary sources of information, in line with available resources and if judged sufficiently reliable, comparable and relevant, and continue its focus on providing high-quality information on the broad range of financial instruments at the disposal of SMEs and entrepreneurs. For example, one or several indicators on trade finance, supply chain finance, finance provided through online alternative platforms and business angel investments could be included, if appropriate sources of data can be identified.

Furthermore, in the context of the recovery from the COVID-19 crisis, the subsequent energy crisis, and the growing importance on supporting SMEs for the green and digital transition, other indicators have also become relevant. For example, more information on public support schemes could be considered, such as public grants received by SMEs and entrepreneurs, as well as the conditions and the eligibility criteria used to provide this support.

Inclusion of more disaggregated data

The Scoreboard now seeks to collect disaggregated data on SME and entrepreneurship finance and financing conditions. These efforts, in addition to being in line with the 2022 Updated High-Level Principles on SME Financing and the OECD Recommendation on SME Financing, are a crucial improvement for the

Scoreboard, considering the significant heterogeneity of the SME population and the impact that these underlying characteristics have on access to finance and financing conditions.

In order to obtain a better picture of the availability of more granular data in the Scoreboard countries, a survey was conducted as part of a stocktaking exercise and as an input for the longer-term objective of including more detailed information in the Scoreboard report. In total, 25 countries participated in the survey. Based on the survey results, four levels of disaggregation are being explored:

- The *geographical location* of the company, TL 2 regions (based on the OECD nomenclature), which mostly corresponds to NUTS 2 regions in the EU.
- The *gender* of the principal owner, making a distinction between firms that are primarily owned (not necessarily managed) by women and firms that are primarily owned by men; "dual ownership" is a third category.
- The main *sector of operation*, using NACE Level 1 sectors as the reference.
- *Firm size,* i.e. going beyond the classic dichotomy between SMEs and large companies to look into data disaggregated by smaller size bands (e.g. micro vs. small vs. medium).

Data collection and related analysis has started by geographical location and by gender of the principal owner. The 2023 Scoreboard Highlights was the first edition to present the first early findings and this 2024 edition presented more insights on the disaggregated data by TL2 regions. The collection of subnational and gender disaggregated data on access to finance responds to: i) a growing interest in documenting how financing conditions change across different regions of a same country, and how these variations affect enterprise development and productivity and may justify different or differentiated policies ii) a growing opportunity to address the gap in the collection and diffusion of gender-disaggregated data which is increasingly crucial for policymakers to target and design policies that effectively address gender disparities in the offer and uptake of finance from SME owners and entrepreneurs.

Yet the results of the Scoreboard pilot exercise revealed that there is a discrepancy between the political priority attached to the issue of gender, and the official data currently being collected on this dimension, which is extremely limited. Across the OECD, work on gender is being stepped up, including through a strategic document outlining the corporate priorities and contributions in this area, in which better data is a core objective. In this context, the Scoreboard can make an important contribution to driving the agenda forward. In this context, the OECD is collaborating with other international initiatives which seeks to strengthen information on access to finance by women-owned businesses.

The collection of additional dimensions (e.g. sector of operation and firm size) is foreseen to be incorporated in the near future. Overall, the incorporation of these dimensions will provide a better understanding of SME and entrepreneurship finance trends, would significantly continue to strengthen the usefulness of the Scoreboard, contribute to a better understanding of the heterogeneity of SME segments, enrich the evidence base and support policy efforts focused on SME and entrepreneurship financing. The rest of this section explains the relevance of including these four levels of disaggregation in the Scoreboard.

Subnational perspective

Enterprise financing conditions at the local level reflect local economic conditions. SMEs in lagging regions typically find it more difficult to receive a loan and, when they receive one, are charged higher interest rates than SMEs in better-off regions. This does not necessarily imply geographical discrimination, but rather reflects financial performance of the borrower (internal factors) and/or higher perceived credit risk by the lenders due to a less favourable local business environment (external factors), as shown for example by higher rates of nonperforming loans in lagging regions. Equity finance is also geographically concentrated, depriving growth-oriented SMEs and start-ups in more peripheral regions from much needed growth capital. While technology could in principle allow for a greater distance between investors and entrepreneurs, a recent report by the British Business Bank finds that in 82% of equity investment stakes, the investor had an office within two hours travel time of the company that they were backing (British Business Bank, 2021[2]).

Gender perspective

Women entrepreneurs have long-faced barriers in financial markets, and these barriers have been persistent over time and across contexts. For example, women run one in three small enterprises worldwide, yet many of them rely only on their personal finances to fund their operations (IFC, 2014[3]). Compared to men, women have a lower success rate when applying for debt financing, and when they do, they often receive less money, pay higher interest rates, and have to put up more collateral (Thébaud and Sharkey, 2016[4]; Lassébie et al., 2019[5]) (OECD, forthcoming[6]). The gender gap is also seen when women-owned businesses try to access equity financing, with the proportion of women receiving venture capital funding being considerably less than the proportion of men, as well as the amount of funding that they receive being on average lower than what men-owned businesses receive (Pitchbook, 2023[7]) (Female Founder Fund, 2022[8]).While the availability of enterprise financing data by the gender of the business owner is scarce, it is crucial to work in this direction, for example by central banks asking commercial banks to collect and share aggregate information on the distribution of business loans by the gender of the borrower.

Sector perspective

Financing needs and access to finance opportunities change depending on the main activity and industry in which a business operates. SMEs in sectors that rely more intensively on physical assets, such as manufacturing, can be expected to receive credit more easily, as capital assets can be pledged as collateral. Asset-based financing is also more easily available to these enterprises. Companies whose business model hinges on intangible assets (IA) (e.g. patents and trademarks), on the other hand, are at a disadvantage in credit markets, as these assets are firm-specific and difficult to use as collateral in traditional debt relations. The availability of alternative sources of finance, from equity finance to private debt, is particularly important for IA-intensive companies, which are often major drivers of growth. Equity finance, in addition to being geographically concentrated, is also sector-concentrated in knowledge-intensive industries, such as ICT, biotechnologies and medical services. Interestingly, however, the sector distribution of high-growth firms is much less concentrated than the sector distribution of equity investments, suggesting the existence of an industry mismatch between the allocation of equity finance and the distribution of high-growth firms.

Firm size perspective

The rationale behind the *OECD SME and Entrepreneurship Financing Scoreboard* is that SMEs are disadvantaged compared to larger companies in access to external finance, making it relevant to assess trends in the SME finance gap and policies that can bridge this gap. However, a closer look would show that micro and small enterprises face the most constraints, whereas access to finance and financing conditions for mid-sized companies are closer to those available for larger companies. Typical problems of credit markets, such as information asymmetries or lack of collateral, are much more prominent among smaller SMEs. To the extent possible, efforts should seek to go beyond the classic dichotomy of SMEs and larger companies by collecting more granular information on credit and equity finance by smaller firm-size classes.

References

AIFI (2020), *Il mercato italiano del private equity e del venture capital*, Associazione Italiana del Private Equity, Venture Capital e Private Debt, https://www.aifi.it/visualizzaallegatodocumenti.aspx?chiave=u10jlmi71yQ3jShJ6O2Nz9nr8MV48g. [15]

British Business Bank (2021), *Regions and Nations Trackers: Small Business Finance Markets*, https://www.british-business-bank.co.uk/research/regions-and-nations-tracker-2021/. [2]

Bruegel (2021), *European Union countries' recovery and resilience plans*, https://www.bruegel.org/publications/datasets/european-union-countries-recovery-and-resilience-plans/. [10]

European Commission (2023), *SME Relief Package*, https://single-market-economy.ec.europa.eu/system/files/2023-09/COM_2023_535_1_EN_ACT_part1_v12.pdf. [1]

Female Founder Fund (2022), *2021 Review of Funding for Female Founders*, https://blog.femalefoundersfund.com/2021-review-of-funding-for-female-founders-b3008c13d390. [8]

Halabisky, D. and I. Basille (forthcoming), *Policy brief on access to finance for inclusive and social entrepreneurship*. [17]

IFC (2014), *Women-Owned SMEs: A Business Opportunity for Financial Institutions*, https://financialallianceforwomen.org/download/women-owned-smes-a-business-opportunity-for-financial-institutions/. [3]

Lassébie, J. et al. (2019), "Levelling the playing field : Dissecting the gender gap in the funding of start-ups", *OECD Science Technology and Industry Policy Paper*, No. 73, OECD Publishing, Paris, https://doi.org/10.1787/23074957. [5]

NESTA (2009), *The Vital 6 Per Cent: How High-Growth Innovative Businesses Generate Prosperity and Jobs*, National Endowment for Science, Technology and the Arts, https://media.nesta.org.uk/documents/vital-six-per-cent.pdf. [16]

O'Callaghan, B. (2021), *Global Recovery Observatory Methodology*, https://doi.org/20210201-Global-Recovery-Observatory-Draft-Methodology-Document-.pdf (ox.ac.uk). [18]

O'Callaghan, B. (2020), *Global Recovery Observatory*, https://recovery.smithschool.ox.ac.uk/tracking/. [9]

OECD (2021), *COVID-19 Government Financing Support Programmes for Business [DAF/CMF(2021)6/REV2]*, http://COVID-19 Government Financing Support Programmes for Businesses: 2021 Update (oecd.org). [14]

OECD (2021), *Focus on green recovery*, https://www.oecd.org/coronavirus/en/themes/green-recovery#climate-action. [12]

OECD (2020), *COVID-19 Government Financing Support Programmes for Businesses*, OECD, Paris, http://www.oecd.org/finance/COVID-19-Government-Financing-Support-Programmes-for-Businesses.pdf. (accessed on 28 February 2021). [11]

OECD (2015), *New Approaches to SME and Entrepreneurship Financing: Broadening the Range of Instruments*, OECD Publishing, Paris, https://doi.org/10.1787/9789264240957-en. [19]

OECD (forthcoming), *Addressing gender disparities in access to finance for business creation*, OECD Publishing. [6]

Pitchbook (2023), *US VC female founders dashboard*, https://pitchbook.com/news/articles/the-vc-female-founders-dashboard. [7]

Thébaud, S. and A. Sharkey (2016), "Unequal Hard Times: The Influence of the Great Recession on Gender Bias in Entrepreneurial Financing", *Sociological Science*, Vol. 3. [4]

Wuppertal Institute, E3G (2021), *Green Recovery Tracker*, https://www.greenrecoverytracker.org/. [13]

Notes

[1] OECD (2009), *OECD Factbook 2009: Economic, Environmental and Social Statistics*, OECD Publishing, Paris, http://dx.doi.org/10.1787/factbook-2009-en

[2] For more information on how the World Bank classify countries please visit https://datahelpdesk.worldbank.org/knowledgebase/articles/378834-how-does-the-world-bank-classify-countries.

[3] See Annex C in OECD (2017), Entrepreneurship at a Glance 2017, OECD Publishing, Paris, for a detailed discussion on the international comparability of venture capital data.

[4] Recent studies by the World Bank provide evidence that loan size is an adequate proxy for size of the firm accessing the loan. See for instance Ardic O.P., Mylenko N., Saltane V. (2012), "Small and medium enterprises: a cross-country analysis with a new data set", Pacific Economic Review, Vol. 17, Issues 4, pp. 491-513.